Lecture Notes of the Institute for Computer Sciences, Social Informatics and Telecommunications Engineering 519

The LNICST series publishes ICST's conferences, symposia and workshops.
LNICST reports state-of-the-art results in areas related to the scope of the Institute.
The type of material published includes

- Proceedings (published in time for the respective event)
- Other edited monographs (such as project reports or invited volumes)

LNICST topics span the following areas:

- General Computer Science
- E-Economy
- E-Medicine
- Knowledge Management
- Multimedia
- Operations, Management and Policy
- Social Informatics
- Systems

José-Luis Guisado-Lizar ·
Agustín Riscos-Núñez ·
María-José Morón-Fernández ·
Gabriel Wainer
Editors

Simulation Tools and Techniques

15th EAI International Conference, SIMUtools 2023
Seville, Spain, December 14–15, 2023
Proceedings

 Springer

Editors
José-Luis Guisado-Lizar (ID)
Universidad de Sevilla
Seville, Spain

Agustín Riscos-Núñez (ID)
Universidad de Sevilla
Seville, Spain

María-José Morón-Fernández (ID)
Universidad de Sevilla
Seville, Spain

Gabriel Wainer (ID)
Carleton University
Ottawa, IL, USA

ISSN 1867-8211 ISSN 1867-822X (electronic)
Lecture Notes of the Institute for Computer Sciences, Social Informatics
and Telecommunications Engineering
ISBN 978-3-031-57522-8 ISBN 978-3-031-57523-5 (eBook)
https://doi.org/10.1007/978-3-031-57523-5

This Springer imprint is published by the registered company Springer Nature Switzerland AG
The registered company address is: Gewerbestrasse 11, 6330 Cham, Switzerland

Paper in this product is recyclable.

Preface

We are delighted to introduce the proceedings of the 15th edition of the European Alliance for Innovation (EAI) International Conference on Simulation Tools and Techniques (SIMUtools 2023). This conference brought together researchers, developers, and practitioners from around the world who are leveraging and developing research work in the fields of systems modeling and simulation, including modeling techniques, simulation software, combination of artificial intelligence and simulation, application of high-performance computing to simulation, simulation performance, and applications to a wide variety of fields, including for example wildfire risk, water infrastructures, road traffic, electric vehicles, logistics, medical sciences, and communication networks. The conference was dedicated to fostering interdisciplinary collaborative research in these areas and its application domains.

SIMUtools 2023 was hosted at the Technical School of Computer Engineering of the University of Seville (Seville, Spain) on 14th and 15th December 2023. The technical program consisted of 23 full papers in oral presentation sessions at the main conference track. Aside from the high-quality technical paper presentations, the technical program also featured two keynote speeches. The first one, entitled "Why Sim-Learnheuristics? Solving Optimization Problems under Stochastic and Dynamic Scenarios", was given by Angel A. Juan, from the Universitat Politécnica de Valencia (Valencia, Spain). The second one, entitled "Modeling and Simulation of Cellular Networks: formalizing the models", was given by Gabriel Wainer, from Carleton University (Ottawa, Canada).

Coordination with the Steering Committee Chair, Imrich Chlamtac, and the Steering Committee Co-Chairs, Gabriel Wainer, Helen D. Karatza, José Luis Sevillano Ramos, and José-Luis Guisado-Lizar, was essential for the success of the conference. We sincerely appreciate their constant support and guidance. It was also a great pleasure to work with such an excellent Conference Manager, Veronika Kissova, and Organizing Committee team, formed by José-Luis Guisado-Lizar, Agustín Riscos-Núñez, María-José Morón-Fernández, David Ragel Díaz-Jara, David Orellana Martín, Daniel Cascado Caballero, Elena Cerezuela Escudero, Daniel Cagigas Muñiz, Luis Valencia Cabrera, Betsaida Alexandre Barajas, from the University of Seville (Spain), and Gabriel Wainer, from Carleton University (Canada), for their hard work in organizing and supporting the conference. In particular, we are grateful to the Technical Program Committee, who completed the peer-review process for the technical papers and helped to put together a high-quality technical program. We are also grateful to all the authors who trusted us and submitted their papers to the SIMUtools 2023 conference.

We strongly believe that SIMUtools provides a good forum for all researchers, developers, and practitioners to discuss all science and technology aspects that are relevant to simulation tools and techniques. We also expect that future SIMUtools conferences will be as successful and stimulating, as indicated by the contributions presented in this volume.

December 2023

José-Luis Guisado-Lizar
Agustín Riscos-Núñez
María-José Morón-Fernández
Gabriel Wainer

Organization

Steering Committee

Imrich Chlamtac	University of Trento, Italy
Gabriel Wainer	Carleton University, Canada
Helen D. Karatza	Aristotle University of Thessaloniki, Greece
José Luis Sevillano Ramos	University of Seville, Spain
José-Luis Guisado-Lizar	University of Seville, Spain

Organizing Committee

General Chair

José-Luis Guisado-Lizar	University of Seville, Spain

General Co-chairs

Agustín Riscos-Núñez	University of Seville, Spain
María-José Morón-Fernández	University of Seville, Spain
Gabriel Wainer	Carleton University, Canada

TPC Chairs

José-Luis Guisado-Lizar	University of Seville, Spain
Agustín Riscos-Núñez	University of Seville, Spain
María-José Morón-Fernández	University of Seville, Spain

Sponsorship and Exhibit Chair

Elena Cerezuela Escudero	University of Seville, Spain

Local Chair

Betsaida Alexandre Barajas	University of Seville, Spain

Workshops Chair

Daniel Cascado Caballero   University of Seville, Spain

Publicity and Social Media Chair

David Orellana Martín   University of Seville, Spain

Publications Chair

Daniel Cagigas Muñiz   University of Seville, Spain

Web Chair

David Ragel Díaz-Jara   University of Seville, Spain

Posters and PhD Track Chair

Luis Valencia Cabrera   University of Seville, Spain

Technical Program Committee

Agustín Riscos-Núñez	University of Seville, Spain
Alonso Inostrosa Psijas	Universidad de Valparaiso, Chile
Álvaro Romero Jiménez	University of Seville, Spain
Andrea D'Ambrogio	University of Rome Tor Vergata, Italy
Betsaida Alexandre Barajas	University of Seville, Spain
Cristina Ruiz-Martin	Carleton University, Canada
Daniel Cagigas Muñiz	University of Seville, Spain
Daniel Cascado Caballero	University of Seville, Spain
David Orellana Martín	University of Seville, Spain
David Ragel Díaz-Jara	University of Seville, Spain
Dingde Jiang	University of Electronic Science and Technology of China, China
Domenico Talia	University of Calabria, Italy
Elena Cerezuela Escudero	University of Seville, Spain
Ezequiel Pecker-Marcosig	Universidad de Buenos Aires, Argentina
Fernando Díaz del Río	University of Seville, Spain
Francesco Quaglia	Università di Roma Tor Vergata, Italy
Franco Davoli	University of Genoa, Italy

Contents

Transportation and Logistics

Medical Sciences

Network Simulations

Simulation Tools and Methods

A DEVS-Based Methodology for Simulation and Model-Driven Development of IoT

Iman Alavi Fazel[(⊠)] [iD] and Gabriel Wainer[iD]

Carleton University, 1125 Colonel By Dr, Ottawa, ON K1S 5B6, Canada
`{imanalavifazel,gwainer}@cmail.carleton.ca`

Abstract. The Internet of Things (IoT) has emerged as a promising technology with diverse applications across industries, including smart homes, healthcare services, and manufacturing. However, despite its potential, IoT presents unique challenges, such as interoperability, system complexity, and the need for efficient development and maintenance. This paper explores a model-driven development (MDD) approach to design IoT applications by employing high-level models to facilitate abstraction and reusability. Specifically, we adopt a methodology based on Discrete Event System Specification (DEVS), a modular and hierarchical formalism for MDD of IoT. In our work, different DEVS models are developed to address distinct functional aspects of the devices, encompassing data retrieval, data serialization/deserialization, and network connectivity. The developed models, along with a DEVS simulator, are then used for both simulation and deployment. To create a comprehensive simulation environment, the paper introduces two additional models for simulating the MQTT protocol, including its Quality of Service (QoS) mechanism.

Keywords: IoT · DEVS · Model-driven development · MDD

1 Introduction

The Internet of Things (IoT), characterized as an internet-accessible network of sensors and actuators, has emerged as a promising solution in numerous areas. In addition to its established application within home automation, IoT has been used in sectors such as healthcare, supply chains, and manufacturing [1]. What is referred to as the fourth industrial revolution, or Industry 4.0, is backed by IoT technologies which results in more autonomy and enhanced efficiency of industrial plants and processes.

Due to the nature of these systems, it is challenging to design, implement, and verify their components and their interconnections, in particular interoperability, the ability of these systems to properly work and communicate together [2]. In addition, there are various difficulties related mainly to the distributed nature, heterogeneity, and the presence of "human-in-the-loop" in these systems [3]. To help with the design, different life cycle phases should be automated, as manual efforts for development, deployment, and maintenance of the plethora of devices are prone to errors [4].

© ICST Institute for Computer Sciences, Social Informatics and Telecommunications Engineering 2024
Published by Springer Nature Switzerland AG 2024. All Rights Reserved
J.-L. Guisado-Lizar et al. (Eds.): SIMUtools 2023, LNICST 519, pp. 3–17, 2024.
https://doi.org/10.1007/978-3-031-57523-5_1

Model-driven development (MDD) approaches can overcome these challenges. Using these methods, the code for devices is designed using high-level models instead of platform-specific programs. These models can be expressed in various formats such as graphical and textual or with formal or informal semantics. However, the goal of all of them is to create an abstraction over specific code implementation. After their design and analysis, these models will eventually be transformed into executable code that can be run on the hardware. In MDD, the use of high-level models provides *abstraction*, *separation of concern,* and *reusability* to the development cycle [5, 6].

This paper presents a methodology based on Discrete Event System Specification (DEVS) for model-driven development of IoT devices. To achieve this, a series of DEVS models were developed, each performing a specific functional aspect of the devices. These tasks encompassed capabilities such as retrieving data from ADC channels, serializing/deserializing the data (such as to and from JSON or XML), and providing network connectivity. These models, alongside a DEVS simulator, would then be flashed onto the devices for deployment. We developed prototype models for the widely used ESP32 microcontrollers, but they can be extended to other platforms. For simulation purposes, we include two models for MQTT brokers and clients, replicating MQTT at a high level (including its acknowledgment mechanism for Quality of Service - QoS). The models for MQTT communication facilitate the collection of information about network traffic and the feasibility of an event within a specified time frame.

An advantage of using DEVS lies in the ability to reuse models with similar interfaces and behavior, for both simulation and deployment on the device. Furthermore, if the DEVS models perform hardware-independent tasks, the same implementation code for the models can be used for both scenarios. Utilizing DEVS for model-driven development additionally enables us to leverage a set of techniques and methods that have been developed for the verification and validation of their behavior [7–9].

The rest of the paper is organized as follows. In Sect. 2, some previous work on model-driven development of IoT alongside a short description of DEVS is presented. Section 3, provides the DEVS specification of the developed models. A simple case study comprising of moisture sensor and an irrigation system is presented in Sect. 4. In Sect. 5, the implementation of the DEVS models is discussed. Lastly, Sect. 6, summarizes the paper and discusses future directions.

2   Related Work

High-level models have found diverse applications in the design and development of IoT technologies. These models have been employed to capture the characteristics of specific components of the infrastructure, such as network connectivity and resource allocation schemes, as well as to model the complete behavior of a node. The models were then used for purposes such as simulation, verification, and code generation. In this section, we present some of the previous research that used high-level models in the context of IoT [10].

Authors in [11] developed a framework called IFogSim, which used models of sensors and actuators to simulate different resource management strategies within the fog computing paradigm. This framework is an extension of CloudSim and is based on discrete-event simulation (DES). Another CloudSim-based simulator [12] considers the big data aspect of these devices using MapReduce. SimTalk [13], a simulation software, facilitates the emulation of environments that can be a combination of virtual and interconnected IoT devices using graphical representations of the actuating systems in the network. A survey by [14] presents 31 simulators for Wireless Sensor Networks (WSNs) which employ a form of model for the sensor nodes, propagation medium, or communication technologies.

The use of models in the form of model-driven development (MDD) of IoT applications was the focus of other works in the literature. The authors used various kinds of models such as the one based on visual notations, to textual formats with domain-specific languages (DSLs) to design IoT applications. These models also differed in their semantics being formal, expressed as mathematical techniques, or informal, such as the one that uses plain language [15]. Some research in this category further used models for verification using methods such as simulation and model checking to ensure the correct behavior of the system. In what follows, some of these works are presented.

In [16], the authors presented a DSL that allows developers to define ports, properties, and Statecharts in text-based format, and later use a set of tools to automatically transform models and generate code. In [17], a UML-based approach was used to generate wrappers, enabling the integration of diverse IoT elements. Research in [5] introduced a framework to enable node-centric and rule-based programming through a DSL, providing reusability, flexibility, and maintainability. Authors in [18] presented a method for designing and analyzing IoT applications to verify their correctness and QoS using SysML4IoT, a framework consisting of a SysML profile and a model-to-text translator that converts the models for a model checker.

In our work, we applied the DEVS formalism for model-driven development and simulation of IoT devices. DEVS can be viewed as finite-state machines where transitions between states occur based on new input to the system or expiration of their lifespan [19]. A model of interest can be broken down into atomic models, each responsible for specific behavior. The atomic models can then be coupled together to create the complete model of interest. The modular nature of DEVS enables us to design and test atomic models individually, and then integrate them with the other models.

Some authors have previously applied DEVS formalism to the IoT domain. In a study by [20], the authors proposed methods to simulate moving IoT nodes more efficiently, and used DEVS for modeling the wireless communications aspect of the devices. In [21], a novel approach was introduced, aimed at improving energy efficiency in smart buildings based on user location. Authors in [22] used DEVS for modeling botnets using Markov Chains. Their model behaved similarly to the spread of Mirai and Torii botnets. A DEVS model of smart home networks, was used to determine the optimal working hours for energy consumption [23], as well as a DEVS-based IoT management system that provides users with metrics of power consumption [24]. Research in [25] explored a simulation acceleration method for a DEVS-based hybrid system using multiple CPUs and GPU cores. Their simulation environment was a fire-spreading application comprised of IoT sensor networks. DEVS was also used to model a Fog computing environment and showed that combining fog and cloud computing can enhance the user experience by offloading tasks to the fog nodes [26].

Our work differs from the previous research in that we employed DEVS to develop models for simulation, and ultimately for deployment on the devices. We also modeled the MQTT protocol using DEVS, another key contribution of this work.

3   Methodology

As discussed earlier, our goal was to apply DEVS for the simulation as well as the operation of IoT devices. To achieve this, we developed two sets of DEVS models with identical interfaces, state variables, and state transitions. One set of models was designed to be used for the simulation environment, and the other set for deployment. Moreover, any model that performed a hardware-agnostic task was reused in both sets. For simulating the DEVS models, we adopted Cadmium, a header-only C++ library[1]. Cadmium has the advantage of having a real-time version, which we later used to execute the DEVS model on the IoT device. In this study, we chose the ESP32 microcontroller for devices which is a popular choice in the industry.

3.1   Deployment Models

ADC Model
ADC is a model that periodically reads the ADC channel of the device and transmits its value through an output port, defined as a floating-point number proportional to the analog input signal, depicted in Fig. 1. This model can optionally receive a Boolean input to toggle its state between outputting data or becoming passive.

Fig. 1. The ADC atomic model.

Wrapper Model
The Wrapper model receives raw data and creates a set of values consisting of a value (for instance, from the ADC), an ID, and a type of channel. Then, it sends this set as its output. The input and output ports of this model are depicted in Fig. 2.

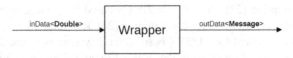

Fig. 2. The Wrapper atomic model.

---

[1] Source code for the Cadmium library can be found at https://github.com/SimulationEvery where/cadmium.

In the implementation, we used instances of a user-defined C++ class named *Message* to represent this information. For example, an object of this type could be comprised of the following fields:

- data (as Double): **24.0**
- id (as String): **"adc1"**
- type (as String): **"temperature"**

Base Model

The Base model performs the main computation of the IoT device. For instance, for IoT sensor nodes, this model is responsible for collecting different ADC channels and creating a final output to be later transmitted over the network. In other applications, this model can receive commands that have been transmitted from the network and control the connected actuators to the board. Hence, the definition of the internal and external transition functions of this model is dependent on the specific application. However, its interface, i.e., the input and output ports, is the same among its different applications. This model has two sets of input and output ports. One set of ports is defined to provide communication with ADC and/or actuator models of the device, and the other set is for sending and/or receiving objects of type *MQTTMessage*. The fields of this type contain the data (as a JSON string), the MQTT topic, and the desired QoS level for the MQTT message. For instance:

- data (as String): **{data: 25.4, type: "temperature", unit: "C"}**
- topic (as String): **/home/garden/sensor1**
- QoSLevel (as Integer): **2**

In an example of the sensor node, this Base model can receive sensor readings for one or more ADC channels and then perform some form of sensor fusion algorithm. This operation can involve simple averaging or any other complex computations. Eventually, the result of the computation is set as the *data* field of the *MQTTMessage* object out of the model.

The input and output ports of this model are depicted in Fig. 3.

Fig. 3. Base DEVS model

Connection Model

The Connection model provides network connectivity for the board. This model receives *MQTTMessage* objects as input, which are produced by the Base model, and then transmits them to an MQTT broker accessible on the network. Conversely, it can also receive data from an MQTT Broker and dispatch as *MQTTMessage* instances to the Base model. Moreover, on the ESP32 board, the implementation of this model causes the device to initially connect to a Wi-Fi Access Point during initialization.

3.2 Simulation Models

In what follows, the descriptions of the equivalent simulation models are discussed. The ADC model in the simulation environment has the same specification as the deployment model, except it produces pseudo-random numbers in its output function. The Wrapper and Base models are identical for both simulation and deployment. For the Connection model, a coupled model mimics the functionality of an MQTT client in the simulation environment including the state changes in its connections. This model was complemented by the Network Medium and MQTT Broker model. The Network Medium model is a queueing network model that captures the latency of the network transmission, and the MQTT broker provides communication for multiple MQTT clients connected to it. The subsequent sections provide details about these models.

MQTT Client

The MQTT Client establishes communication with the device model on one end and with the MQTT broker on the opposite one. The type of data exchanged with the device is *MQTTMessage*, as discussed in the previous section, while with the broker, it is of type *MQTTPacket*. Objects of type *MQTTPacket* contain fields such as the packet ID and packet type, in accordance with the MQTT protocol specification. The exchange of objects of this type allows us to perform proper state changes similar to how they occur in actual implementations of this protocol. *MQTTPacket* objects are comprised of:

- **type** (as an MQTTPacketType): Specifies the type of the MQTT packet, such as PUBLISH, PUBREL, PUBREC, etc.
- **body** (as a map of String to String): Depending on the type of the packet, maps the required fields, such as "packetID" and "Payload", to their corresponding values.
- **newPublishPacket** (as a Boolean): A flag that designates whether the packet is a newly created PUBLISH packet for the client, or it is a PUBLISH packet that was received from the broker.

For instance, an MQTTPacket object has the following fields:

- **type**: PUBLISH
- **body**:

```
{
  {"packetID", 100-},
          {"topic", "/home/kitchen/sensor"}
          {"DUPFlag", true}
          {"QoSLevel", 2}
          {"retain", true}
          {"payload", "{ data: 10, sensor_type: \"temperature\"}"}
}
```

- **newPublishPacket**: true

The MQTT client is a coupled model composed of two atomic DEVS models: the *Base* and the *Acknowledgement Buffer*. The Base model transmits and receives MQTT packets to and from the Broker. In this process, whenever a packet with a QoS level of 1 or 2 is received, the Base model also sends a copy of the packet to the Acknowledgement Buffer model. The Acknowledgment Buffer stores information about packets and their connection states by maintaining a variable that maps each packet ID to its current connection phase. Additionally, this model keeps track of the last timestamp at which the packets arrive. Whenever the timer for a particular packet expires, the Acknowledgment Buffer generates a new acknowledged packet and sends it to the Base model. The Base model will then forward any received packets from the Acknowledgment Buffer to the clients. The MQTT client model is depicted in Fig. 4.

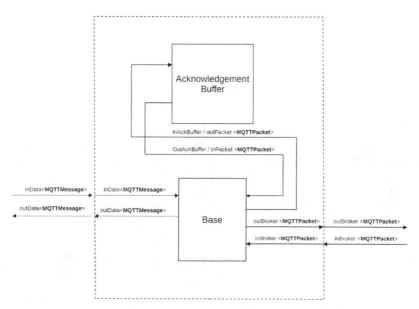

Fig. 4. MQTTClient DEVS model

Network Medium

The network medium is connected by an array of input and output ports to the MQTT clients and by one set of input and output ports to the broker. The model receives *MQTTPacket* objects from clients and then adds them to a queue. The packets in this queue will be dispatched after a certain time interval, which is determined by the exponential distribution function. This model sends objects of type *BrokerMessage* to the MQTT broker, which contains the *MQTTPacket* objects and the index of the input array in which the packets have arrived. Similarly, the Network Medium model can receive objects of type *BrokerMessage* from the MQTT broker model, which, after the expiry of the service time, will be forwarded to the intended client. The MQTT broker distinguishes between different clients based on the index of the input/output array with which they communicate. Therefore, during the simulation, clients should remain connected to specific input and output ports of the model (Fig. 5).

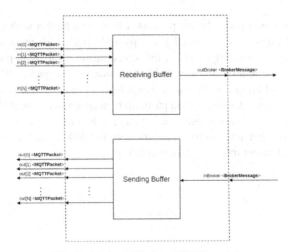

Fig. 5. Network Medium DEVS model.

MQTT Broker

The MQTT Broker receives *BrokerMessage* objects from the Network Medium model. Depending on the packet type, it performs the appropriate connection state change or broadcasts it to different clients. Similar to the MQTT client model, the MQTT Broker is a coupled model comprised of two atomic models: the *Base* and the *Acknowledgment Buffer*. The Base model stores the list of topics to which clients are subscribed and updates this list upon receiving a new SUBSCRIBE packet. Alternatively, when a PUBLISH packet arrives, the Base model inspects the topic of the packet and broadcasts a set of PUBLISH messages to every client that was previously subscribed to that topic. Other types of packets, including the newly generated PUBLISH packets with QoS levels 1 or 2, are then forwarded to the Acknowledgment Buffer. The Acknowledgment Buffer, in turn, updates the connection state for the packet ID, generates an appropriate acknowledgment packet, and sends it to the Base model. The Base model simply forwards any packet it receives from the Acknowledgment Buffer to the clients. In the Acknowledgment Buffer, a state variable is also present to keep track of the last timestamp when the packet was received. Upon its expiry, the model regenerates the acknowledgment packet for the Base model. The input and output ports of this model are depicted in Fig. 6.

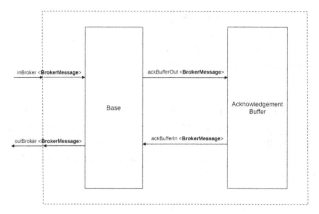

Fig. 6. MQTTBroker DEVS model

4 Implementation

To implement the DEVS model in Cadmium, the first step was defining the model's state using a user-defined C++ type. For instance, the state for the Sensor nodes in our implementation was defined as:

```
struct SensorState {
    double sigma;
    ConnectionPhase phase;
    Message<double> newMessage;
    vector<string> topicsToSubscribe;
    vector<string> topicsToPublish;

    SensorState(vector<string> topicsToPublish,
      vector<string> topicsToSubscribe = {})
        : sigma(std::numeric_limits<double>::max()),
          newMessage(),topicToPublish(topicToPublish),
            listOfTopicsToSubscribe(listOfTopicsToSubscribe) {
              if(listOfTopicsToSubscribe.size() > 0) {
                phase = ConnectionPhase::
                        DATA_AVAILABLE_FOR_SUBSCRIBE;
                sigma = 0;
              }
}
```

Where *ConnectionPhase* is an *enum* with the following definition:

```
enum class ConnectionPhase {
    IDLE,
    DATA_AVAILABLE_FOR_PUBLISH,
    DATA_AVAILABLE_FOR_SUBSCRIBE
};
```

An instance of *SensorState* holds information about sigma, a variable that was used in the time advance function, its connection phase, and other data used as state variables in this model. After defining these data types for different states, the DEVS models were created by declaring classes inherited from Cadmium's Atomic template class. In the case of the Sensor model, the class was declared as:

```
class Sensor : public Atomic<SensorState>
{ /* … */ }
```

To complete the definition of the DEVS model, the input and output ports were then defined, and the virtual member functions of the *Atomic* class, such as the internal and external transition were overridden. The type of Port objects specified using a template argument determines the values they send or receive. These types can be primitive types, such as double and int, or any other user-defined types. In the example of the Sensor model, these ports were defined as:

```
Port<MQTTMessage> outMQTT;
Port<MQTTMessage> inMQTT;
```

In our implementation, a list of ports that send and receive objects of the same type was represented using a 'std::vector' of ports. For example, the ports of the buffer models in the Network Medium model were declared as:

```
std::vector<Port<MQTTPacket>> receivingBufferIn;
std::vector<Port<MQTTPacket>> sendingBufferOut;
```

After defining the ports, the models were coupled together using Cadmium's *add-Coupling* function. Furthermore, to facilitate the coupling between the MQTT client and broker, a function was defined that kept track of the coupled ports and assigned free ones to the models. The signature of the function was as follows:

```
void assignFreePort(std::shared_ptr<MQTTClient> mqttClient,
    std::shared_ptr<MQTTBroker> mqttBroker,
        std::shared_ptr<PropagationMedium> networkMedium);
```

The final step was to create a top model consisting of all inner submodels coupled together. Then, to execute the models in the simulation, an object of type *RootCoordinator* was instantiated, and the start() member function was called. For instance:

```
auto model = make_shared<TopLevelModel>("top");
auto rootCoordinator = cadmium::RootCoordinator(model);
auto logger = make_shared<cadmium::CSVLogger>("log.csv", ";");
rootCoordinator.setLogger(logger);
rootCoordinator.start();
rootCoordinator.simulate(std::numeric_limits<double>::
                                            infinity());
rootCoordinator.stop();
```

In contrast, if we wanted to run the models for their operation on the devices, an object of *RealTimeRootCoordinator* was created. This was done via:

```
auto realTimeRootCoordinator =
  cadmium::
  RealTimeRootCoordinator
  <cadmium::ChronoClock<std::chrono::steady_clock> >
                                    (model, clock);

realTimeRootCoordinator.start();
realTimeRootCoordinator
        .simulate(std::numeric_limits<double>::infinity());
realTimeRootCoordinator.stop();
```

5   Measuring Levels of Soil Moisture

A case study was conducted in which a sensor node periodically captured the moisture levels of the soil using its ADC channel, and an actuator that triggered the irrigation system when the moisture fell below a specified threshold. Communication between the sensor and the actuator was established using the MQTT protocol. Before deployment on the boards, these models were executed in a simulation environment. This section provides information about the simulation setup and presents the results. Furthermore, to complete the simulation environment, an additional DEVS model was developed to simulate the behavior of gardening soil. This model stored the moisture value, as well as transitions to change this value. The sensor node was connected to this model to retrieve moisture readings, while the actuator sent irrigation commands to this model. Specifically, when the actuator initiated a command to start irrigation, the model's internal transition function consistently incremented the moisture level, unless a subsequent signal was received, indicating the termination of irrigation. The input and output ports of the soil model are depicted in Fig. 7.

At the beginning of the simulation, the actuator first subscribes to the topic */garden/moisture_sensor*, and the sensor model starts reading the moisture value from the soil model and publishes them to the same topic. Whenever the moisture level falls below 15, the actuator sends a signal to the soil model to initiate the irrigation system.

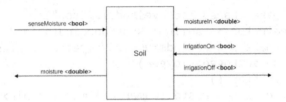

Fig. 7. Soil DEVS model

5.1 Simulation Result

The simulation ran for 10 sensor readings. To showcase the packet retransmission mechanism, an additional simulation was run with a condition added to a buffer of the Network Medium, causing intentional packet drops based on a certain probability. Namely, packets with a packet ID divisible by 3 had a 50% chance of being dropped. Table 1 depicts the timestamp of the PUBCOMP packets being received by the Broker when data was being published to the actuator model in both simulation runs.

Table 1. Timestamp of the received PUBCOMP message from the sensor node

Packet ID	Timestamp of the PUBLISH	Timestamp of PUBCOMP without retransmission	Timestamp of PUBCOMP with retransmission
1	1	1.55052	1.48447
2	2	2.47999	2.91148
3	3	3.60933	7.56755
4	4	4.52406	4.38234
5	5	5.74917	5.60835
6	6	6.59165	11.7505
7	7	7.65689	8.83374
8	8	8.38723	8.97219
9	9	9.59758	11.5696
10	10	10.2355	11.7876

As Table 1 shows, the PUBCOMP packets that required retransmission were received by the broker with a significant delay. The total number of packets exchanged between models is shown in Fig. 8.

By applying realistic conditions for packet drops, we can estimate the arrival of the packets at the destination. Furthermore, the total number of packets that need to be transmitted to and from the device can be used to estimate the power consumption of the devices.

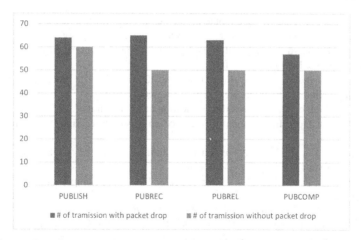

Fig. 8. Number of packets exchanged in the simulation with and without retransmission.

6   Conclusion

In this work, we applied Discrete Event System Specification (DEVS), a modular and hierarchical formalism for the model-driven development of IoT devices. We developed two sets of models to be used in both simulation and deployment on the device. Each model was responsible for a specific functional aspect of the device, and their composition created the complete application. In our case study, we applied the models in a simulation environment that included a sensor node and an actuator for an irrigation system. The results of the simulation showed timestamps for different events occurring in the system and provided metrics related to packet transmission in the MQTT protocol.

For our future work, we aim to develop models that implement more functionalities of IoT devices and for a wider range of hardware. The conditions that cause packet retransmission can be further investigated to be based on real scenarios. Hence, the metrics obtained from the simulations would more closely resemble the deployment environment.

References

1. Da Xu, L., He, W., Li, S.: Internet of Things in industries: a survey. IEEE Trans. Ind. Inf. **10**(4), 2233–2243 (2014)
2. Noura, M., Atiquzzaman, M., Gaedke, M.: Interoperability in Internet of Things: taxonomies and open challenges. Mob. Netw. Appl. **24**, 796–809 (2019)
3. Udoh, I.S., Kotonya, G.: Developing IoT applications: challenges and frameworks. IET Cyber-Phys. Syst. Theory Appl. **3**(2), 65–72 (2018)
4. Patel, P., Cassou, D.: Enabling high-level application development for the Internet of Things. J. Syst. Softw. **103**, 62–84 (2015)
5. Nguyen, X.T., Tran, H.T., Baraki, H., Geihs, K.: FRASAD: a framework for model-driven IoT application development. In: 2015 IEEE 2nd World Forum on Internet of Things (WF-IoT), pp. 387–392. IEEE (2015)

6. Doddapaneni, K., Ever, E., Gemikonakli, O., Malavolta, I., Mostarda, L., Muccini, H.: A model-driven engineering framework for architecting and analysing wireless sensor networks. In: 2012 Third International Workshop on Software Engineering for Sensor Network Applications (SESENA), pp. 1–7. IEEE (2012)

7. Saadawi, H., Wainer, G.: Verification of real-time DEVS models. In: Proceedings of the 2009 Spring Simulation Multiconference, pp. 1–8. Citeseer (2009)

8. Labiche, Y., Wainer, G.: Towards the verification and validation of DEVS models. In: Proceedings of 1st Open International Conference on Modeling & Simulation, pp. 295–305. Citeseer (2005)

9. Olsen, M.M., Raunak, M.S.: A method for quantified confidence of DEVS validation. In: SpringSim (TMS-DEVS), pp. 135–142 (2015)

10. Manrique, J.A., Rueda-Rueda, J.S., Portocarrero, J.M.: Contrasting Internet of Things and wireless sensor network from a conceptual overview. In: 2016 IEEE International Conference on Internet of Things (iThings), pp. 252–257. IEEE (2016)

11. Gupta, H., Vahid Dastjerdi, A., Ghosh, S.K., Buyya, R.: IFogSim: a toolkit for modeling and simulation of resource management techniques in the Internet of Things, Edge and Fog computing environments. Softw. Pract. Experience **47**(9), 1275–1296 (2017)

12. Sotiriadis, S., Bessis, N., Asimakopoulou, E., Mustafee, N.: Towards simulating the Internet of Things. In: 28th International Conference on Advanced Information Networking and Applications Workshops, pp. 444–448. IEEE (2014)

13. Lin, Y.-W., Lin, Y.-B., Yen, T.-H.: Simtalk: simulation of IoT applications. Sensors **20**(9), 2563 (2020)

14. Nayyar, A., Singh, R.: A comprehensive review of simulation tools for wireless sensor networks (WSNs). J. Wirel. Netw. Commun. **5**(1), 19–47 (2015)

15. Arslan, S., Ozkaya, M., Kardas, G.: Modeling languages for Internet of Things (IoT) applications: a comparative analysis study. Mathematics **11**(5), 1263 (2023)

16. Harrand, N., Fleurey, F., Morin, B., Husa, K.E.: ThingML: a language and code generation framework for heterogeneous targets. In: Proceedings of the ACM/IEEE 19th International Conference on Model Driven Engineering Languages and Systems, pp. 125–135 (2016)

17. Thramboulidis, K., Christoulakis, F.: UML4IoT—a UML-based approach to exploit IoT in cyber-physical manufacturing systems. Comput. Ind. **82**, 259–272 (2016)

18. Costa, B., Pires, P.F., Delicato, F.C., Li, W., Zomaya, A.Y.: Design and analysis of IoT applications: a model-driven approach. In: 14th International Conference on Dependable, Autonomic and Secure Computing, pp. 392–399. IEEE (2016)

19. Zeigler, B.P., Praehofer, H., Kim, T.G.: Theory of Modeling and Simulation. Academic Press (2000)

20. Im, J.H., Oh, H.-R., Seong, Y.R.: Simulation of a mobile IoT system using the DEVS formalism. J. Inf. Process. Syst. **17**(1), 28–36 (2021)

21. Maatoug, A., Belalem, G., Mahmoudi, S.: A location-based fog computing optimization of energy management in smart buildings: DEVS modeling and design of connected objects. Front. Comp. Sci. **17**(2), 172501 (2023)

22. Barakat, G., Al-Duwairi, B., Jarrah, M., Jaradat, M.: Modeling and simulation of IoT botnet behaviors using DEVS. In: 2022 13th International Conference on Information and Communication Systems (ICICS), pp. 42–47 (2022)

23. Albataineh, M., Jarrah, M.: DEVS-IoT: performance evaluation of smart home devices network. Multimed. Tools Appl. **80**, 16857–16885 (2021)

24. Albataineh, M., Jarrah, M.: DEVS-based IoT management system for modeling and exploring smart home devices. In: 2019 Sixth International Conference on Internet of Things: Systems, Management and Security (IOTSMS), pp. 73–78. IEEE (2019)

25. Kim, S., Cho, J., Park, D.: Accelerated DEVS simulation using collaborative computation on multi-cores and GPUs for fire-spreading IoT sensing applications. Appl. Sci. **8**(9), 1466 (2018)
26. Etemad, M., Aazam, M., St-Hilaire, M.: Using DEVS for modeling and simulating a Fog Computing environment. In: 2017 International Conference on Computing, Networking and Communications (ICNC), pp. 849–854. IEEE (2017)

Performance Evaluation of a Legacy Real-Time System: An Improved RAST Approach

Juri Tomak$^{(\boxtimes)}$ ⓘ, Adrian Liermann, and Sergei Gorlatch

University of Muenster, Münster, Germany
{jtomak,a_lier03,gorlatch}@uni-muenster.de

Abstract. A challenging aspect in optimizing legacy distributed systems with strict real-time requirements is how to evaluate the performance of the system running in a production environment without disrupting its regular operation. The challenge is even greater when the System Under Evaluation (SUE) runs within a resource-sharing environment and, thus, is affected by the resource usage of other software running in the same environment. Current performance evaluation methods dealing with this challenge rely on data collected by Application Performance Monitoring (APM) tools that are not always available in existing systems and hard to establish when the system is already in production. In this paper, we improve the initial, proof-of-concept implementation of our RAST (Regression Analysis, Simulation, and load Testing) approach to evaluate the response time of a distributed system using the available system's request logs. In particular, we greatly improve the prediction model based on machine learning. Our use case is a commercial alarm system in productive use, developed and maintained by the GSelectronic company in Germany. We experimentally demonstrate that our improvements significantly enhance RAST's capability to adequately predict the system performance and verify the strict requirements on the response time. We make our model and software freely available in order to enable reproducing our experiments.

Keywords: performance evaluation · real-time requirements ·
regression analysis · simulation · distributed system

1 Introduction

Evaluating performance, e.g., the response time[1], of a legacy real-time software system that runs in a production environment is a great challenge as the system's regular operation is not allowed to be disrupted by the evaluation. A further challenge to performance evaluation is when the System Under Evaluation (SUE)

---

[1] Response time is the time interval between a sent request and the received response to it; it usually includes network latency and the request's processing time.

This work was supported by the DFG project PPP-DL at the University of Muenster.

J.-L. Guisado-Lizar et al. (Eds.): SIMUtools 2023, LNICST 519, pp. 18–33, 2024.
https://doi.org/10.1007/978-3-031-57523-5_2

runs within a resource-sharing environment, where the performance of the SUE is significantly affected by the resource usage of other software running in the same environment.

In our work, we are interested in evaluating the performance of existing, real-time software to decide what parts of it and how should be improved to comply with strict real-time requirements.

Current performance evaluation methods traditionally rely on data collected by Application Performance Monitoring (APM) tools [1,6,8,15]. These data usually contain low-level metrics of resource utilization, like CPU-, or RAM-utilization, or detailed information regarding network requests, like their size in bytes. The collected data are then used for creating a prediction model for the system's response time. However, we consider systems that often do not provide an APM and its integration is too complicated. Our target software only implements request logging, i.e., incoming network requests and their responses are logged, including their type, timestamp and executing thread. Beyond that, there is no further information regarding the requests, like the payload size.

As an alternative to using an APM, we introduce in [22] the RAST (Regression Analysis, Simulation, and load Testing) approach and its initial implementation as a proof of concept. The idea of RAST is to utilize log files (in the literature called request logs or access logs) that are typically created by the System Under Evaluation (SUE). In contrast to an APM, these log files provide only information about when a request was received by the system, when its processing was finished (or alternatively when the response was sent), and the request type. Using these data, RAST creates a prediction model for the time needed for processing network requests, e.g., HTTP requests, that the system processes. RAST automatically determines the optimal prediction model for the analyzed system using the provided request logs; it chooses the best regression algorithm via cross-validation of common regression algorithms, such as: Linear, Lasso, Ridge, Decision tree, and Elastic net regression. The prediction model is deployed in the Simulator of RAST, which simulates the system and takes the same requests as the SUE, and then uses the prediction model to predict the request's processing time and to delay the server's response accordingly. The Load Tester component of RAST is based on our load-testing approach [21]: it generates network requests, sends them to the SUE or the Simulator and measures the response time.

Our aim in presenting RAST is to provide a comprehensive and configurable toolset, encompassing common practices in log transformation, prediction model generation, Simulation, and Load Testing, to researchers engaged in performance evaluation of mission-critical legacy systems. Our initial version of RAST, introduced in [22], served as a proof-of-concept. This paper addresses its initial limitations with the following contributions:

- We implement common training data preprocessing methods, as well as automatic hyperparameter optimization via the grid search method [3]. To enhance flexibility, each individual method can be activated or deactivated via configuration settings.

– To assess the impact of each implemented method on the R^2 score [19], we conduct experiments using a commercial alarm system as a case study. Additionally, we identify the RAST configuration that yields the most substantial improvements over the previous version, achieving the highest R^2 score of 0.792 (with an ideal score of 1.0). Notably, this represents a remarkable 47% improvement over the best score of 0.63 obtained in the initial proof-of-concept implementation.

– To facilitate accessibility and reproducibility, we publish our improved, full RAST implementation on GitHub [20]. Additionally, we provide pre-trained models from our case study in both PMML and JSON formats, widely used data interchange formats for models. This further supports the reproducibility and reliability of our experiments.

In the rest of the paper, Sect. 2 provides an overview of our RAST approach and highlights the key features and improvements implemented in comparison to the initial, proof-of-concept version. Section 3 describes an alarm system's typical architecture and performance requirements and how our target alarm system of the GS company group works. Section 4 showcases various configurations of RAST and their influence on the achieved model's R^2 score. Section 5 presents our experiments with the new RAST implementation for evaluating the alarm system performance and finding the system's saturation point, i.e., the maximum number of Alarm Devices (ADs) that can be simultaneously handled while complying with the real-time requirements. Section 6 concludes the paper and outlines future work.

2   The RAST Approach: Overview and the Improved Implementation

Figure 1 illustrates the six components of RAST – our approach that combines Regression Analysis, Simulation, and load Testing to evaluate performance (in particular, the response time) of a production real-time system.

In this paper, we focus on our improvements to Pipeline A (2). For further details about the components (1), (3)–(6), refer to the caption of Fig. 1 and [22].

Figure 2 depicts two components – Log-Transformer and Prediction-Model-Creator – inside of Pipeline A of RAST and the data flow between the components, indicating our newly implemented components in bold font. The new components can be selectively activated or deactivated via the configuration file so that we can precisely study their influence on the prediction quality.

The component Log-Transformer (LT) in Fig. 2 creates a database with training data from the contents of the log files. The dedicated LT component allows the Prediction-Model-Creator component to become more generic, because processing the specific SUE details is offloaded to LT.

Training data are produced by the LT component and then are taken by Predictive-Model-Creator (PMC) that creates a prediction model by using regression analysis (Fig. 2). The goal of the prediction model is to predict the request's processing time by the system. This time depends upon the amount of concurrent requests and their types.

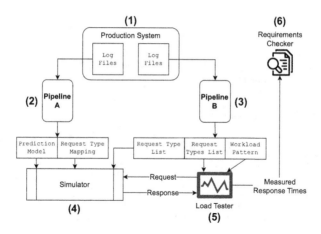

Fig. 1. The RAST components and connections: The analyzed system transfers its log files to Pipelines A and B that process the logs and produce the prediction model, the request type mapping, the list of all request types, and the pattern of system's workload; these are transmitted to Simulator and Load Tester. Load Tester produces a synthetic workload, sends requests to Simulator, measures the response times, and sends them to Requirements Checker that verifies if they comply with the performance requirements. When receiving a request, Simulator verifies request's type and transforms it to a numerical value for the prediction model. Simulator utilizes the prediction model for delaying the response for the time needed by the analyzed system for processing the corresponding request.

Our prediction model includes a regression algorithm with its parameters that are calculated by regression analysis (for example, linear regression and its coefficients). Our regression analysis employs a variety of machine-learning methods for predicting a continuous outcome variable using the values of one or several predictor variables [18].

It is essential for the choice of suitable predictor variables in our RAST approach that we can observe the variables at simulation run time in order to generate an input vector for our prediction model. While the target of our approach is the processing time, the predictor variables include the amount of concurrent requests at the beginning of the request, the amount of finished concurrent requests during the request processing, and the request's type.

Proper data preprocessing is an important factor in creating high-quality prediction models [10]. The PMC component implements two common data preprocessing methods: outlier detection and removal, and zero removal. The PMC component employs the standard deviation method for outlier detection and removal [4]: it calculates the mean and standard deviation of the processing times and it removes all values that lie from the mean more than three-times the standard deviation away. The PMC component offers two approaches for outlier detection: global and request. Global outlier detection considers all processing times whereas the request outlier detection, introduced in the new version, takes

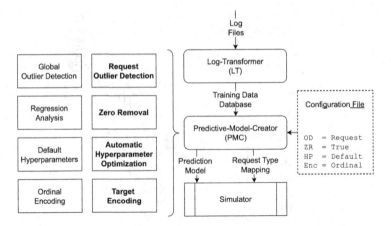

Fig. 2. Components of Pipeline A in RAST. Compared to the initial version [22], our new PMC component adds a request outlier detection method that is more precise than global outlier detection, adds a zero removal method, and performs automatic hyperparameter optimization. A configuration file enables choosing the preferred methods.

the processing times of each individual request type. In addition, the updated PMC component can perform zero removal which removes all database records with a processing time of zero, as they are often considered to be flawed measurements.

After removing outliers from the data, the PMC component compares common regression algorithms, called *estimators* in the following. Each estimator takes as input the training data and determines the optimal model parameters for a particular regression algorithm. This process in which the model parameters for the prediction model are learned via training is controlled by the values of hyperparameters. Hyperparameters are specific to the chosen estimator. Examples of such hyperparameters are the depth of a decision tree or the alpha value of ridge regression. The choice of proper hyperparameters has a great impact on the quality of a prediction model [3]. By default, RAST uses the default hyperparameters for the regression algorithms provided by the *scikit-learn* library [16], whereas in the new version, automatic hyperparameter optimization via grid search [3] can be activated. Grid search exhaustively searches for the optimal hyperparameters from a predefined set of hyperparameter combinations for a given estimator. We use Grid search in conjunction with five-fold cross-validation [19]. This involves performing cross-validation for each combination of hyperparameters and estimators, resulting in a score for each of them. We select the best estimator using the scores, and we export the best found estimator as a file, thus enabling the Simulator to use our prediction model.

Since many regression algorithms operate only on numerical data, PMC component modifies all textual requests in the training data to numeric values when loading the data. This modification assigns a unique number to each type of request. Every assignment is memorized in a hash map, so generating the request type mapping. PMC can use two different ways to generate the unique number: by ordinal encoding or target encoding [17], the latter being introduced in the new version. Ordinal encoding is a method that assigns a numerical value to each distinct request type incrementally. The first request type is assigned the number one, the second is assigned two, and so on. However, when ordinal encoding is used with nominal data, such as request types, it introduces an order that does not exist in reality. For instance, a request type x_i is not inherently less or greater than a request type x_{i-1} or x_{i+1}, $\forall i \in (1, 2, ..., \text{number\_of\_requests})$. This limitation makes ordinal encoding less suitable for nominal data. For nominal data, other encoding techniques, such as target encoding, are more appropriate [17]. Target encoding calculates the mean value of all response times for each request type and assigns this value to the respective request type. To improve accuracy, an additional smoothing step is often applied by multiplying the mean value with the relative frequency of the request type. In contrast to ordinal encoding, target encoding takes the influence of the request type on the response time into account, resulting in a more accurate encoding. This consideration is expected to positively influence the prediction model's quality. After the completion of Pipeline A, our Simulator gets the prediction model and the request type mapping.

3   An Alarm System as the Use Case

Our use case is illustrated in Fig. 3: a typical production-quality alarm system. A so-called Alarm Device (AD) is installed at the customer's home. When detecting a breach of some safety criterion, e.g., burglary or fire, or an AD's own malfunction, AD sends an alarm message to the Alarm Receiving Software (ARS) that runs in the Alarm Receiving Center (ARC), a computer center that is the endpoint for the messages from ADs.

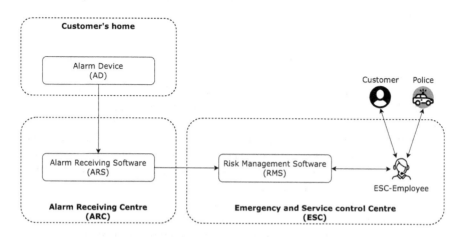

Fig. 3. A production-quality alarm system as our use case

ARS receives and processes alarm messages and then they are forwarded to the Risk Management Software (RMS) that runs in the Emergency and Service control Center (ESC). After an alarm message was processed by ARS, an acknowledgment is sent to the corresponding AD, such that no message resending is needed. The employees of ESC may take respective counter-measures as agreed with the customer.

Our use case in this paper is a production-quality software for alarm systems developed and maintained by the GSelectronic company [9] – one of the leading providers in Germany. It handles per day about 13.000 alarms received from more than 82.000 alarm devices working 24/7 all over Germany.

Nowadays, the software system supported by GSelectronic is a very large, quite complex, and not always well documented legacy distributed system that consists of about 80 executables and libraries written in C++, C#, BASIC, and Java, counting altogether more than $1.5 \cdot 10^6$ lines of code. The majority of the previous software developers are no longer available; furthermore, the system misses automated testing mechanisms, e.g., unit tests. In other words, we deal with the worst case of a legacy system, which is defined in the literature as "a large software system that we don't know how to cope with but that is vital to our organization" [14].

Therefore, our practical goal of performance evaluation for a productive alarm system poses several serious challenges:

1. Resource-sharing environment: the ARS is only one of altogether 12 server programs constituting the target SUE. Moreover, the system simultaneously runs anti-virus and backup software. These programs run in virtual machines (VM) and share system resources, e.g., CPU time, network bandwidth, memory, etc.;
2. Database-centric architecture: all servers' programs in the system use the same database instance, which can thus become a bottleneck;
3. The system has software bugs, is under continuous development, while the test environment is a legacy IT infrastructure.

Our measurements and company's statistics show that only 3% of the requests processed by the system are indeed processed by ARS, while the vast majority of requests go to other server software. Due to this high workload in background, one usually has to face unreliable performance measurements for the ARS. In the following, we show how our RAST approach can rectify this problem.

The timing behavior of an alarm system must follow the EN 50136 standard [7]. The *response time* between AD and ARS is the most relevant performance metric: it shows how timely the system responds to a request. Traditionally, according to the ISO/IEC 2382 standard [11], response time is defined as the time interval between a request and *any* response. However, the EN 50136 standard for alarm systems defines the response time as the time interval between an alarm message (request) sent and a *positive* acknowledgment (response) received, i.e., negative responses and timeouts do not count: ARS must meet the agreed real-time requirements in presence of failures and high workloads. The precise requirement on the response time in the EN 50136 standard for alarm systems is currently: the arithmetic average of all response times taken in any time interval is not allowed to exceed 10 sec, and the maximum response time must be under 30 sec.

In this paper, our objective is to determine the *saturation point* of the ARS, i.e., the maximum number of simultaneous Alarm Devices (ADs) that can be handled by the system. In the practical sense, the GSelectronic company plans to upgrade about 25.000 outdated ADs to a modern version, so the company desires to have a confirmation in advance that the system will be able to handle the increased workload of modern devices. A modern AD sends requests for health checking much more frequently (every 20 to 90 sec compared to once per day); moreover, much more data are exchanged during each request.

4   Training the Optimal Prediction Model

In this section, we: a) describe the process of training the optimal prediction model, b) showcase the influence on the R^2 score with different configurations for outlier detection, encoding, and hyperparameters, and c) compare the results of the new RAST implementation described in this paper vs. the initial, proof-of-concept implementation presented in [22]. To ensure a fair comparison, we utilize the same estimators as in our initial implementation.

For our training, we utilize one node of the PALMA II ("Parallel Linux System for Muenster Users" abbreviated in German) supercomputer provided by the University of Muenster. The node is equipped with Intel Xeon Gold 6140 18C processors with 2.30 GHz of which we utilize 36 CPU cores as well as 192 GB of RAM. Our PMC component utilizes multiple cores at two different stages:

- When automatic hyperparameter optimization is active, the grid search is performed with 36 so called jobs, i.e., up to 36 hyperparameter/estimator combinations are evaluated in parallel;
- The regression analysis and cross-validation process is implicitly parallelized by the *scikit-learn* library.

To make our results comparable, we use the same request logs for both implementations which we compare. The logs include 5 out of 12 server programs of the system, as only these programs produce request logs. Each request processed by these programs generates two lines of text in the log file, one for the begin of processing a request, one for its end. One line of text in the log file is usually named a log entry. From the selected server programs, we use 180 log files from 30 days spanning a 13-month period between Dec 2020 and Jan 2022. The selected days capture all of the different business workflows performed by the company throughout the year, including monthly and yearly accounting tasks, daily operations such as alarm message processing and customer handling, and other relevant workflows. Altogether, our considered log files feature about $40 \cdot 10^6$ log entries. The amount of resulting rows in the training database is about half of the amount of log entries, since one pair of log entries is used to calculate the processing time of a request, which means that our training database consists of around 20 million rows and 4 columns of data: the amount of parallel requests at the request beginning (PR 1 N), the amount of parallel requests finished during the request's processing (PR 2 N), the type of the request (CMD), and its processing time. We refer to the ordinal encoded request type as CMD O and to the target encoded request type as CMD T.

As an initial step of comparison between various configurations, we configure the PMC component with the exactly same settings as in our initial study (global outlier detection, no zero removal, and default hyperparameters). We do so to validate that our new RAST implementation produces identical results to its predecessor. Moreover, this provides us with a benchmark against which to measure our improvements.

Table 1 shows the estimators and their respective R^2 scores. We observe identical scores to our initial case study [22] with the DecisionTree Regression being the best and Ridge Regression having a lower score, by 0.089. Lasso and ElasticNet Regression are effectively useless with this configuration. Thus, our new implementation, when used with the predecessor's configuration, successfully produces identical results, demonstrating its successful implementation.

Table 1. Baseline R^2 scores of the estimators when using CMD 0, PR 1 N, PR 2 N as predictor variables, global outlier detection, and default hyperparameters. These scores are identical to the results of our initial study [22].

Estimator (regression type)	R^2 Score
Ridge	0.537
Lasso	−0.000
ElasticNet	−0.000
DecisionTree	0.626

Table 2 shows the improved R^2 scores for our next configuration of the PMC component: using request outlier detection, zero removal, and keeping the default hyperparameters. To assess the influence of zero removal and the different outlier detection methods, we show the R^2 scores for each combination, highlighting our target configuration in bold font.

The reason for this improvement is that request outlier detection is more precise than global outlier detection. For example, consider two requests, x and y, of type T, with processing times of 10 ms and 12 ms, and two requests, a and b, of type M, with processing times of 100 ms and 1000 ms respectively. Global outlier detection would remove both requests a and b, as it neglects the type of request. In contrast, request outlier detection only eliminates request b. Furthermore, zero removal eliminates around 2 million rows from the database, signifying that roughly 10% of our training data consisted of faulty measurements. Yet, the

Table 2. R^2 scores of the estimators when using CMD 0, PR 1 N, PR 2 N as predictor variables, and default hyperparameters. Columns (1)–(4) represent different combinations of zero removal (ZR) and outlier detection method. Column (1) shows the values from Table 1 for easier comparison, depicting the results for no zero removal (ZR) and global outlier detection (GOD). A comparison between Columns (2) and (1) reveals that ZR seemingly has no discernible effect. Columns (3) and (1) show that request outlier detection (ROD) significantly enhances the R^2 score, resulting in an improvement of around 0.2 for all estimators except of Lasso Regression. Column (4) shows the scores for zero removal and request outlier detection. Compared to (3), we observe a marginal improvement for all estimators except Lasso Regression. This underscores that zero removal marginally enhances the R^2 score when implemented alongside request outlier detection. This implies that zero removal boosts the R^2 score specifically when coupled with request outlier detection, albeit with minimal impact due to our specific dataset. The DecisionTree Regression remains the best and Ridge Regression slightly worse, although the difference between their scores has shrunk to 0.053. ElasticNet Regression has significantly improved, but is still far behind Ridge and DecisionTree Regression, with Lasso still being useless.

Estimator	(1) R^2 Score, No ZR, GOD	(2) R^2 Score, ZR, GOD	(3) R^2 Score, No ZR, ROD	(4) R^2 Score, ZR, ROD
Ridge Regression	0.537	0.537	0.756	**0.761**
Lasso Regression	−0.000	−0.000	−0.000	**−0.000**
ElasticNet Regression	−0.000	−0.000	0.263	**0.264**
DecisionTree Regression	0.626	0.626	0.811	**0.814**

R^2 score only improves when zero removal is used in conjunction with request outlier detection. This outcome can be attributed to the idiosyncrasies of our specific training data, and thus, we do not generalize that zero removal is only efficacious when paired with a specific outlier detection method.

In our third configuration, we use target encoding of the request type instead of ordinal encoding. Table 3 shows the R^2 scores compared to the previous configurations. The increased score of Ridge Regression can be attributed to the use of target encoding instead of ordinal encoding for the nominal data of request types. Ordinal encoding can introduce an artificial order to the request types, which might lead to a distortion of the model parameter estimated by the Ridge Regression.

Table 4 shows the R^2 scores of our final configuration: we activate automatic hyperparameter optimization for both ordinal and target encoding. We observe that, with this configuration, every estimator has a better score than the best baseline score in Table 1.

To summarize the improvements presented in this paper, cleaning the training data with a better outlier detection method and also removing zero values have together the biggest impact on the prediction quality of the model. Automatic hyperparameter optimization significantly improves the scores of ElasticNet and Lasso Regression, but only slightly improves Ridge and DecisionTree Regression. Target encoding improves Ridge Regression, but has little to no impact on the scores of the other examined estimators.

Table 3. R^2 Scores of the Estimators when using CMD T, PR 1 N, PR 2 N as predictor variables, request outlier detection, zero removal, and default hyperparameters. Compared to Table 2 we use target encoding on the request type instead of ordinal encoding with the result that the R^2 scores of ElasticNet and Lasso Regression are unchanged compared to the previous configuration. The score of the DecisionTree Regression is very slightly lower by 0.004 and Ridge Regression increased by 0.031. The gap between their scores has shrunk further to 0.018.

Estimator	R^2 Score
Ridge Regression	0.792
Lasso Regression	−0.000
ElasticNet Regression	0.264
DecisionTree Regression	0.810

Table 4. R^2 Scores of the Estimators when using CMD O or CMD T, PR 1 N, PR 2 N as predictor variables, request outlier detection, zero removal, and optimized hyperparameters. Compared to Tables 2 and 3 we activate automatic hyperparameter optimization and observe a significant improvement for ElasticNet and Lasso Regression with an improvement of 0.484 for ElasticNet and 0.676 for Lasso Regression for both encodings. The Ridge Regression remained the same. The DecisionTree Regression slightly improved by 0.006 for ordinal encoding and 0.001 for target encoding.

Estimator	R^2 Score CMD O	R^2 Score CMD T
Ridge Regression	0.761	0.792
Lasso Regression	0.676	0.676
ElasticNet Regression	0.748	0.748
DecisionTree Regression	0.820	0.821

The enhancements introduced in this paper improve the R^2 score of the Ridge Regression by 47% and the R^2 score of the DecisionTree Regression by 31%. ElasticNet and Lasso Regression initially had a score of 0, but with our improvements they have a higher score than the best baseline score of 0.626.

5   Experiments: Alarm System's Saturation Point

This section describes experiments aimed at determining the saturation point of our legacy alarm system using the prediction models described in the previous section. We rely on the testing infrastructure developed in our previous work [21,22], based on the popular load testing tool *Locust* [5], together with our own supplementary *shell* and *Python* scripts for automating and visualizing the results. Our testing infrastructure implements the Load Tester, Simulator, and Requirements Checker components of the RAST approach shown in Fig. 1. We observed a performance issue with the initial version of the Simulator component: when approaching the system saturation point, the CPU core running the simulator process became fully utilized. As a result, the simulation results could not accurately represent the real system, despite having a high R^2 score for the prediction model. The two main reasons for the high CPU utilization are caused by the simulator implementation in Python. First, Python in combination with CPython as the popular Python runtime is an interpreted language and, thus, inherently slower compared to compiled languages. Second, Python's Global Interpreter Lock (GIL) of CPython prevents a Python process from using multiple CPU cores, even when utilizing multiple threads on a multicore CPU [2]. Therefore, in this paper we re-implement the simulator in the compiled language Kotlin, and we employ the popular *Ktor* library [12] which utilizes multiple CPU cores, thus, solving the performance issues.

To ensure consistent comparison between our new findings and those reported in our previous work [22], we perform our experiments twice - once utilizing the prediction model (PM1) obtained with the initial version of RAST, and then employing the enhanced prediction model (PM2) presented in this paper. We use the same hardware as in our initial study: an HP Proliant dl380 G7 server equipped with two Intel Xeon X5690 processors with 3.46 GHz. We conduct all of our experiments within a virtual machine (VM) that has 8 virtual CPU cores with 16 GB of RAM. We run the Simulator and the Load Tester on the same computer. We also use the popular *mininet* tool [13] for simulating network bandwidth and latency. Our *mininet* topology (hosts, switches, and links) and the link parameters (bandwidth, delay, packet loss, jitter) reflect the properties of our production alarm system. The process of experiment running on our test infrastructure is encapsulated in a single *shell* script that uses *mininet's* built-in functions to establish a *mininet* topology and launch the Simulator and Load Tester components. We allow free access to our source code, *mininet* configuration, and server's parameters GitHub [20].

The goal of our load test is to evaluate the number of alarm devices that can be handled by the system while meeting the real-time requirements under the production workload. The workload generated by the Load Tester has two parts: the system workload generated by alarm devices sending alarm messages and the background workload generated by the other programs running at the same time. Our load tester uses the workload pattern extracted from the production system to generate the background workload; in our case study, it sends 70 requests per second that are randomly selected from 349 different request types. The system workload is gradually increased by simulating the alarm devices, each sending a request every 20 s, and increasing their amount over time, until we reach the critical workload, such that Requirements Checker of RAST reports that the required response time limit is exceeded. In this manner, we determine the saturation point of the system.

The Load Tester component distributes the system workload among three *Locust* workers, each running as a separate Python process. We experimentally choose the number of workers to be three, with the goal to utilize only as few CPU cores for the experiment as necessary. In our setup, the system workload, the background workload, and Simulator utilize five CPU cores, leaving three remaining cores for *mininet* and other system processes. The system workload runs for 10 min and then the Load Tester reports the measurements to Requirements Checker. The time of 10 min proves to suffice for each AD to send 30 requests during the experiment. We observe that running the test longer shows no significant influence on the results. If the real-time requirements are met, i.e., the mean and the maximum response times are within the standard requirements described in Sect. 3, Load Tester increases the amount of ADs by 200 (the initial number is 200 too) and repeats the system workload run. The experiment ends once Requirements Checker reports the saturation point. Once the saturation point is found, the Load Tester component goes back to the previous amount of ADs, and then it increases the amount of ADs by 20 in order to get finer-grained results.

Figure 4 shows the experimental results for our both prediction models, i.e., PM1 (previous) and PM2 (new). The top diagram shows the results for PM1, the bottom diagram for PM2. In each load test executed, the mean and maximum response times are shown as a blue and an orange curve, respectively. We observe that both models yield similar results and the system's saturation point lies around 1240–1340 ADs, depending on the model used. The maximum response time increases quickly and not monotonically. In our experiments, we observe that this behavior happens when several hundred ADs simultaneously send requests within a time frame of less than a second. This behavior is hard to reproduce consistently due to the non-deterministic scheduling of hundreds of ADs and the short time frame in which it occurs. The low average response time suggests that these situations are rare events in the experiment. To mitigate this issue, we repeat the experiment for each model nine times and calculate the average values of all reported average and maximum response times. After nine repetitions, we do not observe any changes in the found saturation point.

Our results show that, although PM2 has a significantly higher R^2 score than PM1, the difference in the measured saturation point is minimal in our experiment. We expect this difference to become more noticeable with a higher number of simulated ADs.

Our study also shows that the value of PR 2 N, which represents the amount of parallel requests that ended while the current request was processed, fluctuates significantly, even for the same number of ADs. These fluctuations are evident in the non-monotonic behavior of the maximum response time shown in Fig. 4, where the maximum response time can be lower for a greater number of ADs. Although our prediction variables produce a high R^2 score, these fluctuations suggest that the adopted prediction variables are still insufficient. Our future research will include other commonly used prediction variables, such as the average amount of requests per sec, to improve the model's accuracy.

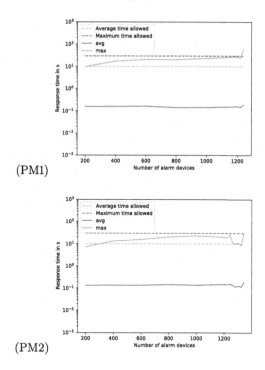

(PM1)

(PM2)

Fig. 4. Average and maximum response times depending on the number of ADs for both prediction models. Both models yield similar results, with an average response time (blue curve) between 0.1 s and 0.2 s. The maximum response time (orange curve) exceeds the allowed maximum response time at 1,240 ADs for PM1, with the response time of 61.151 s, and 1,340 ADs for PM2, with the response time of 30.379 s. (Color figure online)

6   Conclusion and Future Work

In this paper, we develop and implement several improvements of RAST – our approach to performance evaluation of legacy real-time systems by combining Regression Analysis, Simulation, and load Testing. These improvements enable training an adequate prediction model for a specific System Under Evaluation. We apply our enhancements to a commercial legacy alarm system which runs already in a production environment and poses strict real-time requirements. We evaluate various RAST configuration settings and report how they affect the model's R^2 score. We demonstrate significantly improved accuracy of performance evaluation due to our new developments.

The results from our prediction model generation indicate a significant improvement of accuracy over our initial study, with R^2 scores increasing for all tested models. For instance, the Ridge Regression improved from 0.537 to 0.792, while the Decision Tree Regression rises from 0.626 to 0.821. Additionally, both Elastic Net and Lasso Regression started out at 0 but were then increased to respective values of 0.748 and 0.676. Notably, the performance of each model surpassed the highest-performing model from our initial study, which was 0.626. Overall, these findings demonstrate the effectiveness of our proposed methodology.

Our experimental results show that, under usual operating conditions, our evaluated alarm system can successfully handle the workload of up to 1340 Alarm Devices (ADs) while meeting the real-time requirements of the EN 50136 standard. Thus, the company's long-term goal of managing 25000 modern ADs is currently at risk. However, we are now still at an early development stage of our RAST approach: in particular, the current model performs predictions based on only three predictor variables, which leads to fluctuations in the measured response time. Thus, the saturation point obtained with our current prediction model may still not represent the real system accurately enough, despite a high R^2 score.

In our future work, we will extract more predictor variables, like the average amount of requests/sec, from the log files, in order to improve the prediction model. Also, we plan to implement the RAST approach for different (open-source) software systems, in order to estimate its validity for other types of systems and thereby allow for better reproducibility of our experimental results.

References

1. Aichernig, B.K., et al.: Learning and statistical model checking of system response times. Softw. Qual. J. **27**(2), 757–795 (2019)
2. Beazley, D.: Understanding the Python GIL. In: PyCON Python Conference (2010)
3. Belete, D.M., Huchaiah, M.D.: Grid search in hyperparameter optimization of machine learning models for prediction of HIV/AIDS test results. Int. J. Comput. Appl. **44**(9), 875–886 (2022). https://doi.org/10.1080/1206212X.2021.1974663
4. Brownlee, J.: How to remove outliers for machine learning (2020). https://machinelearningmastery.com/how-to-use-statistics-to-identify-outliers-in-data/
5. Byström, C., et al.: Locust. https://docs.locust.io/en/stable/what-is-locust.html
6. Courageux-Sudan, C., Orgerie, A.C., Quinson, M.: Automated performance prediction of microservice applications using simulation. In: MASCOTS 2021, pp. 1–8 (2021). https://doi.org/10.1109/MASCOTS53633.2021.9614260
7. DIN EN 50136-1:2012-08: Alarm systems - alarm transmission systems and equipment - part 1: General requirements for alarm transmission systems (2012)
8. Grohmann, J., et al.: Monitorless: predicting performance degradation in cloud applications with machine learning. In: Middleware 2019, pp. 149–162. ACM (2019). https://doi.org/10.1145/3361525.3361543
9. GS. https://www.gselectronic.com/
10. Huang, J., et al.: An empirical analysis of data preprocessing for machine learning-based software cost estimation. Inf. Softw. Technol. **67**, 108–127 (2015). https://doi.org/10.1016/j.infsof.2015.07.004
11. ISO/IEC: ISO/IEC 2382:2015: Information technology - Vocabulary. Technical report, ISO (2015)
12. JetBrains: Ktor (2022). https://github.com/ktorio/ktor

13. Keti, F., Askar, S.: Emulation of software defined networks using mininet in different simulation environments. In: ISMS 2015, pp. 205–210 (2015). https://doi.org/10.1109/ISMS.2015.46
14. Matthiesen, S., Bjørn, P.: Why replacing legacy systems is so hard in global software development: an information infrastructure perspective. In: CSCW 2015, pp. 876–890. ACM (2015)
15. Okanović, D., Vidaković, M.: Software performance prediction using linear regression. In: Proceedings of the 2nd International Conference on Information Society Technology and Management, pp. 60–64. Citeseer (2012)
16. Pedregosa, F., et al.: Scikit-learn: machine learning in Python. J. Mach. Learn. Res. **12**, 2825–2830 (2011)
17. Potdar, K., et al.: A comparative study of categorical variable encoding techniques for neural network classifiers. Int. J. Comput. Appl. **175**(4), 7–9 (2017). https://doi.org/10.5120/ijca2017915495
18. Regression analysis essentials for machine learning. https://www.sthda.com/english/articles/40-regression-analysis/
19. Scikit-learn Development Team: Model selection and evaluation. https://scikit-learn.org/stable/model_selection.html
20. Tomak, J.: Performance Testing Infrastructure (2022). https://github.com/jtpgames/Locust_Scripts
21. Tomak, J., Gorlatch, S.: Measuring performance of fault management in a legacy system: an alarm system study. In: Calzarossa, M.C., Gelenbe, E., Grochla, K., Lent, R., Czachórski, T. (eds.) MASCOTS 2020. LNCS, vol. 12527, pp. 129–146. Springer, Cham (2021). https://doi.org/10.1007/978-3-030-68110-4_9
22. Tomak, J., Gorlatch, S.: RAST: evaluating performance of a legacy system using regression analysis and simulation. In: MASCOTS 2022, pp. 49–56 (2022). https://doi.org/10.1109/MASCOTS56607.2022.00015

KNXsim: Simulator Tool for KNX Home Automation Training by Means of Group Addresses

Juan A. Gómez-Pulido[1](✉) [iD] and Alberto Garcés-Jiménez[2] [iD]

[1] Department of Technologies of Computers and Communications,
Universidad de Extremadura, 10003 Cáceres, Spain
jangomez@unex.es

[2] Department of Computing Sciences, Universidad de Alcala,
28805 Alcala de Henares, Spain

Abstract. The growth of home automation makes it necessary to train qualified personnel in the knowledge and use of the most important standards, among which KNX is the leader in Europe. The programming of home automation services with KNX is based on the concept of group addresses, which allow defining the behavior of the domotic devices for a previously defined facility. This training is complex and usually requires a physical domotic facility where the previously programmed design can be tested, which makes the learning process difficult for the students. In this article we show the development and characteristics of a multi-platform simulator that recreates the real operation of an automated facility for any programming scheme defined by the student, validating it by means of a virtual installation that includes different devices usually involved in home automation. This simulator has allowed the generation of a wide range of cases of use in the training of the most usual domotic services.

Keywords: Simulation · Home automation · KNX · Group address

1 Introduction

Home automation (or Domotics) [7] is a technological area that deals with the development and integration of automated systems in all types of facilities, with the aim of efficiently managing services such as security, energy, communications, comfort, etc. This area of knowledge is undergoing a fast technological growth and social deployment, with a strong projection in innovation. For this reason, academic institutions include its study in practically all engineering degrees: industrial, telecommunications, computer science, electronics, etc.

In the early 1990s, Europe promoted the "European Installation Bus" (EIB) home automation standard, which evolved into the EIB Konnex standard, better known as KNX [1]. It is an open standard, oriented to the technical management of buildings and homes. Most of european domotized facilities are deployed by using the KNX standard.

© ICST Institute for Computer Sciences, Social Informatics and Telecommunications Engineering 2024
Published by Springer Nature Switzerland AG 2024. All Rights Reserved
J.-L. Guisado-Lizar et al. (Eds.): SIMUtools 2023, LNICST 519, pp. 34–43, 2024.
https://doi.org/10.1007/978-3-031-57523-5_3

KNX allows for highly scalable designs and can be used in installations of any size, large or small. KNX facilities are very flexible, as they allow components from different manufacturers to be connected. The compliance of domotic devices with this standard is managed by the KNX Association [3], which currently has more than 500 members in 190 countries.

The design of a domotic system based on KNX architecture can be planned schematically and the devices involved can be programmed manually. However, this procedure is complex, not very flexible and subject to failures. It is important to note that the operation of a KNX system depends on how the so-called Group Addresses (GA) are used and assigned. The concept of GA is fundamental, as its understanding will enable engineers to design a correct domotic system.

The automation of the design and programming processes of a KNX system is mostly done by means of the Engineering Tool Software (*ETS*) [5], which relies on GAs for the definition and operation of the domotic services. This powerful tool allows to design any KNX configuration and to program it; however, it lacks the ability to simulate the designed system for validation before programming the real facility. In other words, we will only know that the domotic services will work according to our specifications when we program it in the real environment. This limitation makes the possibility of using simulators attractive.

This paper shows the development of the *KNXsim* simulator, which allows to simulate the real behavior of domotic services as they have been programmed using GAs. This simulator was mainly designed for training purposes, in order to facilitate the understanding of the concept of group addresses and its experimentation without the need of having the physical home automation facility.

2   Related Works

ETS is the main software tool devoted to the design and programming of KNX-based home automation systems. It is a powerful and professional tool, but lacks the ability to perform simulations. To fill this gap, KNX Association developed the *KNX Virtual* [2] tool. This software performs a simulation of the system, although it has two limitations in regards to a comprehensive academic purpose. On the one hand, *KNX Virtual* can only run under the Windows operating system, so computers with the Linux O.S. (quite common in academic, student and laboratory environments) would not be able to install this simulator. On the other hand, the visual environment is not very user-friendly, as it consists of a set of rectangles that need to be conceptually associated with the different home automation devices, which have to be imagined. In addition, *KNX Virtual* requires a previous study in its use and does not facilitate the understanding of the concept of group addresses, a basic concept in this domain.

KNX simulator [4] is a powerful online simulation tool designed to learn KNX through practice without the need of having physical devices. Its beautiful visual environment and high level of user interaction facilitates the learning process. This tool is mainly focused on the selection of real home automation devices, their connectivity and simulated operation. However, the design of the installation to be programmed (including the definition of the group addresses) still requires the use of the *ETS* tool.

In this sense, unlike *KNX simulator*, *KNXsim* facilitates the learning of KNX home automation systems under the paradigm of group addresses without the need of other tools, such as *ETS*. This way, *KNXsim* provides a conceptual and academic approach as a first step for a better knowledge that will facilitate the later use of *ETS* and/or *KNX simulator*.

3   Methodology

3.1   Domotic Approach

The simulator proposes a house with a particular domotic architecture, not defined by the user in terms of its elements and physical connections. Therefore, the simulator was designed to allow operational, but not constructive, flexibility.

This design approach was chosen because, as mentioned above, the simulator was developed mainly for training purposes. It is intended to facilitate the understanding of the concept and handling of group addresses for home automation, which is perfectly covered by a rigid physical architecture, as long as it is broad enough to cover the most common domotic services.

This approach allows to generate a wide set of use cases of group addresses, where different operational approaches for the same domotic purpose can be explored. In this way, training of group address is simplified if the same physical home automation structure is always used as a starting point.

3.2   Architecture of the Domotic House

Figure 1 shows the domotic architecture of the facility that will be used by the simulator, in terms of its functional elements and connections. In this case, the installation represents a home.

There are several types of elements:

- Sensors. The sensors are the domotic devices that receive information from the environment (temperature, luminosity, touch, etc.) and send the corresponding values to the domotic bus. Thus, the domotic system will make the appropriate decisions according to the way it was programmed.
- Loads. The loads are electromechanical devices that can be controlled by a home automation system for purposes of climate control, security, comfort, etc. For example, loads are lights, alarms, taps, doors, blinds, etc. We remark that the loads are not domotic devices, but devices that are controlled by the domotic devices.
- Actuator. 8-channel binary output switch. This device controls the on/off switching of the loads according to the values received from the sensors.
- Buses. Electrical power line and KNX bus. The first one feeds electrically the actuators and the loads. The second connects the sensors and the actuator to enable communication among them.

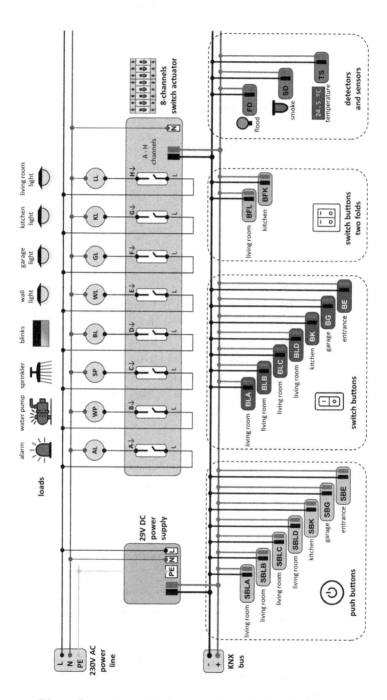

Fig. 1. Domotic architecture considered by the simulator.

Table 1. Devices involved in the domotized house.

ID	Device
Loads:	
AL	alarm
WP	water pump
SP	sprinkler
BL	blinks
WL	wall light
GL	garage light
KL	kitchen light
LL	living room light
Sensors:	
FD	flood detector
SD	smoke detector
TS	temperature sensor
Switch buttons:	
SBLA	switch button A in living room
SBLB	switch button B in living room
SBLC	switch button C in living room
SBLD	switch button D in living room
SBK	switch button in kitchen
SBG	switch button in garage
SBE	switch button in entrance
Push buttons:	
BLA	push button A in living room
BLB	push button B in living room
BLC	push button C in living room
BLD	push button D in living room
BK	push button in kitchen
BG	push button in garage
BE	push button in entrance
Push buttons 4-fold:	
BFL	push button-four in living room
BFK	push button-four in kitchen

Table 1 lists the visible devices involved in the user's interaction with the home automation system.

Figure 2 shows the domotic house from the end user's point of view, where all the sensors and loads are visible. The simulator uses this view for the validation

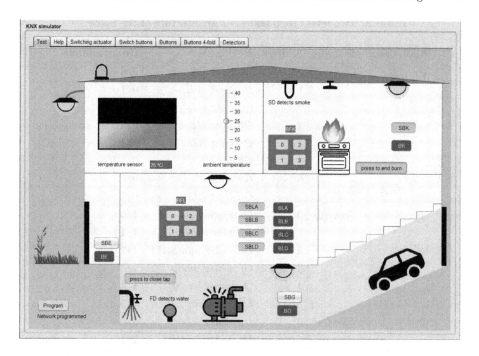

Fig. 2. Simulator view of the domotic house.

of the domotic behaviour as the group addresses have been programmed. The simulator provides, for this view, a set of buttons that allow the user interaction to control the house, as well as the necessary mechanisms to define environmental events that condition the domotic behavior, such as ambient temperature, smoke generation, water flooding, etc.

Table 2 shows the group addresses architecture of the house. As we said before, *KNXsim* considers a fixed architecture of a domotic system. This requires the definition of a table of group addresses (in our case, of two levels), which assign to each address a meaning in terms of the operability of the associated load. The group addresses have been classified into three domains of home automation services: lighting, security and comfort.

3.3   Simulator Workflow

Figure 3 shows the workflow developed for the simulator. The user of the tool has two options: to design the home automation application and to test its operation.

The user designs the home automation application by modeling the scene, i.e. designing the links between the actuator channels and the sensors by means of the corresponding group addresses. Once this modeling is done, the group addresses are automatically sent to the home automation devices (switch actuator, buttons, and detectors), which generate signals that indicate valid events. If the group address selections are incorrect or they have not yet been selected, these signals

Table 2. Two-level group addresses architecture of the house.

Main group	Meaning	Address	Meaning	Group address
0	Lighting	0	On light WL	0/0
		1	Off light WL	0/1
		2	On light GL	0/2
		3	Off light GL	0/3
		4	On light KL	0/4
		5	Off light KL	0/5
		6	On light LL	0/6
		7	Off light LL	0/7
1	Security	0	On alarm AL	1/0
		1	Off alarm AL	1/1
		2	On water pump WP	1/2
		3	Off water pump WP	1/3
		4	On sprinkler SP	1/4
		5	Off sprinkler SP	1/5
2	Comfort	0	Up blinks BL	2/0
		1	Down blinks BL	2/1

are not sent. Therefore, the simulator will only act on the domotic system when it receives valid events.

The result of these events on the domotic house is only generated when the test order is received by the user, and this order will only arrive if there are valid events. This will prevent the simulator from activating non-configured or erroneous applications.

The simulator generates the results by visualizing the effects that the domotic devices and the environmental conditions generate on the loads. An undesired result can be achieved if the configuration of the group addresses for the designed scene is not correct, in which case this scene has to be redesigned by selecting the correct set of group addresses.

4   Results

The simulator was programmed using the Java language [6] and the Netbeans [8] graphics library. In this way, the application can run independently of the operating system, which favors its dissemination in any academic installation.

Currently, *KNXsim* is used as a teaching tool in the lab practices of the Domotics subject, that belongs to the Degree on Telecommunication Engineering of the University of Extremadura, Spain. In addition to the application installed on the laboratory computers, students have a wide range of practice scripts to implement use cases in the programming of home automation services. Each

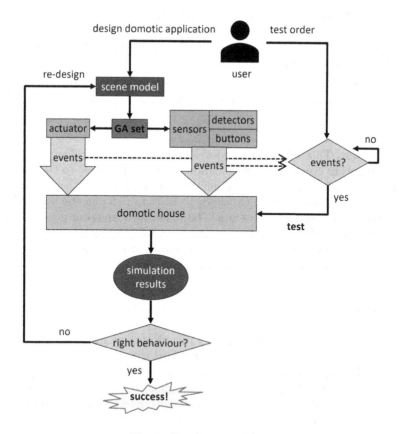

Fig. 3. Simulator workflow.

practice is based on some specifications, with which the student must program the appropriate group addresses for each domotic device. This programming is not deterministic, but the specified result must be so. In this way, the student's understanding and creativity are favored in order to reach the same end.

The following list shows some of the use cases considered in the practices for the students according to the timetable of the subject. These cases were selected as they cover basic domotic services present in many homes:

- Lighting control based on user interaction.
- Lighting control based on door opening.
- Alarm control based on smoke, flood or intrusion detection.
- Sprinkler control based on fire detection.
- Water pump control based on the detection of flooding in the garage.
- Blinds opening degree control according to the outdoor temperature.

Nevertheless, other use cases different from those listed and many other combinations can be configured from the same domotic devices and loads available

Table 3. Features comparison of KNX simulator tools.

Feature	KNXsim	KNXsimulator	KNX virtual
Realistic graphical interface	Yes	Yes	No
Platform	All	online	Windows only
Supports group addresses	Yes	No	No

in the simulator. This will favor the development of projects where the student will autonomously create home automation services of interest to the user.

Table 3 shows a comparison of the simulator with the alternatives described in Sect. 2 in terms of basic operational characteristics from a didactic point of view, which is the main purpose of KNXSim. The simulator stands out in two features: it has been developed to be used under any operating system that supports Java (e.g. Windows and Linux) and to use group addresses as a fundamental element for designing home automation applications.

5   Conclusions

The *KNXsim* simulator was developed to facilitate the learning of the design of domotic systems based on the KNX standard through the concept of group addresses. This tool fills a gap in *ETS*, the main software devoted to the programming of these systems: *ETS* does not allow a simulation prior to the programming of the physical installation. This means, on the one hand, that anomalous behaviors can only be detected if we have access to the real system once it has been programmed; on the other hand, debugging times are longer, as a real validation is always required. Other tools allow prior simulation, but are more difficult to use or have a more professional approach.

In addition to allowing a simulation of domotic behavior, KNXsim was developed with the purpose of facilitating training in domotic programming by means of group addresses. This simulator, intended for academic environments, presents a user-friendly environment, easy to understand and operate, and a set of manuals and practice scripts for the student.

The current experience is that students understand the concept of group addresses and become familiar with KNX-based systems better and more quickly. Nevertheless, we want to go further into this educational area, proposing some indicators to analyze the impact of this tool on student learning regarding to traditional learning methods. Also, we want to analyze the usability facts of real professional users in the domotic area.

Acknowledgements. The authors thank the support of Fundacion General CSIC and the State Research Agency, Spain, under the contracts 0551-PSL-6-E (iFriend project) and PID2022-137275NA-I00 (X-BIO project) respectively, by the resources used for developing the simulator.

Author contributions. Juan A. Gómez-Pulido: Conceptualization; Methodology; Investigation; Software; Computational; Writing; Supervision. Alberto Garcés-Jiménez: Ideas; Testing; Writing-review.

References

1. KNX Handbook for Home and Building Control, 6th edn. KNX Association (2015)
2. ETS6 and KNX Virtual for testing and learning about KNX. Technical report, KNX Association (2023)
3. KNX Association: Mission and Objectives (2023). https://www.knx.org/knx-en/for-professionals/What-is-KNX/Our-mission/. Accessed Sept 2023
4. KNX Simulator, S.L.: KNX Simulator (2023). https://www.knxsimulator.com. Accessed Sept 2023
5. Meier, M., Szczensny, C.: The Ultimate Guide to KNX Programming: One of fastest, easiest and cheapest ways to learn KNX programming and ETS 5. Voltimum (2018)
6. Sharan, K., Davis, A.: Beginning Java 17 Fundamentals: Object-Oriented Programming in Java 17 (2022). https://doi.org/10.1007/978-1-4842-7307-4
7. Spivey, D.: Home Automation For Dummies. O'Reilly (2015)
8. Wielenga, G.: Beginning NetBeans IDE: For Java Developers. Apress (2015)

Development of a 3D Visualization Interface for Virtualized UAVs

Chloé Rivière[1], Jamie Wubben[2]([envelope])[ID], Carlos T. Calafate[2][ID],
and Tahiry Razafindralambo[1][ID]

[1] Reunion Island and Indian Ocean Engineering School (ESIROI),
University of Reunion Island, Reunion Island, France
chloe.riviere@esiroi.re, tahiry.razafindralambo@univ-reunion.fr
[2] Computer Engineering Department (DISCA), Universitat Politecnica de València,
46022 Valencia, Spain
{jwubben,calafate}@disca.upv.es

Abstract. Nowadays, Unnamed Aerial Vehicles (UAVs) are used in many different fields, ranging from agriculture and entertainment to parcel delivery, among others. For several of these tasks, the UAVs are programmed to follow a specific path, as defined in their flight missions. In addition, as more sophisticated solutions begin to be adopted, new protocols should be developed to handle possible collisions among UAVs, as well as to create UAV swarms. However, directly testing new protocols on UAVs can be hazardous and time consuming. Therefore, many investigators first perform simulations. Although different UAV simulators exists, not all of them offer a 3D rendering of the UAVs in the target flight environment. Hence, in this work, we present a real-time 3D visualization interface that can be easily coupled to any simulator. In this way, we offer developers a powerful way to validate their solutions and make in-depth analysis.

Keywords: UAV simulator · 3D visualization · ArduSim · Unity

1 Introduction

Unnamed Aerial Vehicles (UAVs), more commonly known as drones, have experienced a huge adoption in recent years by both particulars and professionals, for different reasons, and in different fields. According to the field and their intended use, the UAVs need specific algorithms to, e.g., avoid collisions, perform surveillance on a specific area, etc.

The process of testing these new algorithms is complex and prone to frequent failures. As such, attempting to perform tests on real UAVs is a time-consuming and costly endeavor. For this reason, especially in the initial stages, simulation is preferred. Different UAV simulation tools have been made available in recent years, such as AirSim [10], which allows controlling UAVs and many other vehicles in a 3D environment, or tools which are specific for UAVs like Gazebo [6].

© ICST Institute for Computer Sciences, Social Informatics and Telecommunications Engineering 2024
Published by Springer Nature Switzerland AG 2024. All Rights Reserved
J.-L. Guisado-Lizar et al. (Eds.): SIMUtools 2023, LNICST 519, pp. 44–55, 2024.
https://doi.org/10.1007/978-3-031-57523-5_4

In particular, our focus in this work in on ArduSim [3], an UAV emulation tool developed to model interactions between UAVs based on wireless communications. However, ArduSim lacks a proper 3D visualization interface, complicating the proper validation of novel protocols under development. Hence, in this work, we address this challenge by developing a new component for ArduSim: a new 3D visualization interface. More specifically, the visualization interface allows seeing if, for example, a UAV swarm has the formation wanted, and if their coordinates on the map are correct.

We created this interface to extend the capabilities of our simulator ArduSim. Nevertheless, there are more simulators that do not provide a 3D interface. Hence, we created our interface in such a way that it is open, meaning that it can be easily connected to other simulators as well. Our new 3D tool is able to (i) render multiple UAVs at the same time, (ii) render buildings, and the terrain, (iii) and work in real-time.

The remainder of this paper is organized as follows: the following section will present the most relevant works in the field of UAV simulation, with greater emphasis on the OpenStreetMap project. Afterward, in Sect. 3, we explain how our application is developed, we go over its features, and detail how it should be used. Then, in Sect. 4, we perform various experiments in order to test the limits of our tool. Finally, Section Sect. 5 concludes the paper and refers to future works.

2   Related Work

With all the interest around UAV topics in recent years, a plethora of protocols have been developed using UAV simulators. Currently, we can find several UAV simulators, and some of them have a 3D or 2D visualization built-in. For instance, InDrone [1] is a UAV simulator that has only visualizes the UAVs in 2D. This requires less computational power and, although it is useful in many cases, sometimes 3D rendering is necessary in order to fully analyze the behaviour of the UAV flight paths. For instance, when simulating collision avoidance, take-off algorithms, landing, etc.

Other well-known UAV simulators do include a 3D visualization. For instance, FlightGear [8], and Gazebo [6]. However, in their simulators, the 3D visualization is completely built-in. This is a problem for two reasons. First, one must always use the 3D user interface, which makes performing many tests more-time consuming. Secondly, it does not allow users to easily integrate different simulators at the same time. This might become important in the future when we want to simulate UAVs, rovers, and boats at the same time. Hence, we propose a 3D visualization interface that can be easily connected to any simulator.

A common feature in many simulators is the choice and generation of the map/environment. Often the map is build using real building information (e.g. OpenstreetMap) and the ground is artificially created by a script [4].

There are different libraries that allow for a easy creation of the map. As seen in the Table 1, the most convenient choice for the OpenStreetMap was the

Table 1. Map Information sources.

Name	License	Library for Unity	References
OpenIndoor	Free	No	[7]
Streets GL	Free	No	[2]
Esri OpenStreetMap 3D Scene Layers	Proprietary	No	[9]
Map SDK Mapbox	Free	Yes	[5]

Map SDK for Unity from MapBox [5], which enables a direct implementation, and provides various examples of using the map for the Unity game engine.

3 Application Development and Design

In this section, we will explain how we developed our 3D interface. We will start by the architecture, then go over the different features our 3D visualization tool offers, and finally explain how a user can interact with the tool.

3.1 Architecture

Our entire tool was created using the Unity game engine. This allowed us to develop the tool faster, and also to make use of many libraries that are compatible with all major platforms (Windows, Linux, and macOS). As stated before, the intention of this visualization interface is to only visualize the UAVs and their environment. The actual simulation of the drones is performed by ArduSim [3]. Hence, this visualization tool requires some data from ArduSim in order to accurately display the UAVs. It is worth reiterating that our goal is that this tool can be used for other simulators as well. In order to facilitate this, the data that this visualization tool requires is received via web sockets. Notice that communication through web sockets is both straightforward and universally used.

In order for our tool to work, messages must be sent (using JSON) to this web socket. The messages only have to contain the x, y, and z coordinates (in UTM format), and a unique number in order to identify the drone. From the moment our visualization tool receives the first message, it will create a drone instance and place it on the desired location (based on the UTM coordinates). If new data is received, the drone's location will be updated. It is obvious that, in order for the drone to move smoothly, the simulator should send messages frequently.

Furthermore, our visualization tool supports two different types of maps (and the option to disable the map completely). The first type of map that we include in our tool uses information from OpenStreetMap in order to accurately display buildings, streets, etc. In order to do so, we relied on the map SDK (software development kit) from MapBox. In order to initialize the map, we use the first

UTM position received as the center of the virtual world. Then, we render the world around this first drone. The specific area that will be rendered depends on the position of the camera and the field of view of the camera. When the UAV moves, the map will automatically update and render new parts of the virtual world when needed. In Fig. 1a, we show what this virtual world looks like.

Besides this type of map, we also have the option to use information from Digital Elevation Maps (DEMs). These maps consist of information about the terrain level (sometimes they also include buildings). The advantage of these types of files is that (i) they are readily available, and (ii) we can accurately display the terrain level. This might be important when researchers are simulating a drone flight in the mountains. Since these files only provide the elevation level (above sea level) for specific coordinates, some processing was needed. First of all, at the beginning of the experiment, this file needs to be read, and the elevation data needs to be retrieved and stored in local memory. This processing takes some time, but it only has to be done once. Afterward, we create our virtual world by rendering multiple triangles. Since we have the elevation information of many points, we are able to create a smooth surface. In Fig. 1b, we provide a visual representation.

(a) Map view with MapBox.   (b) Map view with DEM.

Fig. 1. The two different maps that are available.

3.2   Features

Besides choosing between the two maps, our visualization tool also includes a few extra features. First of all we have different cameras so that the user analyzes the UAVs from different perspectives. We include four different types of views: a static view, a "following view", a focused view, and a view from a camera placed on a UAV. In Fig. 2 we show the different type of views. As one can image, the static view remains at one place, the following view follows the UAVs from a distance, the focused view is a close up view for one specific UAV, and finally the drone view is a first person view taken from a camera attached to the UAV. This drone view gives a more realistic aspect to the interface by allowing the user to have the view of the UAV camera as in a real life use.

To further explain where the cameras are placed for each specific view, we include Fig. 3. In this figure, one can clearly see the different camera views.

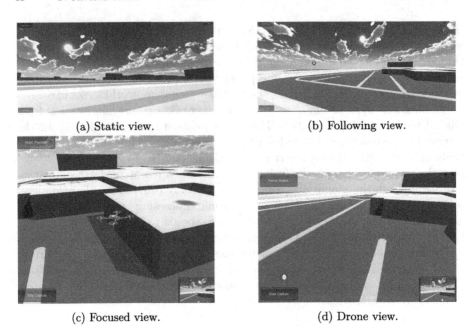

<table>
</table>

(a) Static view.   (b) Following view.

(c) Focused view.   (d) Drone view.

Fig. 2. The different views available in our visualization tool.

Since there are different types of views, we can easily lose sight of one UAV. For this reason, we included small flags on top of the UAVs (including their ID). This flag is placed differently depending on one criterion: whether the UAVs are in the camera's field of view or not. For UAVs in the camera's field of view, the flag is displayed when the distance between the camera and the UAV in each axis (x, y, z) exceeds a fixed distance. To place the flag correctly on the screen (above the UAV), the UAV's position in the 3D world is converted to a 2D position on the screen. This conversion is made possible by a function of the camera in Unity. For UAVs that remain outside the camera's field of view, the corresponding flags are placed on the right or left side of the screen. This would tell users in which direction they need to turn the camera to see the UAVs. Such direction in determined by first calculating the direction between the camera and the UAV; based on this direction, we can calculate the angle between the camera and the UAV. To this angle we add the angle of rotation of the camera; thus, if this angle is below or above a certain threshold, we know in which direction the camera must be turned, and on which side of the screen we need to place the flag.

Finally, we also include an option to record a video. This will provide the user the ability to review the simulation later on. The user has 4 states regarding the recording: not recording, currently recording, paused recording, and finished recording. At the end of the recording, if the option to send video has not been disabled, the recorded video will be sent to a dedicated server via a web socket.

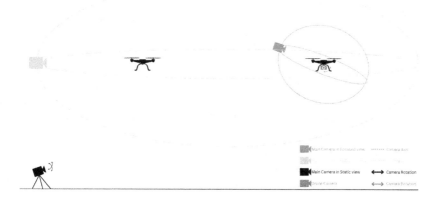

Fig. 3. Static view and camera rotation features.

The recording of the simulation is done using a library (Rock VR) created for Unity. This library allows recording the field of view of any designated camera. Despite the fact that the library only records the flow of a specific camera and the UI elements, this library has been chosen due to the fact that it is free, and works out of the Unity environment, in contrast to the Unity editor recording which only works in the Unity environment. This in an important element, especially when users merely intend to run the executable, and not work within the Unity environment.

3.3   User Interface

The simulator provides many opportunities for user interaction. These interactions allow the user to tailor the interface to their needs. Many of these interactions are optional and intuitive to use (click on a button, move the mouse). We can find some of these interactions in Fig. 4.

Before starting the simulation, the user has the opportunity to make some configurations. These configurations will not be editable during the simulation. In these pre-configurations we will find the choice of map type, the scale of the map, the choice of the camera path for saving the recording, the possibility of sending the video to a server or not, the rendering quality of the simulation, and the possibility of hiding or showing the UAV flags. The user can leave the focused view with a double click/tap, or by pressing the space bar, which will set the main camera to the selected view type and "destroy" the UAV camera.

4   Evaluation

In this section, we proceed to validate the developed application by performing different types of tests to determine how different loads/features affect the CPU

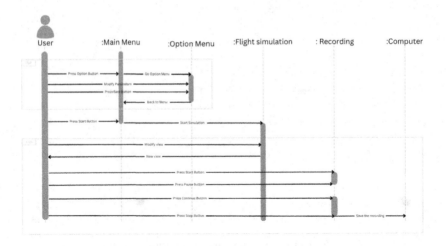

Fig. 4. User interaction options.

and RAM use. Notice that both CPU and RAM are critical resources, being intimately related to an adequate execution of the application. Hence, these tests will have a series of experiments with different numbers of UAVs, while other tests will vary the different map options, the rendering quality, and the recording option. Each test was repeated on a laptop (see specifications, Table 2). In order to have accurate results, each experiment was repeated three times with a simulation of 2 UAVs for 30 s (except when stated otherwise). The CPU and RAM usage was collected every 5 s.

Table 2. Hardware used for experiments.

Feature	Value	Feature	Value
Processor	Intel(R) Core(TM) i5-8265U	Speed	1.60 GHz (1.80 GHz max)
Cores	4	Hyper-Threading	Yes
RAM	8 GB	HHDD	237 GB
GPU	Intel UHD Graphics 620	Screen resolution	1920 × 1080
OS	Windows 10 Professional		

4.1 Impact of the Rendering Quality

For all the different qualities tested, the same configuration was used: Mapbox map, following view, without recording, and with the same UAV scheme. This test shows whether the quality of the video selected affects the CPU or the RAM during the simulation. Figure 5 illustrates the results achieved with 6 different rendering qualities:

- VL (Very Low)
- L (Low)
- M (Medium)

- H (High)
- VH (Very High)
- U (Ultra)

These different qualities affect the frame rate, anti-aliasing (which allows for smooth edges), shadow rendering, and more.

From Fig. 5a we find that the rendering quality of the interface has a major impact on the use of CPU; we can specifically see the gap for the first quality level (VL) to the fourth (H). Concerning the last three, High, Very High and Ultra, they present a similar CPU usage. From Fig. 5b we can also see that the different qualities do not affect RAM usage.

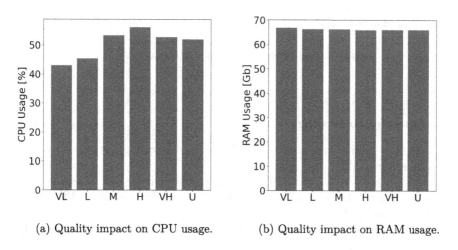

(a) Quality impact on CPU usage.   (b) Quality impact on RAM usage.

Fig. 5. Impact of video quality on CPU and RAM.

4.2 Impact of the Map

The tests detailed below were carried out by fixing the configuration as follows: same rendering quality, following view, and no recording. This way, only the map itself is changed. Our purpose is to determine if the map choice has an effect on the CPU or the RAM usage during the simulation.

Figure 6a shows that the different maps do not have a significant impact on the use of CPU; in contrast, in Fig. 6b we can see an increase of the RAM usage for the DEM map due to the reading of the DEM file (needed for the ground elevation data).

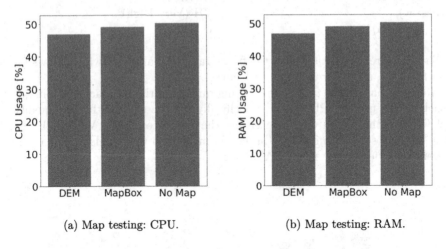

(a) Map testing: CPU.   (b) Map testing: RAM.

Fig. 6. Impact of maps' usage on CPU and RAM.

4.3   Impact of Recording

The tests that follow were carried out by fixing the configuration as follows: same rendering quality, and following view. This way, only the impact of the recording and the sending would be measured. Our purpose is to determine if the recording and the sending of the video have an effect on the CPU or the RAM usage during the simulation.

Figure 7a shows that the recording and sending are tasks that significantly increase the CPU usage. Similarly, in Fig. 7b we can notice the increase of the RAM usage according to the space needed during the recording for the data of the video and for the sending of the video, which required the reading of the video data for the conversion of the video while sending.

4.4   Impact of the Number of UAVs

The tests that follow were carried out to determine how many UAVs we can visualize in real time using our interface. Hence, we have tested increasing the number of UAVs in the experiment, while testing with different rendering qualities, and again measuring both CPU and RAM usage. The *following* view was chosen, and we also made one test with recording on.

Figure 8a shows that the CPU usage reaches its maximum with about 15 UAVs, independently of the rendering quality; yet, the movement of the camera for each view still remains smooth with up to 25 UAVs. Above 25 UAVs, the simulation is not smooth anymore, failing to represent mobility realistically. In terms of RAM usage, Fig. 8b demonstrates that the number of UAVs is not a

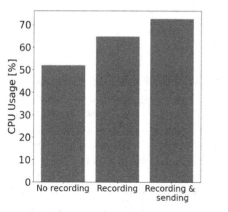
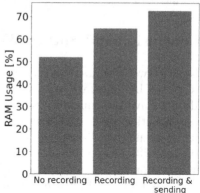

(a) Recording and sending: impact on CPU.

(b) Recording and sending: impact on RAM.

Fig. 7. Impact of recording and sending on CPU and RAM.

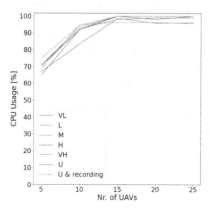
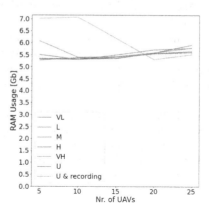

(a) CPU use for different UAVs.

(b) RAM use for different UAVs.

Fig. 8. Impact of increasing the number of UAVs on CPU and RAM.

factor having a significant impact on simulation. Hence, in most cases, only CPU limits should be accounted for.

In this test we have also noticed that, if we enable recording, the limit of UAVs to be used is just under 15 UAVs. This lower limit is associated to the high needs in terms of CPU usage associated to the recording process. Above 15 UAVs, the CPU can no longer handle adequately both the real-time UAV simulation and the recording process itself. This can also be seen in Fig. 8b:

above 15 UAVs, the use of RAM decreases when recording is enabled because the interface can no longer record adequately.

5   Conclusion and Future Work

In this paper, we have presented a new 3D UAV visualization interface that can be easily used by different UAV simulators. In this way, good UAV simulators that do not have the capability to render UAVs in 3D can now use our tool to do so. Additionally, this allows for the rendering of the UAV to be executed on a different machine. With the use of this 3D UAV visualization interface, investigators will now be able to analyze their simulations in a better way. With our visualization tool, the surrounding (buildings, streets, etc.) of the UAVs is automatically built. Furthermore, we have different cameras in order to inspect the UAV from different angles. One of these cameras is a first person view camera, which provides a realistic view of what the UAV sees. Furthermore, videos can be recorded from every camera.

We performed various tests in order to validate our visualization tool. Results show that our 3D interface allows visualizing in real-time up to 25 UAVs with the best rendering quality; tests also highlighted the huge consumption of the CPU and the RAM during the recording, which limited the overall number of UAVs to 15.

To improve the current interface, it would be interesting to test other libraries for the recording to find a way to reduce the use of CPU and RAM associated to this process. Also, to have a more realistic simulation, it will also be interesting to have different types of UAVs with different weights and characteristics.

Acknowledgement. This work has been partially supported by R&D project PID2021-122580NB-I00, funded by MCIN/AEI/10.13039/501100011033 and "ERDF A way of making Europe". It was also supported by ERASMUS+, as a cooperation project between the Universitat Politècnica de València (UPV), Spain, and the Reunion Island and Indian Ocean Engineering School (ESIROI).

References

1. Eiris, R., Albeaino, G., Gheisari, M., Benda, W., Faris, R.: InDrone: a 2D-based drone flight behavior visualization platform for indoor building inspection. Smart Sustain. Built Environ. **10**(3), 438–456 (2021)
2. Esri: Streetgl map online. https://streets.gl
3. Fabra, F., Calafate, C.T., Cano, J.C., Manzoni, P.: ArduSim: accurate and real-time multicopter simulation. Simul. Model. Pract. Theory **87**, 170–190 (2018)
4. Hong, W.T., Lee, P.S.: Mesh based construction of flat-top partition of unity functions. Appl. Math. Comput. **219**(16), 8687–8704 (2013)
5. Laksono, D., Aditya, T.: Utilizing a game engine for interactive 3D topographic data visualization. ISPRS Int. J. Geo Inf. **8**(8), 361 (2019)

6. Meyer, J., Sendobry, A., Kohlbrecher, S., Klingauf, U., von Stryk, O.: Comprehensive simulation of quadrotor UAVs using ROS and Gazebo. In: Noda, I., Ando, N., Brugali, D., Kuffner, J.J. (eds.) SIMPAR 2012. LNCS (LNAI), vol. 7628, pp. 400–411. Springer, Heidelberg (2012). https://doi.org/10.1007/978-3-642-34327-8_36
7. OpenIndoor: Openindoor github (2022). https://github.com/open-indoor
8. Perry, A.R.: The flightgear flight simulator. In: Proceedings of the USENIX Annual Technical Conference, vol. 686, pp. 1–12 (2004)
9. Piccione, M., Fuhrmann, S.: Using Esri cityengine (2016). https://esri.com/about/newsroom/MultiMedia%20LLCarcuser/creating-a-3d-campus-scene-using-esri-cityengine/
10. Shah, S., Dey, D., Lovett, C., Kapoor, A.: AirSim: high-fidelity visual and physical simulation for autonomous vehicles. In: Hutter, M., Siegwart, R. (eds.) Field and Service Robotics. SPAR, vol. 5, pp. 621–635. Springer, Cham (2018). https://doi.org/10.1007/978-3-319-67361-5_40

Test-Driven Simulation of Robots Controlled by Enzymatic Numerical P Systems Models

Radu Traian Bobe[1]($\boxtimes$) [iD], Marian Gheorghe[2] [iD], Florentin Ipate[1] [iD],
and Ionuț Mihai Niculescu[1] [iD]

[1] Department of Computer Science, Faculty of Mathematics and Computer Science,
University of Bucharest, Str Academiei 14, 010014 Bucharest, Romania
radu.bobe@s.unibuc.ro, florentin.ipate@unibuc.ro

[2] Faculty of Engineering and Informatics, University of Bradford, Bradford,
West Yorkshire BD7 1DP, UK
m.gheorghe@bradford.ac.uk
https://www.ifsoft.ro/~florentin.ipate/,
https://www.bradford.ac.uk/staff/mgheorghe,
https://ionutmihainiculescu.ro/

Abstract. The simulation of robots behavior and the use of robust models are very important for building controllers. Testing is an important aspect in this process. In this paper, a test-driven approach for designing robot controllers based on enzymatic numerical P systems models is introduced. Four such models are defined and tested using three distinct scenarios. The paper reveals an effective way of using modelling, simulation and testing in a coherent way.

Keywords: Membrane computing · Numerical P systems · Enzymatic numerical P systems · Robot controllers · Simulation · Search-based software testing

1 Introduction

Membrane computing is a branch of a more general research area, called *natural computing*. Natural computing investigates computational models inspired by phenomena and processes occurring in nature. Membrane computing, introduced by Gh. Păun [13], is a biological-inspired computational paradigm, investigating models that abstract out from the structure and functionality of the living cells. The field evolved rapidly in its first decade, focusing on theoretical developments of several classes of membrane systems (or P systems), various applications in computer science, graphics, economics and biology, as well as on relationships with other classes of computational models. A handbook reporting the key developments in membrane computing at the end of the first decade of research in the field has been published [15]. The main classes of membrane systems (P systems), *cell-like*, *tissue-like* and *neural-like* P systems, reflect the structure

© ICST Institute for Computer Sciences, Social Informatics and Telecommunications Engineering 2024
Published by Springer Nature Switzerland AG 2024. All Rights Reserved
J.-L. Guisado-Lizar et al. (Eds.): SIMUtools 2023, LNICST 519, pp. 56–69, 2024.
https://doi.org/10.1007/978-3-031-57523-5_5

of living cell, tissue and brain, respectively. Real-life applications of membrane computing in various areas have been investigated in [24].

A new class of membrane systems, namely *numerical P systems*, has been introduced, with the aim of modelling economics phenomena, in a nature-inspired computational setting [14]. Later on an extension of this model has been considered, *enzymatic numerical P system*, which looks appropriate for modelling robot controllers [11]. Some robot controllers have been designed based on enzymatic numerical P systems [12,22]. A simulator, called Pep [17], for running enzymatic numerical P systems has been provided and utilized in various controllers [3,12,22].

Software applications tend to have a considerable role in solving problems in various aspects of the life. Given the importance of these applications, it is important to ensure the product quality and functionality and this is mostly addressed through software testing. This becomes an important part of the software development life-cycle, aiming to validate that the requirements of the software product are fulfilled, by identifying undesired behavior. A largely used testing approach is search-based testing [8]. A relatively new tool for search-based testing, especially for autonomous systems, is AmbieGen [6].

In this paper, we propose an approach for building simulators for a robot controller designed to handle enzymatic numerical P system models. Four models are built using the formalism provided in [11]. The development process of designing the models is driven by a number of scenarios, one of these, the most complex, uses the testing tool AmbieGen for generating use cases and for testing the model-based systems. In some sense, our approach is similar to *"test-driven development"* [5], improvements being added only after studying the performance of the models during the previous tests. The behavior of the controller and the enzymatic numerical P system models designed for an *E-puck* educational robot [10], is visualized with Webots, a robot simulation tool.

The paper is structured as follows: Sect. 2 presents the definition of the enzymatic numerical P system model used in the paper. Section 3 introduces the working environment, including the tools used. Section 4 describes the four enzymatic numerical P system models, while Sect. 5 illustrates the testing approach along with the results for three scenarios. Finally, Sect. 6 presents the conclusions and future work.

2   Enzymatic Numerical P System Definition

The enzymatic numerical P systems are special classes of membrane systems, that share with the rest of the models only the membrane structure, in the form of a tree. The compartments contain *variables* instead of objects and their values are processed by *programs* replacing the rewriting and communication rules [11]. As in any membrane system, the compartments are delimited by membranes. Subsequently, we use them interchangeably. A global clock controls the systems through discrete time units.

The enzymatic numerical P system (EN P system) is defined by the tuple:

$$\Pi = (m, H, \mu, (Var_1, Pr_1, Var_1(0)), \ldots, (Var_m, Pr_m, Var_m(0))) \qquad (1)$$

where:

- $m \geq 1$ is degree of the system Π (the number of membranes);
- H is an alphabet of labels;
- μ is membrane structure (a tree);
- Var_i is a set of variables from membrane $i, 1 \leq i \leq m$;
- $Var_i(0)$ is the initial values of the variables from region $i, 1 \leq i \leq m$;
- Pr_i is the set of programs from membrane $i, 1 \leq i \leq m$.

The program $Pr_{l_i,i}, 1 \leq l_i \leq m_i$ has one of the following forms:
  i) non-enzymatic

$$F_{l_i,i}(x_{1,i}, \ldots, x_{k,i}) \rightarrow c_{1,i}|v_1 + c_{2,i}|v_2 + \cdots + c_{m_i,i}|v_{m_i}$$

where $F_{l_i,i}(x_{1,i}, \ldots, x_{k,i})$ is the production function, $c_{1,i}|v_1 + c_{2,i}|v_2 + \cdots + c_{m_i,i}|v_{m_i}$ is the repartition protocol, and $x_{1,i}, \ldots, x_{k,i}$ are variables from Var_i. Variables $v_1, v_2 \ldots v_{m_i}$ belong to the compartment where the programs are located, and to its upper and inner compartments, for a particular compartment i. If a compartment contains more than one program, only one will be non-deterministically chosen.
  ii) enzymatic

$$F_{l_i,i}(x_{1,i}, \ldots, x_{k,i})|_{e_i} \rightarrow c_{1,i}|v_1 + c_{2,i}|v_2 + \cdots + c_{m_i,i}|v_{m_i}$$

where e_i is an enzymatic variable from Var_i, $e_i \notin \{x_{1,i}, \ldots, x_{k,i}, v_1, \ldots, v_{m_i}\}$. The program can be applied at time t only if $e_i > min(x_{1,i}(t), \ldots, x_{k,i}(t))$. The programs that meet this condition in a compartment will be applied in parallel.

When the program is applied by the system at time $t \geq 0$, the computed value

$$q_{l_i,i}(t) = \frac{F_{l_i,i}(x_{1,i}(t), \ldots, x_{k,i}(t))}{\sum_{j=1}^{n_i} c_{j,i}}$$

representing the *unitary portion* that will be distributed to the variables $v_1, \ldots, v_n$, proportional to coefficients $c_{1,i}, \ldots, c_{m_i,i}$, where $c_{j,i} \in \mathbf{N}^+$ and the received values will be $q_{l_i,i}(t) \cdot c_{1,i}, \ldots, q_{l_i,i}(t) \cdot c_{m_i,i}$.

The value of each of the variables from $t - 1$, occurring in the production functions is *consumed*, reset to zero, and its new value is the sum of the proportions distributed to variable through the repartition protocols, if it appears in them or remain at value zero.

3   Research Environment and Tools

The research environment allowing to implement our simulation approach consists of several tools that serve the purpose of this investigation.

EN P system models are simulated with a tool called Pep [17] allowing to define them in domain specific language and then execute the systems in accordance with the semantics of the models. This tool allows us to implement the robot controller environment and execute it.

The controller is meant to equip an E-puck robot [10]. Important for our study is the fact that the robot has two motors attached to the body along with two wheels; the speed value is changeable and handled by the controller. It also includes eight infrared proximity sensors placed around the body and a GPS attached to the turret slot in order to assess the coordinates at each step and use them for the simulation. For the purpose of our investigation a simulator is used instead of the E-puck robot. In this case, Webots, a robot simulation tool is used, allowing to construct complex environments [9]. A special mechanism, called PROTO [16], allows to build special objects within the environment.

A third tool utilized in this investigation is AmbieGen, an open-source tool relying on evolutionary search methods for the generation of test scenarios [6,7]. The software is written in Python and uses evolutionary search [23] and multi-objective algorithms for search-based test generation [2].

We now briefly described how these tools are integrated.

PeP simulator containing EN P system model is integrated with E-puck controller.

The pseudocode version of the main loop in our controller, taken from [1], appears below.

Algorithm 1. Simulation steps performing algorithm

1: **repeat**
2:     **for** i=1 to number_of_sensors **do**
3:         $sensor\_membrane(i) \leftarrow value(i)$
4:     run one simulation step
5:     read lw, rw from P system
6:     $leftMotor \leftarrow lw$
7:     $rightMotor \leftarrow rw$
8: **until** the end of the road or E-puck goes out of the road

---

AmbieGen provides the test generation scenarios with roads, as *.json* files, plus test outcome, maximum curvature coefficient etc.

In the Webots graphic interface, the simulation can be visualized on inputs provided by AmbieGen. More details about the tools and the way they work together are available from [1].

Remark 1. All the models used in this experiment and test scenarios along with the results are available in our GitHub project [18].

4   Enzymatic Numerical P System Models

In this section we will present our models used to control the robot. The controller receives data from proximity sensors, that measure distances to obstacles from the environment, to determine the direction of movement of a differential two wheeled robot, E-puck, in our case.

The proximity sensor has a range of 4 cm; if the obstacles are further than this limit the sensor returns the value of 0. The proximity sensors are placed on the left and right side of the robot in the direction of its movement at different angles.

The basic model was taken from [3] and adapted to make a rotation move when an obstacle is near, in order to avoid it and continue the movement. The equations that calculate the linear and angular velocity are shown below:

$$leftSpeed = cruiseSpeed + \sum_{i=1}^{n} weightLeft_i \cdot prox_i \tag{2}$$

$$rightSpeed = cruiseSpeed + \sum_{i=1}^{n} weightRight_i \cdot prox_i \tag{3}$$

The $leftSpeed$ and $rightSpeed$ are the speeds of the two wheels of the robot, whilst n is the number of sensors. Each sensor has constant weight values, empirically chosen to conduct the robot to the desired behavior.

This basic model encountered considerable difficulties to pass the road tests generated by AmbieGen, being capable to move without hitting the margins just on straight roads or very little curved roads. The model was formally described and more experiments have been done in our previous work [1], where it is referred as Π_{M_1}.

Considering the limitations of Π_{M_1}, the model we present next is an improvement on the first one.

4.1   Basic Model with Rotation

Analyzing the initial model, we observed that the speed of the wheel on the side with an obstacle increased reported to weights. Thereby, this caused a sort of rotation in the opposite direction of the obstacle but not sufficient to pass the test.

The main change of our model was to introduce the compartment w, calculating the product of the travel speed and the sum of the weights. In this way, after rotating in the opposite direction when detecting an obstacle, the robot will continue the test, moving forward with a constant velocity.

This is certainly an improvement, especially when the robot is challenged on roads, but as presented next, there were still some issues that aimed us to introduce another model.

Let us consider the following function:

$$f(x) = \begin{cases} 1, & \text{if } x = 0 \\ 0, & \text{otherwise} \end{cases}$$

This function will be used in the equations describing the behavior of the model and in the production functions from the programs.

The equations describing the behavior are:

$$weightLeft = \sum_{i=1}^{n} weightLeft_i \cdot prox_i \tag{4}$$

$$weightRight = \sum_{i=1}^{n} weightRight_i \cdot prox_i \tag{5}$$

$$leftSpeed = cruiseSpeed \cdot weightLeft + f(weightLeft) \cdot cruiseSpeed \tag{6}$$

$$rightSpeed = cruiseSpeed \cdot weightRight + f(weightRight) \cdot cruiseSpeed \tag{7}$$

The model is defined as follows:

$$\Pi_{M_2} = (m, H, \mu, (Var_1, Pr_1, Var_1(0)), \ldots, (Var_m, Pr_m, Var_m(0))) \tag{8}$$

where:

- $m = 3k + 3, k = 6$;
- $H = \{s, w, s_c\} \cup \bigcup\limits_{i=1}^{k} \{c_i, s_i, w_i\}$;
- $\mu = [[[[]_{s_1} []_{w_1}]_{c_1} \cdots [[]_{s_k} []_{w_k}]_{c_k} []_{s_c}]_w]_s$;
- $Var_s = \{x_{s_l}, x_{s_r}\}, Var_w = \{x_{w_l}, x_{w_r}, e_w\}, Var_{s_c} = \{x_{s_c}\}$,
  $Var_{c_i} = \{x_{c_i,s_l}, x_{c_i,s_r}, x_{c_i,w_l}, x_{c_i,w_r}, e_{c_i}\}, 1 \le i \le k$,
  $Var_{s_i} = \{x_{s_i,i}\}, 1 \le i \le k$,
  $Var_{w_i} = \{x_{w_i,w_l}, x_{w_i,w_r}, e_{w_i}\}, 1 \le i \le k$;
- $Var_i(0) = 0, 1 \le i \le m$;
- $Pr_s = \{0 \cdot x_{s_l} \cdot x_{s_r} \to 1|x_{s_l} + 1|x_{s_r}\}$;
  $Pr_w = \{x_{s_c} \cdot x_{w_l} + f(x_{w_l}) \cdot x_{s_c}|e_w \to 1|x_{w_l}$,
  $\qquad x_{s_c} \cdot x_{w_r} + f(x_{w_r}) \cdot x_{s_c}|e_w \to 1|x_{w_r}\}$;
  $Pr_{s_c} = \{x_{s_c} \to 1|x_{s_c}\}$;
  $Pr_{c_i} = \{x_{c_i,s_l} \cdot x_{c_i,w_l}|e_{c_i} \to 1|x_{s_l}$,
  $\qquad x_{c_i,s_r} \cdot x_{c_i,w_r}|e_{c_i} \to 1|x_{s_r}\}, 1 \le i \le k$;
  $Pr_{s_i} = \{3x_{s_i,i} \to 1|x_{s_i,i} + 1|x_{c_i,s_l} + 1|x_{c_i,s_r}\}, 1 \le i \le k$;
  $Pr_{w_i} = \{2x_{w_i,w_l}|e_{w_i} \to 1|x_{w_i,w_l} + 1|x_{c_i,w_l}$,
  $\qquad 2x_{w_i,w_r}|e_{w_i} \to 1|x_{w_i,w_r} + 1|x_{c_i,w_r}\}, 1 \le i \le k$;

The meaning of the variables from the model is the following:

○ x_{s_l} and x_{s_r} from the region s represent $leftSpeed$ and $rightSpeed$, the sum of the products are accumulated in s;

○ x_{s_c} from the compartment s_c is *cruiseSpeed*;

○ each pair of weights, *weightLeft$_i$* and *weightRight$_i$*, resides in the regions w_i, $1 \le i \le k$;

○ for each proximity sensor, *prox$_i$*, a compartment is defined, namely s_i, containing a single variable, $x_{s_i,i}$, $1 \le i \le k$;

○ the products are calculated by two distinct programs, *weightLeft$_i$ · prox$_i$*, and *weightRight$_i$ · prox$_i$*, $1 \le i \le k$, in the compartments c_i.

4.2   Refined Model

During the test phase of the above presented model, we observed that even though the robot avoids the obstacles (road borders, in case of generating roads with AmbieGen), it tends to have a "zig-zag" motion going from the proximity of a border to the proximity of the other one. Considering this, an immediate adjustment was to recenter the robot after avoiding an obstacle and reaching the center of the road, so the robot will go straight until it encounters a new obstacle.

We made this adjustment by introducing a new membrane, called *Direction*. The membrane has seven variables, called *directionLeft, directionRight, angle, state, distance, angleStep, distanceStep*, which will be detailed when giving the formal definition of the model. In order to obtain the desired behavior, we used differential drive kinematics equations [20]. The *state* variable aims to reproduce a finite state machine inside the production function of the membrane, with the following states:

a) state 0 - the robot is moving in a straight line
b) state 1 - the robot is moving in the presence of an obstacle
c) state 2 - the robot is moving to approximately the center of the lane
d) state 3 - the robot is recentering on the lane

Before introducing the mathematical definition of the described model, we firstly defined four functions needed in the production functions (Table 1):

Table 1. Functions used in the model

$sgn(x)$	$sgn(x) = \begin{cases} 1, & \text{if } x = 1 \\ 0, & \text{if } x = 0 \\ -1, & \text{if } x = -1 \end{cases}$
$not(x,y)$	$not(x,y) = \begin{cases} 1, & \text{if } x \ne y \\ 0, & \text{otherwise} \end{cases}$
$gt(x,y)$	$gt(x,y) = \begin{cases} 1, & \text{if } x > y \\ 0, & \text{otherwise} \end{cases}$
$eq(x,y)$	$eq(x,y) = \begin{cases} 1, & \text{if } x = y \\ 0, & \text{otherwise} \end{cases}$

Also, we used the constant *len* which represents the axle length of the robot. For E-puck this is equal to 52 mm.

The model is defined as follows:

$$\Pi_{M_3} = (m, H, \mu, (Var_1, Pr_1, Var_1(0)), \ldots, (Var_m, Pr_m, Var_m(0))) \quad (9)$$

where:

- $m = 3k + 4, k = 6$;
- $H = \{s, d, w, s_c\} \cup \bigcup_{i=1}^{k} \{c_i, s_i, w_i\}$;
- $\mu = [[[[[]s_1[]w_1]c_1 \cdots []s_k[]w_k]c_k[]s_c]w]d]s$;
- $Var_s = \{x_{s_l}, x_{s_r}\}, Var_d = \{x_{d_l}, x_{d_r}, x_a, x_{st}, x_{dst}, x_{as}, x_{ds}, e_{ds}, e_{dw}, e_d\}$,
  $Var_w = \{x_{w_l}, x_{w_r}, e_w\}, Var_{s_c} = \{x_{s_c}\}$,
  $Var_{c_i} = \{x_{c_i,s_l}, x_{c_i,s_r}, x_{c_i,w_l}, x_{c_i,w_r}, e_{c_i}\}, 1 \le i \le k$,
  $Var_{s_i} = \{x_{s_i,i}\}, 1 \le i \le k$,
  $Var_{w_i} = \{x_{w_i,w_l}, x_{w_i,w_r}, e_{w_i}\}, 1 \le i \le k$;
- $Var_i(0) = 0, i \in \{s, w, s_c\} \cup \bigcup_{i=1}^{k} \{c_i, s_i, w_i\}, Var_{d_{e_d}}(0) = 100, Var_{d_i}(0) = 0$,
  $i \in Var_d \setminus \{e_d\}$;
- $Pr_s = \{0 \cdot x_{s_l} \cdot x_{s_r} \to 1|x_{s_l} + 1|x_{s_r}\}$;
- $Pr_d = \{not(x_{st}, 3) \cdot x_{d_l} + eq(x_{st}, 3) \cdot ((x_{d_l} + |x_{as}|) \cdot sgn(x_{as}))|_{e_{ds}} \to 1|x_{s_l}$,
  $not(x_{st}, 3) \cdot x_{d_r} + eq(x_{st}, 3) \cdot ((x_{d_r} + |x_{as}|) \cdot sgn(-x_{as}))|_{e_{ds}} \to 1|x_{s_r}$,
  $gt(x_{as}, 0) \cdot x_{as}|_{e_{ds}} \to 1|x_{as}$,
  $x_{d_l}|_{e_{dw}} \to 1|x_{s_l}$,
  $x_{d_r}|_{e_{dw}} \to 1|x_{s_r}$,
  $e_{ds} \cdot e_{dw} \cdot 0|_{e_d} \to 1|e_{ds} + 1|e_{dw}$,
  $not(x_{d_r} - x_{d_l}, 0) \cdot \frac{x_{d_r} - x_{d_l}}{2len} + eq(x_{d_r} - x_{d_l}, 0) \cdot x_a + x_a \cdot 0|_{e_{dw}} \to 1|x_a$,
  $not(x_{d_r} - x_{d_l}, 0) \cdot \frac{x_{d_r} - x_{d_l}}{4} + eq(x_{d_r} - x_{d_l}, 0) \cdot x_{as}|_{e_{dw}} \to 1|x_{as}$,
  $not(x_{d_r} - x_{d_l}, 0) \cdot \lfloor|\frac{4}{2len}|\rfloor \cdot 3 + eq(x_{d_r} - x_{d_l}, 0) \cdot x_{ds} + x_{ds} \cdot 0|_{e_{dw}} \to 1|x_{ds}$,
  $eq(x_{st}, 1) \cdot 2 + eq(x_{st}, 2) \cdot not(x_{dst}, 0) \cdot 2 + eq(x_{st}, 2) \cdot eq(x_{dst}, 0) \cdot 3+$
  $eq(x_{st}, 3) \cdot gt(x_{dst}, 0) \cdot 3 + eq(x_{st}, 3) \cdot eq(x_{dst}, 0) \cdot 0|_{e_{ds}} \to 1|x_{st}$,
  $x_{st} \cdot 0 + 1|_{e_{dw}} \to 1|x_{st}$,
  $x_{dst} \cdot 0 + 180|_{e_{dw}} \to 1|x_{dst}$,
  $eq(x_{st}, 2) \cdot gt(x_{dst}, 0) \cdot (x_{dst} - 1) + eq(x_{st}, 1) \cdot x_{dst}|_{e_{ds}} \to 1|x_{dst}$,
  $eq(x_{st}, 3) \cdot gt(x_{ds}, 0) \cdot (x_{ds} - 1) + not(x_{st}, 3) \cdot x_{ds}|_{e_{ds}} \to 1|x_{ds}$;
- $Pr_w = \{x_{s_c} \cdot x_{w_l}|_{e_w} \to 1|x_{d_l}$,
  $f(x_{w_l}) \cdot x_{s_c}|_{e_w} \to 1|x_{d_l}\}$,
  $x_{s_c} \cdot x_{w_r}|_{e_w} \to 1|x_{d_r}$,
  $f(x_{w_r}) \cdot x_{s_c}|_{e_w} \to 1|x_{d_r}\}$,
  $(f(x_{w_l}) \cdot f(x_{w_r})) \cdot x_{s_c} \cdot 100|_{e_w} \to 1|e_{ds}$,
  $(not(x_{w_l}, 0) \cdot not(x_{w_r}, 0)) \cdot x_{s_c} \cdot 100|_{e_w} \to 1|e_{dw}$;
- $Pr_{s_c} = \{x_{s_c} \to 1|x_{s_c}\}$;
- $Pr_{c_i} = \{x_{c_i,s_l} \cdot x_{c_i,w_l}|_{e_{c_i}} \to 1|x_{s_l}$,
  $x_{c_i,s_r} \cdot x_{c_i,w_r}|_{e_{c_i}} \to 1|x_{s_r}\}, 1 \le i \le k$;

$$Pr_{s_i} = \{3x_{s_i,i} \rightarrow 1|x_{s_i,i} + 1|x_{c_i,s_l} + 1|x_{c_i,s_r}\}, 1 \leq i \leq k;$$
$$Pr_{w_i} = \{2x_{w_i,w_l}|e_{w_i} \rightarrow 1|x_{w_i,w_l} + 1|x_{c_i,w_l},$$
$$2x_{w_i,w_r}|e_{w_i} \rightarrow 1|x_{w_i,w_r} + 1|x_{c_i,w_r}\}, 1 \leq i \leq k;$$

As observed, the main difference in the membranes structure is made by the new region called *direction*. Next we present the meaning of the variables used in it:

- x_{d_l} and x_{d_r} represent *directionLeft* and *directionRight*;
- x_a and x_{as} represent *angle* and *angleStep*;
- x_{dst} and x_{ds} represent *distance* and *distanceStep*;
- x_{st} represents the *state* of the simulated finite state machine

4.3   Extended Refined Model

Experiments carried out with the second model proved that when the robot approaches perpendicularly the obstacle, it remains locked into that obstacle. This limitation is caused by the values of weights, which have values of opposite sign, and sum is cancel each other out. This situation can be easily explained by the position of the proximity sensors that are facing the obstacle perpendicularly.

To solve this problematic behavior we defined two more production functions inside *Weight* compartment. These functions are distributed to *directionRight* and *directionLeft* variables, as follows:

$$directionLeft = eq(|weightLeft|, |weightRight|) \cdot gt(|weightLeft|, 0) \cdot$$
$$\cdot\, gt(|weightRight|, 0) \cdot weightLeft \cdot cruiseSpeed \cdot 0$$
$$directionRight = eq(|weightLeft|, |weightRight|) \cdot gt(|weightLeft|, 0) \cdot$$
$$\cdot\, gt(|weightRight|, 0) \cdot weightRight \cdot 0 + cruiseSpeed$$

In this way, we ensure that the robot will not get stuck when perpendicularly facing an obstacle, as the speed of the right wheel (guided by *directionRight* variable) will move the robot to the left.

An interesting step would be to automatically decide what direction to follow in this situation (e.g., if an obstacle is near on the left, a better decision should be to activate the *directionLeft* variable, thus moving the robot to the right).

5   Simulation Results

In this section we will present some scenarios designed to challenge the robot as well as their results. Considering the way we defined and integrated the models, these simulation scenarios guided us to refine intermediate variants of models based on the results.

In this experiment we opted for three scenarios and all of them are defined by the type of the area E-puck needs to go through. These are introduced as follows:

a) *corridors*
b) *a square*
c) *roads generated by AmbieGen*

The first two scenarios were created in a simple manner, using the areas that E-puck should cover being defined using Webots embedded shapes. The last scenario is the most complex one, taking the roads generated by AmbieGen and integrating them in a Webots world.

As stated above, our approach combines robot testing and simulation, using AmbieGen for road generation. The tool offers flexibility in choosing the parameters needed by the genetic algorithm. Some of them are set as constant values in the source code and other aspects (e.g., allowed out of bound percentage, map size, generation time) can be set easily from the command line, when launching the tool. Taking into consideration the default values from AmbieGen, we performed some trials and noticed that the same would fit our needs in road generation. More details about these values and how to use the tool were presented in [1,4].

As mentioned before, this approach encapsulates three main types of scenarios, *a corridor, a square* and *roads generated by AmbieGen*. For *corridor* and *square* we simulated two situations. In the first situation, the robot starts in a straight line from the middle of the corridor or from the middle of the square. For simplicity, let us call this types of tests *corridor straight* and *square straight*.

The other situation assumes that the robot also starts from the middle of the corridor, respectively square, but with an angle of 15°. Let us refer to these test types as *corridor angle* and *square angle*.

Table 2 contains the simulation results for each model, starting with the basic one, Π_{M_1}. It includes the test types presented in the above paragraph and four roads generated by AmbieGen and imported to Webots. We chose these roads from a larger suite, opting for different curvatures in order to better observe the behavior of each model.

Table 2. Experimental results

Test type	Π_{M_1}	Π_{M_2}	Π_{M_3}	Π_{M_4}
Corridor straight	Failed	Failed	Failed	Passed
Corridor angle	Failed	Passed	Failed	Passed
Square straight	Failed	Failed	Passed	Passed
Square angle	Failed	Passed	Passed	Passed
Road 1	Failed	Passed	Passed	Failed
Road 2	Failed	Passed	Passed	Passed
Road 3	Failed	Passed	Passed	Failed
Road 4	Passed	Passed	Passed	Failed

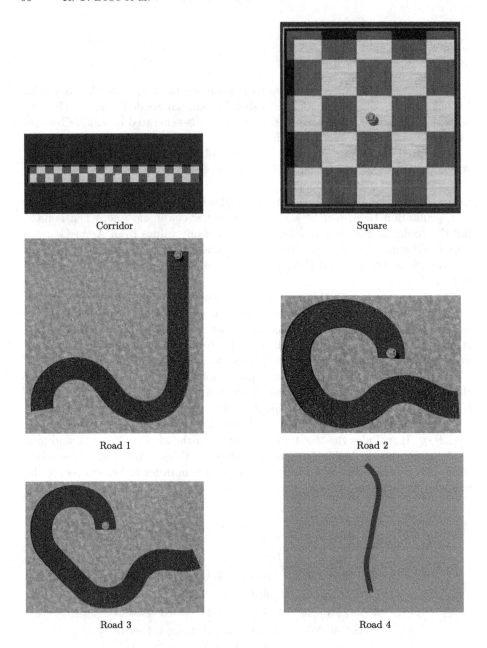

Fig. 1. Test cases as represented in Webots

When analyzing the experimental results, we noticed that the basic model, Π_{M_1}, has the worst performance compared to the other three models. This basic model passed just one test, Road 4, which is the simplest one (as presented in Fig. 1).

Another observation that can be extracted from the experimental results recorded in Table 2 is that the second model, Π_{M_2}, has an improved performance in terms of passing the road tests. The improvement consists in a rotation that is performed when the road is curved (i.e., the proximity sensors detect an obstacle). Additional road tests were added to [19].

The refocusing movement added to the behavior of the third model, Π_{M_3}, conducted to a natural movement on the roads, all the roads being also passed for this model. Nevertheless, it can be observed that this modification of the membrane structure (with the addition of the membrane *direction*) made Π_{M_3} to fail the *corridor angle* challenge, but pass the *square straight*, failed by Π_{M_2}.. In the end, the last model, Π_{M_4}, came with an improvement in passing the corridor and square tests, due to the property of moving even if the obstacle is in the front of the robot (placed perpendicularly), the situation when the robot gets stuck in front of an obstacle being handled. However, the adjustments made came with a few disadvantages in passing road tests, the robot moving to the left and failing the test at the moment the robot direction is perpendicular to one of the borders. In many instances, this scenario was frequently observed, serving as the underlying cause for the model's failure to pass three out of the four road test examples.

Figure 1 illustrates the experimental tests discussed above. A video representation of each model performance on these tests can be found at [21].

6   Conclusions and Future Work

This paper illustrated our approach to model, simulate and test a robot controller based on enzymatic numerical P systems. As we already introduced two models and the working environment in our previous work [1], we formally described each additional model and the reasons which made us to implement them.

As presented above, each model was constructed taking into consideration the limitations discovered during the testing phase of the previous ones. We also emphasize the capabilities of each model in a comparative manner, testing them in three challenging scenarios with different features.

Concerning our future work, we intend to involve in our experiments other types of P systems in order to obtain a more natural functioning of the robot. We analyze the possibility to dynamically assign weights values depending on the situation (e.g., taking a decision when the robot is close to an obstacle and there is another obstacle nearby). The palette of different P systems types is encouraging but there are some limitations in the area of available tools for simulating them, this constituting another aspect that we investigate.

References

1. Bobe, R.T., Ipate, F., Niculescu, I.M.: Modelling and search-based testing of robot controllers using enzymatic numerical p systems. In: Cheval, H., Leuştean, L., Sipoş, A. (eds.) Proceedings 7th Symposium on Working Formal Methods, Bucharest, Romania, 21–22 September 2023. Electronic Proceedings in Theoretical Computer Science, vol. 389, pp. 1–10. Open Publishing Association (2023). https://doi.org/10.4204/EPTCS.389.1

2. Deb, K., Pratap, A., Agarwal, S., Meyarivan, T.: A fast and elitist multiobjective genetic algorithm: NSGA-II. IEEE Trans. Evol. Comput. **6**(2), 182–197 (2002). https://doi.org/10.1109/4235.996017

3. Florea, A.G., Buiu, C.: Modelling multi-robot interactions using a generic controller based on numerical P systems and ROS. In: 2017 9th International Conference on Electronics, Computers and Artificial Intelligence (ECAI), pp. 1–6 (2017). https://doi.org/10.1109/ECAI.2017.8166411

4. Gambi, A., Jahangirova, G., Riccio, V., Zampetti, F.: SBST tool competition 2022. In: Proceedings of the 15th Workshop on Search-Based Software Testing, pp. 25–32 (2022). https://doi.org/10.1145/3526072.3527538

5. George, B., Williams, L.: A structured experiment of test-driven development. Inf. Softw. Technol. **46**(5), 337–342 (2004). https://doi.org/10.1016/j.infsof.2003.09.011

6. Humeniuk, D., Antoniol, G., Khomh, F.: AmbieGen tool at the SBST 2022 tool competition. In: Proceedings of the 15th Workshop on Search-Based Software Testing, pp. 43–46 (2022). https://doi.org/10.1145/3526072.3527531

7. Humeniuk, D., Khomh, F., Antoniol, G.: AmbieGen: a search-based framework for autonomous systems testing. arXiv preprint arXiv:2301.01234 (2023). https://doi.org/10.48550/arXiv.2301.01234

8. Khari, M., Kumar, P.: An extensive evaluation of search-based software testing: a review. Soft Comput. Fusion Found. Methodol. Appl. **23**(6), 1933–1946 (2019). https://doi.org/10.3233/ICA-190616

9. Michel, O.: Cyberbotics Ltd. Webots^{TM}: professional mobile robot simulation. Int. J. Adv. Robot. Syst. **1**(1), 5 (2004). https://doi.org/10.5772/5618

10. Mondada, F., et al.: The e-puck, a robot designed for education in engineering. In: Proceedings of the 9th Conference on Autonomous Robot Systems and Competitions, pp. 59–65. IPCB: Instituto Politécnico de Castelo Branco (2009)

11. Pavel, A., Arsene, O., Buiu, C.: Enzymatic numerical P systems - a new class of membrane computing systems. In: 2010 IEEE Fifth International Conference on Bio-Inspired Computing: Theories and Applications (BIC-TA), pp. 1331–1336. IEEE (2010). https://doi.org/10.1109/BICTA.2010.5645071

12. Pérez-Hurtado, I., Martínez-del Amor, M.A., Zhang, G., Neri, F., Pérez-Jiménez, M.J.: A membrane parallel rapidly-exploring random tree algorithm for robotic motion planning. Integr. Comput.-Aided Eng. **27**(2), 121–138 (2020). https://doi.org/10.3233/ICA-190616

13. Păun, G.: Membrane Computing: An Introduction. Springer, Heidelberg (2002). https://doi.org/10.1007/978-3-642-56196-2

14. Păun, G., Păun, R.: Membrane computing and economics: numerical P systems. Fundam. Inform. **73**(1–2), 213–227 (2006). http://content.iospress.com/articles/fundamenta-informaticae/fi73-1-2-20

15. Păun, G., Rozenberg, G., Salomaa, A. (eds.): The Oxford Handbook of Membrane Computing. Oxford University Press, Oxford (2010)

16. Webots reference manual. https://cyberbotics.com/doc/reference/proto
17. Florea, A.G., Buiu, C.: PeP - an open-source software simulator of numerical P systems and numerical P systems with enzymes (2017). https://github.com/andrei91ro/pep
18. Github project. https://github.com/radubobe/Research/tree/main/Modelling
19. Github simulation results folder. https://github.com/radubobe/Research/tree/main/Modelling
20. Hellstrom, T.: Kinematics equations for differential drive and articulated steering. Umea University (2011). https://www8.cs.umu.se/kurser/5DV122/HT13/material/Hellstrom-ForwardKinematics.pdf
21. Simulation of E-puck controlled by Enzymatic Numerical P Systems models in Webots. https://youtu.be/FA7snrqaKKs
22. Wang, X., et al.: Design and implementation of membrane controllers for trajectory tracking of nonholonomic wheeled mobile robots. Integr. Comput.-Aided Eng. **23**(1), 15–30 (2016). https://doi.org/10.3233/ICA-150503
23. Whitley, D., Rana, S., Dzubera, J., Mathias, K.E.: Evaluating evolutionary algorithms. Artif. Intell. **85**(1–2), 245–276 (1996). https://doi.org/10.1016/0004-3702(95)00124-7
24. Zhang, G., Pérez-Jiménez, M.J., Gheorghe, M.: Real-Life Applications with Membrane Computing. Springer, Cham (2017). https://doi.org/10.1007/s00500-017-2906-y

PySPN: An Extendable Python Library for Modeling & Simulation of Stochastic Petri Nets

Jonas Friederich[1(✉)] [iD] and Sanja Lazarova-Molnar[1,2] [iD]

[1] Mærsk Mc-Kinney Møller Institute, University of Southern Denmark, Odense, Denmark
jofr@mmmi.sdu.dk
[2] Institute AIFB, Karlsruhe Institute of Technology, Karlsruhe, Germany
lazarova-molnar@kit.edu

Abstract. Stochastic Petri Nets (SPNs) are a powerful formalism, widely used for modeling complex systems in various domains, ranging from manufacturing and logistics to healthcare and computer networks. In this paper, we introduce *PySPN*, a flexible and easily extendable *Python* library for Modeling & Simulation (M&S) of SPNs. *PySPN* aims to provide researchers, engineers, and simulation practitioners with a user-friendly and efficient toolset to model, simulate, and analyze SPNs, facilitating the understanding and optimization of stochastic processes in dynamic systems.

Keywords: Stochastic Petri nets · Modeling & Simulation · Python

1 Introduction

SPNs are a popular formalism for system M&S due to their ability to capture concurrency, synchronization, and stochastic behavior. SPNs are an extension of Petri nets, developed in the 1960s by Carl Adam Petri, and are used today in many domains such as manufacturing [12] and healthcare [14]. Existing tools for SPN M&S, however, often suffer from usability issues and limited extensibility.

GUI-based solutions like *GreatSPN* [1], *Oris* [9], or *CPN Tools* [11] offer user-friendly interfaces and facilitate quick modeling of Petri nets. However, they lack the flexibility and customization required for specific use cases. Conversely, command-line-interface-based solutions, such as *SNAKES* [10], *gspn-framework* [2], or *PNet* [4], are often domain-specific or have complex software architectures.

PySPN [6] fills this gap by offering an open-source, easy-to-use, and extensible library that integrates seamlessly with the *Python* ecosystem, empowering users to efficiently explore and analyze stochastic processes in a wide range of applications.

Our previous work on data-driven Digital Twins [7] and data-driven reliability modeling [8] in the manufacturing domain motivated the development of

J.-L. Guisado-Lizar et al. (Eds.): SIMUtools 2023, LNICST 519, pp. 70–78, 2024.
https://doi.org/10.1007/978-3-031-57523-5_6

this library. In the referenced work, we demonstrate the potential of SPNs to be used in combination with techniques such as Process Mining for data-driven model extraction and continuous validation.

The remainder of this paper is organized as follows: In Sect. 2, we provide a comprehensive technical overview of *PySPN*. Subsequently, in Sect. 3, we illustrate the application of our developed library using a two-server queuing system. Lastly, in Sect. 4, we summarize this work and discuss potential future expansions of *PySPN*.

2   Library Overview

Our library focuses on discrete-event systems, where system changes occur at discrete points in time as a result of completing particular activities in the system. These activities are associated with transitions, which can either fire instantly when certain conditions are met (immediate transitions) or have firing delays determined by probability distribution functions (timed transitions). Beyond transitions, a SPN comprises a finite number of places, a finite number of arcs, and an initial state, denoted by the initial marking of the Petri Net. Formally, the class of SPNs that can be modeled using the library is defined as:

$$SPN = (P, T, A, G, m_0)$$

where:

- $P = \{P_1, P_2, .., P_m\}$ is the set of places, drawn as circles;
- $T = \{T_1, T_2, .., T_n\}$ is the set of transitions along with their distribution functions or weights, drawn as bars;
- $A = A^I \cup A^O \cup A^H$ is the set of arcs, where A^O is the set of output arcs, A^I is the set of input arcs and A^H is the set of inhibitor arcs and each of the arcs has a multiplicity assigned to it;
- $G = \{g_1, g_2, .., g_r\}$ is the set of guard functions which are associated with different transitions;
- and m_0 is the initial marking, defining the distribution of tokens in the places.

Each transition is represented as $T_i = (type, F)$, where $type \in \{timed, immediate\}$ indicates the type of the transition, and F is either a probability distribution function if the corresponding transition is timed, or a firing weight or probability if it is immediate. *PySPN* currently supports empirical distributions, as well as several theoretical distributions such as *exponential, normal,* and *Weibull*. The sets of arcs are defined such that

$$A^O = \{a_1^o, a_2^o, ..., a_k^o\}, \ A^I = \{a_1^i, a_2^i, ..., a_j^i\} \text{ and } A^H = \{a_1^h, a_2^h, ..., a_i^h\}$$

where:

$$A^H, A^O \subseteq P \times T \times \mathbb{N}^+ \text{ and } A^I \subseteq T \times P \times \mathbb{N}^+.$$

Figure 1 illustrates the directory structure of *PySPN*. *spn.py* defines the necessary classes for constructing a SPN, including places, transitions, input and output arcs, inhibitor arcs, guard functions, memory policies, and the SPN itself. *spn_simulate.py* implements the SPN simulation algorithm based on the discrete-event simulation paradigm [3]. In order to retrieve firing times for timed transitions during simulation, *RNGFactory.py* includes a factory method returning a random sample of a probability distribution function. We have employed the scientific computing library *scipy* [13] for defining distribution functions and obtaining random samples. *scipy* defines theoretical distribution functions with a consistent set of parameters, making it easy to extend our tool with other, not yet implemented, distributions. Furthermore, *scipy*'s *.ecdf* function can be employed to define empirical cumulative distribution functions based on underlying data samples. *spn_io* defines methods for printing a textual description of a SPN, printing statistics, printing a simulation protocol, and importing and exporting SPNs using *Python's pickle* format. Lastly, *spn_visualization.py* includes a method to create a graphical representation of a SPN using the *graphviz* [5] library. For further information about the tool and how to get started, we refer the reader to the documentation on *GitHub* [6].

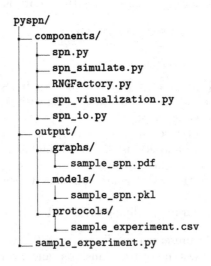

Fig. 1. Directory structure of *PySPN*.

3   Application Example

To illustrate the capabilities of *PySPN*, we use the popular model of a two-server queueing system (Fig. 2). In this particular model, *Server1* operates at a faster speed than *Server2*, but *Server2* has the capability to process two entities simultaneously, whereas *Server1* can only process one entity at a time. A guard function is implemented on the *TApproach_Server2* immediate transition, only enabling the transition if there are at least two entities present in the queue.

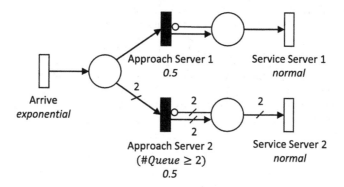

Fig. 2. SPN of a two-server queueing system.

By modeling, simulating, and analyzing the described model, several insights into the performance and behavior of the system can be gained, for example:

- **Performance Metrics:** throughput (rate at which entities are served and leave the system), queue length, and waiting times.
- **Resource Utilization:** utilization of each server (fraction of time a server is busy serving entities).
- **Sensitivity Analysis:** by varying the arrival times, service times, and number of servers the impact of these parameters on the system can be analyzed. This can help in optimizing resource allocation to minimize queue lengths, waiting times, or other performance metrics.
- **Bottleneck Identification:** Bottlenecks (model components that limit the overall system performance) can be identified and potentially mitigated.

In Listing 1 we show, how to implement the SPN for the described model using *PySPN*. The process of modeling a SPN follows a clear structure: After importing the required components (lines 1–3), a SPN object is instantiated (line 5). Then, places and transitions are instantiated (lines 7–25) and added to the SPN object (lines 27–35). Next, the places and transitions are connected by arcs (lines 37–45). Finally, the modeled SPN can be simulated (line 47). The simulation function (i.e., *simulate*) takes as arguments the SPN object, the maximum time to run the simulation, the output verbosity, and whether to write a protocol file to store the marking for each discrete state transition during the simulation.

```
1 from components.spn import *
2 from components.spn_simulate import simulate
3 from components.spn_visualization import draw_spn
```

```
 4
 5  spn = SPN()
 6
 7  p1 = Place(label="Queue", n_tokens=0)
 8  p2 = Place(label="Server1", n_tokens=0)
 9  p3 = Place(label="Server2", n_tokens=0)
10
11  t1 = Transition(label="Arrive", t_type="T")
12  t1.set_distribution(distribution="expon", a=0.0, b=1.0/1.8)
13  t2 = Transition(label="Approach Server 1", t_type="I")
14  t2.set_weight(weight=0.5)
15  t3 = Transition(label="Approach Server 2", t_type="I")
16  def guard_t3():
17      if p1.n_tokens >= 2:
18          return True
19      else: return False
20  t3.set_weight(weight=0.5)
21  t3.set_guard_function(guard_t3)
22  t4 = Transition(label="Service Server 1", t_type = "T")
23  t4.set_distribution(distribution="expon", a=0.0, b=1.0/0.9)
24  t5 = Transition(label="Service Server 2", t_type = "T")
25  t5.set_distribution(distribution="expon", a=0.0, b=1.0/0.9)
26
27  spn.add_place(p1)
28  spn.add_place(p2)
29  spn.add_place(p3)
30
31  spn.add_transition(t1)
32  spn.add_transition(t2)
33  spn.add_transition(t3)
34  spn.add_transition(t4)
35  spn.add_transition(t5)
36
37  spn.add_output_arc(t1,p1)
38  spn.add_input_arc(p1,t2)
39  spn.add_input_arc(p1,t3,multiplicity=2)
40  spn.add_output_arc(t2,p2)
41  spn.add_output_arc(t3,p3,multiplicity=2)
42  spn.add_input_arc(p2,t4)
43  spn.add_inhibitor_arc(t2,p2)
44  spn.add_input_arc(p3,t5,multiplicity=2)
45  spn.add_inhibitor_arc(t3,p3,multiplicity=2)
46
47  simulate(spn, max_time = 100, verbosity = 2, protocol = True)
```

Code Listing 1. Two-server queue example.

We executed a simulation run of the described two-server queuing model using the arguments shown in Listing 1 (line 47). As can be seen form the listing, the simulation time is set to be 100 time units, the output verbosity is set to be 2 and a protocol file is to be written and stored.

In Fig. 3, we display an excerpt of the generated terminal output during the simulation. At a verbosity level of 2, basic information regarding the simulation run, such as the initial marking and the firing of transitions is returned. The initial marking describes the distributions of tokens in each of the three places (i.e., 0 for *Queue*, *Server 1*, and *Server 2*).

```
Starting simulation...
Simulation time limit = 100

Marking at time 0
Place Queue, #tokens: 0
Place Server 1, #tokens: 0
Place Server 2, #tokens: 0

Transition Arrive fires at time 0.08
Transition Approach Server 1 fires at time 0.08
Transition Service Server 1 fires at time 0.45
Transition Arrive fires at time 0.56
Transition Approach Server 1 fires at time 0.56
Transition Arrive fires at time 0.59
Transition Arrive fires at time 0.83
Transition Approach Server 2 fires at time 0.83
Transition Arrive fires at time 0.87
Transition Arrive fires at time 0.89
...
```

Fig. 3. Excerpt of the terminal output for the simulation run.

Table 1 shows an excerpt of the generated simulation protocol file. The protocol shows the changes of the markings at discrete points in time for the three places throughout the simulation. For this two-server queuing model, the marking of the place *Queue* corresponds to the number of entities waiting in the queue and the marking of the places *Server 1*, and *Server 2* corresponds to the number of entities being processed by the servers (i.e., either 0 or 1 for *Server 1* and 0 or 2 for *Server 2*).

Based on the generated protocol, Fig. 4, displays a graph depicting the discrete changes in queue size (i.e., marking of the place *Queue*) throughout the simulation.

4 Summary and Outlook

In this paper, we introduced *PySPN*, a *Python* library for M&S of SPNs. *PySPN* aims to provide a user-friendly and extensible toolset for researchers, engineers, and simulation practitioners to model, simulate, and analyze SPNs, facilitating the understanding and optimization of stochastic processes in dynamic systems.

PySPN offers a comprehensive set of features, including support for immediate and timed transitions, various probability distribution functions, inhibitor

Table 1. Excerpt of the generated protocol file.

Place	Time	Marking
...	...	...
Queue	5.6	2
Queue	5.6	0
Server 2	5.6	0
Server 2	5.6	2
Queue	6.05	0
Queue	6.05	1
Server 1	6.15	1
Server 1	6.15	0
Queue	6.15	1
Queue	6.15	0
Server 1	6.15	0
Server 1	6.15	1
...	...	...

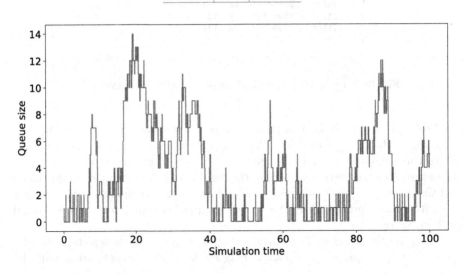

Fig. 4. Changes in queue size throughout the simulation.

arcs, guard functions, and more. It integrates seamlessly with the *Python* ecosystem, making it easy to extend and adapt for specific use cases.

Looking ahead, PySPN has potential for further development and expansion. Some avenues for future work include:

- **Parallel Simulation:** Implementing parallel and distributed simulation techniques to enable the efficient simulation of large-scale and highly concurrent systems.
- **Advanced Analysis Tools:** Developing additional tools and libraries for advanced analysis of SPNs, including sensitivity analysis, optimization algorithms, and statistical inference.
- **Enhanced Visualization:** Improving the visualization capabilities of PySPN to provide more detailed and customizable representations of SPNs, facilitating better insights into model behavior.

Furthermore, we are aiming to provide a more comprehensive review and comparison of related tools for SPN M&S in the future.

References

1. Amparore, E.G., Balbo, G., Beccuti, M., Donatelli, S., Franceschinis, G.: 30 years of GreatSPN. In: Fiondella, L., Puliafito, A. (eds.) Principles of Performance and Reliability Modeling and Evaluation. SSRE, pp. 227–254. Springer, Cham (2016). https://doi.org/10.1007/978-3-319-30599-8_9
2. Azevedo, C.: cazevedo/gspn-framework. https://github.com/cazevedo/gspn-framework
3. Banks, J., Carson, J., II., Nelson, B., Nicol, D.: Discrete-Event System Simulation, 5th edn. Pearson, Upper Saddle River (2009)
4. Chay, Z.E., Goh, B.F., Ling, M.H.: PNet: a Python library for Petri net modeling and simulation, February 2023. https://doi.org/10.48550/arXiv.2302.12054
5. Ellson, J., Gansner, E., Koutsofios, L., North, S.C., Woodhull, G.: Graphviz—open source graph drawing tools. In: Mutzel, P., Jünger, M., Leipert, S. (eds.) GD 2001. LNCS, vol. 2265, pp. 483–484. Springer, Heidelberg (2002). https://doi.org/10.1007/3-540-45848-4_57
6. Friederich, J.: PySPN (2023). https://github.com/jo-chr/pyspn
7. Friederich, J., Francis, D.P., Lazarova-Molnar, S., Mohamed, N.: A framework for data-driven digital twins of smart manufacturing systems. Comput. Ind. **136**, 103586 (2022). https://doi.org/10.1016/j.compind.2021.103586
8. Friederich, J., Lazarova-Molnar, S.: Data-driven reliability modeling of smart manufacturing systems using process mining. In: 2022 Winter Simulation Conference (WSC), pp. 2534–2545, December 2022. https://doi.org/10.1109/WSC57314.2022.10015301
9. Paolieri, M., Biagi, M., Carnevali, L., Vicario, E.: The ORIS tool: quantitative evaluation of non-Markovian systems. IEEE Trans. Software Eng. **47**(6), 1211–1225 (2021). https://doi.org/10.1109/TSE.2019.2917202
10. Pommereau, F.: SNAKES: a flexible high-level Petri nets library (tool paper). In: Devillers, R., Valmari, A. (eds.) PETRI NETS 2015. LNCS, vol. 9115, pp. 254–265. Springer, Cham (2015). https://doi.org/10.1007/978-3-319-19488-2_13
11. Ratzer, A.V., et al.: CPN tools for editing, simulating, and analysing coloured Petri nets. In: van der Aalst, W.M.P., Best, E. (eds.) ICATPN 2003. LNCS, vol. 2679, pp. 450–462. Springer, Heidelberg (2003). https://doi.org/10.1007/3-540-44919-1_28
12. Tüysüz, F., Kahraman, C.: Modeling a flexible manufacturing cell using stochastic Petri nets with fuzzy parameters. Expert Syst. Appl. **37**(5), 3910–3920 (2010). https://doi.org/10.1016/j.eswa.2009.11.026

13. Virtanen, P., et al.: SciPy 1.0: fundamental algorithms for scientific computing in Python. Nat. Methods **17**(3), 261–272 (2020). https://doi.org/10.1038/s41592-019-0686-2

14. Wang, J.: Patient flow modeling and optimal staffing for emergency departments: a Petri net approach. IEEE Trans. Comput. Soc. Syst. **10**(4), 2022–2032 (2023). https://doi.org/10.1109/TCSS.2022.3186249

Replacing Sugarscape: A Comprehensive, Expansive, and Transparent Reimplementation

Nathaniel Kremer-Herman[1]([⊠])(iD) and Ankur Gupta[2](iD)

[1] Seattle University, Seattle, WA 98122, USA
nkh@seattleu.edu
[2] Butler University, Indianapolis, IN 46208, USA
agupta@butler.edu

Abstract. We provide the definitive implementation of the seminal agent-based societal simulation *Sugarscape*. Our implementation is fully-featured open source software [5] that aims to make Sugarscape available for use by researchers across disciplines. It includes an extensive validation of all results shown in *Growing Artificial Societies* [2]. We also discuss the significant challenges in modernizing this groundbreaking body of work.

Keywords: sugarscape · computational social science · simulation validation · agent-based simulation

1 Introduction

Sugarscape was originally developed in 1996 and evaluated in *Growing Artificial Societies* [2]. It is an agent-based simulation platform that explored how societies might express *emergent behavior* based solely on the actions of individual agents. Sugarscape is a seminal work that has wide reach across many disciplines that require a carefully considered and feature-rich agent-based simulation.

Sugarscape is a two-dimensional $n \times m$ grid[1] landscape, where each grid cell contains some amount of the two available resources *sugar* and *spice*. These resources are metaphors for wealth and are gathered by agents who then consume sugar and spice over time. In Sugarscape, agents can lead long, rich lives where they interact with the environment and other agents.[2]

We present the following results:

1. We introduce the definitive implementation of Sugarscape and provides the full functionality displayed in [2].
2. Our implementation uses modern software development standards, is modular, transparently reproducible, and is highly configurable and customizable.
3. We tested all of the emergent behaviors described in [2]. We showcase several instances of our validated Sugarscape features.

---

[1] The grid is a *torus*. For example, an agent walking too far west ends up on the eastern side of the grid.

[2] Or, life can be *solitary, poor, nasty, brutish, and short* [4].

J.-L. Guisado-Lizar et al. (Eds.): SIMUtools 2023, LNICST 519, pp. 79–92, 2024.
https://doi.org/10.1007/978-3-031-57523-5_7

2   Related Work

The modeling of artificial life has a long lineage. John von Neumann's foundational work on self-reproducing automata [10] is insightful in the myriad ways he presaged then-future considerations of artificial life but also in his noting of the computational power necessary to meaningfully compute realistic, incredibly complex automata. An early workshop held by Langton et al. [8] helped jump-start the study of artificial life. The impact of this initial workshop is still felt as the conference of the same name still convenes today. One of the initial and most significant attempts at using agent-based simulation for studying *social* phenomena was made by Thomas Schelling [11]. Epstein and Axtell extended the fundamentals from Schelling and took inspiration from John Conway's Game of Life [3] to create Sugarscape [2]: an agent-based simulation to observe emergent social behaviors. These early works were constrained by the computational power available at the time.

The Sugarscape model remains relevant decades after its creation. One recent work uses Sugarscape to explore implementing computational ethics [9]. Lasquety-Reyes provides an initial implementation of the Aristotelian virtue *temperance* as a quantitative formulation using the PECS (physical, emotional, cognitive, and social) model to represent the moderation of an agent's internal desires. Serrano and Satoh introduce a different extension to Sugarscape that models the effects differing pension and social security policies may have on society [12]. Kurakin [6] provides yet another extension called Technoscape to model a phenomenon studied by economic historians: the uneven coalescing of resources, trade power, and technology into the hands of a select few economic powerhouse states (represented as *cities* of agents in Sugarscape). The applications of Sugarscape are diverse, but none of these papers were able to leverage the true power of the fully-featured Sugarscape implementation.

3   Brief Overview of Sugarscape

The Sugarscape environment is a two-dimensional $n \times m$ grid. An initial allocation of the two resources *sugar* and *spice* is placed in each grid cell. These resources regenerate per-cell at preconfigured rates. Based on these user-defined regeneration rates, one can simulate particularly harsh or bountiful environments. Vanilla Sugarscape agents are born inherently greedy. Their sole aim is to live as long as possible. Every simulation timestep, an agent consumes their held sugar and spice according to their respective *metabolisms* for each. They also move a number of cells according to their *vision* to gather more resources. A faithful reimplementation of Vanilla Sugarscape would include additional, toggleable features for the environment (e.g. seasons, pollution, or disease) and for agents (e.g. trade, combat, or reproduction).

Vanilla Sugarscape is an elegant baseline for studying agent-based behavior because it demonstrates rich social dynamics ranging from simple, short-term behavioral rules to elaborate, long-term agent planning. It does a remarkable job reinforcing our understanding of real world social phenomena. The level of abstraction in the simulation provides strong metaphors for the real world while remaining readily computable as it is driven by discrete numerical values [2].

Multiple versions of Sugarscape exist today. However, to the best of our knowledge, all publicly available versions remain incomplete. A popular implementation [13] of Sugarscape is provided with NetLogo[3], but it only replicates experiments from the first two chapters of *Growing Artificial Societies*. Most literature we found uses the NetLogo version (including the recent works noted previously [6,9,12]). Lange [7] implemented Sugarscape in Python with more functionality, but it was still not a complete representation of the book. His work inspired our own efforts in this area.

From private conversation with Epstein and Axtell, they consider the Bigbee [1] implementation (written in Java) to be the definitive edition of Sugarscape. However, even though it implements the majority of the features in [2], it *also* remains incomplete. We offer the first *complete* version of Sugarscape since the original implementation. Our software is freely available (along with validations of all experiments presented in the source book) in our code repository [5].

Table 1 compares the previously mentioned Sugarscape implementations and our own based on which features can be found in the software. We use the chapters of the source book represented in the code as a shorthand. Since the first and last chapter of the book do not introduce new features to the simulation, the experiments we reference are only found in Chaps. 2–5.

Table 1. Sugarscape Versions and Implemented Book Chapters

Implementation	Chapter 2	Chapter 3	Chapter 4	Chapter 5
NetLogo [13] Sugarscape	✓	X	X	X
Python 2 Sugarscape [7]	✓	✓	X	X
MASON-Sugarscape [1]	✓	✓[a]	✓	X
Our Implementation	✓	✓	✓	✓

[a] MASON-Sugarscape does not implement the combat feature found in Chap. 3.

4   Vanilla Sugarscape Features

We provide a brief overview of *Vanilla Sugarscape*, the original implementation of Sugarscape described in *Growing Artificial Societies* [2]. Vanilla Sugarscape has various features which can be selectively turned on or off. We categorize these features as those which affect the environment and those which affect agents. Many of these options are not simply Boolean switches; rather, one can assign a magnitude to the effect (such as setting the agents' maximum age range).

---

[3] NetLogo is a programming model and development environment for agent-based modeling which comes preloaded with various examples.

Agents are born, live in, interact with, and eventually die in the environmental landscape. The set of configured features enabled at the start of the simulation have quite pronounced effects on the resulting emergent societal behaviors.

4.1   Environment Features

The environment has toggleable features which may be enabled in a given simulated instance. Each has profound impacts for agents as they interact with the environment. These impacts are also expressed at the societal level.

Replacement. If an agent dies, a new agent is generated and placed randomly in the environment. By default, agents are *not* replaced in Sugarscape.

Seasons. Without loss of generality, seasons periodically shift between the northern and southern hemisphere of the environment. Hemispheres cycle between dry and wet seasons, which affect the resource regeneration rate of cells.

Pollution. Pollution is generated at a cell when an agent harvests sugar and spice from the cell and when they consume resources at the cell. This forever harms the cell's regeneration rate. Diffusion of pollution is also toggleable and governs how severely the pollution spreads to surrounding cells.

4.2   Agent Features

Agents consume sugar and spice according to their *metabolism* at each timestep. They die if they do not have enough resources to consume. In Vanilla Sugarscape, agents can move up to their *vision* to gather additional resources. We describe the following configurable agent features, which could have profound impacts on agent behavior:

Reproduction. Neighboring agents of appropriate age with sufficient resources can each expend some of their resources to produce *offspring*.

Trading. Agents can trade their sugar for spice and *vice versa*. Trading in Vanilla Sugarscape is always fair, meaning no agent can make a profit from trading.

Loans. Agents can loan resources to other agents with a specified repayment schedule and interest rate.

Inheritance. When an agent dies, their wealth and debt is passed along to another agent (usually their offspring). Inheriting debt provides more security for lenders should an agent starve or die of old age.

Culture. Agents have a bit vector of tags which represents their tribal affiliation. When agents meet in Vanilla Sugarscape, they exert cultural pressure upon each other that may change their tribal affiliations.

Combat. Only possible when *culture* is active. Agents may kill others from different tribes to take their resources. Agents consider the risk of retaliation before they kill.

Disease. Agents are born with an immune system, represented as a bit vector. Vanilla Sugarscape seeds some initial agents with starting diseases. Agents have a chance to contract diseases from neighboring agents; agents that recover from a disease are more resistant to reinfection.

4.3   Emergent Behavior in Vanilla Sugarscape

Emergent behavior refers to the behavior of groups of agents (a *society*) that transcend the available actions of any individual agent in the group. Vanilla Sugarscape agents exhibit observable collective social behaviors.

Group Migration. Since agents can only move orthogonally in the grid, societies that make diagonal migratory movements over time are exhibiting emergent behavior. These societies are incentivized to move toward a resource rich area of the grid when their current location becomes barren. Agents that cannot migrate instead hibernate, attempting to wait out the dry spell in hopes that the landscape recovers. Migrators bunch up and behave similar to a *flyer* in Conway's Game of Life [3].

With the season environment feature turned on, half the environment's sugar peaks do not replenish for a certain number of timesteps. This feature intensifies the need for agents to migrate or hibernate: agents with high vision flee during offseasons, whereas agents with low vision typically hibernate.

Formation of Tribes. Tribal formation is another example of emergent behavior that is best seen through the movement patterns of individual agents. Tribes are a consequence of agent tags. There are no explicit rules determining how agents *form* tribes. Rather, there is a simple mechanism for agents to influence each other's tags. When agents with very similar tags interact, they may stick together and become a tribe to avoid being attacked by agents with dissimilar tags. Aside from the tribal value as a protective group, they may instead become a hunting party and use their numbers to pick off lonely agents with dissimilar tags.

Stable Economy. We also observe the creation of an *ad hoc* (yet functional) economy as an emergent behavior. When the trading feature is enabled, agents can exchange goods with one another, and their valuation of sugar and spice stabilizes over time to create a healthy, dependable market for a fair exchange of goods. This free market value is synthesized from the bottom up as opposed to being dictated by some centralized arbiter. The evolution of this system is another example of emergent behavior. Thematically, this pattern is true of many other agent behaviors: introduce a simple rule, agents adhere to it collectively, and an emergent *social* behavior develops corresponding to that rule.

5   Validation of Vanilla Sugarscape

We validate Vanilla Sugarscape by recreating the experiments from the source material [2] in our implementation. Due to space constraints, it is not realistic to present all of our validation efforts, though we did test every experiment from Vanilla Sugarscape. All resources needed to reproduce our validations may be found in our source code repository [5].

Table 4 (found in Appendix A) lists the full set of validated examples found in the repository. We showcase three experiments from Vanilla Sugarscape here: seasonal migration, constrained reproduction, and disease transmission. Table 2 can be used when interpreting our Sugarscape visualizations; more saturated cell colors indicate the presence of a higher number of its associated resources:

Table 2. Visualization Color Legend

Cell Color	Meaning
Yellow	Sugar
Brown	Spice
Tan	Both sugar and spice
White	No sugar or spice
Other	Agent properties under study

Vanilla Sugarscape, although insightful, is not inherently easy to validate, in part since its documentation is incomplete. As a result, it is impossible to know the initial configuration for any particular result or rationale behind underlying design decisions for a given experiment. We address that deficiency in our reimplementation of Sugarscape and provide details as we go along. We parameterize our pseudo-random number generator with the fixed seed value of 12345 to establish a uniform baseline for initial conditions across experiments. We further organize all configurable parameters (such as agent max age ranges, maximum combat rewards, and resource growback) into a single configuration file. In this way, we produce a completely deterministic instance of Sugarscape.

Our descriptions of agent behavior in this paper are conveyed in qualitative, not quantitative terms, which mirrors the source text [2]. When considering the results of any experiment on any given seed, there will always be a few agents whose behavior reflects a blend of the influences that inform a particular experiment. As a result, agents may migrate more slowly or express a reproductive behavior that appears to oscillate between two relatively equal paths towards optimal resource collection. Our observational goal when considering *emergent* behavior is to focus more on *majority trends* that govern agents, rather than the much lower frequency of actions of agents in the minority. In some sense, if we incorporate this minority behavior to a larger extent, we risk overfitting societal behavior based on this minority noise.

5.1   Seasonal Migration

The *seasons* environmental feature splits the world into northern and southern halves. At any given timestep, half of the world is experiencing a dry season where the sugar regeneration rate is severely reduced. Simultaneously, the other half of the world experiences a wet season where the sugar regeneration rate is normal. The two seasons switch at a regular timestep interval.

We describe the activity in this scenario in Fig. 1. Agents (indicated by red cells) are initially placed at random across the landscape. The south begins in a wet season, and we see the agents concentrate at the southern sugar peak. The northern agents either migrate south (given high enough vision to explore) or hibernate (given low enough metabolism to survive). Once the seasons change, we see mass migration from south to north.

Southern agents who can explore (having high vision) migrate north and find plentiful resources. Those who cannot (having low vision *and* low metabolism) hibernate through the dry season. Agents with both lower vision and high metabolism become scavengers, picking off the few remaining resources in the south. Due to natural selection, scavengers are the most likely to perish in the seasonal change. Figure 1 shows the environment in the initial stages of the southern wet season, the beginning of the seasonal transition, the agents migrating and hibernating, and finally a return to a southern wet season. This result verifies the behavior explained and demonstrated in pages 44–46 of *Growing Artificial Societies*.

5.2   Constrained Reproduction

Agents have multiple factors which impact their ability to reproduce. They have a fertility window that dictates the age range they can reproduce. Reproduction also has a configurable resource cost (in sugar and spice) that parents share. The cost to reproduce is based on their starting sugar and spice holds. In pages 64–66 of the source book, the authors study the effect of reducing an agent's fertility window by 10 timesteps. This change led to wild oscillations in population which, over the course of many generations, eventually stabilized.

Figure 2 shows a similar effect happening under the initial conditions. The population explodes in an initial boom due to plentiful access to resources and

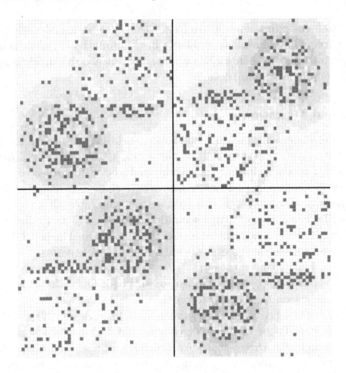

Fig. 1. Seasonal Migration in Sugarscape (Color figure online)

a population that reaches fertility age at roughly the same time. Soon after, the starting generation gets old and begins to die. We see our first big dip in population between timesteps 60 and 100, which corresponds to the maximum age range for agents.

The next generation experiences a similar pattern, though the population boom is not as pronounced. The dampened effect happens because resources are more scarce, since they are spread across more overall agents; also fewer agents have a synced fertility window. Additionally, there are fewer agents who are coming of age for this second boom. After three generations, we see the population has become more or less stable. Society is now less prone to generational death, since agents are more evenly distributed across all ages. At the end of the simulation, we find that the population has reached a steady state, which validates the results in pages 64–66 of *Growing Artificial Societies.*

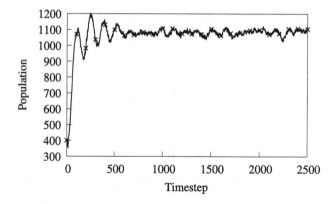

Fig. 2. Constrained Reproduction in Sugarscape

5.3 Disease Transmission

Diseases impact agent behavior by negatively affecting their attributes: increasing metabolism, reducing vision, rendering agents temporarily infertile, or other harmful effects. Diseases are also *highly* contagious since neighboring agents contract a random disease that the acting agent is carrying. Agents either die or recover from a given disease and become immune to it for a time. Diseases may be eradicated (most likely due to herd immunity), may become endemic to the society, or they may kill the society.

We compare Fig. 3 to the experiment on page 148 of [2], which shows an initial death event, eventual eradication of disease, and a final population recovery. An initial set of 10 diseases are placed on random agents. Red colored agents represent the sick while blue represents the healthy. At the beginning of the simulation, disease spreads *rapidly*, which causes an initial mass death. At this stage, a majority of the living population (a mere 165 agents) had contracted at least one new disease. The population battles disease over time, eventually leading to roughly 20 surviving agents either immune to infection or far enough away from a disease carrier to avoid further infection. Once rid of disease, society rapidly recovers and the population booms.

5.4 Further Validation with Random Seeds

In all the previous experiments, we use seed 12345 to validate our results; however, it is possible that this seed is an anomaly and does not represent the average case behavior. To that end, Table 3 shows abbreviated results on an additional 20 randomly generated seeds. A ✓ indicates the same or similar behavior as seed 12345, whereas an X indicates behavior that was meaningfully different. For example, all seeds successfully demonstrated the migrators and hibernators behavior of the seasons experiment.

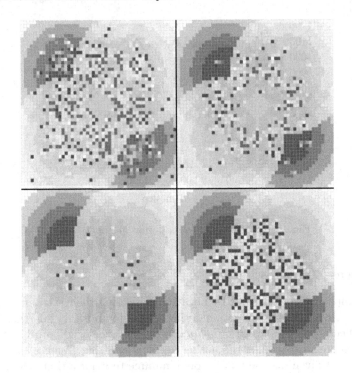

Fig. 3. Disease Transmission in Sugarscape

For the constrained reproduction experiment, seeds that differed from 12345 had especially resilient initial conditions and did not see the large population swings indicated in *Growing Artificial Societies*. The changes to the fertility window in these seeds appear to have made no meaningful difference.

For the disease transmission experiment, the authors of *Growing Artificial Societies* suggest the outcome as either an eradication of disease or endemic disease with a stable population. However, the two seeds with different behavior (12881 and 22744) completely died out from sickness. Seed 24022 nearly had endemic disease (as page 149 of the source book indicates), but the population eventually eradicated all disease.

5.5 Deviations from Vanilla Sugarscape

Although our implementation of Sugarscape largely matches the behavior of the original, there are cases where we deviate. The two most apparent deviations come from the trade and lending mechanisms which have uplifting effects on the number of agents the environment can support. This concept is called the society's *carrying capacity*. In both cases, on pages 111–112, the authors of the source book share data showing that trade and lending increase carrying capacity by 10% to 25%.

Table 3. Validating Vanilla Sugarscape with Random Seeds

Seed	Seasons	Reproduction	Disease
14133	✓	✓	✓
5172	✓	✓	✓
32209	✓	X	✓
23128	✓	✓	✓
15362	✓	✓	✓
12881	✓	✓	X
1484	✓	X	✓
19522	✓	✓	✓
23231	✓	✓	✓
24022	✓	✓	✓
5568	✓	✓	✓
13461	✓	X	✓
31844	✓	✓	✓
8885	✓	X	✓
21500	✓	✓	✓
28307	✓	✓	✓
28548	✓	✓	✓
22744	✓	✓	X
27167	✓	✓	✓
26341	✓	✓	✓

Magnitudes aside, this concept seems intuitively apparent: if an agent has a need for a resource, they could satisfy that need by trading with or borrowing from a neighbor, rather than depending on what is currently available in the environment. With more opportunities for agents to address their needs, we would *expect* a corresponding higher carrying capacity and higher reproduction to meet it.

In contrast, we were not able to find *any* seeds that demonstrate this significant uplift in carrying capacity. Our experiments show that increases from trade and lending average around 3%, with a maximum increase of 5% for all seeds we tested. Worse still, a few seeds saw a marginal *decrease* in carrying capacity!

We offer some possible reasoning for this mismatch. Epstein and Axtell focused their exposition on presenting the conceptual ideas clearly, and likely omitted many design and configuration details in the pursuit of a more accessible description of the complex and interconnected nature of the economic features of Vanilla Sugarscape. As experts in economic theory, Epstein and Axtell may have also written for an experienced audience, and we were unable to reconstitute that domain expertise. Finally, the authors of Vanilla Sugarscape were computationally limited by the hardware and software of the day, leading to potentially quite different design decisions from our implementation.

5.6   Additional Features in Our Implementation

We make many fundamental improvements to the underlying engine for Vanilla Sugarscape. For example, nearly all agent features (such as base interest rate or loan duration) now use a numeric range rather than a single value which allows for more granular behavioral variation. We also provide wholly new configurable parameters, such as `aggressionFactor` and `tradeFactor`, which indicate the likelihood an agent will engage in combat or trade respectively. A value of zero means the behavior is not present in the agent, with larger values indicating increasing prioritization of the associated action.

We also enhance the tracking of most agent interactions. Each agent keeps detailed records of their parents, children, neighbors, friends, lenders, borrowers, and traders throughout their lifetimes. We also maintain how often agents visit, trade, reproduce with, lend, etc. with each agent they meet. Though we do not use these tracking improvements in our current work, they provide us with a treasure trove of data we can investigate for future work.

The most significant, albeit simple, change is to consider resources as real numbers rather than integers. Trading and lending more cleanly map to exchanges of real number values rather than integer representations since rounding can punish agents when considering a loan or commencing a trade. The granularity of the trade or loan impacts its viability. In particular, it is more difficult to make a fair trade when agents cannot use fractional resource values to balance transactions. This change to the engine has profound implications on the realism for the Sugarscape simulation, making it a higher fidelity model for real world computations. Nevertheless, our observations on emergent behavior closely match the experiments in [2] and validate our approach.

5.7   Technical Details in Our Implementation

Our version of Sugarscape is written in Python 3. We chose this language to lower the barrier to entry for domain researchers who likely have more Python experience than other programming languages. The software repository [5] provides a `Makefile` to automate much of the setup and running process. The software requires a local `Bash` installation. Additionally, the Python code uses the `Tkinter` module *only* if it is run using the GUI as the module is conditionally imported.

The simulation takes a JSON (JavaScript Object Notation) configuration file as an optional input parameter and optionally produces a JSON log file as output. The code repository comes with a default configuration with most features enabled as well as the full set of examples from the source book [2] we have validated. The full details for running the software can be found in the included `README` in the repository.

6   Conclusions

Given its myriad applications across many different disciplines, Sugarscape serves as an important and feature-rich cornerstone to inspiring new and innovative work that requires a carefully considered agent-based simulation. It is therefore incumbent upon the research community to maintain a modern, extendable, and robust version.

We humbly submit that we have created the *definitive version* of Sugarscape, together with the tools necessary to further research in the area. Our goals were to increase verification standards, integrate transparency, and provide a modern, modular software style that supports deep and meaningful customization. Along the way, we verify many of the results of [2], which are more easily reproduced in our software. Our code and validations are publicly available [5], and we invite the community to explore and use this seminal framework to study societal behavior.

Acknowledgements. We would like to thank Willem Hueffed, Maria Milkowski, and Joshua Palicka for their contributions to our Sugarscape software repository. This work was supported in part by the Seattle University Undergraduate Summer Research Award and the Holcolm Award Research Fund at Butler University.

A   Appendix: Table of Validated Examples

Table 4. Full Set of Validated Examples

Example	Book Page Number(s)
Resource Collection with Immediate Growback	21–26
Resource Collection with Constant Growback	28–30
Seasonal Migration	43–45
Pollution	45–50
Reproduction	55–58
Constrained Reproduction	64–66
Inheritance	67–68
Cultural Tagging	72–79
Combat with Unlimited Reward	82–83
Combat with Limited Reward	86–90
Sugar & Spice	96–99
Trading	101–107
Trading & Agent Replacement	120–122
Trading & Pollution	127–129
Agent Foresight	129–130
Lending	131–133
Disease Transmission	141–147

References

1. Bigbee, A., Cioffi-Revilla, C., Luke, S.: Replication of Sugarscape using MASON. In: Terano, T., Kita, H., Deguchi, H., Kijima, K. (eds.) Agent-Based Approaches in Economic and Social Complex Systems IV. ASS, vol. 3, pp. 183–190. Springer, Tokyo (2007). https://doi.org/10.1007/978-4-431-71307-4_20

2. Epstein, J.M., Axtell, R.: Growing Artificial Societies: Social Science From the Bottom Up. Brookings Institution Press, Washington, D.C. (1996)

3. Games, M.: The fantastic combinations of John Conway's new solitaire game "life" by Martin Gardner. Sci. Am. **223**, 120–123 (1970)

4. Hobbes, T.: Leviathan: Or the Matter, Forme and Power of a Commonwealth Ecclesiasticall and Civil. A. Crooke, London (1651)

5. Kremer-Herman, N., Gupta, A., Palicka, J.: Sugarscape (2023). https://github.com/digital-terraria-lab/sugarscape

6. Kurakin, P.: Technoscape: a multi-agent model of all-human global web. In: 2022 15th International Conference Management of Large-Scale System Development (MLSD), pp. 1–5. IEEE (2022)

7. Lange, H.: Sugarscape (2022). https://github.com/langerv/sugarscape

8. Langton, C.G.: Artificial life. In: Langton, C.G. (ed.) Artificial Life: The Proceedings of an Interdisciplinary Workshop on the Synthesis and Simulation of Living Systems, held September, 1987, Los Alamos, New Mexico, pp. 1–48. Addison-Wesley, Redwood City (1989)

9. Lasquety-Reyes, J.A.: Towards computer simulations of virtue ethics. Open Philos. **2**(1), 399–413 (2019)

10. von Neumann, J.: Theory of Self-Reproducing Automata. University of Illinois Press, Champaign (1966)

11. Schelling, T.C.: Micromotives and Macrobehavior. W. W. Norton & Company, October 1978

12. Serrano, E., Satoh, K.: An agent-based model for exploring pension law and social security policies. In: Sakamoto, M., Okazaki, N., Mineshima, K., Satoh, K. (eds.) JSAI-isAI 2019. LNCS (LNAI), vol. 12331, pp. 50–63. Springer, Cham (2020). https://doi.org/10.1007/978-3-030-58790-1_4

13. Tisue, S., Wilensky, U.: NetLogo: design and implementation of a multi-agent modeling environment. In: Proceedings of Agent, vol. 2004, pp. 7–9 (2004)

Artificial Intelligence and Simulation

Generative AI with Modeling and Simulation of Activity and Flow-Based Diagrams

Abdurrahman Alshareef[1]([✉]), Nicholas Keller[2], Priscilla Carbo[2], and Bernard P. Zeigler[2]

[1] Department of Information Systems, College of Computer and Information Sciences, King Saud University, Riyadh 11543, Saudi Arabia
`ashareef@ksu.edu.sa`
[2] RTSync Corp., Chandler, AZ 85226, USA
{`nicholas.keller,priscilla.carbo,zeigler`}`@rtsync.com`

Abstract. In systems engineering and model-based design, the complexity and interrelationships across different system elements always demand continuous elaboration and expansion in various overlapping domains. We examine how such a phenomenon can be assisted with generative AI and benefit from large language models (LLMs), such as GPT-4. We demonstrate ways of incorporating generated text and outputs from LLMs into the modeling process. The approach can customize the GPT-4 model with an activity metamodel specified in Eclipse Ecore or predefined activity diagrams encoded in a textual format for learning from instances. Alternatively, the descriptive text from the LLM can be provided as input to a parser, resulting in an activity that can be readily transformed into a discrete event system specification (DEVS) model with simulation capability. We will discuss how the process can be enhanced in a simulation environment, thus offering the opportunity to examine a variety of scenarios and arguments for incorporating generative AI or general AI as a collaborative agent in the domain of interest. One scenario could begin with a simplified text describing a generic process, yielding an approximate representation as a starting point for further elaboration by modelers to a complex specification through a systematic, guided, and well-defined framework. We demonstrate the approach with activity and flow-based diagrams in a manner applicable to SysML, UML, and systems engineering at large.

Keywords: Activity Diagram · Generative AI · DEVS · SysML · UML · Systems Engineering · Ecore

1 Introduction

We examine how generative AI can offer valuable assistance in constructing simulation models. Such assistance can take multiple forms, from trivially generating plain textual descriptions to making critical maneuvering decisions and

© ICST Institute for Computer Sciences, Social Informatics and Telecommunications Engineering 2024
Published by Springer Nature Switzerland AG 2024. All Rights Reserved
J.-L. Guisado-Lizar et al. (Eds.): SIMUtools 2023, LNICST 519, pp. 95–109, 2024.
https://doi.org/10.1007/978-3-031-57523-5_8

threat recognition tasks. In the case of large language models (LLMs), it can help distinguish between boilerplate and logic infused in models. It can help in repetitive tasks that may vary in significance to different modelers with different domain backgrounds and perspectives. The assessment can also take a more profound form and facilitate discussion and experiments related to problems regarding domain-neutral and multi-domain modeling along with platform-independent modeling all the way through to Artificial General Intelligence (AGI) with advanced planning capabilities.

In systems engineering and software modeling, generative AI offers an opportunity to facilitate the creation of models in design frameworks like the System Modeling Language (SysML) and Unified Modeling Language (UML) at large. Corpora of such documents must have been subject to the aggregations of LLMs. Basic inquiries demonstrate that. However, they are contributing to the body of knowledge in these models in a collective manner. Given the scale of such models, they are susceptible to biases and specific patterns from various resources, which we plan to investigate in this paper with simulation. To address potential failures and threats, research has been initiated for safety and responsibility, such as responsible AI [9] and safe and beneficial AI [13].

For activities and activity diagrams, in particular, the task demands more effort to navigate through intricacies posed by challenging problems of interpretations, semantics, transformations, and code generation [1]. Currently, GPT-4 cannot generate executable code or real instances from an activity diagram. Moreover, different parallelization schemes and algorithmic complexity, as evident in any sophisticated activity modeling, require advanced handling and presumably a degree of reasoning and validation. However, ongoing efforts, such as in GPT-4, attempt to enhance LLMs with these capabilities. Here, we demonstrate ways they can assist simulation modeling and approximate design in the preparatory sense or earlier stages of model development, as well as in intrinsic elements of the process, such as random number generation and sampling.

The general frame of learning and perception has been subject to examination by simulation research [14]. More recent research [10,19] seeks to infuse generative adversarial network (GAN) into agent-based and traffic simulations to enhance synthetic populations and sampling. In addition, major developers [12] in such technology use simulated tests and exams to evaluate and benchmark the performance of their models where valuable insights can highlight and guide future decisions for further improvement and acquisitions. The simulation element, as a plugin, framework, or environment, can significantly contribute to the whole ecosystem and guide optimizations in data and logic with discipline and confident assessment of alternative designs.

2   Common LLMs

Commonly known as ChatGPT, the GPT-4, a member of the Generative Pre-trained Transformer (GPT-n) family, is the most recently released LLM model by OpenAI [12]. The model fundamentally uses a deep neural network for natural language understanding. It initially has a knowledge cutoff as of September 2021. GPT-4 Turbo extended its knowledge to April 2023. Thus, the training data consists of information from the internet up until that date. GPT-3 (GPT-4 predecessor) uses 175 billion parameters [8], and the number of parameters in GPT-4 has yet to be released. Simulating exams taken by humans was one of the performance benchmarks conducted to evaluate and assess such models. The model accepts prompts in different forms, such as images or texts. In this work, we primarily experimented with using the textual form for all prompts. However, we also experimented with textual forms that are handwritten and captured in pictures. We plan to extend that and examine various visual inputs, such as images, slides, diagrams, charts, or infographics, in future works.

Google developed PaLM [4], a Transformer model trained with the Pathways system, an advanced design utilizing many TPUs (Tensor Processing Unit). Bahram et al. [2] presented the Pathways design developed for distributed dataflow and computation accelerators for machine learning (ML). The novelty in such design comes primarily from a distinction between the data plane and the control plane while warranting parallel execution despite sharding. In [4], PaLM uses 540 billion parameters to train the neural network. We used PaLM 2 branded as Bard in some of the experiments.

3 Related Work

We looked for works that use ChatGPT or other LLMs to create models in specific modeling languages and for activity diagrams in particular. Some recent research uses LLMs and other technologies to automatically or semi-automatically generate code, UML, and SysML. In [3], the authors test its ability to re-create existing class diagrams through iterative prompting. They conclude that ChatGPT can handle only relatively small models, is inconsistent, and does not comprehend all UML concepts. They also observe that its performance depends highly on the specific UML syntax and is much better with OCL (Object Constraint Language). Given that the performance of ChatGPT is highly dependent upon the specific domain, we considered it worthwhile to explore its applicability to activity diagrams.

In [17], the authors use BERT-based (Bidirectional Encoder Representations from Transformers [6]) language models to generate requirements tables from U.S. federal aeronautical regulations. It does this primarily through named entity recognition and chunking sentences into linguistic elements such as noun phrases, verb phrases, and much more. This method cannot generate activity diagrams, although it can be used to aid in generating SysML requirements tables. Their technique generates requirements from documentation but cannot create that documentation or requirements tables from scratch like ChatGPT can. In [15], authors discuss the potential data curation role that could benefit AI-enabled aerospace systems along with challenges for concept development and MBSE (Model-Based System Engineering.)

In [22], the authors are concerned with extracting SysML from system documentation. Unlike [17], they use statistical methods instead of a large language model. Their approach relies upon frequency-inverse document frequency (tf-idf) and part-of-speech tagging. They can only generate block definition diagrams, internal block diagrams, and requirement diagrams. Like [17], they rely more on existing documentation.

GitHub's copilot uses an LLM to write code from natural language prompts. We consider our work to align with this approach with application to SysML and UML. Copilot helps generate code with a considerable success rate [20]. This performance is likely possible for SysML with current models or further training. Although practical, it is prone to producing errors. However, recent research has found that experienced developers best use the copilot as an AI pair programmer [5]. Junior developers may fail to identify the errors that the copilot produces. We expect a similar dynamic with our SysML and UML generation tool once it matures while valuing human expertise, inputs, and logic. Our work also addresses some limitations in natural language requirement descriptions highlighted in [18] while relying on the DEVS formalism [21] as an underlying and core guiding principle.

4   Possible Use Cases of Generative AI for Activity Diagrams

As illustrated in Fig. 1, we consider three possibilities in which generative AI can assist in the modeling of activity and flow-based diagrams.

The first possibility is where we input examples or the metamodel to the LLM and use it to generate instances that comply with the deduced schema. The second one is where we use it to generate a generic text describing the desired activity model and then parse the resulting text according to a set of given syntactical rules using our code generation facility. We consider the third possibility for future work in which we train, and transfer learn the LLM with additional knowledge about languages and simulation modeling processes using reinforcement learning.

4.1   Customizing GPT-4 to Generate Activity Diagrams

Inserting the Ecore metamodel can be a starting prompt. Then, subsequent queries follow through with requests to generate model instances. In this case, an instance can be generic or domain-specific. A generic instance consists of various activity elements and probably has a generic naming pattern. We had to add particular keywords to create a full-fledged instance without using informal texts or pseudocode. Within the resulting file, it used an XPath-like style for referencing. Since we use Sirius for editing, we changed the referencing style to use an ordered list instead and use element indices. Moreover, since the model has constraints specified using the Acceleo query language, we had to explicitly insert instructions explaining those constraints in a natural language.

Alternatively, inserting instance example as the input string can also be the starting prompt. In this case, akin to post-training reinforcement learning, we expect the GPT-4 to deduce the metamodel and the overall schema and infer that from one or multiple examples. It is also reasonable to expect the GPT-4 to generate a similar instance without going through deduction. The example model needs to include the various elements in the activity metamodel and our proposed activity editor with features supporting the specification of the simulation experiments and visualization options. A combinatorial design of the example with permutation coverage of all possible parameterizations of variables with finite domains would suffice in giving the GPT-4 comprehensive insights about variations.

4.2   Parsing Textual Flow and Activity Descriptions

We use the GPT-4 in its generic sense to produce a textual description of the activity of interest. We feed the resulting text as a string to the code generator equipped with basic parsing functionality that would, therefore, transform it into a full-fledged activity model. A wide range of options can be used here to implement such a process, including but not limited to the reuse of the GPT-4 itself. Preliminary, we generate activity with various nodes and flows given the basic structure of the given string, such as new lines and numbering. A drawback of this method is that it may include less transfer learning and training to the general GPT-4 model. However, this drawback might be advantageous in domains where a certain level of privacy is required. A more apparent separation exists between the generative AI and other modeling components. Figure 1 visualizes the ways we followed in this paper to produce the desired experiments through activity modeling.

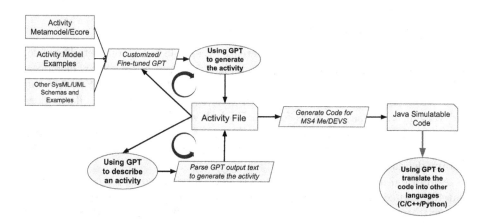

Fig. 1. GPT-4 (or any LLM) assistance in the simulation modeling development

5   Model Generation and Simulation Experiments

We design our simulation experiments while delegating some development tasks
to GPT-4, as Fig. 2 explains. It is not surprising to note that the results of each
approach differ. For example, the instance obtained after prompting the Ecore
metamodel differs from the result obtained after actual instance model training. We used both GPT-4 and PaLM 2. However, we demonstrate the models
obtained by employing GPT-4 and plan to explore further variations in future
development.

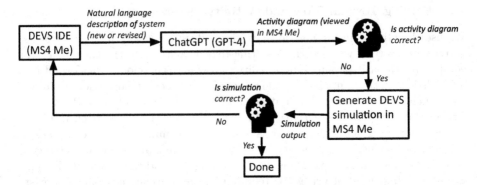

Fig. 2. An overall description of using GPT-4 with activity modeling and simulation
in MS4 Me.

5.1   Prompt Engineering

After promoting the Ecore schema, it created a simple but incomplete instance.
In the second prompt, it created a fully-fledged instance but with few elements,
only one instance of each class, that is, one *Flow, Action, Sync, Select, Input
Parameter*, and *Output Parameter* with generic names post-fixed with indices
and varying value assignments for the Boolean attributes. *Action* is a type of
activity node, while *Sync* is a common type for fork and join nodes, and *Select*
is a common class for decision/choice and merge nodes. More details about the
metamodel can be found in [1].

Additional instructional prompts were necessary to produce a correctly populated instance. More instructions were needed to create more extensive activities with more elements. There were issues with flow specifications in which
identifiers for source and destination nodes did not exist. The instance initially
followed an XPath-like referencing scheme. We instructed it to create an ordered
list of behaviors to comply with the Eclipse Sirius [7] visual editor. Since some
constraints on the metamodel were originally specified using the Acceleo query
language without being part of the Ecore schema, these constraints were vio-
lated. Using natural language, we prompted the GPT-4 with such constraints.

And it complied. More prompts were given to fix specific mistakes in the activity or to add missing flows. Most of the resulting instances did not use parallel flows or hierarchical structures. Figure 3 shows the final resulting activity.

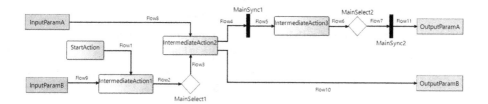

Fig. 3. The generated generic activity. Notice that some elements, such as the fork and join, have been misplaced or roughly added.

We could easily see some basic issues in the generated activity. While the activity is syntactically correct, it does not contain parallel flows after the *Main-Sync1* node, regardless of characterizing the node as a sync, where the node could initiate the parallel flows. Some actions receive multiple incoming flows. It would be better if such flows were processed with control nodes to describe the dictation of the desired control explicitly. Nevertheless, having such a model at the initial step and without making a substantial effort can be valuable. Automation of tedious aspects in modeling and minimizing the entry barriers can offer significant value in some domains.

Figure 4 shows the three resulting activities after prompting the GPT-4 with an example activity. The entered example activity is for an airport check-in process and has one input and one output parameter. After entering the text, we started with a text asking the model to deduce the syntax from the entered example activity and then produce an example for making coffee. Figure 4a shows the first result. Figure 4b shows the result after promoting the GPT-4 to add sync nodes. Figure 4c shows the resulting activity after adding a prompt for adding parallel flows. Notice that the resulting activities still do not have a proper use of parallel flows with reasonable description at the example level.

5.2   Syntactical Parsing of the GPT-4 Output String

A safer option is to use GPT-4 as is and focus on producing the simpler, non-nuanced parts of the activity and flow descriptions in simple English. Then, we encoded a designated parser for the output string as part of our code generation facility. The advantage of such an approach is ensuring correctness relative to our metamodel, schema, and DEVS specification. The drawback is its limited ability

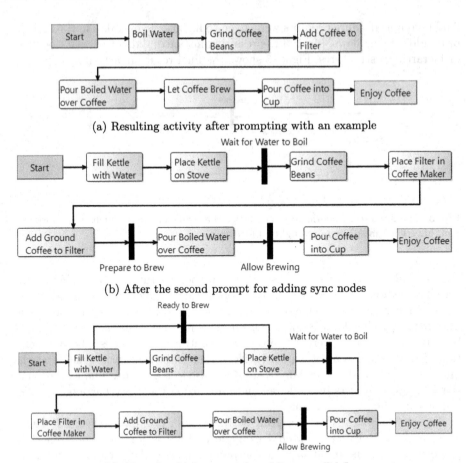

(a) Resulting activity after prompting with an example

(b) After the second prompt for adding sync nodes

(c) After the third prompt for adding parallel flows

Fig. 4. Generating an activity after promoting GPT-4 with an example activity that is an instance of the activity Ecore metamodel. Again, notice the misplacement of some nodes.

to parameterize the various parameters and stochastic specifications supported in the activity editor. How to incorporate such aspects in the parsing process needs to be clarified. However, some aspects have already been addressed in DEVS natural language and ongoing research in natural language processing and programming language development.

The approach focuses on gaining the low-hanging fruits of GPT and LLM while maintaining the rigor found in mathematical modeling. The overall perspective is to delegate parts of the model development tasks to generative AI and the language model, in particular for aspects that are akin to the LLM function like naming, helping modelers to adopt a more pragmatic perspective and shifting their focus toward what they deem more relevant to their domain of interest such as logic, creative and critical thinking, tactical design, and reasoning. The warranted flexibility has the potential to align well with the virtues of domain generic, domain-neutral, multi-domain, and platform-independent modeling. It allows modelers to select what to delegate to GPT with some flexibility, especially in capturing requirements that might be specified in various forms and preferences and using different tools, editors, and documentation standards and techniques. Figure 5a shows the basic transformation of text into an activity where modelers can, therefore, infuse more logic, control, and flow routes using the full design experience with the activity editor in the MS4 Me environment. See the resulting activity after the enhancement in Fig. 5b.

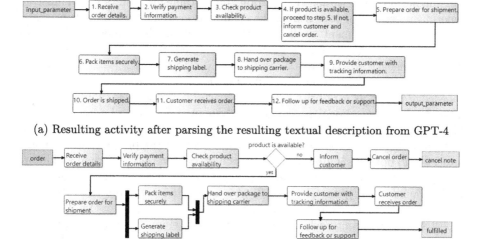

(a) Resulting activity after parsing the resulting textual description from GPT-4

(b) The same activity after manual enhancement using the full design experience in the activity editor within MS4 Me

Fig. 5. Parsing the generated string for online order activity. Correctness can be ensured in this approach with additional supporting features.

All of the aforementioned generated activities are now readily simulatable in the MS4 Me environment and DEVS-compliant according to the earlier activity specification [1]. We plan to examine the simulation results of models constructed in such a manner. Comparing them with results from ordinary models can provide more insights into LLMs and their interrelationships with model development.

5.3 The Case for Using Generative AI to Capture Requirements in Visual Forms with Perceptive Model Generation

This case would ultimately cover various visual forms of requirements to facilitate model rapid development. We will demonstrate briefly in this paper and plan to extend it in future works and projects. The grand plan for such an endeavor aims to utilize the recent developments in GPT models to transform the current model development lifecycle in general and for systems engineering in particular. Starting by simply using the GPT model to capture the specification in a variety of forms, such as documents, figures, diagrams, and handwritten sketches or notes in audio formats. The job then is to thoroughly digest those entries in a refinement process to ensure the meaningfulness of the resulting models and simulations. We managed to obtain some promising results for small-scale experiments and plan to continue the examination with larger models at scale. The resulting experiment applies to other sections in this paper. In Fig. 6, we demonstrate the overall lifecycle of simulation models in such systems along with their counterpart experiments.

We note that addressing existing challenges pertinent to domain-specific knowledge comes as a priority in the approach of such a cycle. The envisioned AI-enabled system prioritizes the general human expertise and domain experts while enhancing their productivity and filling the technical gaps for them as a way towards a systems engineering approach with overlapping interdisciplinary subjects and domains. Our current approach covers a variety of formal and informal specifications and can extend further seamlessly to cover more elements in a wide range of subjects. The SysML acts as a collective approach for capturing system requirements and communicating mental models across multi-faceted expertise from different backgrounds. The resulting simulations and lessons from the conducted experiments can feed through the system iteratively until reaching the desired goal, where the simulation models can gradually and eventually evolve into a fully-fledged system in the production phase with optimized designs to maximize potential.

5.4 Generative AI and Simulation: Potential Benefits

The importance of simulation as a profound perspective and benchmark tool for assessing systems with AI models and components is undeniable. The idea of enhancing the generative elements in AI models has been entertained in the past [14] with competitive or cooperative reactions in contexts such as game theoretic simulation and cognizant simulation with AI. Recent generative AI development and the advancement in GAN and GPUs can benefit from tools with simulation capacity to perform necessary assessments and evaluation of such systems and with more disciplined testing and adversarial testing mechanisms. The demand for such techniques is urgent, especially when using generative AI with planning capacity in critical domains, given the evidence of such models producing harmful content in so-called hypothetical scenarios [12]. We need not take human-in-loop intervention for granted but instead develop models and conduct research to

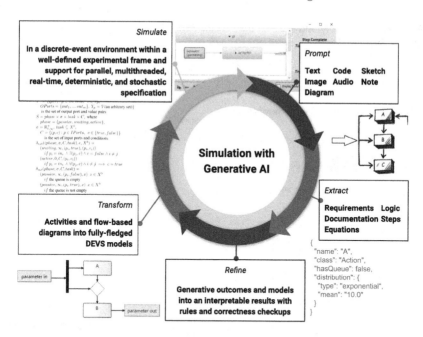

Fig. 6. An illustration of the envisioned lifecycle to capture systems in SysML, UML, Activities, DEVS, DEVS Markov, Queuing, etc., with stronger accounts for timing toward an AI-enabled system with an advanced planning capacity.

uncover more about the black box [11] in ways, no matter how small, that in no way undermine the crucial part of human experience and knowledge but rather signify it. The interrelationships amongst such an ecosystem are complementary and multi-directional. New integrative and incorporative studies are needed to produce tools and techniques to account for the recent development with rigorous simulation support.

Figures 7 and 8 visualize our current approach to the subject in this paper. We treat each element with examination to any redundant, overlapping, or unique role of each. Most of our effort so far in trying to utilize GPT-4 accounts for early stages and starting points in model development. The blue curve in Fig. 7 illustrates the effects of using GPT-4 in the early stages to stimulate critical thinking and facilitate aspects of communicating mental models in a way that could benefit the initial conceptualizations of models and systems under study. However, the curve seems to converge at some points where the LLM may not produce additional utility or even starts to produce inaccurate results. It is possible to consider the resulting models as approximations of actual systems or models that can have alternative representations using more rigorous probabilistic, deterministic, or cognitive manifestations. Figure 8 illustrates the overlapping, unique, or redundant roles we encountered throughout our prompts engineering, simulation modeling, and experimental design.

Achieved Complexity and
Size of System/Model

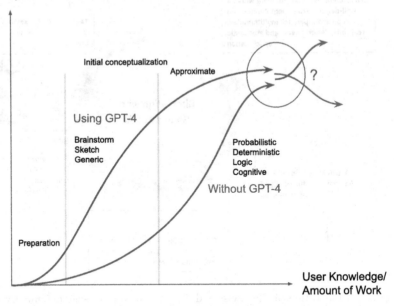

Fig. 7. Roles of using GPT and impact on learning curve

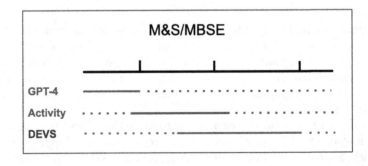

Fig. 8. Our current approach for stages of integrative GPT-4, activity, and DEVS, for M&S MBSE.

LLMs for large scale activities indicates an attractive endeavor to explore infinite variations in design with the possibility to restrain large models. Such a task could offer an ideal setting where handling activities with large amounts of elements and interconnecting components can be complicated for humans. In this setting, queries about the model metadata can be informative and constructive. In a recently submitted article that is currently under review, we tested and explored our tool and code generator for a manually developed activity with 161 actions, 118 end flow, 46 fork/join, 8 decision/merge, 18 input, and 8 output parameters, resulting in 321 Java code files. We plan to match this capacity with LLMs to enhance the modelers' grasp over large models often encountered in system engineering domains with advanced, flexible, representative knowledge and reasoning.

6   Challenges and Limitations

Although the landscape of generative AI and the use of LLMs is rapidly changing, we attempt to observe and document some of the currently existing limitations we have seen and encountered in our experiments. Amid all the handiness that could come about in using such models, the problem of domain expertise and questions about the level of generality remains quite pressing. The issue can be better discussed in the context of a boilerplate and rules of transformation and translation. Some questions may arise in these contexts to ignite a thorough discussion about the degree of cognition and generative usefulness where both are attained to an extended level.

From the activity modeling perspective, the obtained texts and results from GPT-4 in different ways demonstrate different aspects. The resulting activities from inserting the Ecore metamodel differ from those obtained after inserting an example activity. This particular distinction mimics, in a way, the previous research efforts made to acquire domain-general and domain-neutral modeling [16]. In the Ecore case, the generated activity contains a variety of values that may not be deemed particularly useful. For example, since the seed value is a long data type, the model ignored the default value and gave a different value at each round. Some instructions had to be given in a particular manner to attain correctly specified models where the given details might be subject to the question in the simulation environment. In this kind of context, the question about the degree of customization or fine-tuning without losing generality remains relevant. Further research efforts and experiments can be beneficial and necessary for the overall model improvement.

The current results from GPT-4 are mostly better suited to serve as a starting point for an approximate representation in a manner that is also akin to bootstrapping but in a less data-dependent sense and more toward reasoning, logic, and cognition capacity while using simulation as an essential element of the whole scheme to force the cognitive perspective through it. Enhancements are often necessary to render it more inclusive and aware of the existing body of knowledge. This study's proposed integrative simulation framework could contribute to the model-assisted safety pipeline [12] and examine reliability and dependency issues, such as over-reliance on specific components of the system and potential tradeoffs in centralized schemes from a system-theoretic vantage point.

6.1   Towards Fine-Tuning and Transfer Learning

Tailoring to specific domains is currently quite costly. It demands substantial domain-specific pre-training and reinforcement learning. Accounting for such an issue demands using sophisticated environments and architectures with a degree of maturity in concepts such as modularity, hierarchy, and iterative development.

Future work will involve fine-tuning existing models or retraining new variants. While developing a specialized model can be costly, there can be some tangible benefits regarding privacy, control, and curating. The hypothetical separation between generative and deterministic, possibly rule-based, aspects in the model can be handy in aerospace, defense, and healthcare domains. However, it is at the cost of segregating from the larger corpus. Such a decision must account for long-term benefits and data-curating techniques that could result in better collective future models in a strategic, large-scale sense with valid representatives of the body of knowledge. This concern proves to be persistently an open problem. Moreover, simulation capability helps discover and explore its dimensions and scale. The position of such capability can take different places and positions across different technical and conceptual layers and facilitate the expansion and growth of the more extensive system toward an AI and LLM with a more integrated cognitive capacity.

References

1. Alshareef, A.: Activity specification for time-based discrete event simulation models. Technical report, Arizona State University (2019). https://keep.lib.asu.edu/items/157772. Accessed 30 Sept 2023
2. Barham, P., et al.: Pathways: asynchronous distributed dataflow for ML (2022)
3. Cámara, J., Troya, J., Burgueño, L., Vallecillo, A.: On the assessment of generative AI in modeling tasks: an experience report with ChatGPT and UML. Softw. Syst. Model. 1–13 (2023)
4. Chowdhery, A., et al.: PaLM: scaling language modeling with pathways (2022)
5. Dakhel, A.M., Majdinasab, V., Nikanjam, A., Khomh, F., Desmarais, M.C., Jiang, Z.M.J.: GitHub copilot AI pair programmer: asset or liability? J. Syst. Softw. **203**, 111734 (2023)
6. Devlin, J., Chang, M.W., Lee, K., Toutanova, K.: Bert: pre-training of deep bidirectional transformers for language understanding (2019)
7. Eclipse Foundation: Sirius (2023). https://eclipse.dev/sirius/. Accessed 30 Sept 2023
8. Floridi, L., Chiriatti, M.: GPT-3: its nature, scope, limits, and consequences. Mind. Mach. **30**, 681–694 (2020)
9. Google Research: Responsible AI. Google AI Blog (2023). https://research.google/teams/responsible-ai/
10. Kotnana, S., Han, D., Anderson, T., Züfle, A., Kavak, H.: Using generative adversarial networks to assist synthetic population creation for simulations. In: 2022 Annual Modeling and Simulation Conference (ANNSIM), pp. 1–12. IEEE (2022)
11. Editorial, N.: ChatGPT is a black box: how AI research can break it open. Nature **619**, 671–672 (2023)
12. OpenAI: GPT-4 technical report (2023)
13. OpenAI: Safety and responsibility (2023). https://openai.com/safety
14. Ören, T.I., Zeigler, B.P.: Artificial intelligence in modelling and simulation: directions to explore. Simulation **48**(4), 131–134 (1987)

15. Raz, A.K., Blasch, E.P., Guariniello, C., Mian, Z.T.: An overview of systems engineering challenges for designing AI-enabled aerospace systems. In: AIAA Scitech 2021 Forum, p. 0564 (2021)
16. Sarjoughian, H.S., Alshareef, A., Lei, Y.: Behavioral DEVS metamodeling. In: 2015 Winter Simulation Conference (WSC), pp. 2788–2799. IEEE (2015)
17. Tikayat Ray, A., Pinon-Fischer, O.J., Mavris, D.N., White, R.T., Cole, B.F.: aerobert-ner: named-entity recognition for aerospace requirements engineering using bert. In: AIAA SCITECH 2023 Forum, p. 2583 (2023)
18. Wach, P., Salado, A.: The need for semantic extension of SysML to model the problem space. In: Madni, A.M., Boehm, B., Erwin, D., Moghaddam, M., Sievers, M., Wheaton, M. (eds.) Recent Trends and Advances in Model Based Systems Engineering, pp. 279–289. Springer, Cham (2022). https://doi.org/10.1007/978-3-030-82083-1_24
19. Wu, C., et al.: Spatiotemporal scenario generation of traffic flow based on LSTM-GAN. IEEE Access 8, 186191–186198 (2020)
20. Yetistiren, B., Ozsoy, I., Tuzun, E.: Assessing the quality of GitHub copilot's code generation. In: Proceedings of the 18th International Conference on Predictive Models and Data Analytics in Software Engineering, pp. 62–71 (2022)
21. Zeigler, B.P.: DEVS representation of dynamical systems: event-based intelligent control. Proc. IEEE **77**(1), 72–80 (1989)
22. Zhong, S., Scarinci, A., Cicirello, A.: Natural language processing for systems engineering: automatic generation of systems modelling language diagrams. Knowl.-Based Syst. **259**, 110071 (2023)

Wildfire Risk Mapping Based on Multi-source Data and Machine Learning

Ghinevra Comiti$^{(\boxtimes)}$, Paul-Antoine Bisgambiglia[iD], and Paul Bisgambiglia

University of Corsica, CNRS UMR SPE, Corte, Corse, France
{COMITI_G,BISGAMBIGLIA_PA}@univ-corse.fr

Abstract. The management and prevention of forest fires are crucial in fire-prone regions such as Corsica, a French island in the Mediterranean. In this study, an approach to mapping wildfire vulnerability is presented using different data sources, including meteorological, temporal, geographical and economic datasets. These heterogeneous datasets are seamlessly integrated to produce a comprehensive forest fire vulnerability map for Corsica. The methodology involves the collection and pre-processing of a variety of data, such as historical forest fire events, meteorological variables, land cover data, socio-economic indicators and temporal factors. Machine learning models are used to visualise the complex relationships between these variables and predict wildfire susceptibility. Finally, we were able to create a daily fire susceptibility map for the island of Corsica.

Keywords: Machine Learning · Wildfire · Map

1 Introduction

Forest fires have a catastrophic impact on the environment, the economy and even people's lives. In recent decades, these fires have become more intense, more frequent and more deadly under the influence of climate change. Therefore, understanding and preventing wildfires has become an important scientific topic and many papers have addressed this issue [2].

The island of Corsica, our study island, is particularly affected by this problem: More than 75,000 hectares of forest burned in 2021 alone. The Mediterranean climate (cold winters with little precipitation and very hot and dry summers) favours the development of forest fires. For this reason, some researchers at the University of Corsica had the idea of launching the GOLIAT project, a multidisciplinary project aimed at better understanding forest fires in order to prevent them. The acronym GOLIAT stands for "Group of Tools for Fire Fighting and Regional Planning". It is a multidisciplinary project involving researchers from various fields: Physics, Biology, Economics, History, Computer Science, etc.

Supported by "Collectivité de Corse" CdC through the GOLIAT project.

J.-L. Guisado-Lizar et al. (Eds.): SIMUtools 2023, LNICST 519, pp. 110–119, 2024.
https://doi.org/10.1007/978-3-031-57523-5_9

The aim is to put scientific knowledge at the service of professionals in the field (firefighters, foresters, etc.) by creating tools that these professionals can use on a daily basis. This is why many employees are also members of the GOLIAT project.

In this context, our goal was to create a forest fire risk map: a map that would show us the fire risk for every place on the island for every day. But first we had to answer a (seemingly) simple question: How can we define "risk"?

Academically, the concept of "risk" refers to a state of uncertainty in which certain possibilities include the occurrence of a loss, disaster or other undesirable outcome [19]. It is an integral part of various areas such as finance, business, insurance and everyday life. Risk consists of two key components: probability and impact.

Probability refers to the likelihood or chance that a certain event or outcome will occur. Impact refers to the extent or severity of the possible consequences of that event or outcome. This definition is very broad and general. If we apply it to the prevention of forest fires, the "probability" component would represent the likelihood of a fire occurring and the "impact" component would represent the vulnerability of a particular place: the presence of people, infrastructures that should be protected, etc.

Although this is a two-component problem, our current software focuses mainly on predicting the probability of fire occurrence. However, taking into account the vulnerability of the location could be an interesting improvement for the future of the method.

To create our forest fire risk map, we used a 2 × 2 km resolution grid to divide our area. Each grid cell is assigned a forest fire risk between 0 and 1, with 0 representing a very low risk and 1 representing a very high risk. Each grid cell is also linked to the data of the respective day and shows whether a forest fire has occurred or not. This data is fed into a machine learning model for classification. This model is able to tell us, based on the data we provide it with, how likely it is that a fire will break out on a particular date and location. Of course, these models can make mistakes. Therefore, we want to try out different models and choose the best one in terms of certain precision metrics, which we will discuss later in this document.

Once we have an optimal machine learning model, we select a day and run the model for each cell in our grid for that day. Each cell is associated with a forest fire risk between 0 and 1, which we use to create a choropleth map. We now have a tool that allows us to create a wildfire risk map for any given day, assuming the data is available.

In the following sections, we will first look at the background work. Then we will present our solution in detail, starting with an explanation of the methodology used and ending with the applications of our method.

2   Background

The quantity and nature of the data to be processed are essential parameters in selecting a machine learning model. Related works have shown a wide variety of data to be useful [6,13,15]. The relevant data can vary significantly from one study to another and appear to depend on the specific characteristics of each location (geography, climate, population, etc.). Therefore, we relied on studies conducted in regions similar to Corsica (high altitude variation, Mediterranean climate, low population density) and identified the relevant variables [6,9,15,16, 18]. They are listed below:

- The coordinates of the fire: the fire is identified either by a point or by its position on a grid. Often, the position on a grid dividing the relevant territory is used when we are trying to create a map, as is the case in our situation.
- Temperature: most commonly, the average temperature of the given day is used.
- Wind strength: here, as well, the average wind strength over the day is taken into consideration.
- Wetness: Wetness plays a great role on ignition and spreading probability of the fire. Indeed, wet fuel will ignite less easily and more slowly.
- Topography: altitude affects the vegetation cover and influences the available fuel and consequently the potential for a fire to ignite and spread [12,15]. In addition, the degree of slope also plays an important role, as a fire will spread more quickly if it follows a slope.
- Land Use: this is about categorizing the type of land on the island [9,15,16]. Certain types of land, such as urban or cultivated areas, are less prone to fires than others, such as bushes.
- Day of the week: in Europe, more than 80% of fires are of human origin [3,6,18]. This means that human activity has a significant impact on the risk of fire. The day of the week has a major influence on human activity. Towards the end of the week, for example, people spend more time in nature, where their activities can lead to the ignition of fires. The day of the week is therefore likely to be an important criterion.
- Unemployment rate: in certain studies, it is assumed that the unemployment rate is a factor that contributes to the ignition of forest fires [12]. This could be because unemployed people are less employed and therefore have more time to fuel conflicts with their neighbours, e.g. by starting fires on their properties.
- Road density: some studies have also shown the effects of road density [9,15]. Roads concentrate human activities, especially in summer, in touristic places like Corsica. Therefore, this seems to be an interesting parameter to consider.
- Vegetation: vegetation serves as the medium for fire propagation [9]. Thus, it has a direct impact on the probability of ignition as well as the spread of a potential forest fire.

We were able to obtain this data from the relevant authorities. Then we had to use it to train the model. But first we had to select model. There is indeed a wide range of machine learning models. Since our goal here is to classify cell grids, we focused on classification methods. Also for efficiency and transparency reasons, we focused on supervised machine learning. After reviewing related work and the literature, a few potential models emerged:

- Random Forest: a Random Forest is an ensemble machine learning algorithm that combines multiple decision trees to improve predictive accuracy and reduce overfitting [14,17]. Random Forest creates multiple random subsets of the dataset through a process called bootstrapping. For each subset, it builds a decision tree using a random subset of features at each node of the tree. When making predictions, each tree in the forest independently predicts the output, via majority voting. Finally, Random Forest combines the predictions from all the individual trees to produce a more robust and accurate prediction.
- Adaboost: AdaBoost, short for Adaptive Boosting, is another ensemble machine learning algorithm used for binary classification [10]. It works a little bit like Random Forest, except Adaboost trains its learners sequentially and assigns weight to the data, paying more attention to often misclassified data. It makes Adaboost more powerful, but also more prone to overfitting.
- Gradient Boosting: Gradient boosting is a machine learning technique that builds a predictive model in a stage-wise fashion by combining the predictions of multiple weak models, typically decision trees [11]. Like the two previous models, it combines the predictions of several individual models to improve overall predictive performance.

The workflow is recapitulated in Fig. 1. We made the choice to try all of these models and chose the more performant one to use in our application. Our definition of "performant" will be detailed afterward.

3   Method

In this section, we will give further details on the method we used to create our map.

As mentioned in previous sections, we selected and gathered a wide range of data. Those data were obtained from relevant authorities: Copernicus [1] for weather data, the French governmental opensource data website "data.gouv" [5] for road, topography and land use, French forest database [4] for vegetation and the National Institute of Statistics and Economical Studies [7] for unemployment rate.

To locate fire and relevant data, we decided to divide the map to a 2 × 2 km grid. We chose this particular grid format because it's the one that is already used to locate fires in France. To each grid cell are assigned data of the area. We consider that each cell grid, each day, is a data entry [8]. We assign to this entry all the relevant data of the grid cell, and a boolean "fire", set to "True" if a fire happened at this time and location and to "False" instead.

Using this method, we found ourselves with a tremendous amount of data where "fire" is set to "False", because obviously, there are more days without fire

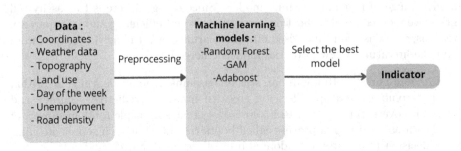

Fig. 1. Strategy used to answer our problematic.

than with fire. If one wants to do machine learning, this huge data imbalance can be problematic. Indeed, it could introduce a bias, and the model might be bad at generalization. Thus, it is essential to have a pretty well-balanced dataset. To this end, we deleted part of our "no fire" data. We now have a balanced dataset with 27 500 examples of fires and 27 500 examples of "no fire", that will help us to train our model. Now, the next step would be to choose a model.

Once the data was prepared, we had to train the models and see which one performed best. We used the scikit-learn library. The first step was dividing the data into two sets, a training set and a validation set. Then, we created instances of the models we're interested in. To capable the parameters, we used the GridSearchCV function of the scikit-learn library. This function tests a model with different sets of parameters, to determine which parameters give the best results. We ensure that all our models have optimal parameter settings, enabling us to easily compare them.

To compare the models, we decided to use their AUC. AUC stands for "Area Under the (Receiver Operating Characteristic) Curve." It is a commonly used metric in machine learning and statistics to evaluate the performance of a binary classification model. The Receiver Operating Characteristic (ROC) curve is a graphical representation of a model's ability to distinguish between the two classes it is trying to classify, typically the positive class (e.g., presence of a fire) and the negative class (e.g., absence of a fire). The AUC varies between 0 and 1, with 0.5 being the performance achieved by random choice.

After a careful comparison of the models, the Random Forest appeared to be the one with the best AUC. It was around 0.80, which is considered quite good. Gradient Boosting was behind with around 0.70, and Adaboost was pretty close with a score of about 0.75.

Once we had selected our model, we also tried to optimize its recall. Recall is a performance metric that allows you to evaluate the effectiveness of a binary classification model, especially when one of the classes is of greater importance or when you want to minimize the number of false negatives. This is our case: it would indeed be dramatic to "miss" a fire by underestimating the risk in a given area. On the other hand, it would also be problematic to overestimate the risk, as this could lead to a fragmentation of forces. We have therefore tried to find a kind of balance between recall and another metric, precision, which focuses on minimising false positives, while still prioritizing recall. A target that has been chosen in similar articles and seems quite reasonable to us (and which we have therefore tried to replicate) is to achieve a recall of over 0.9 and a precision of over 0.6, which is already an honourable value in this field [8].

4   Application

We then generated the risk map. We edited it for a day for which we had data, the 8th of July 2009. Then, we compared it with the fires that really happened this day. The result is represented in Fig. 2, with the blue stars being the location of the actual fires happening that day.

As we can observe, the predictions for this day seem pretty accurate. Most of the fires are located in places where the fire risk is above 0.7, or 0.6 for three of them. Only one is located in a place where the fire risk is below that (about 0.4 to 0.5). No fire happened in locations where the fire risk is above 0.8, but we can argue that those places are already identified by the capable authorities as being very prone to fire, and are thus very closely monitored.

The prefecture of the island already publishes its own forest fire risk map. It is published every summer day on the prefecture's website. This map, based exclusively on meteorological data, is shown in the Fig. 3. As we can see, it is far less accurate than our map, which makes it less useful for the staff on the ground. This is actually the main reason why this project was launched in the first place.

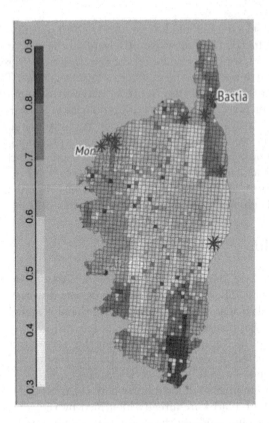

Fig. 2. The fire risk map edited for the 8th of July 2009. The blue stars represent the actual fires. (Color figure online)

We were also able to obtain from the model the contribution of each variable to the result. These data may be of crucial importance. Indeed, knowing which variables have an influence on fire susceptibility allows us to prevent fire more efficiently. These contributions are represented in Fig. 4.

As we can observe in Fig. 4, the contribution can be very different from a variable to another. Road density, time of the day, geographical and meteorological values seem to play a pretty important role, as well as altitude variables. On the other hand, day of the week, unemployment rate, vegetation and land use don't seem very meaningful. We can try to explain some of those results. For instance, the lack of importance of the "day of the week" variale can be explained because fires often happen during summer, when there are a lot of tourists on the island. The day of the week is way less meaningful for this population, who doesn't work at the moment and is thus more free. For the vegetation, we can argue that the Corsican vegetation is pretty homogenous. Furthermore, the vast majority of fires are forest fire (more than 90% of them) which can explain why land use isn't of great importance as well.

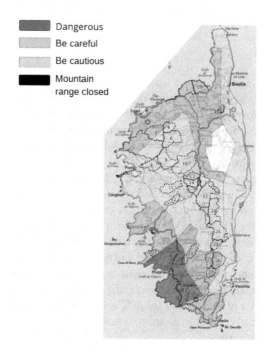

Fig. 3. The prefecture's map.

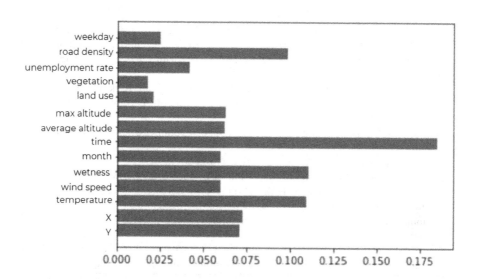

Fig. 4. The relative contribution of variables to our model.

We can conclude that our method can help us to prevent fires, and in addition, to better understand our territory and how to protect it.

5   Conclusion

To summarise, we have proposed a method to predict the probability of forest fires for a given day at different locations in Corsica. This method involves the collection and processing of a large dataset containing historical records of forest fires, meteorological parameters, land cover information, socio-economic indicators and temporal aspects. Using machine learning models, we calculate a forest fire risk between 0 and 1. This risk is calculated for each of our grid cells. We then use these numbers to create a choropleth map. The map created is a great tool to help decision makers make better decisions, and for the public to get information before going on a hike or other outdoor activity.

The prospects for this project include a phase of method validation and consolidation, in which we will assess the accuracy of the method in more detail. We will also take a closer look at the current map and the predictions and accuracy differences between the two maps. In addition, we would like to combine the map's hazard prediction with more traditional simulation techniques for the high fire risk areas identified in the map. This would allow us to predict fire risk more efficiently. Finally, before the map is made available to the public, it needs to be validated in practise.

References

1. Accueil copernicus. https://www.copernicus.eu/en
2. Evolving Risk of Wildfires in Europe - Thematic paper by the European Science & Technology Advisory Group (E-STAG). https://www.undrr.org/publication/evolving-risk-wildfires-europe-thematic-paper-european-science-technology-advisory
3. Fire — Free Full-Text — Forest Fire Susceptibility and Risk Mapping Using Social/Infrastructural Vulnerability and Environmental Variables. https://www.mdpi.com/2571-6255/2/3/50
4. French forest database, national institute of geograophy. https://geoservices.ign.fr/bdforet
5. French governemental data. https://www.data.gouv.fr/fr/
6. Full article: Modelling temporal variation of fire-occurrence towards the dynamic prediction of human wildfire ignition danger in northeast Spain. https://www.tandfonline.com/doi/full/10.1080/19475705.2018.1526219
7. National institute of statistics and economical studies. https://www.insee.fr/fr/accueil
8. Apostolakis, A., Girtsou, S., Giannopoulos, G., Bartsotas, N.S., Kontoes, C.: Estimating next day's forest fire risk via a complete machine learning methodology. Remote Sens. 14(5), 1222 (2022). https://doi.org/10.3390/rs14051222. https://www.mdpi.com/2072-4292/14/5/1222

9. Carmona, A., González, M.E., Nahuelhual, L., Silva, J.: Spatio-temporal effects of human drivers on fire danger in Mediterranean Chile. Bosque **33**(3), 31–32 (2012). https://doi.org/10.4067/S0717-92002012000300016

10. Friedman, J., Hastie, T., Tibshirani, R.: Additive logistic regression: a statistical view of boosting (with discussion and a rejoinder by the authors). Ann. Stat. **28**(2), 337–407 (2000). https://doi.org/10.1214/aos/1016218223. https://projecteuclid.org/journals/annals-of-statistics/volume-28/issue-2/Additive-logistic-regression--a-statistical-view-of-boosting-With/10.1214/aos/1016218223.full

11. Friedman, J.H.: Greedy function approximation: a gradient boosting machine. Ann. Stat. (2001)

12. Ghorbanzadeh, O., Blaschke, T., Gholamnia, K., Aryal, J.: Forest fire susceptibility and risk mapping using social/infrastructural vulnerability and environmental variables. Fire **2**(3), 50 (2019). https://doi.org/10.3390/fire2030050. https://www.mdpi.com/2571-6255/2/3/50

13. Jain, P., Coogan, S.C., Subramanian, S.G., Crowley, M., Taylor, S., Flannigan, M.D.: A review of machine learning applications in wildfire science and management. Environ. Rev. **28**(4), 478–505 (2020). https://doi.org/10.1139/er-2020-0019. https://cdnsciencepub.com/doi/full/10.1139/er-2020-0019

14. Kam, H.T.: Random decision forests. In: Proceedings of 3rd International Conference on Document Analysis and Recognition (1995)

15. Pourtaghi, Z.S., Pourghasemi, H.R., Aretano, R., Semeraro, T.: Investigation of general indicators influencing on forest fire and its susceptibility modeling using different data mining techniques. Ecol. Ind. **64**, 72–84 (2016). https://doi.org/10.1016/j.ecolind.2015.12.030. https://www.sciencedirect.com/science/article/pii/S1470160X15007359

16. Rodrigues, M., Jiménez, A., de la Riva, J.: Analysis of recent spatial-temporal evolution of human driving factors of wildfires in Spain. Nat. Hazards **84**(3), 2049–2070 (2016). https://doi.org/10.1007/s11069-016-2533-4

17. Safavian, S., Landgrebe, D.: A survey of decision tree classifier methodology. IEEE Trans. Syst. Man Cybern. **21**(3), 660–674 (1991). https://doi.org/10.1109/21.97458. http://ieeexplore.ieee.org/document/97458/

18. Vilar, L., Camia, A., San-Miguel-Ayanz, J., Martín, M.P.: Modeling temporal changes in human-caused wildfires in mediterranean europe based on land use-land cover interfaces. Forest Ecol. Manag. **378**, 68–78 (2016). https://doi.org/10.1016/j.foreco.2016.07.020. https://www.sciencedirect.com/science/article/pii/S0378112716303760

19. Šotić, A., Rajić, R.: The Review of the Definition of Risk, vol. 3, no. 3 (2015)

An Intelligent Ranking Evaluation Method of Simulation Models Based on Graph Neural Network

Fan Yang[1,2] , Ping Ma[1,2], Jianchao Zhang[3], Huichuan Cheng[3], Wei Li[1,2(✉)], and Ming Yang[1,2]

[1] Control and Simulation Center, Harbin Institute of Technology, Harbin 150080, China
fleehit@163.com
[2] National Key Laboratory of Complex System Modeling and Simulation, Harbin 150080, China
[3] Chinese Aeroengine Research Institute, Beijing 101304, China

Abstract. To validate the alternative simulation models and select the most credible one when the models have multivariate and correlated outputs, an intelligent ranking evaluation method of simulation models based on Graph Neural Network (GNN) is proposed. The process of ranking evaluation is divided into three parts: graph structure conversion for evaluation data, feature extraction based on Graph Representation Learning (GRL) and ranking evaluation based on feature distance. A graph structure modeling method is presented to provide the pre-define graph structure for further GRL primarily. Next the interdependencies and dynamic evolutionary patterns among variables are captured by GNN so that the graph representations of evaluation data can be obtained. Then ranking evaluation is achieved by similarity measurement of the graph representations. In the end, the effectiveness of the proposed method on feature extraction of evaluation data and simulation models ranking is illustrated through an application example on a prediction model for aerodynamic parameters of a certain flight vehicle.

Keywords: Ranking Evaluation of Simulation Models · Multivariate and Correlated Outputs · Graph Neural Network (GNN)

1 Introduction

Simulation is an important means of assisting complex systems in design, development, analysis, evaluation, optimization, and decision-making [1] and has been widely used in various fields such as military, manufacturing, medical, transportation, etc. In practical applications, the uncertainty of model parameters and the diversity of modeling methods may lead to the ranking and selection problem of alternative simulation models. It is necessary to validate the credibility of multiple alternative simulation models and select the most credible one [2].

Simulation result validation method is generally used for the simulation model validation. The principle of the method is to obtain the credibility of the simulation model

J.-L. Guisado-Lizar et al. (Eds.): SIMUtools 2023, LNICST 519, pp. 120–130, 2024.
https://doi.org/10.1007/978-3-031-57523-5_10

by measuring the consistency between simulation outputs and reference outputs. The evaluation data of continuous system simulation such as aircraft motion simulation and guidance control system simulation are mostly in the form of time series with correlation [3]. However, the existing multivariate validation methods generally focus on the validation of multivariate static data [4, 5], such as multivariate Bayesian hypothesis testing [6], probability integral transformation (PIT) and area metric [7], principal component analysis and area metric [8], etc.

The validation of multivariate simulation results is essentially a similarity measurement problem for multivariate time series (MTS). Some common methods achieve multivariate result validation by synthesizing the validation result of univariate [9] while ignoring the correlation between multiple variables. Some other methods analyze the similarity after reducing the dimension of multivariate outputs [3, 10] which may lead to loss of information, and some of these methods may be computationally inefficiency for large kernel matrix [3]. There is also a type of simulation result validation method based on data feature [11]. However, it is difficult to select suitable features for evaluation data artificially. There is still a lack of effective validation methods for multivariate dynamic outputs with correlation.

Deep learning can autonomously and quickly learn effective features in multi-level abstraction process. Recently, Graph Neural Network (GNN) has received increasing attention in modeling MTS to achieve MTS prediction [12, 13] and anomaly detection [14, 15] due to high capability in dealing with relational dependencies [16]. How to use GNN to extract the features of the evaluation data from different models could be considered as a supervised and graph-level Graph Representation Learning (GRL) task to be study. In addition, GNNs are generally performed on data with a pre-defined graph structure while the relationships among output variables are generally unknown. How to convert evaluation data into graph-structured data is also a problem that needs to be solved.

In summary, we expect to achieve ranking evaluation of multiple alternative simulation models under correlation based on data feature and extract the features of evaluation data by GNN. Firstly, we propose a graph structure modeling method based on distance correlation coefficient to provide the pre-define graph structure for further GRL. Then, we adopt GRL method based on Graph Isomorphism Network (GIN) [17] to extract the features of evaluation data. Next, the alternative simulation models could be ranked by comparing the similarity of the features corresponding to different simulation models and the real system.

The rest of the paper is organized as follows. The ranking evaluation method based on GNN is presented in Sect. 2, including the problem description in Sect. 2.1, the graph structure modeling method in Sect. 2.2, the feature extraction method in Sect. 2.3 and the ranking evaluation method in Sect. 2.4. Then, an application example is enumerated to verify the effectiveness of the proposed method in Sect. 3. Finally, the conclusion and the future work are given in Sect. 4.

2 Ranking Evaluation Method Based on GNN

2.1 Problem Description

Suppose that S denotes the system, and $\mathbf{Y} = \left[\mathbf{y}_1, \mathbf{y}_2, \ldots, \mathbf{y}_M\right]^{\mathrm{T}}$ represents M outputs of S. $S_s = \{S_{s1}, S_{s2}, \ldots S_{sA}\}$ and S_r are regarded as the alternative simulation models and the real system. Let the real system and all alternative simulation models run repeatedly under several given inputs, $\mathbf{Y}_{sa} = \left[\mathbf{y}_{sa1}, \mathbf{y}_{sa2}, \ldots, \mathbf{y}_{saM}\right]^{\mathrm{T}}$ and $\mathbf{Y}_r = \left[\mathbf{y}_{r1}, \mathbf{y}_{r2}, \ldots, \mathbf{y}_{rM}\right]^{\mathrm{T}}$ represent the M outputs of $S_{sa}(a = 1, 2, \ldots A)$ and S_r respectively while only dynamic outputs are considered in this problem. $\mathbf{Y}_{sa}$ is a $T \times M \times N_s$ matrix representing M simulation output variables across T timestamps each having N_s samples for aleatory uncertainty. Similarly, $\mathbf{Y}_r$ is a $T \times M \times N_r$ matrix representing M reference output variables across T timestamps each having N_r samples for aleatory uncertainty. Suppose that $C(\mathbf{Y}_{sa}, \mathbf{Y}_r)$ denotes the credibility of the simulation model S_{sa} which is measured by the consistency between $\mathbf{Y}_{sa}$ and $\mathbf{Y}_r$. S_{sa} is the most credible one when $C(\mathbf{Y}_{sa}, \mathbf{Y}_r)$ is largest in $\{C(\mathbf{Y}_{s1}, \mathbf{Y}_r), C(\mathbf{Y}_{s2}, \mathbf{Y}_r), \ldots C(\mathbf{Y}_{sA}, \mathbf{Y}_r)\}$.

To solve the ranking evaluation problem of multiple alternative simulation models, we adopt GNN to extract the features of evaluation data and obtain ranking evaluation result by comparing feature distance. The outputs of each alternative simulation model can be represented by some graphs while reference outputs can be represented by other graphs. Given two sets of graphs $\mathbf{G}_{sa} = \left\{\mathbf{G}_{sa}^1, \mathbf{G}_{sa}^2, \ldots \mathbf{G}_{sa}^{N_s}\right\}$, $\mathbf{G}_r = \left\{\mathbf{G}_r^1, \mathbf{G}_r^2, \ldots \mathbf{G}_r^{N_r}\right\}$ and assuming that $\mathbf{h}_{Gsa}$ and $\mathbf{h}_{Gr}$ represent the features of two sets of outputs respectively, $D(\mathbf{h}_{Gsa}, \mathbf{h}_{Gr})$ represents the corresponding feature distance. It is certain that the smaller $D(\mathbf{h}_{Gsa}, \mathbf{h}_{Gr})$ is, the larger $C(\mathbf{Y}_{sa}, \mathbf{Y}_r)$ is.

An overview of ranking evaluation framework is shown in Fig. 1. The process of ranking evaluation mainly includes three stages, data convertion, feature extraction and similarity comparison. We convert the evaluation data into graph structured data and then learn the graph representations which can effectively represent the features of the evaluation data. Furthermore, ranking evaluation of the alternative simulation models could be achieved by comparing the similarity of graph representations corresponding to different simulation models and the real system.

2.2 Graph Structure Modeling for Evaluation Data

The evaluation data need to be converted from two-dimensional form to graph structure for further GRL. Graph is a non-linear data structure which has proved useful for analyzing multivariate and correlated data. Let $\mathbf{G} = (\mathbf{V}, \mathbf{E})$ denotes a graph which consists of a finite non empty set of nodes $v_i \in \mathbf{V}$ and edges $e_{ij} \in \mathbf{E}$. And $e_{ij} = (v_i, v_j)$, which means that e_{ij} denotes the edge between v_i and v_j. In order to analyze the evaluation data, we proposed a graph structure modeling method in which output variables and their correlation are represented by nodes and edges respectively.

Given $\mathbf{y}^n$, a sample of the evaluation data, the component $\mathbf{y}_i^n (i \in [1, M])$ is a $1 \times T$ matrix which represents the i_{th} output variable across T timestamps. In the corresponding graph $\mathbf{G}^n$, $\mathbf{y}_i^n$ is represented by a node $v_i \in \mathbf{V}$. The number of nodes in the graph corresponds to the number of output variables and thus $\mathbf{V} = \{v_1, v_2, \ldots, v_M\}$.

$$\mathbf{y}_i^n = \left[y_i^n(1) \, y_i^n(2) \ldots y_i^n(T)\right] \tag{1}$$

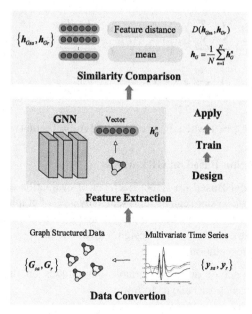

Fig. 1. An overview of ranking evaluation framework.

The graph structure can describe the relationships among multiple variables. There exists an edge $e_{ij}(i, j \in [1, M])$ between node v_i and v_j when the correlation between $\mathbf{y}_i^n$ and $\mathbf{y}_j^n$ exceeds a certain threshold. We adopt the distance correlation coefficient [18] to measure the correlation. The larger the distance correlation coefficient, the higher the correlation between the two variables. Besides, the threshold could be set differently in different problems.

The adjacency matrix, $\mathbf{A} = \{A_{ij}\} \in \mathbb{R}^{M \times M}$, is a storage structure that uses a matrix to represent the relationships among the nodes in a graph and the local-level representations are learned based on the adjacent relationships. Each element A_{ij} represents the relationship between node v_i and v_j. If $A_{ij} = 1$, there exists an edge between v_i and v_j, and $A_{ij} = 0$ otherwise.

We set the value of A_{ij} based on the distance correlation coefficient of the corresponding paired nodes and the given threshold m_d. Given the outputs of the i_{th} variable and the j_{th} variable in a sample of outputs $\mathbf{y}_{sa}^n$ or $\mathbf{y}_r^n$, we can obtain the distance correlation coefficient between node v_i and v_j in the corresponding graph. The distance correlation coefficient is calculated as follow:

$$dCor(\mathbf{y}_i, \mathbf{y}_j) = \frac{dCov(\mathbf{y}_i, \mathbf{y}_j)}{\sqrt{dCov(\mathbf{y}_i, \mathbf{y}_i)dCov(\mathbf{y}_j, \mathbf{y}_j)}} \quad (2)$$

where $dCor(\mathbf{y}_i, \mathbf{y}_j) \in [0, 1]$, $\mathbf{y}_i = \{y_i(p)\}$ and $\mathbf{y}_j = \{y_j(q)\}$ represent two variables, and $dCov^2(\mathbf{y}_i, \mathbf{y}_j) = S_1 + S_2 - 2S_3$ with S_1, S_2, S_3 defined as follows:

$$S_1 = \frac{1}{T^2} \sum_{p=1}^{T} \sum_{q=1}^{T} |y_i(p) - y_i(q)||y_j(p) - y_j(q)| \quad (3)$$

$$S_2 = \frac{1}{T^2} \sum_{p=1}^{T} \sum_{q=1}^{T} |y_i(p) - y_i(q)| \frac{1}{T^2} \sum_{p=1}^{T} \sum_{q=1}^{T} |y_j(p) - y_j(q)| \tag{4}$$

$$S_3 = \frac{1}{T^3} \sum_{p=1}^{T} \sum_{q=1}^{T} \sum_{o=1}^{T} |y_i(p) - y_i(o)| |y_j(p) - y_j(o)| \tag{5}$$

Furthermore, let $A_{ij} = 1$ when $dCor > m_d$, and $A_{ij} = 0$ otherwise.

2.3 Feature Extraction Based on GRL Model

Design of GRL Model Based on GIN. Each set of evaluation data corresponding a simulation model or real system can be represented by a set of graphs based on the graph structure modeling method. Given a set of graphs, and a positive integer D (the expected graph embedding size), our goal is to design a GRL model to learn a D-dimensional distributed graph representation.

To avoid the impact of different variable magnitudes on the results of feature extraction, normalize each variable as follow:

$$\mathbf{y}_i = \frac{\mathbf{y}_i - y_{\min}}{y_{\max} - y_{\min}} \tag{6}$$

where $\mathbf{y}_i$ is a sample of evaluation data corresponding to node v_i, $y_{\max}$ and $y_{\min}$ denote the maximum and minimum element in $\mathbf{y}_i$ respectively.

GIN is adopted to extract local features for its higher graph-level representational power. In GIN, the representation of nodes is updated by concatenating their own features with the features of neighbor nodes [19] and inputting them into an MLP for nonlinear transformation. Then the entire graph embedding could be calculated by readout function based on the representation of nodes.

We design the GIN layers according to output variables. When the number of output variables is large, the layers of GIN can be increased to obtain more information in larger scale subgraph. We input the preprocessed data into the GIN layers as Eq. (7), then the k_{th} GIN layer $g^{(k)}$ updates the representation of node v_i as Eq. (8):

$$\mathbf{h}_i^{(0)} = \mathbf{y}_i \tag{7}$$

$$\begin{aligned} \mathbf{h}_i^{(k)} &= g^{(k)}(\mathbf{h}_i^{(k-1)}, \mathbf{h}_j^{(k-1)} | j \in \mathbf{N}_i) \\ &= MLP^{(k)}((1 + \varepsilon^{(k)}) \cdot \mathbf{h}_i^{(k-1)} + \sum_{j \in N_i} \mathbf{h}_j^{(k-1)}) \end{aligned} \tag{8}$$

where $MLP^{(k)}$ represents the MLP in the k_{th} GIN layer $g^{(k)}$, $\boldsymbol{\varepsilon}^{(k)}$ is trainable aggregation parameter in the k_{th} GIN layer $g^{(k)}$, $\mathbf{h}_i^{(k-1)}$ is the output of the $(k-1)_{th}$ GIN layer $g^{(k-1)}$, and $\mathbf{N}_i$ is a set of nodes adjacent to v_i.

After applying L GIN layers, we can consider the output of the last layer $\mathbf{h}_i^{(L)}$ ($i = 1, 2, ...M$) as the updated node representations which represent the local features. This process can be described as Eq. (9).

$$g(\mathbf{h}_i^{(0)}) = \mathbf{h}_i^{(L)} (i = 1, 2, ...M) \tag{9}$$

It is necessary to summarize these patch representations into the representation of the entire graph by a readout function so that we can obtain a fixed length feature vector as follow for further similarity measurement.

$$\mathbf{h}_G = readout(\mathbf{h}_i^{(L)}|i = 1, 2, ...M) \tag{10}$$

In the majority of GRL models, $readout(\cdot)$ can be a simple function such as sum, mean, max, etc. or a more sophisticated graph-level pooling function [20, 21]. In this work, we use sum as the readout function to catch global information. Overall, we have designed the structure of GNN for feature extraction as Fig. 2.

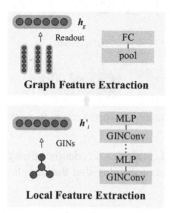

Fig. 2. Structure of GRL model.

Training and Application of GRL Model. We hope that the trained GRL model can effectively extract the features of the evaluation data and the features of the evaluation data from the same simulation model are similar while the features of the evaluation data from different simulation models are dissimilar. Then we could apply the trained GRL model to extract the features of the simulation outputs and the reference outputs and compare the consistency of two sets of features. Hence the ranking evaluation problem of multiple alternative simulation models is transformed into the evaluation data multi-categorization problem and the class of labels are equal to the number of simulation models. There may be a variety of input conditions for simulation experiments, however we assign the evaluation data generated from the same simulation model to the same labels regardless of the input conditions.

In the training stage, we input the graph-structured simulation outputs into the designed GRL model to obtain graph representation. In order to ensure that the graph representation can effectively represent the features of the evaluation data to support the subsequent similarity measurement task, the cross-entropy loss is used as the objective function as Eq. (11) and the stochastic gradient descent algorithm is used to train the

GRL model as shown in Fig. 3.

$$L = \frac{1}{N} \sum_n \sum_{a=1}^{A} y_{na} \log(p_{na}) \tag{11}$$

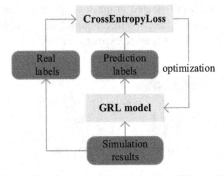

Fig. 3. Training and optimization for GRL models.

Where A is the number of categories, y_{na} denotes the symbolic function as Eq. (12), and p_{na} denotes the predicted probability that the sample y_n belongs to category a as Eq. (13).

$$y_{na} = \begin{cases} 0 \ y_n \text{ is not generated from model } S_{sa} \\ 1 \ y_n \text{ is generated from model } S_{sa} \end{cases} \tag{12}$$

$$p_{na} = -\log(\frac{e^{x_a}}{\sum_{i=0}^{A} e^{x_i}}) = -x_a + \log(\sum_{i=0}^{A} e^{x_i}) \tag{13}$$

Then the trained model can be applied to extract the features of evaluation data. In the application stage, we input two sets of graph-structured data which represent simulation outputs and reference outputs into the trained GRL model to obtain two sets of graph representations, $\mathbf{h}_{Gsa}^n (n = 1, 2, ...N_s, a = 1, 2, ..., A)$ and $\mathbf{h}_{Gr}^n (n = 1, 2, ...N_r)$.

2.4 Ranking Evaluation Based on Feature Distance

Since the two sets of graph representations $\mathbf{h}_{Gsa}^n (n = 1, 2, ...N_s)$ and $\mathbf{h}_{Gr}^n (n = 1, 2, ...N_r)$ can effectively represent the features of the outputs from the simulation model S_{sa} and reference outputs, the validation result of S_{sa} can be obtained by comparing the similarity of two sets of graph representations. To obtain the overall features of the simulation outputs from S_{sa} and the reference outputs, we calculate the mean of two sets of graph representations due to multi samples as follows:

$$\mathbf{h}_{Gsa} = \frac{1}{N_s} \sum_{n=1}^{N_s} \mathbf{h}_{Gsa}^n \tag{14}$$

$$\mathbf{h}_{Gr} = \frac{1}{N_r} \sum_{n=1}^{N_r} \mathbf{h}_{Gr}^n \tag{15}$$

Then 2-norm distance is adopted to measure the feature distance $D(\mathbf{h}_{Gsa}, \mathbf{h}_{Gr})$ as Eq. (16). The distance between $\mathbf{h}_{Gsa}^n$ and $\mathbf{h}_{Gr}^n$ represents the consistency between the corresponding simulation outputs $\mathbf{Y}_{sa}$ and reference outputs $\mathbf{Y}_r$ so that $D(\mathbf{h}_{Gsa}, \mathbf{h}_{Gr})$ can be used to describe $C(\mathbf{Y}_{sa}, \mathbf{Y}_r)$. And the smaller $D(\mathbf{h}_{Gsa}, \mathbf{h}_{Gr})$ is, the larger $C(\mathbf{Y}_{sa}, \mathbf{Y}_r)$ is.

$$D(\mathbf{h}_{Gsa}, \mathbf{h}_{Gr}) = \|\mathbf{h}_{Gsa} - \mathbf{h}_{Gr}\|_2 \tag{16}$$

Furthermore, we can rank multiple alternative simulation models by comparing the value of $\{D(\mathbf{h}_{Gs1}, \mathbf{h}_{Gr}), D(\mathbf{h}_{Gs2}, \mathbf{h}_{Gr}), ..., D(\mathbf{h}_{GsA}, \mathbf{h}_{Gr})\}$. The smaller $D(\mathbf{h}_{Gsa}, \mathbf{h}_{Gr})$ is, the more credible the simulation model S_{sa} is.

3 Experimental Studies

In this section, we evaluate the effectiveness of the proposed ranking evaluation method by an application example on the aircraft aerodynamic parameter prediction model. There are four simulation models in the experiment including an identification model and three prediction models, and the prediction models include the 5-s prediction model, the 8-s prediction model, and the 10-s prediction model. The prediction models are used to predict the outputs at the current moment according to the historical information a few seconds ago. Given the labels of these four models are model 1, model 2, model 3, model 4.

Compared to the prediction models, the identification models are significantly more credible. In addition, among three prediction models, the longer the prediction time, the less credible the prediction model is. It is obvious that the ranking result of the four models should be in the order of model 1, model 2, model 3 and model 4 so that we apply the proposed method to evaluate these simulation models to validate the effectiveness of the method.

We select three outputs for simulation ranking evaluation including lift coefficients, drag coefficients and moment coefficients. Given 3 input conditions, let these four models run 10 times under each condition respectively while the real system run 5 times under each condition so that 135 sets of outputs in the range of 10 s to 90 s with a sampling interval of 0.02 s were obtained. Each set of evaluation data is a 4001 × 3 matrix representing 3 output variables across 4001 timestamps. The first two dimensions of each variable in the four simulation models are taken for observation before training, and the data distribution is shown in Fig. 4.

We analyze the correlation between paired variables by reference data based on Eq. (2)–Eq. (5), and the mean of the paired distance correlation coefficients among the three variables are 0.971, 0.989, 0.991 respectively. The value of each element in the adjacency matrix could be set as 1 with $m_d = 0.9$. There are significant correlations among the three variables and it is in good agreement with practice. After that we have completed the data convertion.

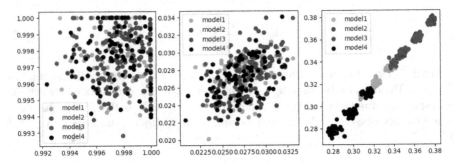

(a) Value of lift coefficients (b) Value of drag coefficients (c) Value of moment coefficients

Fig. 4. The distribution of original outputs.

Two GIN layers are adopted for feature extraction and the simulation outputs are used for training which is a 4001 × 3 × 120 matrix. The parameters of each layer are set as Table 1 after training and optimization. Training terminates when the number of iterations reaches 400.

Table 1. The parameters of GNN.

layer	Linear1	Linear2
ginconv_1	[4001,1024]	[1024,256]
ginconv_2	[256,64]	[64,64]

Then we can get the change of the loss value during the training process and the distribution of the first two dimensions of the evaluation data feature at the end of training (see Fig. 5). The feature distributions of the outputs of the same model under different conditions are close while the feature distribution of the outputs of different models are farther away. It shows that the GRL method can effectively extract the features of multivariate correlated variables.

Inputting the reference data which is a 4001 × 3 × 15 matrix into the trained GRL model, then the features of the reference data can be obtained. Furthermore, the feature distance could be calculated based on Eq. (14–16). The features corresponding to the outputs under the three conditions are taken to calculate the feature distance respectively, and the results are shown in Table 2.

It means that the sorting result of the above simulation models is model 1, model 2, model 3 and model 4 which is consistent with the fact. It can be seen that the ranking evaluation method of simulation models based on GNN can effectively achieve the ranking evaluation under the multivariate and correlated outputs.

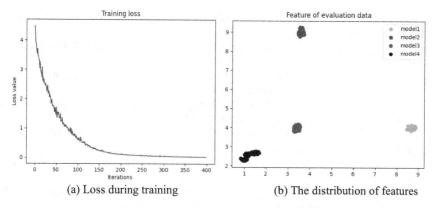

(a) Loss during training   (b) The distribution of features

Fig. 5. Results of training based on GNN.

Table 2. Feature distance under different conditions.

	Model1	Model2	Model3	Model4
Condition1	0.15	2.33	3.82	6.33
Condition2	0.63	2.56	3.90	6.50
Condition3	1.70	2.46	3.97	6.17
Mean	0.83	2.45	3.90	6.33

4   Conclusions

To solve the ranking and selection problem of multiple alternative simulation models with multivariate and correlated outputs, an intelligent ranking evaluation method of simulation models based on GNN has been presented. We propose a ranking evaluation framework to illustrate the process of ranking evaluation for multiple alternative simulation models in which there are three stages including data convertion, feature extraction and similarity comparison.

The proposed method is applied to ranking four models about the aircraft aerodynamic parameter prediction. Obviously, the method is effective to extract the features of the evaluation data and rank multiple alternative simulation models with multivariate and correlated outputs. The future work would focus on solving the ranking evaluation of simulation models with the multivariate, heterogeneous and correlated outputs.

Funding Information.   National Science and Technology Major Project(J2019-I-0004-0005).

References

1. Sargent, R.G.: Verification and validation of simulation models. J. Simul. **7**(1), 12–24 (2013)
2. Fan, Y., Ping, M., Wei, L., et al.: An intelligent ranking evaluation method for simulation models based on twin networks. Syst. Eng. Electron. **45**(07), 2060–2068 (2023)

3. Yuchen, Z.: Research on Verification Methods for Complex Simulation Models. Harbin Institute of Industry, Harbin (2019)
4. Rebba, R., Mahadevan, S.: Validation of models with multivariate output. Reliab. Eng. Syst. Saf. **91**(8), 861–871 (2006)
5. Oberkampf, W.L., Barone, M.F.: Measures of agreement between computation and experiment: validation metrics. J. Comput. Phys. **217**(1), 5–36 (2006)
6. Jiang, X.M., Mahadevan, S.: Bayesian wavelet method for multivariate model assessment of dynamic systems. J. Sound Vib. **312**(4–5), 694–712 (2008)
7. Wei, L., Zhenzhou, L., Wei, C.: New validation metrics for models with multiple correlated responses. Reliab. Eng. Syst. Saf. **127**, 1–11 (2014)
8. Luyi, L., Zhenzhou, L.: A new method for model validation with multivariate output. Reliab. Eng. Syst. Saf. **169**, 579–592 (2018)
9. Kai, Z., Jie, H., Zhenfei, Z.: Multivariate response analysis for dynamic system model validation. J. Shanghai Jiao Tong Univ. **02**, 191–195 (2015)
10. Haiying, W.: Research on verification method of multi variable uncertainty simulation results. Harbin Institute of Technology, Harbin (2016)
11. Shenglin, L., Wei, L., Ming, Y., Ping, M.: Validation method for multivariate output simulation models considering correlation. J. Autom. **45**(09), 1666–1678 (2019)
12. Xiulin, G., Xiaoyu, H., Lingyu, X.: Graph correlated attention recurrent neural network for multivariate time series forecasting. Inf. Sci. **606**, 126–142 (2022)
13. Zonghan, W., Shirui, P., Guodong, L.: Connecting the dots: multivariate time series forecasting with graph neural networks. In: The ACM SIGKDD International Conference on Knowledge Discovery and Data Mining, pp. 753–763 (2020)
14. Liwei, Z., Qingkui, Z., Bo, L.: Hybrid anomaly detection via multihead dynamic graph attention networks for multivariate time series. IEEE Access **10**, 40967–40978 (2022)
15. Jun, Z., Siqi, W., Xiandong, M., et al.: Stgat-Mad: spatial-temporal graph attention network for multivariate time series anomaly detection. In: ICASSP 2022 - 2022 IEEE International Conference on Acoustics, Speech and Signal Processing, pp. 3568–3572. Singapore, Singapore (2022)
16. Mikalsen, K.Y., Bianchi, F.M., Soguero, R.C.: Time series cluster kernel for learning similarities between multivariate time series with missing data. Pattern Recognit. **76**, 569–581 (2018)
17. Xu, K., Hu, W., Leskovec, J., et al.: How powerful are graph neural networks? In: International Conference on Learning Representations (2019)
18. Szekely, G.J., Rizzo, M.L., Bakirov, N.K.: Measuring and testing dependence by correlation of distance. Ann. Stat. **35**(6), 2769–2794 (2008)
19. Gilmer, J., Schoenholz, S.S., Riley, P.F.: Neural message passing for quantum chemistry. In: International Conference on Machine Learning, pp. 2053–2070 (2017)
20. Zhitao, Y., Jiaxuan, Y., Christopher, M., et al.: Hierarchical graph representation learning with differentiable pooling. In Advances in Neural Information Processing Systems, pp. 4800–4810 (2018)
21. Muhan, Z., Zhicheng, C., Marion, N., et al.: An end-to-end deep learning architecture for graph classification. In: In Thirty-Second AAAI Conference on Artificial Intelligence (2018)

Simulation of Drinking Water Infrastructures Through Artificial Intelligence-Based Modelling for Sustainability Improvement

Carlos Calatayud Asensi[1] , José Vicente Berná Martinez[2](✉) ,
Lucia Arnau Muñoz[2] , Vicente Javier Macián Cervera[1],
and Francisco Maciá Pérez[2]

[1] Aguas de Valencia S.A., Avda. Marqués del Turia, 46005 València, Spain
{ccalatayud,jmacian}@globalomnium.com
[2] University of Alicante, Carretera San Vicente del Raspeig s/n, 03690 Alicante, Spain
{jvberna,lucia.arnau,pmacia}@ua.es

Abstract. The development of control systems for critical infrastructures requires testing and validating the proposals before using them in real environments. This work proposes the development of a new control system with an approach based on sustainability, which uses multi-agent systems as a basis, and which breaks away from traditional proposals focused on optimising energy costs. This new approach requires a thorough validation before its possible deployment, as it is based on distributed components that make independent decisions to generate complex emergent behaviour. In order to test its viability, a simulator has also been developed alongside the control system, which allows the behaviour of each agent to be analysed by subjecting it to tests using real data from the scenario to be controlled. Through this tool it is possible to observe each agent in the fulfilment of its functions, validate its behaviour, and check that the control system guarantees the supply of drinking water to a city, using the data obtained from that city as input. Through the simulator it is possible to analyse and represent different configurations of the control system over an infrastructure, thus being able to select the best option for the environment.

Keywords: WASUSI-MAS · Water supply simulator · Multi agent systems

1 Introduction

The use of artificial intelligence (AI) models makes it possible to make highly accurate estimates of the behaviour of complex non-linear systems, where hundreds of variables and actors involved need to be considered. AI is becoming increasingly important in resource management contexts, such as river flow prediction [1], energy management in construction [2] or solid waste management [3], where numerous technical, climatic, environmental, demographic, socio-economic and legislative parameters are involved. Today, one of the scarcest resources that must be managed efficiently is undoubtedly

J.-L. Guisado-Lizar et al. (Eds.): SIMUtools 2023, LNICST 519, pp. 131–146, 2024.
https://doi.org/10.1007/978-3-031-57523-5_11

water, and more specifically drinking water. This is because, in recent years, water resources on a global scale have come under considerable pressure due to altered hydrological conditions and the spread of pollution resulting from climate change [4]. As a result, there are numerous studies that address the need to optimise water infrastructure management through all kinds of techniques, but most commonly through an energy optimisation approach [5]. This is because energy consumption in such systems is significant, and improving pump performance can greatly reduce energy costs [6]. In such work where optimisation must utilise large amounts of data, situations and conditions, IA plays a fundamental and very useful role in modelling, automating, and optimising critical water management applications [7].

However, today, an optimisation approach based solely on the energy efficiency of drinking water infrastructures does not meet the needs of environmental sustainability. This is because, energy optimisation is based on taking advantage of the hours when energy costs are lowest for the accumulation of drinking water in large reservoirs, i.e., producing the most water when energy is cheap [8]. There are several problems with this approach. Firstly, the stored water has been extracted from the ground, which decreases the water in aquifers and increases their deterioration, worsening water quality [9]. A sustainability-based approach dictates that only the water needed for consumption is abstracted, thus using aquifers as natural water reservoirs, which are even protective against surface pollutants and conserve water quality [10]. Secondly, by keeping the reservoirs filled to the maximum using cheap energy, the stored water exerts pressure on water infrastructures and pumping stations, which in the case of reservoirs that have their inlet at the bottom means that the higher the level in the reservoir, the more energy the pumps have to use to lift the water [11]. The use of storage tanks with their inlet/outlet at the bottom is beneficial for the maintenance of pressures in the infrastructure and therefore their use is common [12]. Figure 1 shows a classic drinking water supply infrastructure scheme, where groundwater is pumped to an above-ground reservoir that supplies a city. The more water is stored in the tank, the higher the water pumps have to pump.

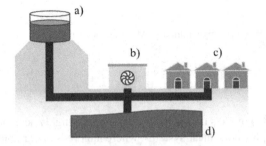

a) Water tank with bottom inlet
b) Water pumps
c) Urban area
d) Aquifer

Fig. 1. Schematic of an infrastructure based on an overhead storage facility.

And thirdly, by having the storage at the maximum, when water consumption is high, inertia is produced that the pumping systems have to overcome. For example, during the first hours of the night when people come home from work, water is consumed in showers and kitchens, this generates an inertia of water towards the city, but when the water level in the reservoir drops and as energy is cheap at that time, water is pumped into the reservoir. This causes the pumps to be fighting against the inertia of the consumed water, which means higher energy consumption and unwanted overpressure towards the city. Figure 2 illustrates this effect.

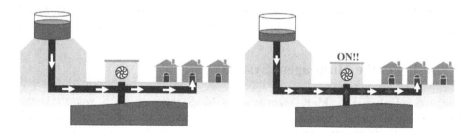

Fig. 2. Pumping start time where the pumping inertia is opposite to the consumption inertia.

To combat these three problems, this paper proposes the design of intelligent control systems capable of handling multiple objectives and priorities among them dynamically, through a multi-agent system (MAS). Multi-agent systems are an important branch of distributed artificial intelligence [13] that allows the decomposition of complex systems into different independent agents that collaborate with each other to achieve objectives. Each agent implies that it possesses local knowledge and information only about its own interests and goals, as it does not have to contain information from the whole system. This circumstance is beneficial in the management of infrastructures that may be distributed, very large, or that may change and evolve over time [14]. MAS is not only a field within IA, but also a field of research in associative areas such as economics, philosophy, sociology, or biology, where agent technology is used to achieve complex tasks in a distributed way, with solid results for years [15]. We can find works using MAS related to distributed energy infrastructure management. In renewable energy optimisation for hybrid systems, the study [16] proposes a MAS system where agents model the infrastructure elements and generate the optimal behaviour for the infrastructure. In [17], the creation of a simulator for an energy management system is proposed, where the agents model the communication between the elements, the execution of actions and the infrastructure components, and it is implemented through FIPA. Even the use of MAS has shown valid results in highly distributed, heterogeneous, and variable scenarios [18] where multi-level MAS systems coordinate multi-energy microgrid infrastructures.

The main distinction of our work is that the focus will be on minimising water storage to avoid unnecessary exploitation of aquifers, minimising the pressure due to the height of the stored water sheet and controlling overpressure. For this purpose, a simulator of a MAS has been developed in this work, which allows validating the control system by comparing it with the real behaviour and thus being able to check the points of improvement. Furthermore, this modelling has been carried out using the infrastructure and real data obtained from a small town of approximately 5,000 inhabitants in southeastern Spain. As it is based on a real scenario, the results allow us to quantify the benefit obtained on the real aquifers and infrastructures and thus validate the proposal.

The rest of the article is organised into the following sections: Sect. 2 contains a preliminary study of the characteristics of multi-agent systems, together with the definition of the necessary parameters for their design and implementation; Sect. 3 shows the objectives that the system must fulfil, each of them being an independent agent, with a series of parameters that condition each agent in its task; Sect. 4 explains the development of the simulator, from the technologies used to a certain level of code used; Sect. 5 finally draws the main conclusions of the work and sets out the lines of future work.

2 Design of the Multi-agent System

Our proposal is based on a Multi-agent Systems (MAS) approach. MASs were developed to solve large problems where data may be distributed and of different nature. In addition, they are particularly suited to problems with multiple methods of solving, multiple perspectives and/or multiple elements that can provide a solution to the problem. The purpose is to achieve objectives through a distributed system of sound, communication, processing, and control [19]. The use of the MAS paradigm in complex systems related to sensorisation has shown that it enables the generation of complex behaviour and is even capable of dealing with unknown situations [20], which means that it is not necessary to consider all possible states of the system, but rather to model the behaviour appropriately. The use of MAS as a possible solution to water resource management is relatively recent, as shown by the work of [21], but in this case, only optimisation focused on consumption is used, without considering other variables or the flexibility of the system to change both infrastructures and efficiency approach.

Our system is based on the definitions of [22], where each agent is described as an α element able to obtain information from its environment, what we call the $Percept_\alpha$, obtaining a perceived state Φ_α from the global environment. It can store this new perceived state, what we call Mem_α, in an internal state Σ_α, which will be the result of combining the perceived data and its own knowledge up to that moment. Using this perceived information and its own internal state, it can make decisions, called $Decision_\alpha$, and finally based on the decided action, execute it in the $Exec_\alpha$ system. Using formal definitions, developed for our proposal, an agent α is defined as:

$$\alpha = \langle \Phi_\alpha, \Sigma_\alpha, P_\alpha, \Gamma_\alpha, Percept_\alpha, Mem_\alpha, Decision_\alpha, Exec_\alpha \rangle \tag{1}$$

where:

- $\Phi_\alpha = \langle \varphi_1, \varphi_2, \varphi_3, \ldots, \varphi_n, \rangle$ and φ_i is a list of signal-value pairs of perceptions of the world, the information that an agent will extract from its context and that comes either from the managed system or from other agents producing new information.
- $\Sigma_\alpha = \langle \varsigma_1, \varsigma_2, \varsigma_3, \ldots, \varsigma_n, \rangle$ and ς_i is a list of signal-value pairs internal to the system, the information it will store internally.
- $P_\alpha = \langle \rho_1, \rho_2, \rho_3, \ldots, \rho_n, \rangle$ and ρ_i is a list of signal-value pairs that define an action, an intention to change.
- $\Gamma_\alpha = \langle \gamma_1, \gamma_2, \gamma_3, \ldots, \gamma_n, \rangle$ and γ_i is a list of output signal-value pairs, called influences, which constitute the centre's attempt to change the state of the world by outputting new values it wishes to change in some element.

- $Percept_\alpha: W \rightarrow \Phi_\alpha$ function that generates a perception from the state of the world W.
- $Mem_\alpha: \Phi_\alpha \rightarrow \Sigma_\alpha$ function that generates a new internal state from the perceived state.
- $Decision_\alpha: \Phi_\alpha \times \Sigma_\alpha \rightarrow P$ function that generates an action from the perceived and internal state.
- $Exec_\alpha: P \rightarrow \Gamma$ function that generates an influence from the action taken.

The execution of a given action by an agent at a given time does not directly imply the alteration of the state of the system but has to be taken as an attempt to change its state, i.e., to exert an influence γ of change. It is therefore the execution of all the actions decided, i.e., the sum of all the influences of each of the agents taking part in the system that actually generates a change from one state to another. Formally, the future state of the system $\sigma(t + 1)$ can be defined as the reaction, *React*, of the system in its current state $\sigma(t)$ together with the union of all the influences of the agents in the system:

$$\sigma(t + 1) = React(\sigma(t), \bigcup_1^n (\gamma_i)) \text{ where each } \gamma_i \text{ is defined as}$$

$$\gamma_i = Exec_i(Decision_i(Percept_i(\sigma(t)), \varsigma_i(t))) \quad (2)$$

Each influence is independent and asynchronous from the others, i.e. this reaction function (2) will be executed each time a new influence is generated. Although function (2) only shows the union of all influences, there might be influences with higher weights than others, and therefore weights could be added to increase or decrease the impact of each influence. However, as will be seen below, in our case it will be an agent who will control this weighting, so the agent can also dynamically adjust the weights if necessary.

Figure 3 shows the description of the MAS system, and how the reaction function launches an attempt to change the influence on the water infrastructure. Note that the fact that actions are generated does not imply that the direct effect is as expected. For example, the current conditions may demand to start the water pumps, but if at the moment the action is performed the consumption is reduced, an unwanted overpressure may occur, which would be controlled again by the system.

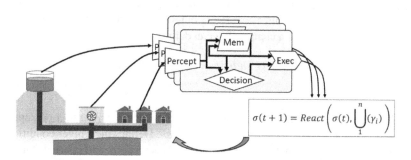

Fig. 3. MAS architecture for water supply control

Once the MAS architecture has been defined, we will define the internal *Percept, Mem, Decision* and *Exec* functions of each agent.

2.1 Percept

This function specifies the list of signals in the world that will be observed by an agent. It will be defined as a list of names of signals to which the agent will react by perceiving the state of the world, when one of them changes. Each agent will therefore define its observation list: $watchList = [singnal1, signal2, ..., signaln]$.

2.2 Mem

The memorisation function is executed whenever there is a substantial change in perception that deserves to be stored. A threshold μ is defined, which when exceeded, generates a new internal state. To compare the current world state with the stored internal state, we use a distance function. Given an agent, and the list of perceived signals (φ) and the stored internal state (ς), at time instant (t), the distance function is defined as:

$$distance = \frac{\sum_1^n \left| \frac{\varphi(t)_i}{\max(\varphi_i)} - \frac{\varsigma(t-1)_i}{\max(\varsigma_i)} \right|}{n} \qquad \text{where | indicates absolute value} \qquad (3)$$

The distance function calculates the difference between a perceived signal and the previous stored state. Furthermore, it divides each signal by its maximum in order to normalise the values and thus not to generate distortions by signals with high values versus signals with small values. Finally, the result of the summation is divided by the number of observed signals, generating a distance value between 0 and 1, where 0 implies that there has been no change and 1 implies that there has been a total change in all signals. *Mem* will store the new state of the world whenever $distance > \mu$. If we want the system to be very sensitive to changes, it will be enough to make $\mu = 0$, and then the system will react to any change. Each agent can be configured with a particular μ.

2.3 Decision

The decision function generates an action in case the centre detects a condition of interest to it. Generating an action implies generating output signals that will try to influence the world, trying to bring about a change. We can define this function as:

$$SetsignalValue(FundD(\varphi, \varsigma)) \; if \; PreD(\varphi, \varsigma) = true \qquad (4)$$

where:

- *PreD* (φ, ς): is a precondition function that relates False or True to a percept and a given internal state: *PreD:* $\Phi_\alpha \times \Sigma_\alpha \to Boolean$. Defines the trigger conditions.
- *FunD* (φ, ς): Function that associates the agent's perception and internal state with a list of output signals that define an action. *FunD:* $\Phi_\alpha \times \Sigma_\alpha \to P_\alpha$. Therefore, each centre will have to determine the signals that generate actions.

2.4 Excec

Finally, the execution function will be defined as a function that outputs the signals generated by *Decision*, provided that a certain execution precondition is met, i.e.:

$$PostE(\rho) \, if \; PreE(\varsigma) = true \tag{5}$$

The *PostE* function generates the output signals or influences. These can be the same signals defined by the action ρ. The *PreE(ς)* function allows the influence intent to be conditioned on the perceived state. If set to "true", influence is always generated.

3   Design of the Agents

To design the actors, it is necessary to specify the figures for the objectives of the system. There is an overall objective that must be met: to ensure water supply. This is achieved by maintaining a minimum level of water in the reservoir, so this objective will take priority over the other goals.

3.1   Goal 1

The first objective is to minimise the amount of water stored. To find out what the minimum and maximum values are, the behaviour of the city has been studied over several months in 2021 and 2022 (Fig. 4). The empirical study indicates that, most of the time, the water level moves approximately 0.5 m, in fact 72% of the measurements are within this range. The minimum level of the reservoir is set at 0.5 m, as below this water level there would be sediment entrainment. Therefore, values between [0.5 - 1] are required to maintain the water level at its optimum point.

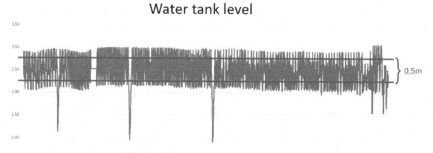

Fig. 4. Water tank level in 2021–2022

3.2 Goal 2

The second objective is to avoid pumping water during periods of peak consumption in the city, thus preventing the pumping stations from working against inertia. To this end, the behaviour of the city's consumption (Fig. 5) has been studied for 2021–2022 and it has been established that, above 50 m³/h of consumption, it is desirable not to switch on the pumps, as long as goal 1 is met.

City consumption m³/h

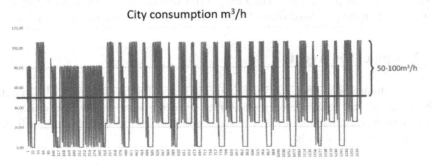

Fig. 5. City consumption in 2021–2022

3.3 Goal 3

The last objective is to maintain the pressure of the infrastructure around a reasonable value, avoiding too high or too low pressure. In this case, the reservoir is located at 47 m above sea level. Therefore, the minimum pressure should be 47 m water column (mwc). Since the maximum height of the tank level is set at 1 m in goal 1, the maximum pressure to be expected is 48 m water column. A margin of ±5% is applied to these values, which is the margin of error of the pressure gauges, so the pressure should be kept between [44.5–50.5] metres water column.

3.4 Agents

The system will be composed of several agents, one managing each objective, plus a coordinating agent, who will be responsible for coordinating the influences of the other agents. Each agent produces an influence on the system, in this case, the influence is the desire for the water pumps to start or stop. Each agent will produce an attempt to modify the state of the system, and we must consider that the intentions can be contradictory, and that is why a coordinating agent is necessary. To define the agents, it is necessary to define the internal functions of each agent.

Agent A_1 is responsible for achieving Goal 1. To do so, it will observe the water level in the tank and when it is close to the limits, it will generate an influence on the pumps, I_1, with a value between $[1, -1]$. Positive values indicate that it wants to start the pumps, a value of 0 indicates no influence, and a negative value indicates that it wants to stop the pumps. The strength of the desire will be between 0 and 1 for positive and between 0 and -1 for negative. Table 1 show the internal definition on A_1.

Agent A_2 will be responsible for Goal 2, so that it will monitor water consumption in the city and when it exceeds 50 m^3/h it will generate an influence, I_2, to detect the motors, i.e., it generates values between $[0, -1]$. In our infrastructures, to know the water consumed by the city, it is calculated by observing the amount of water generated by the pumps when they are on and the amount of water that enters or leaves the tank (positive flow indicates that it enters the tank, negative flow indicates that it leaves the tank) in the tank. Therefore, the water consumed is equal to the water produced by the pumps minus the flow of water in the tank. Table 2 show the internal definition on A_2.

Agent A_3 will manage Goal 3 by monitoring the water pressure. When the pressure is between its normal values, $[44.5–50.5]$ mwc, the agent will produce a neutral influence, 0. When the pressure drops below the minimum, it will generate a maximum influence to start the pumps (value 1), and when the pressure exceeds the maximum, it will generate a maximum influence to stop them (value -1). Table 3 show this.

Table 1. Definition of the internal elements and functions of the agent A_1.

Element	Values	
watchList	HWT (height of water in the tank)	
μ	0,01	
FunD	$I_1 = 1$	if HWT $\leq 0,5$
	$I_1 = 2*(1 - HWT)$	if $0,5 < HWT < 1$
	$I_1 = -1$	if HWT ≤ 1
PostE	I_2	

Table 2. Definition of the internal elements and functions of the agent A_2.

Element	Values	
watchList	WTF (water tank flow), WPF (water pumps flow)	
μ	0,01	
FunD	$I_2 = 0$	if WPF-WTF < 50
	$I_2 = -1$	if WPF-WTF ≥ 50
PostE	I_2	

Table 3. Definition of the internal elements and functions of the agent A_3.

Element	Values	
watchList	WP (water pressure)	
μ	0,01	
FunD	$I_3 = 1$ $I_3 = 0$ $I_3 = -1$	if WP < 44,5 if 44,5 $\leq$ WP $\leq$ 50,5 if WP > 50,5
PostE	I_3	

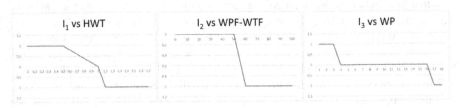

Fig. 6. Influence values of A_1, A_2 and A_3

Figure 6 shows the graphs with the values of the influences produced by each agent.

The coordinating agent AC_1 will be responsible for mediating between all influences, giving priority to I_1 over the others, as maintaining the water supply is mandatory (Table 4).

Table 4. Definition of the internal elements and functions of the agent AC_1

Element	Values
watchList	I_1, I_2, I_3
μ	0
FunD	$I_4 = 0.5*I_1 + 0.3*I_2 + 0.2*I_3$
PostE	I_4

The behaviour of this coordinating agent could be expressed in many ways. It has been chosen to carry out a static weighting of the influences of the rest of the agents, but it could also be dynamic, so that, for example, depending on the season of the year, it would give more weight to I1, so that in summer it gives priority to having stored water, or depending on the time of day to I2, so that, during working hours, it would give more priority to not turning on pumps during the moments of greatest consumption and therefore, of inertia in the water flows.

4   Simulator Development

To validate the proposal, we have developed a MAS simulator, which uses as input the real consumption data of the city of 5000 inhabitants taken as an example. For the development of the system, we have used the Angular framework programmed in TypeScript and libraries of graphical representation of data [23]. These technologies have been chosen for the development of the simulator for two reasons. First, the aim is to use platform-independent web technologies. Secondly, in this way, the logic of the agents is executed on each client's computer, but, if necessary, the logic can be moved to a specialised server, ensuring the scalability of the proposal. Each agent has been designed as a class of type Agent as shown in the Fig. 7.

For each agent, it will only be necessary to define its *FunD* decision function, which generates the corresponding influence. Whenever there is a change in any of the input signals, the agents evaluate the state of the world and make decisions accordingly, generating influences that try to alter the state of the pumps (Fig. 8).

```
export class Agent {
  watchList:string[] = [];              // signals watched
  mu:number = 0;                        // distance threshold
  memory:SignalInterface[] = [];        // internal memory
  perception:SignalInterface[] = [];    // perception of agent
  influence=0;                          // influence of agent
  percept(word:SignalInterface[]){
    this.perception=signalsOfWachList(word);
    this.mem();
  }
  mem() {
    if (distance(perception,memory)>mu) this.memory = perception
    this.decision()
  }
  decision() {
    this.influence = FundD(this.perception, this.memory)
    this.exec()
  }
  exec() { return this.influence }
}
```

Fig. 7. Class Agent used as a base class for all agents.

In the upper area, the initial parameters of HWT, city consumption and initial infrastructure pressure can be set. When starting the simulation (Start button), the system uses the actual city consumption to calculate the status of the pumps. The simulator shows the status of each signal in the graph below. Simulations have been performed using data from 2021 and 2022, with hourly measurements. The results are discussed below.

4.1   Achievement of Goal 1

The behaviour of this agent aims to keep the water level in the tank stable, between 0.5 and 1 m in height. Figure 9 shows the water level (blue line) and the city's consumption

WASUSI-MAS
WAter SUpply SImulator with Multi-Agent System

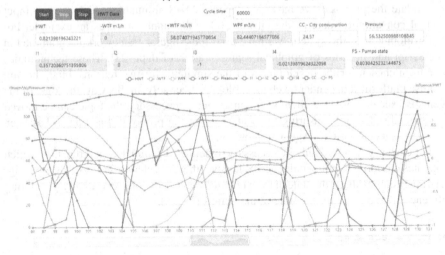

Fig. 8. Interface from WASUSI-MAS.

(green line), and we can see that this level has been always kept stable. Irrespective of the city's consumption demand, at no time has the constant supply been lost, nor has it dropped below 0.5 m, which would have resulted in sediment being washed away.

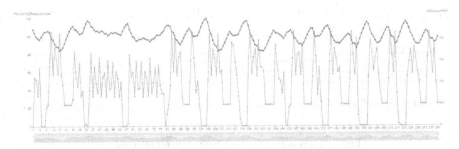

Fig. 9. City consumption and tank level (Color figure online)

Figure 10 shows how the influence generated by agent A_1 decreases when the water level in the tank approaches the maximum values, and how it increases when the water level in the tank decreases.

4.2 Achievement of Goal 2

The A_2 agent aims to reduce the pumps being switched on when there is high consumption in the city, because this prevents the pumps from working against the inertia of the

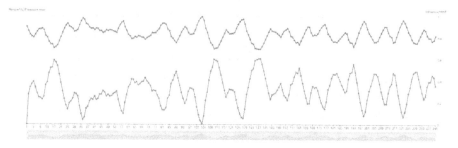

Fig. 10. Water level in the tank against the influence of A1

water flow when it circulates towards the consumption area. In Fig. 11, the influence of A_2 is shown in orange, the city consumption in green, and the pump status in blue. It can be seen that the agent has a negative influence, it tries to stop the pumps when the consumption is high. As soon as the consumption decreases from 50 m^3/h, the agent generates the neutral influence 0, allowing the pumps to be activated according to the rest of the parameters. When the agent A_2 produces the influence 0, the pump can increase its power, this can be seen as the blue line rises in the graph.

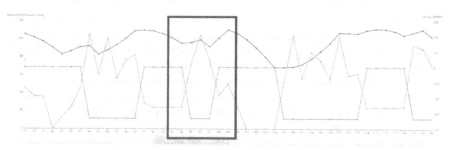

Fig. 11. Pump performance against the influence of A_2 (Color figure online)

4.3 Achievement of Goal 3

The A_3 agent aims to keep the pressure within desirable operating levels between 44.5 and 50.5 mwc. In Fig. 12, the purple line shows the influence of A_3, the dark blue line shows the pump status, and the light blue line shows the pressure in the infrastructure. In this case, A_3 has a negative influence when the pressure is very high, as the pumps are in operation. When the pressure decreases, A_3 generates a neutral influence, leaving the pumps working. Lastly, when the pressure is too low, A_3 produces a positive influence, which boosts the work of the pumps.

The simulator is available in the public repository [24] along with sample data for simulations. This simulator could be used as a basis for the development of other control systems on other infrastructures.

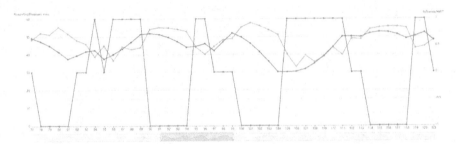

Fig. 12. Evolution of the pressure against the influence of A$_3$ (Color figure online)

5 Conclusions and Future Work

This work has proposed the design and development of a drinking water supply infrastructure simulator, which uses a multi-agent system for its control. The use of MAS allows us to introduce goals to be met by the control system, without the need to worry about the exhaustive modelling of the physical system, or that the goals are consistent with each other. Based on the MAS, a tool has been built, WASUSI-MAS, through which the simulation of the system can be carried out on the data of a real infrastructure. This makes it possible to obtain a control system focused on sustainability, capable of reducing the amount of water stored in the reservoir and maintaining an efficient operating range in the infrastructures, preventing the system from working under adverse circumstances such as high pressures or water inertia. In the simulation, it has been verified that the agents fulfil their goals, generating the desired behaviour. In addition, the simulator has been shared in a public repository so that it can be used freely.

However, when dealing with the management of critical systems, it is necessary to increase the number of tests and simulations, extending to anomalous or exceptional situations, to ensure that the operation will be as desired. Until then, the simulator can be used to propose various improvements to the agents, or to model more complex scenarios or scenarios with new goals. Future work includes increasing the number of tests and the creation of scenarios that are not only based on historical data.

Based on this work, several ways are open. On the one hand, work on the incorporation of prediction agents. The current simulator uses historical consumption data to generate the desired behaviour. This implies that the MAS is limited to being solely reactive. The inclusion of prediction agents could provide a much more sophisticated MAS, with influences based not only on current data, but also on future data. On the other hand, work is underway to generate a library of predefined agents, agents specialised in different goals. This line of work would generate great potential for the simulator, as it would allow the MAS control system to be composed, simulate its operation with real infrastructure datasets, compare different configuration options, and thus be able to generate safe and stable control systems.

Acknowledgments. This work was supported by the UAIND22-01B Project "Adaptive control of urban supply systems" by the Office of the Vice President of Research of the University of Alicante, and ICAR23-06 Project "EWAi. Elderly Wellness Artificial Intelligence" by ICAR Fundation - International Centre for Ageing Research.

References

1. Tikhamarine, Y., Souag-Gamane, D., Ahmed, A.N., Kisi, O., El-Shafie, A.: Improving artificial intelligence models accuracy for monthly streamflow forecasting using grey Wolf optimization (GWO) algorithm. J. Hydrol. **582**, 124435 (2020)
2. Pan, Y., Zhang, L.: Roles of artificial intelligence in construction engineering and management: a critical review and future trends. Auto. Constr. **122**, 103517 (2021)
3. Abdallah, M., Talib, M.A., Feroz, S., Nasir, Q., Abdalla, H., Mahfood, B.: Artificial intelligence applications in solid waste management: a systematic research review. Waste Manag. **109**, 231–246 (2020)
4. Qiu, J., Shen, Z., Leng, G., Xie, H., Hou, X., Wei, G.: Impacts of climate change on watershed systems and potential adaptation through BMPs in a drinking water source area. J. Hydrol. **573**, 123–135 (2019)
5. Oikonomou, K., Parvania, M., Khatami, R.: Optimal demand response scheduling for water distribution systems. IEEE Trans. Ind. Inform. **14**(11), 5112–5122 (2018)
6. Shao, Y., Zhou, X., Yu, T., Zhang, T., Chu, S.: Pump scheduling optimization in water distribution system based on mixed integer linear programming. EJOR (2023)
7. Lowe, M., Qin, R., Mao, X.: A review on machine learning, artificial intelligence, and smart technology in water treatment and monitoring. Water **14**(9), 1384 (2022)
8. Moazeni, F., Khazaei, J.: Optimal operation of water-energy microgrids; a mixed integer linear programming formulation. J. Clean. Prod. **275**, 122776 (2020)
9. Gejl, R.N., Bjerg, P.L., Henriksen, H.J., Hauschild, M.Z., Rasmussen, J., Rygaard, M.: Integrating groundwater stress in life-cycle assessments–an evaluation of water abstraction. J. Environ. Manag. **222**, 112–121 (2018)
10. Trowsdale, S.A., Lerner, D.N.: Implications of flow patterns in the sandstone aquifer beneath the mature conurbation of Nottingham (UK) for source protection. Q. J. Eng. Geol. Hydrogeol. **36**(3), 197–206 (2003)
11. Tiwari, A.K., Kalamkar, V.R., Pande, R.R., Sharma, S.K., Sontake, V.C., Jha, A.: Effect of head and PV array configurations on solar water pumping system. Mater. Today Proc. **46**, 5475–5481 (2021)
12. Rossman, L.A., Grayman, W.M.: Scale-model studies of mixing in drinking water storage tanks. J. Environ. Eng. **125**(8), 755–761 (1999)
13. Wooldridge, M.: An Introduction to Multiagent Systems. Wiley, Hoboken (2009)
14. McArthur, S.D., et al.: Multi-agent systems for power engineering applications—Part I: concepts, approaches, and technical challenges. IEEE Trans. Power Syst. **22**(4), 1743–1752 (2007)
15. Shu, H., Tang, L., Dong, J.: A survey on application of multi-agent system in power system. Power Syst. Technol. **29**(6), 27–31 (2005)
16. Ameur, C., Faquir, S., Yahyaouy, A.: Intelligent optimization and management system for renewable energy systems using multi-agent. IAES Int. J. Artif. Intell. **8**(4), 352 (2019)
17. Basma, A., Benyounes, O.: A simulation energy management system of a multi-source renewable energy based on multi agent system. IAES Int. J. Artif. Intell. **10**(1), 191 (2021)
18. Ahmadi, S.E., Sadeghi, D., Marzband, M., Abusorrah, A., Sedraoui, K.: Decentralized bi-level stochastic optimization approach for multi-agent multi-energy networked micro-grids with multi-energy storage technologies. Energy **245**, 123223 (2022)
19. Knorn, S., Chen, Z., Middleton, R.H.: Overview: collective control of multiagent systems. IEEE Trans. Control Netw. Syst. **3**(4), 334–347 (2015)
20. Berna-Martinez, J.V., Marcia-Perez, F.: Robotic control systems based on bioinspired multi-agent systems. I. J. Adv. Eng. Sci. Technol. **8**(1), 32–38 (2011)

21. Aydin, M.E., Keleş, R.: A multi agent-based approach for energy efficient water resource management. Comput. Ind. Eng. **151**, 106679 (2021)
22. Ferber, J., Weiss, G.: Multi-agent Systems: An Introduction to Distributed Artificial Intelligence, vol. 1. Addison-Wesley, Reading (1999)
23. Official web of ECharts. https://echarts.apache.org/. Accessed 18 Oct 2023
24. WASUSI-MAS Repositori. https://github.com/jvberna/wasusi-mas. Accessed 18 Oct 2023

Transportation and Logistics

Spatio-Temporal Speed Metrics for Traffic State Estimation on Complex Urban Roads

Moritz Schweppenhäuser[1](✉), Karl Schrab[2], Robert Protzmann[1],
and Ilja Radusch[2]

[1] Fraunhofer Institute FOKUS, Kaiserin Augusta Allee 31, 10589 Berlin, Germany
moritz.schweppenhaeuser@fokus.fraunhofer.de
[2] Technical University of Berlin/Daimler Center for Automotive IT Innovations,
Ernst-Reuter-Platz 7, 10587 Berlin, Germany

Abstract. With this paper, we aim to make two main contributions. Firstly, we present a detailed overview of performance metrics used for estimating traffic conditions in urban settings. Compared to highway situations with relatively stable traffic conditions, Traffic State Estimation in urban environments exhibits several challenges, which we discuss in depth. Secondly, through a simulation study, we utilize Eclipse MOSAIC to assess the capabilities and limitations of these metrics. Therefore, we have developed an open-source suite of applications and add-ons for MOSAIC, that will be documented in this paper. Utilizing the publicly available BeST traffic scenario, which encompasses 24 h of realistic urban traffic in Berlin, we present a comparative analysis of average speeds observed on various types of urban roads. Importantly, we made these implementations available to the open-source community, providing a valuable resource for traffic scientists and others who are interested in our contribution.

Keywords: Traffic State Estimation · Simulation · Eclipse MOSAIC

1 Introduction

Road traffic networks in urbanized areas are vulnerable to congestion, especially during morning and evening rush hours. Precise, timely, and robust Traffic State Estimation (TSE) is a crucial means to identify bottlenecks and circumnavigate afflicted areas. Finding suitable metrics to describe the traffic state is a non-trivial task and often multiple metrics are calculated. A substantial body of research regarding TSE was performed for highway settings, which are characterized by relatively consistent traffic patterns, with fewer intersections and traffic signals. Consequently, the traffic state within this context has been extensively studied, yielding diverse models of traffic behavior and associated metrics. Krajezewicz et al. [1] describe common unambiguous metrics used to describe the traffic state.

© ICST Institute for Computer Sciences, Social Informatics and Telecommunications Engineering 2024
Published by Springer Nature Switzerland AG 2024. All Rights Reserved
J.-L. Guisado-Lizar et al. (Eds.): SIMUtools 2023, LNICST 519, pp. 149–165, 2024.
https://doi.org/10.1007/978-3-031-57523-5_12

As the first objective of our paper, we review and summarize related research on TSE in a short survey. We lay our focus on the mean speed as it is one of the key measurements of traffic performance [4] and can also easily be used in cost functions for routing algorithms. Nonetheless, the mean speed measures presented are seldom used in isolation; instead, they serve as inputs for more advanced systems dedicated to traffic state estimation and prediction.

One effective approach for developing such systems is through simulation. Over the past decade, we have been actively engaged in the development of Intelligent Transport Systems using the Eclipse MOSAIC simulation environment [10]. A notable recent outcome of this effort is the open-source BeST scenario, a calibrated representation of 24 h of motorized traffic in Berlin, Germany [11].

The second objective of this paper is to put the theoretically discussed metrics into practical use, specifically within the simulation context. To achieve this, we have implemented a suite of applications and add-ons for MOSAIC. These implementations are utilized in conjunction with the BeST scenario to conduct a thorough comparison, thus assessing the capabilities and limitations of the identified metrics. It is noteworthy that we have also made these implementations available to the open-source community, rendering this paper a concise guide to our code contributions.

The paper is structured as follows. We give a broad introduction to relevant topics of traffic dynamics in Sect. 2. Secondly, we explain the most commonly applied sensor modalities and their implications for mean speed estimation in Sect. 3. Afterwards, in Sect. 4 we conduct an empirical test to highlight differences in the mean speeds. Finally, in Sect. 5 we summarize our findings and highlight our future research interests.

2   Fundamentals of Traffic Dynamics

In the following section, we build on common traffic theory terminology and encourage newer readers to look up the following references [5,7,12] if you encounter difficulties.

Traffic dynamic research often uses so-called space-time diagrams to explain spatio-temporal relations of the traffic flow [12]. Figure 1 depicts two such space-time diagrams. Conventionally, we plot the time on the abscissa and the space on the ordinate. Each of the purple lines represents the trajectory of a vehicle moving along a given route, where steeper segments indicate faster speeds and less steep segments indicate lower speeds. From a given trajectory it is trivial to calculate the average velocity for a segment of its route using Eq. (1).

$$\bar{v} = \frac{\Delta s}{\Delta t} \tag{1}$$

As the traffic state is a highly fluctuations measure, deviating both over space (i.e., different roads/road segments) and over time (i.e., morning and evening peaks vs. midday lows), any statement about it has to be made on segments

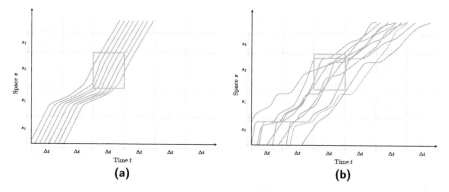

Fig. 1. Exemplary space-time diagrams. (a) shows typical vehicle trajectories on a highway. Whereas, (b) highlights large deviations in vehicle trajectories in urban areas. (Color figure online)

in space and time. Empirically speaking, this means that we consider separate time intervals and traffic network segments, leading to spatio-temporal measurements. This also implies that over these intervals and segments, some form of aggregation has to be applied. Usually, one sets a constant aggregation interval (T) and separates roads into smaller chunks (e.g., from junction to junction, or fixed-length segments). In Fig. 1 this indicated by the Δt's of constant size and the set of road segments $S := \{s_0, \ldots, s_3\}$. With these spatial and temporal segments, many spatio-temporal aggregation intervals have to be considered, one being indicated by the orange squares in Fig. 1. When trying to extract a mean speed for the spatio-temporal interval indicated by the orange square, one faces a couple of issues. In a scenario where we would have access to all exact vehicle trajectories, we would calculate the aggregated average velocity by taking the arithmetic mean of all average velocities within the marked time frame on the marked road segment as shown in Eq. (2).

$$V = \frac{1}{n} \sum_{i=0}^{n} \bar{v}_i = \frac{1}{n} \sum_{i=0}^{n} \frac{\Delta s_i}{\Delta t_i} \tag{2}$$

where V declares the aggregated average velocity and n the amount of vehicles that drive on the marked segment within the marked time interval. Consequently, for each vehicle i, s_i and t_i denote the driven distance within the marked time interval and the time spent on the marked road segment respectively.

However, depending on the sensor modality used vehicle trajectories can at best be estimated and are often only available for a small subset of all vehicles, leading to an incomplete measurement.

When looking at the exemplary trajectories in Fig. 1a and Fig. 1b, it becomes obvious that estimating the traffic state on highways is a much simpler venture compared to urban surface roads [4]. Where we can expect fairly consistent driver behavior on highways, we have to consider large variances in speed, acceleration, and braking behavior on urban roads, due to additional variables like traffic signals, second-row parking, and other obstructions increasing the complexity of an urban scenario. Additionally, Fig. 1 doesn't consider any turns and assumes that all vehicles travel on a concurrent road segment. Turning vehicles further complicate the task of estimating the traffic state.

3   Sensor Modalities

In this section, we will describe the basic functionality and implied use cases of the sensor modalities under test, starting with induction loops in Sect. 3.1 and moving on to Floating Car Data (FCD) in Sect. 3.2. We explicitly regard these sensor modalities separately and omit considerations of fusing the acquired sensor data, as we aim to make out strengths and weaknesses independently. The interested reader may find approaches for fusing sensor data in TSE applications in literature [6, 13].

3.1   Induction Loops

The most widespread, traditional sensor modality comes in the form of induction loops, also known as spot or loop detectors. They function by insetting two metal coils within a short distance from each other below the surface of a road. Using the principle of induction it is possible to detect when a vehicle passes a coil. By knowing the distance between the two coils and stopping the time at passing it is possible to determine the spot speed of a vehicle with high precision.

Due to the high installation price, loop detectors are very sparsely installed and mostly cover major road arteries. Additionally, road administrators usually abstain from installing more than one detector per road segment, which may lead to limited insight into the roads' traffic.

Knowing about how induction loops operate and their cost limitations, we can revisit the space-time diagram from Sect. 2 and illustrate how one would aggregate the mean speed using a loop detector. Figure 2a depicts this by drawing a cross-section through the middle of s_2. The orange crosses along the cross-section indicate the measured spot speeds using the slope of the respective vehicle trajectory at the point of passing. This is a slight simplification as induction loops do not measure spot speeds but rather the average velocity over a very short distance. However, for our purposes, we consider the speed of vehicles over that distance as constant and continue using spot speeds.

Intuitively, to aggregate the marked spot speeds within the marked Δt-interval one would use the arithmetic mean (see Eq. (3)).

$$V_{TMS} = \frac{1}{n} \sum_{\alpha=1}^{n} v_\alpha \tag{3}$$

where n denotes the number of vehicles that pass the detector within a given time interval and v_α the speed of a single vehicle at the time of passing. This arithmetic mean is known in the literature as the *Time Mean Speed* as it aggregates the speeds for a certain duration of time. However, when considering the

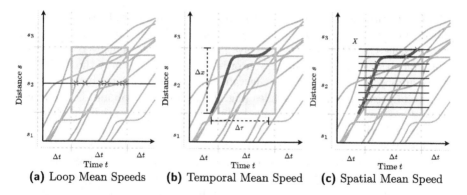

(a) Loop Mean Speeds   **(b)** Temporal Mean Speed   **(c)** Spatial Mean Speed

Fig. 2. (a) illustrates how the samples for the time and space mean speeds are measured. (b) illustrates the calculation of the temporal mean speed Whereas, (c) depicts the calculation of the spatial-mean-speed.

traffic density ρ often the *Space Mean Speed* is used instead of the time mean speed as it delivers better density estimates. The space mean speed considers the same variables but uses the harmonic mean instead of the arithmetic mean (see Eq. (4)).

$$V_{SMS} = \frac{n}{\sum_{\alpha=1}^{n} v_{\alpha}} \tag{4}$$

Note, that even though both presented speeds, especially the space mean speed, are intensively used in practical traffic density analysis, they rarely deliver correct results for density. In reality, density estimates using the time mean speed tend to underestimate the actual density, whereas estimates using the space mean speed tend to overestimate the actual values. For in-depth explanations on these circumstances see [12, Chapter 5].

Another important aspect of the time- and space mean speed is that they originate from traffic-flow theory, which treats moving vehicles similar to a hydrodynamic process in which flow, density, and speed of particles (i.e., vehicles) have a strong correlation. Treating vehicles as particles works sufficiently well on highways, where there is little variance in vehicle speeds and a certain degree of predictability in vehicle movements. In urban scenarios, however, using a single point of measurement will often fail at giving a meaningful insight into the realizable mean speed. The inhomogeneous trajectories in Fig. 2a further visualize this potential flaw.

3.2   Floating Car Data (FCD)

With the increasing availability of GNSS-enabled (Global Navigation Satellite System) devices and broader cell coverage people began to use vehicles as moving (i.e., floating) sensors in the early 2000s [9]. By periodically transmitting position, speed, and heading data to a central service via the cellular network, many vehicles provide a data set called Floating Car Data (FCD). This method of data collection became the de facto standard for many traffic services and is applied in current-day navigation applications like Google Maps and TomTom.

Nonetheless, utilizing the data received from connected vehicles comes with a set of difficulties. On the one hand, sensor inaccuracies, especially those of GNSS sensors, impose a large threat on the validity of collected data. Instead of just trying to improve sensor technologies (e.g., by fusion of GNSS and Inertial measurement systems) an approach called Map-Matching [2] is applied, where the vehicle trajectories are combined with a digital map to infer their most probable positions regarding coordinates but also respective edge and lane positions. The second major difficulty is that crowd-sourced systems such as FCD require a certain percentage of market penetration to deliver broad and reliable estimation results. It is hard to find an exact reference for the minimum penetration rate required, as this depends on the inspected road type and applied algorithms, however, commonly cited thresholds range from 5% to 10% market penetration [4] for reliable highway estimation, meaning every 20th vehicle needs to be connected. In an urban city scenario, this value increases due to higher fluctuations and less coverage in residential areas.

When using FCD as the data source, multiple approaches for mean speed estimation can be applied. These approaches typically examine and aggregate each road segment (i.e., edge or sub-edge) individually by recognizing traversals of said segments.

Commonly, some form of curve fitting is applied using either interpolation or regression (i.e., using polynomial splines) to estimate vehicle movements between received FCD samples. A lower frequency of samples imposes higher uncertainty on the fitted curves. These fitted curves can then be used to infer speed values along a given edge for given vehicles. Yoon et al. [14] introduce the *Temporal Mean Speed* and the *Spatial Mean Speed*, which are calculated using the curve-fitted trajectories of vehicles. These values are calculated separately for each vehicle and later aggregated for specified time intervals, which is depicted in Fig. 2.

The temporal mean speed is simply defined as "[. . .] the average speed over time [. . .]" [14]. It captures the average speed for a single vehicle for one edge, which is formalized in Eq. (5) and visualized in Fig. 2b.

$$v_{\text{temporal}} = \bar{v} = \frac{\Delta x}{\Delta \tau} \qquad (5)$$

Yoon et al. define the spatial mean speed as "[. . .] the average speed over location [. . .]". However, compared to the temporal mean speed, the spatial mean speed follows a more difficult definition as shown in Eq. (6). In this equation, x separates that edge into equidistant segments and X declares the number of these segments spanned within an edge (see Fig. 2c). The distance x typically ranges from 10 m to 15 m. Finally, $v(x)$ defines the instantaneous (i.e., spot) speed at point x derived by the tangential. By averaging these segment speeds, the goal is to gain a perspective on how a vehicle moves in space. For example, if the spatial mean speed of a given vehicle traversal is lower than its temporal mean speed, a more "stop-and-go"-like traffic can be assumed.

$$v_{\text{spatial}} = \frac{1}{X} \sum_{x=1}^{X} v(x) \tag{6}$$

As mentioned in Sect. 2 one is usually interested in an aggregated view of the traffic state as compared to those of individual vehicles. Aggregating the temporal and spatial mean speed for a given time segment has the caveat that traversals of the inspected edge may start before a given time segment. This issue is also visualized in Fig. 2b where the highlighted vehicle trajectory driving on segment s_2 starts within the previous time interval. Most commonly, this issue is disregarded and traversals are accounted towards the aggregation interval in which they finish. It is noteworthy though that this can lead to intervals being more sparsely populated, especially if traffic signals come into play and introduce traffic waves. For this paper we thereby compute V_{temporal} and V_{spatial} for a given edge and a given interval according to Eq. (2) where n includes all vehicles that traversed the edge within the given interval.

$$V_{\text{temporal}} = \frac{1}{n} \sum_{\alpha=1}^{n} v_{\text{temporal}}(\alpha) \tag{7}$$

$$V_{\text{spatial}} = \frac{1}{n} \sum_{\alpha=1}^{n} v_{\text{spatial}}(\alpha) \tag{8}$$

Alternative approaches may omit the curve-fitting step and directly average and aggregate collected samples. These approaches do not face the aforementioned issue, though they can tend to oversimplify the TSE task as only temporal features will be regarded.

4   Simulation Approach

To evaluate, compare, and parameterize a TSE model simulation-based tests can be an effective tool before considering a real-world deployment. Simulation not only allows to catch potential errors and privacy threats at a much lower cost, but it also allows an evaluation of necessary market penetration rates for a functioning system.

4.1   TSE Applications for Eclipse MOSAIC

For simulative tests to deliver significant results simulators for traffic, communication, and other environmental influences have to be modeled as close to reality as possible. The MOSAIC simulation framework [3,10] couples industry-leading FOSS (Free and Open-Source Software) simulators from these domains using a runtime infrastructure based on the IEEE standard for High-Level Architecture (HLA). MOSAIC, additionally, provides a powerful application simulator that allows for fast prototyping and integration of applications in the domains of smart mobility including V2X Communication via ITS-G5 and LTE/5G, autonomous vehicle perception, and e-mobility.

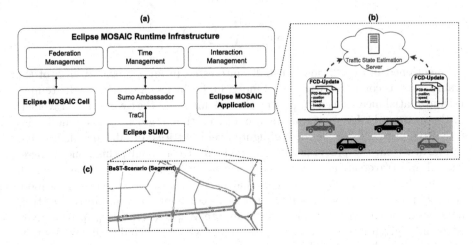

Fig. 3. This diagram gives an overview of all relevant simulators and how they are utilized in hand the TSE applications. **(a)** shows a simplified version of MOSAIC's architecture based on the HLA. **(b)** depicts how the vehicle applications interact with the Traffic State Estimation server using FCD. Finally, **(c)** indicates the functionality of the traffic simulator SUMO. We map our applications on the vehicles controlled by SUMO, which provides realistic FCD traces.

For our evaluation purposes, we couple the microscopic traffic simulator Eclipse SUMO [8] with MOSAIC's integrated Application and Cell simulators. Based on the general FCD approach we modeled the system using MOSAIC's Application simulator (see Fig. 3). The model includes a vehicle application that periodically sends FCD Updates consisting of individual FCD Records and a server application that receives, processes, and aggregates said traces. The server has been designed to be extensible with many processing units, that can act based on newly detected edge traversals or in an event-based manner. The default setup comes enabled with a processor for calculating the Relative Traffic Status Metric (RTSM) defined by Yoon et al. [14], which uses the spatial and temporal mean speed in a threshold-based approach to rate the traffic state. The results of this processor will be stored in a local SQLite database for post-processing and investigation of the collected data. All relevant parameters for both the vehicles, the server, and its processors can be configured using respective JSON configurations, to inspect different key aspects of the system.

In addition to the application-based speed measures (v_{temporal}, v_{spatial}), we configured the traffic simulator SUMO to write ground truth speeds (v_{GT}) and measured speeds of placed induction loops (v_{TMS}, v_{SMS}), which are later used for the comparative study. To ensure reproducibility, the complete application suite as well as all configuration files have been published to GitHub under the following link:

https://github.com/mosaic-addons/traffic-state-estimation.

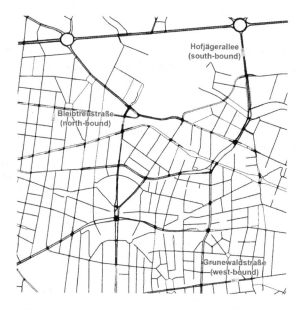

Fig. 4. A map of Charlottenburg indicating loop detector positions for time and space mean speed estimations.

4.2   Experiment Setup

To validate developed applications and the mean speed measurements a traffic scenario has to be established, which mimics real-world road networks and traffic behavior in an urban environment. Therefore, we utilize the BeST scenario [11] which has been modeled for MOSAIC and SUMO and encompasses 24 h of individual motorized traffic in Berlin with around 2.25 million individual vehicle trips.

As we are not focusing on a city-wide evaluation we set up our simulation within the Charlottenburg area of the BeST scenario and simulated an entire day of vehicle movements with 200 000 independent trips. In this test, we configured 100% of vehicles with our FCD solution and set up loop detectors on the marked road segments in Fig. 4 and collected estimations for the time and space mean speed using the configured SUMO output. We selected the marked roads intentionally, to obtain insights on how different measures react to different road types and sizes. Relevant markers for these roads are depicted in Table 1, which indicates how these roads differ from one another. Lastly, we configured SUMO to write a file with reference speed values in the form of edge-wise data which acts as our ground truth. All outputs were aggregated for 15 min intervals as this window size offers a good trade-off between sufficient sample sizes and detailed enough granularity.

4.3   Results

Results of the initial experiment are visualized in Fig. 5 and in Table 2. We colored the measures based on the utilized sensor technology, the ground truth is colored in orange, measures from the induction loops are colored in yellow, and measures retrieved from FCD are colored in purple. We focus on the hours between 6 am to 10 pm as the night hours the network is only sparsely populated and traffic measurements become spotty and irrelevant.

It is apparent that depending on the road type (compare Table 1) the different mean speeds respond differently. On the segment of the *Hofjägerallee* where there are no traffic lights at the end of the edge all measures behave similarly. This is due to the highway-like properties of the road where we can expect nearly constant free-flow speeds along the entirety of the edge on all lanes.

On the segments of the *Grunewaldstraße* and *Bleibtreustraße* a clear split in the measures can be noticed. While the time, space, and spatial mean speeds remain close to the speed limit, the ground truth and temporal mean speeds drop to around 40 km/h on the *Grunewaldstraße* and 22 km/h on the *Bleibtreustraße*. For the time and space mean speed this is easily explained, as the samples are measured close to the center of the segment, where vehicles typically drive close to free flow speed. The spatial mean speed, however, emits this behavior because the distance that vehicles spend in the queue at the traffic signal is small compared to the distance spent driving at free-flow speed.

As the BeST scenario delivers a road network and traffic demand without any major obstructions and slow downs, we are only able to observe measures that reflect this behavior. Figure 5 clearly indicates this as we were only able to measure speeds at and around the speed limit, with expected slowdowns at signalized edges. Also Table 2 shows that average speeds close to the speed limit can be reached. While it is important to be able to measure the free flow characteristics, it is often more relevant to measure impaired traffic situations, as these are the locations one potentially would circumnavigate. How to model these situations and how the TSE system responds to them is part of ongoing research.

In an attempt to highlight the impact of the penetration rate in FCD-based systems, we ran the same scenario with different ratios of (5%, 10%, 30%, 100%) equipped CVs (Connected Vehicles). For this experiment, we solely looked at the temporal mean speed ($v_{temporal}$) as it resembled the ground truth more closely than the spatial mean speed. Results of this test are visualized in Fig. 6.

Table 1. Key markers of the inspected road segments.

street	length	#lanes	speed limit	signalized
Hofjägerallee	399.96 m	3	50 $\frac{km}{h}$	no
Grunewaldstraße	185.37 m	2	50 $\frac{km}{h}$	yes
Bleibtreustraße	182.34 m	1	30 $\frac{km}{h}$	yes

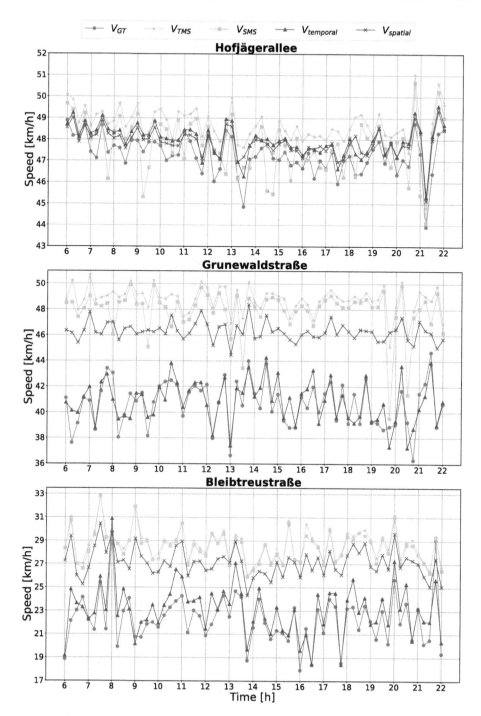

Fig. 5. Different mean speed measures aggregated over 15 min intervals for the street segments highlighted in Fig. 4 using 100% market penetration.

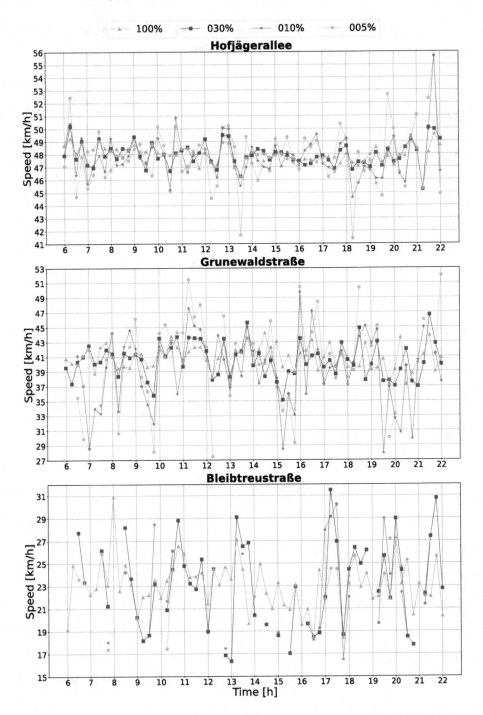

Fig. 6. Temporal mean speed measured with different rates of equipped CVs aggregated over 15 min intervals for the street segments highlighted in Fig. 4.

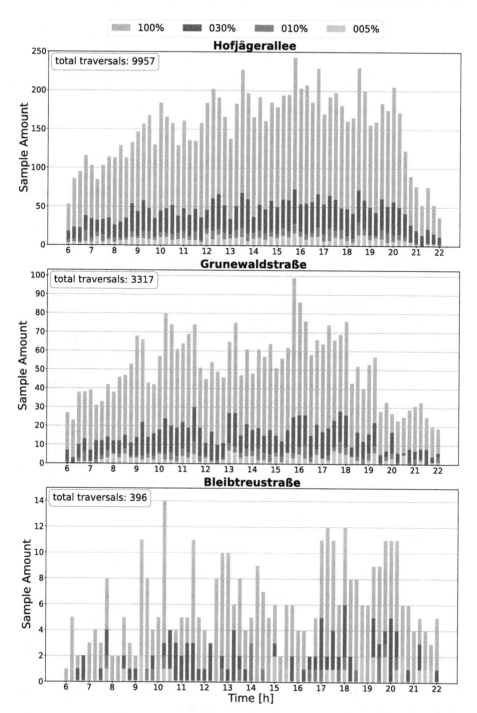

Fig. 7. Samples collected using Floating Car Data aggregated over 15 min intervals for the street segments highlighted in Fig. 4.

Table 2. Measured mean speeds on inspected roads averaged from 6 am to 10 pm.

street	$\bar{V}_{\mathrm{GT}}$	$\bar{V}_{\mathrm{TMS}}$	$\bar{V}_{\mathrm{SMS}}$	$\bar{V}_{\mathrm{temporal}}$	$\bar{V}_{\mathrm{spatial}}$
Hofjägeralle	$47.3\,\frac{\mathrm{km}}{\mathrm{h}}$	$48.7\,\frac{\mathrm{km}}{\mathrm{h}}$	$47.7\,\frac{\mathrm{km}}{\mathrm{h}}$	$48.0\,\frac{\mathrm{km}}{\mathrm{h}}$	$47.9\,\frac{\mathrm{km}}{\mathrm{h}}$
Grunewaldstraße	$40.9\,\frac{\mathrm{km}}{\mathrm{h}}$	$49.0\,\frac{\mathrm{km}}{\mathrm{h}}$	$48.0\,\frac{\mathrm{km}}{\mathrm{h}}$	$40.9\,\frac{\mathrm{km}}{\mathrm{h}}$	$46.3\,\frac{\mathrm{km}}{\mathrm{h}}$
Bleibtreustraße	$22.4\,\frac{\mathrm{km}}{\mathrm{h}}$	$28.6\,\frac{\mathrm{km}}{\mathrm{h}}$	$28.4\,\frac{\mathrm{km}}{\mathrm{h}}$	$23.2\,\frac{\mathrm{km}}{\mathrm{h}}$	$27.2\,\frac{\mathrm{km}}{\mathrm{h}}$

It is evident that the road type and thereby the amount of recorded traversal have a large impact on estimation quality. On the Hofjägerallee even with penetration rates as low as 5% decent estimation is still possible. The Grunewaldstraße on the other hand, seems to reach its threshold between 10% and 5% with more outliers and unsampled intervals. Compared to that, the system fails to collect enough samples on the Bleibtreustraße to get a meaningful speed estimate even at penetration rates around 30%. The acquired estimates at market penetrations of 10% and 5% are only sparsely usable. On the Hofjägeralle and the Grunewaldstraße, the number of outliers increases with decreasing penetration rates and even at 10% we start to see outliers with a significant magnitude. The cited penetration rate thresholds for highway speed estimation of 5% to 10% can only be applied to the Hofjägerallee, due to its highway-like character. On the other two streets, measures based on basic FCD reach their limit sooner.

Figure 7 offers more detailed insights into why a meaningful speed estimation might not be possible at lower penetration rates. While both the Hofjägerallee and the Grunewaldstraße are traversed thousands of times throughout the day, the Bleibtreustraße is only traversed 400 times with intervals where merely two traversals are recorded. This makes it highly unlikely for a CV to traverse the Bleibtreustraße even at penetration rates as high as 30%. Usually, as roads like the Bleibtreustraße don't experience large traffic volumes anyway, less frequent samples aren't influential. Yet, for use cases like incident detection consistent sampling becomes more relevant.

4.4 Summary

To summarize the results, we demonstrated that the published application suite can act as a basis for a simulative assessment of TSE systems, delivering expected results for implemented metrics. We found that on large, heavily frequented roads (e.g., Hofjägerstraße, and highways) loop detectors can deliver decent results and might be worth the investments. However, on these roads, very comparable results can be achieved even with a low market penetration of CVs. Speed estimation on highly frequented, signalized urban street segments is more difficult as speeds fluctuate between and within traversals. Single loop detectors fail to produce proper speed estimations, while an FCD-based solution can still closely reconstruct the actual mean speed on those edges. On smaller, less frequented edges both loop detectors as well FCD-based approaches face difficulties. Despite that, even small amounts of FCD can give an insight into the traffic state throughout the day, while no traffic agency would consider loop detector installation on such roads due to costs. Consequently, for smaller roads, the relevancy of a constantly available TSE has to be considered. For these roads, little traffic is expected anyway and obstructions are rare, meaning that most of the time it is possible to accelerate close to the speed limit and an estimation is not required regardless. However, if a major incident happens even on a smaller road, users would expect a timely reaction by the TSE system to circumnavigate the afflicted area.

5   Conclusion and Outlook

In this paper, we initially offered a review of existing speed metrics for Traffic State Estimation (TSE) and categorized the challenges one faces when considering complex urban environments compared to highways. Due to much larger fluctuations in individual vehicle behavior, metrics have to be chosen more carefully and potentially from multiple sensor sources for urban applications.

Nonetheless, mean speed estimations always offer insights about the traffic state and are highly important for urban TSE. We identified different commonly used sensor modalities, which lead to different mean speed measures as different assumptions have to be made when aggregating lossy data from sensors. We classified the *Time Mean Speed* and the *Space Mean Speed* as common derivations when dealing with induction loop data. More recent applications based on Floating Car Data often rely on curve-fitted approaches, for which we identified the *Temporal Mean Speed* and *Spatial Mean Speed*, derived from the work of Yoon et al. [14].

To empirically test these measures, we pursued a simulation approach (see Sect. 4), utilizing the strengths of Eclipse MOSAIC [3]. We developed an open-source MOSAIC application suite to calculate the aforementioned mean speed metrics for any traffic scenario. The code for these applications is published on GitHub[1], together with configuration files for a simulation setup within the Charlottenburg area of the BeST scenario [11].

Based on the published resources, we conducted a comparative study with urban traffic demand provided by the BeST scenario. We found that inner city speed estimations are dependent on the road that they are measured on. The length, speed limit, lane amount, and traffic signal occurrence at the end heavily influence the magnitude of realizable speeds as well as the variability. Time and space mean speed measured by single loop detectors often fail to capture the latter, as these are limited to a single observation point.

We furthermore showed that FCD-based approaches like the temporal and spatial mean speed are better at capturing the characteristics of entire road segments. As FCD-based systems rely on vehicles as mobile sensors, the equipment rate has to be considered. Our study showed that at rates lower than 15% only partial observations can be made, especially on smaller roads. In the future, we

---

[1] https://github.com/mosaic-addons/traffic-state-estimation.

aim to tackle this research question by enriching the FCD set to improve the data quality and enable smaller fleets to provide a sensible TSE. Concisely, we aim to utilize additional information from perception sensors.

Furthermore, a large-scale, scenario-wide evaluation of implemented TSE metrics is of high importance. While initial efforts have been made in that direction, finding appropriate assessment strategies is a non-trivial task due to the heterogeneous nature of traffic patterns, both in spatial and temporal regards. In addition, we aim to construct and study scenarios with disruptive traffic patterns (e.g., incidents, second-row parking, etc.) in more detail as these are often most relevant for road users and should be detected by any form of TSE.

Acknowledgment. This work was supported by the KIS'M project through the German Federal Ministry for Economic Affairs and Climate Action under grant 45AVF3001E.

References

1. Blokpoel, R.J., Krajzewicz, D., Nippold, R.: Unambiguous metrics for evaluation of traffic networks. In: 13th International IEEE Conference on Intelligent Transportation Systems, pp. 1277–1282. IEEE (2010)
2. Brakatsoulas, S., Pfoser, D., Salas, R., Wenk, C.: On map-matching vehicle tracking data. In: Proceedings of the 31st International Conference on Very Large Data Bases, pp. 853–864 (2005)
3. Eclipse MOSAIC Core Team: Eclipse MOSAIC: A Multi-Domain and Multi-Scale Simulation Framework for Connected and Automated Mobility (2023). https://eclipse.dev/mosaic
4. Ferman, M.A., Blumenfeld, D.E., Dai, X.: An analytical evaluation of a real-time traffic information system using probe vehicles. In: Intelligent Transportation Systems, vol. 9, pp. 23–34. Taylor & Francis (2005)
5. Helbing, D.: Verkehrsdynamik: neue physikalische Modellierungskonzepte. Springer, Cham (2013)
6. Kashinath, S.A., et al.: Review of data fusion methods for real-time and multi-sensor traffic flow analysis. IEEE Access **9**, 51258–51276 (2021)
7. Knoop, V.L.: Introduction to traffic flow theory: an introduction with exercises. Delft University of Technology, Delft, The Netherlands (2017)
8. Lopez, P.A., et al.: Microscopic traffic simulation using sumo. In: 2018 21st International Conference on Intelligent Transportation Systems (ITSC), pp. 2575–2582. IEEE (2018)
9. Schäfer, R.P., Thiessenhusen, K.U., Brockfeld, E., Wagner, P.: A traffic information system by means of real-time floating-car data, vol. 11 (2002)
10. Schrab, K., et al.: Modeling an its management solution for mixed highway traffic with eclipse mosaic. IEEE Trans. Intell. Transp. Syst. **24**(6), 6575–6585 (2023). https://doi.org/10.1109/TITS.2022.3204174
11. Schrab, K., Protzmann, R., Radusch, I.: A large-scale traffic scenario of berlin for evaluating smart mobility applications. In: Nathanail, E.G., Gavanas, N., Adamos, G. (eds.) CSUM 2022. LNITI, pp. 276–287. Springer, Cham (2023). https://doi.org/10.1007/978-3-031-23721-8_24

12. Treiber, M., Kesting, A.: Traffic Flow Dynamics: Data, pp. 983–1000. Models and Simulation, Springer, Heidelberg (2013). https://doi.org/10.1007/978-3-642-32460-4
13. Xing, J., Wu, W., Cheng, Q., Liu, R.: Traffic state estimation of urban road networks by multi-source data fusion: review and new insights. Phys. A **595**, 127079 (2022)
14. Yoon, J., Noble, B., Liu, M.: Surface street traffic estimation. In: Proceedings of the 5th International Conference on Mobile Systems, Applications and Services, pp. 220–232 (2007)

Integrating Efficient Routes with Station Monitoring for Electric Vehicles in Urban Environments: Simulation and Analysis

David Ragel-Díaz-Jara[1]([✉]), José-Luis Guisado-Lizar[1,2][iD],
Fernando Diaz-del-Rio[1,2], María-José Morón-Fernández[1,2],
Daniel Cagigas-Muñiz[1,2], Daniel Cascado-Caballero[1,2][iD],
Gabriel Jiménez-Moreno[1,2], and Elena Cerezuela-Escudero[1,2]

[1] Department of Computer Architecture and Technology, Universidad de Sevilla,
Avenida Reina Mercedes s/n, 41012 Sevilla, Spain
dragel@us.es
[2] Research Institute of Computer Engineering (I3US), Universidad de Sevilla,
Avenida Reina Mercedes s/n, 41012 Sevilla, Spain

Abstract. The electrification of road transportation requires the development of an extensive infrastructure of public charging stations (CSs). In order to avoid them contributing to increased traffic congestion and air pollution in a city, it is very important to optimize their deployment. To tackle this challenge, we present microscopic traffic simulations with a hybrid cellular automata and agent-based model to study different strategies to route electric vehicles (EVs) to CSs, when their battery level is low. EVs and CSs are modeled as agents with capability to demonstrate complex behaviors. Our models take into account the complex nature of traffic and decisions about routes and their predicted behavior. We show that a synthetic city is very useful for investigating the routing behavior and traffic patterns. We have found that a smart routing strategy can contribute to balancing the distribution of EVs among the different CSs in a distributed network, which is the CS layout that produces less traffic congestion. Contrary to our initial expectations, ensuring a balanced distribution throughout the city did not necessarily result in an increase in overall productivity. This observation led to a deeper exploration of the nuances of urban transport dynamics. Furthermore, our study emphasizes the superiority of time-based routing over its distance-based counterpart and highlights the inherent limitations of transportation within a city.

Keywords: Electric Vehicle · Charging · Infrastructure Deployment · Modeling · Simulation

This work is part of the project SANEVEC TED2021-130825B-I00, funded by the Ministerio de Ciencia e Innovación (MCIN), Agencia Estatal de Investigación (AEI) of Spain, MCIN/AEI/10.13039/501100011033, and by the European Union NextGenerationEU/PRTR.

J.-L. Guisado-Lizar et al. (Eds.): SIMUtools 2023, LNICST 519, pp. 166–181, 2024.
https://doi.org/10.1007/978-3-031-57523-5_13

1   Introduction

The transportation sector is responsible for a substantial share of the total carbon dioxide CO_2 equivalents released into the atmosphere. Such greenhouse gas emissions are the cause behind the current global climate crisis, posing a formidable challenge to humanity. Within transportation, road vehicles, which play a major role in our daily mobility, are a significant contributors to this phenomenon. In response to this pressing issue, a shift toward electric vehicles (EVs) is being carried out at a global level. This electrification of road transportation needs the development of an extensive public charging infrastructure. Forecasts for the year 2030 indicate a significant surge in the demand for public charging stations (CSs), far surpassing the current figures. For example, a study conducted by the International Energy Agency indicates that electric vehicles are expected to constitute approximately 55% of all transportation modalities in Europe by 2030 in the existing policies scenario, taking into account different types of vehicles [10].

It is important to optimize the deployment of CSs in a city to avoid them from contributing to increased traffic congestion. In this context, the SANEVEC research project ("A simulation approach to determine the deployment of an urban network of electric vehicle charging stations for environmental and social benefits"), https://grupo.us.es/sanevec/en, funded by the Ministry of Science and Innovation of Spain and by the European Union under the NextGenerationEU program, aims to use simulations and artificial intelligence techniques in order to research, design and implement a computer simulation model to predict the effects of the layout of an urban network of EV CSs on the following aspects of a real city: traffic congestion, air-quality, carbon footprint, and electric grid usage.

Some of the starting hypotheses of the SANEVEC project were established and studied in [6]. In that work, a hybrid microscopic simulation model, based on cellular automata and agent-based modeling, was introduced, which can simulate the behavior of individual vehicles, including EVs and internal combustion engine vehicles (ICEVs), and also the operation of CSs. In that model, each EV is modeled as an agent incorporating a complex behavior involving decisions about factors such as the specific destination of each vehicle, the route to follow, how to navigate there taking into account the local traffic state, when to drive to a CS to recharge the battery, and what station to drive to. A simulator called SIMTRAVEL [7] was also presented and used to study the effects on traffic of different dispositions of CSs in a synthetic city. It was found that the distribution of small or medium-size CSs distributed throughout the city is better than a large central station (or a few of them) in terms of their effect on traffic congestion. However, a drawback was also found: in the distributed CS scenario, there is an uneven distribution of EVs across various stations, leading to saturation at some stations while others retain available chargers. Accordingly, as vehicle density scales, the average queuing time for EVs at a CS, awaiting an available charger, exceeds that observed at a singular, larger station.

In this work, we study different routing strategies to route EVs to CSs when they need to recharge their batteries, using a simulator called PYSIMTRAVEL3 [15], which is based on the previous SIMTRAVEL simulator. Possible strategies could range from deploying informational signs indicating the occupancy of each CS to instituting an intelligent traffic management system that communicates directly with EVs or their users. The objective is to find strategies that can balance the distribution of EVs across different small or medium-size CSs scattered across the city, so that the benefit of distributed CSs (minimizing traffic congestion in the city) can be obtained without the drawback found in the previous study (uneven distribution of EVs across CSs).

The remainder of the paper is organized as follows. Section 2 presents related work. Section 3 describes the methodology. The results are presented in Sect. 4. Finally, Sect. 5 presents the conclusions and future research directions.

2   Related Works

In recent years, many research works have been devoted to this topic due to its importance. For instance, in [5], an optimal allocation problem for charging stations in freight transport is formulated as an NP-hard optimization problem (specifically a Location Set Covering Problem), and tackled using an open-source optimization Python library (spopt). They used a dataset of GPS tracking data collected from a fleet of 61 freight vehicles operating during six months. In the work [9], a multi-period bi-objective optimization model is presented to provide optimal solutions for the placement of charging stations. In [3], the optimal placement and sizing of fast and slow CSs is studied as an optimization problem, in which the cost is determined by CS placement parameters (installation, operation and travel time cost) and penalties for violating power grid constraints. They employed a hybrid evolutionary algorithm combining a chicken swarm optimization and a teaching-learning-based optimization algorithm. In the work [13], GPS-enabled trajectory data were used for the location of CSs, with the objective of minimizing the CO_2 emissions, employing a genetic algorithm. Nonetheless a significant portion of these studies overlook the impact of charging station locations on road congestion. Many also base their analyses on aggregated trajectories of conventional fuel vehicles, neglecting changes that electric vehicles might introduce in driving behaviors.

Our approach is to tackle this challenge by directly simulating traffic using microscopic models. These models individually represent each vehicle and forecast its behavior in response to surrounding vehicular dynamics.

Two main types of microscopic models have been used for traffic: cellular automata (CA) and agent-based models (ABM).

CA are mathematical constructs characterized by their discrete spatial and temporal nature, local interactions, and synchronous parallel dynamic evolution [11]. Their application in modeling vehicle traffic can be traced back to the efforts of K. Nagel and M. Schreckenberg [14], followed by B. Chopard et al. [4], X.G. Li [12], and Y. Zheng [21], among others. In terms of electric vehicle considerations,

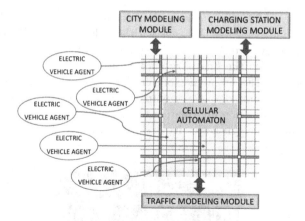

Fig. 1. The simulation model is based on a cellular automaton that represents city roads. EVs are agents that occupy one cell, and in the next time step can move to another nearby cell. CSs are also agents located in a road cell.

Xiang et al. [19] utilized a CA model to evaluate electric demand at a charging station for different traffic flows. However, the scope of their model was somewhat restrictive, including only one road, one intersection, and one charging station. Consequently, they did not examine the impact of the charging station network on traffic patterns.

On the other hand, ABMs simulate the behaviors and interplays of individual components termed agents. Notable examples of the application of ABM in traffic studies include the work of Chen [1] and Waraich [17]. The study by Viswanathan et al. [16] employed an ABM model to explore the optimal placement of charging stations. However, in this work, vehicles followed fixed routes (based on daily traffic data) from a starting point to a destination, compromising its realism. The study by Zhai et al. [20] might be the closest in methodology to our work. They used a hybrid CA-ABM model, but it was not a microscopic model. Each cell was defined as a stretch of a 1 km road that holds multiple cars. Such a coarse-grained model cannot capture intricate traffic dynamics observed in actual urban settings and emergent properties of traffic as a complex system, such as traffic jams, and how they affect traffic density and charging demand.

3   Methodology

Our study employs a cellular automata and agent-based microscopic hybrid model, which was previously introduced in [6]. An implementation of the model has been carried out on the PYSIMTRAVEL3 simulator [15], which is an evolutionized version of the previous SIMTRAVEL simulator [7]. The structure of the simulation model is depicted graphically in Fig. 1. Modelling of the city is based on a cellular automaton.

The city is a square, synthetic, and regular 2D grid of interconnected cells representing streets and vehicles moving through them, useful for investigating routing behavior and traffic patterns that occur in a real city. Therefore, the city roads are divided into square cells with a width of 5 m. The cell state can be either occupied by a vehicle or non-occupied. In this case, periodic boundary conditions are used, so the final structure adopts a 2D toroidal shape, but for future developments, the actual map of a city can be mapped by raster processing onto the 2D mesh proposed above or onto a 1D vector with components capable of storing spatial connection information to emulate the topology of the real city. A representation of the synthetic city is shown in Fig. 2.

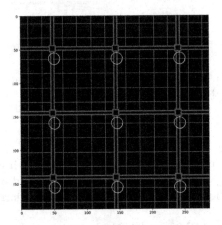

Fig. 2. Road map of the synthetic city showing the location of the 9 CSs. The city includes single lane streets, avenues with two lanes on each direction, and roundabouts with two lanes.

Properties of city cells are inspired by the works of Chopard et al. [2,4]. The city model is built by joining together different tiles (groups of cells), forming different structures. There are different elements in a tile:

- Streets: roads formed by linear configurations of cells in a particular direction, establishing one lane. They can be oriented toward the north, south, east, or west.
- Avenues: bidirectional roads with two lanes of cells for each direction. Vehicle speed in avenues is higher than in streets.
- Intersections: The junctions formed at the convergence of two streets.
- Roundabouts: Established at the nexus of two avenues, they incorporate a central rotational segment of varying radius, with multiple input and output points.

We assume that the energy usage of an EV is directly proportional to speed, following the study by Wu et al. [18], which identified an approximately linear correlation between an EV's power consumption and speed for velocities below 50 km/h. With this premise, on typical streets, EVs move forward by 1 cell when the next cell is unoccupied, depleting 1 unit of their battery energy. On avenues, they advance by 2 cells per time step, consuming 2 energy units.

A snapshot of a typical simulation is shown in Fig. 3. The color codes are shown in Table 1.

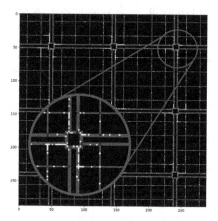

Fig. 3. Snapshot of a simulation of the city with a density of 10% of EVs

Vehicles are modeled as agents with the capability to demonstrate various complex behaviors, including making decisions about routes, recognizing when to visit a CS based on battery levels, and choosing a specific CS. At each step of the simulation, each EV (and thus each agent associated with an EV) evaluates its environment by obtaining information from the 2D matrix representing the current state of the city (own state and location, location of other EVs, remaining energy, route to the assigned target) and produces its next state and next location, which are stored in the 2D matrix representing the next state of the city. Each vehicle occupies a cell and navigates the city governed by a finite state machine. In this work, all vehicles are considered electric vehicles (EVs).

A second type of agents are CSs. The objective of this work centers on tackling challenges associated with the positioning of stations, the dynamics of EV movements, and the charging durations. Therefore, we consider underground CSs, and avoid modeling a queue of vehicles building up on the road outside a station. In this way, CSs are conceptualized as distinct roadway cells that neither consume tangible physical space nor allow vehicles within them to be seen

Table 1. Meaning of color codes for the simulation snapshot shown in Fig. 3

Green	A one-way street
Blue	A street with a bifurcation
Yellow	Charging Station (CS)
White	A car
Red	Safety distance

by external traffic. This design assumes endless capacity for vehicles awaiting or undergoing charging. The time it takes vehicles to recharge within a station depends on the power of the chargers. When every charger at a station is in use, vehicles wait in a queue inside a subterranean facility located under the CS.

At the start of the simulation, each vehicle is assigned a sequence of random cells as targets. In order to ensure repeatability, a single seed for random numbers is taken for the whole program.

More details of the cellular automata and agent-based microscopic hybrid model can be found in [6]. In that work, it was found that a distributed layout of CSs is better than a single large central station in terms of its effect on traffic patterns, because traffic is more fluid. However, a drawback was also found: the distribution of EVs among the different CSs in a distributed layout was not well balanced, so that some stations become saturated, while other ones still have free chargers. As a consequence, it was also found that the time spent by EVs queuing in the CS while waiting for a free charger is higher than for a single station. Therefore, it is important to use smarter routing strategies to balance the distribution of EVs among the different CSs in the distributed network. In the work cited, each EV simply randomly chose the CS to which it would drive when the battery is low.

In the present work, we tackle this problem by studying the effect of different EV routing strategies to CSs. We compare the occupancy of CSs to assess if their usage is well-balanced, i.e., whether the occupancy levels of different distributed CSs (total number of vehicles in the queue) are similar. We also evaluate the effectiveness of the strategies using additional metrics, including productivity. In this context, productivity is defined as the average number of electric vehicles that reach their destination per step in a simulation. This is calculated by dividing the total number of EVs that arrive at their destination by the total number of simulated steps.

We consider the following routing strategies:

1. "Distance": Distance to the CS throughout the shorter path.
2. "Time": Time needed to arrive at the station and obtain a charger.

We do not consider the strategy used in [6] of randomly choosing the CS to which to drive, since it is obviously worse than the strategies considered in this work. The foundation of routing strategies is an A* algorithm [8] that uses heuristics to decide between the various branches it explores. In the Time-based algorithm, the average occupancy of the cells along the route is utilized as a primary determinant. Instead of relying on maximum road speeds, which do not account for dynamic traffic conditions, the average cell occupancy is used. A higher occupancy implies a slower speed, and conversely, a lower occupancy suggests a faster speed.

After trying various heuristics, we opted to use the following one. To ensure that this average occupancy remains dynamic, an exponential moving average (EMA) has been adopted. The EMA has a weight w that modulates the consideration of past data; thus, it is called here "Past Cell Occupancy Weight" (PCOW) or Exponential Weight. In our simulations, two forgetting PCOW factors have been evaluated: 0.5 (which emphasizes the recent information) and 0.95 (which gives more significance to the historical data). The aggregate occupancy of a route leads to good productivity. The heuristic occupancy can be represented by the equation:

$$O_n = w \times O_{n-1} + (1 - w) \times C_n \qquad (1)$$

where:

$$O_n : \text{Heuristic Occupancy at time } n$$
$$O_{n-1} : \text{Heuristic Occupancy at time } n - 1$$
$$C_n : \text{Current Occupancy at time } n$$
$$w : \text{weight}$$

Here, the current occupancy is defined as 0 if there is no vehicle, 1 if there is a vehicle, and $1/speed$ if a vehicle has passed at time n.

We also consider adding the time it would take to be served at the CS. Therefore, it was assumed that a percentage of vehicles use a real-time information system and take that information into account to choose, among the closest CSs, the one that offers the shortest combined travel and waiting time. The term "CS queue query" has been employed here for this percentage. This suggests that they have the ability to utilize an Internet of Things (IoT) application, mobile app, or web service, thus enabling monitoring of the occupancy of nearby CSs.

The possible states of a vehicle in each time step are described in Table 2.

Initially, a sufficient number of vehicles are introduced into the CSs to ensure that the system is in energy balance. That is, the energy received by cars at the chargers should be the same as that of cars still in circulation. In this way, transient states are minimized. Obviously, if a vehicle initially does not have enough energy to reach the nearest CS, it is introduced forcibly.

We perform comprehensive studies, varying parameter configurations, aiming to compare the occupancy of charging stations to assess if their usage is well balanced, and to evaluate the productivity of the simulations. Therefore, for each simulation, we generate two types of partial results:

Table 2. Description of vehicle states.

State	Description
Driving	The vehicle drives without any issues towards its destination
Waiting	The vehicle had to stop due to non-fluid traffic
Destination	The vehicle reaches its destination and remains there for a unit of time
ToCharging	The vehicle is heading to the CS
Queuing	The vehicle enters the CS and queues, waiting for an available plug
Charging	The vehicle is at the CS, charging

– Standard deviation of the queues at the CSs, used to determine if the system is well-balanced (Fig. 5).
– Productivity, which serves as an indicator of the overall performance of the city.

4   Results

We performed tests using a city with six avenues, and with a distributed CS layout composed of 9 evenly distributed stations. Five parameters have been considered in the simulation, and their values can be seen in Table 3.

We carried out experiments with two routing strategies: Distance and Time. Traffic density is the percentage of occupied road cells (that is, containing a vehicle). The "CS Queue Query" and PCOW were previously discussed in the methodology section. The last two parameters only make sense if the strategy is based on Time. The "Number of chargers per charging station" leads to scenarios where available energy ranges from scarce to abundant.

For each parameter configuration, five simulations were conducted with different random seeds. In total, there are 690 simulations ($5 \times 3 \times 2 \times 11 \times 2 + 5 \times 3 \times 2$). For each experiment, we generated two types of results: standard deviation of the queues and productivity, of which we introduce some examples below. We begin by first showcasing a few example graphs from the simulations, followed by aggregate data charts and parameter cross-reference graphs.

The first set of graphs depicts the state of the vehicles throughout the simulation execution. Some basic principles that have been followed along the simulations are the following: 1) Ideally, all EVs should be in the "driving" state, but there should be a constant percentage of EVs in "charging". 2) There are two elements that disrupt this ideal scenario: On the one hand, if there is an energy deficit, we will see the "queuing" segment increase; on the other hand, if traffic becomes congested, the "waiting" segment will grow. 3) When a car reaches its destination, blue dots (labeled "Destination") appear at the bottom. These are hard to spot because of their low frequency, but they are crucial for measuring the simulation's productivity.

The evolution of the number of vehicles in each possible state throughout a simulation under three different scenarios (a stable situation, an energy deficit,

Table 3. Simulation Parameters

Parameter	Values
Strategy	Distance, Time
Number of chargers per charging station	1, 5, 10
Traffic density (percentage of occupied road cells)	5%, 10%
CS Queue Query	0, 0.1, 0.2, 0.3, 0.4, 0.5, 0.6, 0.7, 0.8, 0.9, 1
PCOW	0.5, 0.95

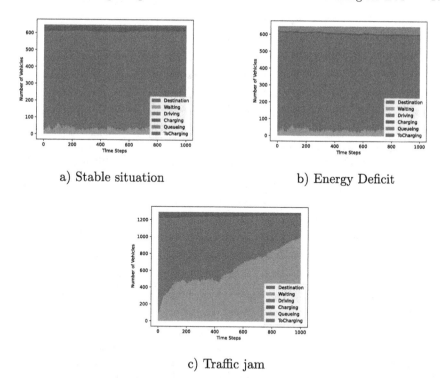

a) Stable situation   b) Energy Deficit

c) Traffic jam

Fig. 4. Evolution of the number of vehicles in each possible state across a simulation for three different situations: a) Stable situation. b) Energy deficit. c) Traffic jam. Parameter values: a): Seed:90. Chargers/CS: 5, Method: Time, Queue Query: 0.1, Traffic Density: 0.05, Exponential Weight: 0.5. b): Seed: 90, Chargers/CS: 1, Method: Time, Queue Query: 0.3, Traffic Density: 0.05, Exponential Weight: 0.5. c): Seed: 12, Chargers/CS: 10, Method: Time, Queue Query: 0.6, Traffic Density: 0.1, Exponential Weight: 0.95

and a congestion situation) is shown in Fig. 4. The results correspond well to the aforementioned principles.

In Figs. 6 and 7, we can see the behavior of traffic density. Strategies based on distance do not have the CS Queue Query parameter, so they are represented as a single point. We can observe that the time-based strategies are superior to the distance-based ones, and although in aggregate terms CS Queue Query does not improve productivity, it does improve the distribution of the queues. We highlight that at 0%, the queue in the distance-based version is better. Therefore, it is essential to combine time-based routing with CS Queue Query.

We can also observe the change in productivity with the density of traffic. If the roads had unlimited capacity, one would expect that productivity would be doubled when density is doubled. We can see in Fig. 6 that this is not what our simulations show. Productivity with a traffic density of 10% is only slightly

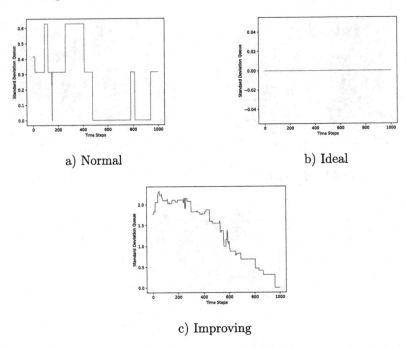

a) Normal   b) Ideal

c) Improving

Fig. 5. Evolution of the standard deviation of the queue occupancy size of the 9 charging stations (CS) in the city throughout the simulation, the x-axis is the time divided by discrete steps, for three different situations: a) Normal, b) Ideal, c) Improving. Parameter values: a): Seed: 34, Chargers/CS: 5, Method: Time, Queue Query: 0.9, Density: 0.05, Exponential Weight: 0.95. b): Seed: 90, Chargers/CS: 10, Method: Time, Queue Query: 0.8, Density: 0.1, Exponential Weight: 0.95. c): Seed: 12, Chargers/CS: 5, Method: Time, Queue Query: 0.7, Density: 0.1, Exponential Weight: 0.95.

better than for a traffic density of 5%, suggesting that the simulated roads have limited transport capacity.

On the other hand, we can see in Fig. 7 that standard deviation of queues is indeed proportional to the traffic density. We can also observe in Figs. 6 and 7 the effect of the CS Queue Query parameter, which indicates the percentage of vehicles that query the queue information system for routing. We can see that the productivity does not benefit from this query. On the other hand, the CS queue balance does improve substantially when CS Queue Query parameter is high. However, a larger improvement is found for low values of this parameter. Therefore, if one is considering the implementation of an information system, there is no need to worry about the adoption rate: a minimal usage percentage can already produce a discernible impact on the equilibrium of the queues at the charging stations.

In Figs. 8 and 9 we can see how the PCOW A * parameter, which calculates cell occupancy, influences the indicators under study.

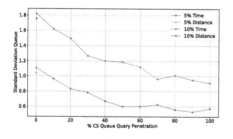

Fig. 6. Study of Queue Distribution. (Color figure online)

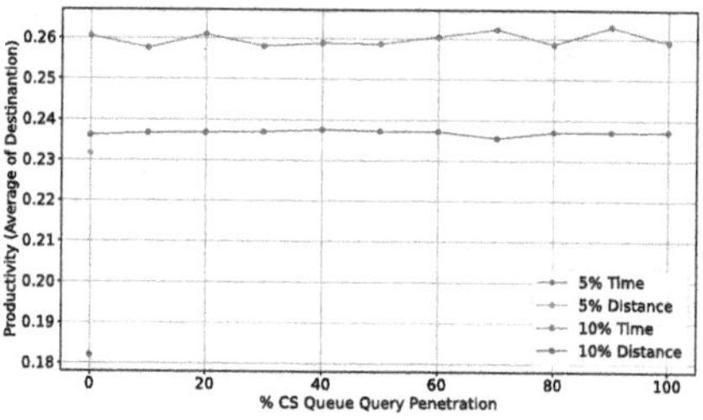

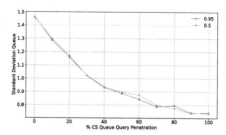

Fig. 7. Study of Productivity. (Color figure online)

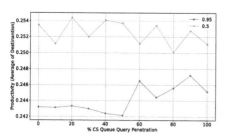

Fig. 8. Productivity for two different values of the PCOW A* parameter (Time Only) (Color figure online)

Fig. 9. Queue Standard Deviation for two different values of the PCOW A* parameter (Time Only) (Color figure online)

The smallest value (0.5, orange) indicates that the update period is shorter, that is, the update is happening more quickly. This value leads to better productivity.

Once again, we observe in Fig. 8 that productivity is not influenced by the number of charging plugs, just as it was the case with traffic density. This is represented in the graphs as horizontal lines. This result suggests that productivity is independent of the queue distribution. At the end of the study, we addressed this issue.

On the other hand, we can see that the standard deviation of the queues (Fig. 9) is not affected by the PCOW A* parameter (the two lines are one above the other).

Finally, we will study the energy restriction. The fewer chargers there are, the greater the energy restriction. More chargers mean more energy, and queues will be shorter. What is the impact of the number of chargers per CS? And its relationship with the CS queue query?

In terms of productivity, Fig. 10(a), we do not observe an improvement when having more charging plugs. It seems that when there is an energy deficit, cars are taken out of circulation, and productivity increases.

However, in terms of queues, Fig. 10(b), when there are fewer chargers (10), the standard deviation is lower because there are fewer vehicles. A possible

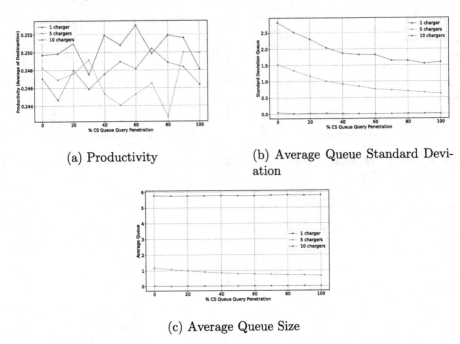

(a) Productivity

(b) Average Queue Standard Deviation

(c) Average Queue Size

Fig. 10. Analysis of energy restrictions based on the number of chargers per charging station (CS) using different metrics

explanation for this might come from queue theory. Under the M/M/1 model, the queue size follows an exponential distribution. However, when estimating the standard deviation of the queue size based on small samples, we tend to underestimate its true value due to the inherent bias of the exponential distribution.

Obviously, when there is an energy deficit as in Fig. 10(c), the average queue sizes are larger. This effect does not occur with 10 chargers; in fact, in this case there are no queues.

In the end, after noting the independence between the distribution of queues and productivity, our aim was to examine the effect of the CS queue query on productivity, as shown in Fig. 11. It is clear that the slope is positive, meaning that as the CS queue query increases, so does productivity. However, the coefficient of determination remains low, indicating that the CS queue query alone does not explain much of the variability in productivity.

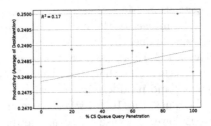

Fig. 11. Productivity vs CS Queue Query Penetration

5   Conclusions and Future Work

We have employed the PYSIMTRAVEL3 simulator, that implements a hybrid cellular automata and agent-based microscopic model. Compared to previous works, this simulator provides microscopic modeling that considers the effects of complex traffic patterns in cities (traffic jams, intersections), unlike previous works that were either limited in the topologies of the cities they can simulate or in the modeling of microscopic traffic effects. In this work, we have used simulations to study different routing strategies for electric vehicles. When the battery level was low, these movements were to the charging stations. We have studied two different strategies, taking into account distance to the CS throughout the shorter path, and time needed to arrive at the station and obtain a charger. In the time strategy, we have taken into account present and past dynamic traffic conditions through the route, and waiting queues at the stations, which can be queried by the vehicles through a real-time information system.

Our initial objective was to balance the distribution of queues in the charging stations as a global improvement strategy. We have found that the better strategy (time) is effective in balancing the queues. However, to our surprise, this did not lead to increased productivity (defined as the average number of electric vehicles that reach their destination per step in a simulation). Answering one question often raises more questions, and while we still believe that reducing the standard deviation in queues is crucial for a more uniform user experience, it raises new questions about transport capacity of the city.

From a policy perspective, implementing a system that queries a real-time information system to obtain information about the current CS queues can enhance the average user experience. To boost productivity, routing services that integrate both traffic and waiting times are essential. Even a slight penetration of such services results in noticeable improvements, and this becomes even more critical during energy deficits or peak hours.

Some key conclusions include:

- Time-based routing is more effective than distance-based.
- CS Queue Query generally balances out the queues, especially during energy deficits, but does not necessarily improve system productivity.
- There seems to be an inherent transport (or production) capacity in the city that is hard to surpass.
- Productivity is mainly improved by adjusting the routing parameters. CS Queue Query's impact on productivity is minor, but it provides a better average service for users.

For future research, we propose:

- Exploring the use of traffic lights to evaluate productivity (i.e., the capacity to increase traffic).
- Analyzing the impact of not only checking the availability of a CS slot, but also scheduling a reservation.

- Studying city topologies in relation to their electrification and solar panel setups.
- Delving into more advanced energy models instead of focusing solely on productivity.
- Adding a rasterization processes in order to simulate realistic city maps using the two-dimensional matrix proposed in this work.
- Performing simulations using real cities and not just synthetic models.

References

1. Chen, B., Cheng, H.H.: A review of the applications of agent technology in traffic and transportation systems. IEEE Trans. Intell. Transp. Syst. **11**, 485–497 (2010). https://doi.org/10.1109/TITS.2010.2048313
2. Chopard, B., Luthi, P.O., Queloz, P.A.: Cellular automata model of car traffic in a two-dimensional street network. J. Phys. A: Math. Gen. **29**(10), 2325–2336 (1996). https://doi.org/10.1088/0305-4470/29/10/012
3. Deb, S., Gao, X.Z., Tammi, K., Kalita, K., Mahanta, P.: A novel chicken swarm and teaching learning based algorithm for electric vehicle charging station placement problem. Energy **220**, 119645 (2021). https://doi.org/10.1016/j.energy.2020.119645
4. Dupuis, A., Chopard, B.: Parallel simulation of traffic in Geneva using cellular automata. In: Virtual Shared Memory for Distributed Architectures, pp. 89–107. Nova Science (2001)
5. Fu, J., Bhatti, H.J., Eek, M.: Optimization of freight charging infrastructure placement using multiday travel data. In: 2023 IEEE 26th International Conference on Intelligent Transportation Systems (ITSC). IEEE (2023)
6. García-Suárez, A., Guisado-Lizar, J.L., Diaz-Del-rio, F., Jiménez-Morales, F.: A cellular automata agent-based hybrid simulation tool to analyze the deployment of electric vehicle charging stations. Sustainability **13** (2021). https://doi.org/10.3390/su13105421
7. García-Suárez, A., Guisado-Lizar, J.L., del Rio, F.D., Jiménez-Morales, F.: Simtravel: Urban traffic simulator based on a hybrid cellular automata and agent-based model (2021). https://github.com/amarogs/simtravel
8. Hart, P.E., Nilsson, N.J., Raphael, B.: A formal basis for the heuristic determination of minimum cost paths. IEEE Trans. Syst. Sci. Cybern. **4**(2), 100–107 (1968). https://doi.org/10.1109/TSSC.1968.300136
9. He, M., Krishnakumari, P., Luo, D., Chen, J.: A data-driven integrated framework for fast-charging facility planning using multi-period bi-objective optimization. In: 2023 IEEE 26th International Conference on Intelligent Transportation Systems (ITSC). IEEE (2023)
10. International Energy Agency: Global EV Outlook 2023 (2023). https://www.iea.org/reports/global-ev-outlook-2023
11. Kroc, J., Jimenez-Morales, F., Guisado, J.L., Lemos, M.C., Tkac, J.: Building efficient computational cellular automata models of complex systems: background, applications, results, software, and pathologies. Adv. Complex Syst. **22**, 1950013 (2019)
12. Li, X.G., Jia, B., Gao, Z.Y., Jiang, R.: A realistic two-lane cellular automata traffic model considering aggressive lane-changing behavior of fast vehicle. Physica A: Stat. Mech. Appl. **367**, 479–486 (2006). https://doi.org/10.1016/j.physa.2005.11.016

13. Liu, Q., Liu, J., Le, W., Guo, Z., He, Z.: Data-driven intelligent location of public charging stations for electric vehicles. J. Cleaner Prod. **232**, 531–541 (2019). https://doi.org/10.1016/j.jclepro.2019.05.388
14. Nagel, K., Schreckenberg, M.: A cellular automaton model for freeway traffic. J. Phys. I France **2**, 2221–2229 (1992). https://doi.org/10.1051/jp1:1992277
15. Ragel-Díaz-Jara, D., et al.: Pysimtravel3: urban traffic simulator for charging stations, electric and combustion vehicles, based on a hybrid cellular automata and agent-based model (2023). https://github.com/sanevec/pysimtravel3
16. Viswanathan, V., Zehe, D., Ivanchev, J., Pelzer, D., Knoll, A., Aydt, H.: Simulation-assisted exploration of charging infrastructure requirements for electric vehicles in urban environments. J. Comput. Sci. **12**, 1–10 (2016). https://doi.org/10.1016/j.jocs.2015.10.012
17. Waraich, R.A., Galus, M.D., Dobler, C., Balmer, M., Andersson, G., Axhausen, K.W.: Plug-in hybrid electric vehicles and smart grids: investigations based on a microsimulation. Transp. Res. Part C: Emerg. Technol. **28**, 74–86 (2013). https://doi.org/10.1016/j.trc.2012.10.011
18. Wu, X., Freese, D., Cabrera, A., Kitch, W.A.: Electric vehicles' energy consumption measurement and estimation. Transp. Res. Part D: Transp. Environ. **34**, 52–67 (2015). https://doi.org/10.1016/j.trd.2014.10.007
19. Xiang, Y., Liu, Z., Liu, J., Liu, Y., Gu, C.: Integrated traffic-power simulation framework for electric vehicle charging stations based on cellular automaton. J. Mod. Power Syst. Clean Energy **6**, 816–820 (2018). https://doi.org/10.1007/s40565-018-0379-3
20. Zhai, Z., Su, S., Liu, R., Yang, C., Liu, C.: Agent-cellular automata model for the dynamic fluctuation of EV traffic and charging demands based on machine learning algorithm. Neural Comput. Appl. **31**, 4639–4652 (2019). https://doi.org/10.1007/s00521-018-3841-2
21. Zheng, Y.L., Zhai, R.P., Ma, S.Q.: Survey of cellular automata model of traffic flow. J. Highway Transp. Res. Dev. **23**, 110–115 (2006)

Comparing the Efficiency of Traffic Simulations Using Cellular Automata

Fernando Díaz-del-Río[1,2]([⊠]) [iD], David Ragel-Díaz-Jara[1],
María-José Morón-Fernández[1,2] [iD], Daniel Cagigas-Muñiz[1] [iD],
Daniel Cascado-Caballero[1] [iD], José-Luis Guisado-Lizar[1,2] [iD],
and Gabriel Jimenez-Moreno[1,2] [iD]

[1] Department of Computer Architecture and Technology, Universidad de Sevilla,
Avenida Reina Mercedes s/n, 41012 Sevilla, Spain
fdiaz@us.es
[2] Research Institute of Computer Engineering (I3US), Universidad de Sevilla,
Avenida Reina Mercedes s/n, 41012 Sevilla, Spain

Abstract. The shift toward electric vehicles requires the development of an extensive public electric charging infrastructure. With the aim of simulating hundreds of configurations for charging stations, street directions, crossing, etc., we need to find the best solution in short periods of time to predict and prevent traffic congestion. Thus, we study different models to discretize and manage vehicle movements using a synchronous cellular automata, with an emphasis in reducing the amount of (frequently accessed) memory and execution time, and improving the thread parallelism. This is guided by the classical lemma of computer architecture "make the common case fast", thus optimizing those code sections where most of the execution time is spent. Experiments carried out for microscopic traffic simulations indicate that compiled languages increase run-time efficiency by more than 70×. Then several strategies are studied, such as storing future velocities of each vehicle so that neighbor vehicles can benefit from this information. Using a single 12-core PC, we get to a total run-time for a unidimensional simulation that is very close to that reached by supercomputers composed of thousands of cores that use interpreted languages. This may also greatly reduce the energy consumed. Although some performance degradation may occur when complex situations are introduced (crossroads, traffic lights, etc.), this degradation would not be significant if the length of the streets were large enough.

Keywords: traffic modeling · cellular automata · computer parallelism · microscopic traffic simulation

Supported by Grant TED2021-130825B-I00 funded by MCIN/AEI/10.13039/501 100011033 and by the "European Union NextGenerationEU/PRTR".

J.-L. Guisado-Lizar et al. (Eds.): SIMUtools 2023, LNICST 519, pp. 182–194, 2024.
https://doi.org/10.1007/978-3-031-57523-5_14

1   Introduction

The transportation sector is responsible for a substantial share of the total equivalents of carbon dioxide CO_2 released into the atmosphere (see data for the European Union in[1]). These greenhouse gas emissions are the cause behind the current global climate crisis, which poses a formidable challenge to humanity. Within transportation, road vehicles, which play a major role in our daily mobility, are a significant contributor to this phenomenon. In response to this pressing issue, a shift toward electric vehicles (EVs) is being carried out at a global level. This electrification of road transportation requires the development of an extensive public charging infrastructure. Forecasts for the year 2030 indicate a significant surge in the demand for public charging stations, far surpassing the current figures. For example, a study conducted by the International Energy Agency indicates that electric vehicles are expected to constitute approximately 55% of all transportation modalities in Europe by 2030 in the scenario of existing policies, taking into account different types of vehicles [2].

It is important to optimize the distribution of urban roads in a city to avoid them contributing to increase traffic congestion.

In this work, we study different models to discretize the movement of vehicles using a synchronous cellular automaton (CA), with an emphasis on the efficiency with respect to reducing both the amount of memory that is to be frequently accessed and the execution time, and to improve the thread parallelism. To do this, we take into consideration the classical lemma of computer architecture "make the common case fast", thus concentrating and optimizing those code sections where it is spent most of the execution time.

The remainder of the paper is organized as follows. Section 2 presents related work. Section 3 presents several ways to simulate and represent vehicle movements and to understand how to make simulation efficient. Section 4 summarizes the definition of data structures to produce an efficient simulation. The results are presented and discussed in Sect. 5. Finally, Section 6 presents the conclusions and future research directions.

2   Related Works

Modern traffic simulation applications focus on microscopic models that simulate the movements of individual vehicles [1]. These models are capable of reflecting various phenomena observed in reality. However, the simulation of detailed models poses a performance challenge that can be solved by using HPC (High Performance Computing) systems or optimizing the part of the code where more than 90% of the execution time is spent.

One of the most well-known microscopic models is the Nagel-Schreckenberg model [6], implemented for parallel execution. The authors tuned the algorithms

---

[1] https://www.europarl.europa.eu/news/en/headlines/society/20190313STO31218/
co2-emissions-from-cars-facts-and-figures-infographics).

for particular processor architectures, achieving good results for different specific computers [5].

Other important findings on parallelization can be found in [10]. The performance analysis of TRANSIM [9] identifies some issues that need to be addressed to achieve good scalability on a large number of processors when information is exchanged between spaces after each time step. GPU implementations are a more recent approach. The problem is that such simulations may not be well suited to GPU or SIMD kernels, due to the inherent random memory accesses, as some authors point out [11].

Other works that parallelize the traffic simulator are: [4], where authors reached a speedup of about 3 using a distributed and synchronized package on four PC computers; [7], where speedup was about 5 using 16 processors; and [3], where a 16 computing nodes (12 cores each) maintain a good speedup up to six nodes, but get stuck for more nodes due to intensive communication.

The above parallel simulators have been written in C, C++ and Java, using OpenMP or native distribution protocols. Only a few papers were written using other languages such as Erlang [12]), which is designed for massively concurrent and asynchronous applications, thus achieving very good scalability on large HPC systems.

3   Representing Vehicle Movements

The classical Nagel-Schreckengberg (Na-Sch) model reproduces the movement of vehicles using a synchronous cellular automata (CA), where space and time are discretized. A common way to simplify the representation of a two-dimensional map is to render and compact it into a one-dimensional vector, where each element (or CA cell) represents an area of a few meters. The vector must contain some special cells to represent crossroads and bifurcations (which must point to at least two cells). However, the number of crossroads and bifurcations is usually much lower than the total number of cells, which implies that speeding up the movement of vehicles along a one-dimensional vector is a critical task.

This model Na-Sch defines the vehicles variables with two pairs of values: The current and next positions of vehicle i ($1 <= i <= N$, N is the number of CA cells) are $x_i(t)$ and $x_i(t + 1)$, and its current and next velocities $v_i(t)$ and $v_i(t + 1)$. Each magnitude corresponds to time steps (t) and (t + 1).

The CA dynamic can be run in parallel and is determined according to the four following rules [6] for a certain vehicle i:

1. Acceleration: $v_i(t + 1) = min(v_i(t) + 1, v_{max})$;
2. Deceleration: $v_i(t + 1) = min(d_i, v_i(t + 1))$;
3. Randomization: $v_i(t + 1) = max(v_i(t + 1) - 1, 0)$ (braking reduces velocity in one unit with probability P_b);
4. Movement: $x_i(t + 1) = x_i(t) + v_i(t + 1)$;

where v_{max} is the maximum speed that i vehicle can reach and d_i is the number of empty cells in front of the vehicle.

Note that these equations are obtained for a simple discretization of a moving particle with a bounded acceleration of one unit, where the third step (randomization) introduces a certain stochastic behavior in the model. Concretely, the most difficult and run-time consuming computing piece of the algorithm is the calculus of the ahead "free" distance d_i. This requires the search for empty cells in front of each vehicle, which implies a loop that necessarily scans the contiguous forward cells at least up to the reachable velocity of the vehicle.

In addition, special attention must be paid when using random numbers. Calling a good random function generator is very time-consuming: in fact, this call usually lasts more than the rest of the code devoted to each cell. High-quality uniform random numbers are not crucial for this kind of simulations: note that movement discretization is actually coarse, and the randomization of the third step is artificial. Therefore, it is preferable to generate previously a vector with a random number for each cell and simply access to one different element for each cell and time step during the simulation (see the explanation later).

The previous equations contain several variables that must be mapped into data structures with the double aim of being efficient and flexible enough to allow the introduction of several functionalities in the simulations. In this section, we proceed with a progressive optimization of the required structures.

First of all, one can part directly from declaring the most simple structures that allow us to run all the CA cell in parallel, and which correspond to the values that equations hold: two pairs of vectors for the current and next positions x_{curr} and x_{next}, and for the velocities v_{curr} and v_{next}, whose index represents the position on the map. As each cell needs to know the current state of its neighborhood to compute its next values, x_{curr} and x_{next} cannot be condensed into a single scalar vector.

Figure 1 represents 3 vehicles in a unidimensional CA, where the calculus of d_i for the two first vehicles and their resultant movements are depicted with arrows. Here, we assume that random braking does not occur. The upper table represents the simple solution that builds the two pairs of vectors.

Although a similar pair of velocity vectors can be the most straightforward solution, both can be condensed into one if we realize that next velocity can be stored in a local variable for each cell, which is stored at the end of a step can be as a last stage. That is, considering $v(t + 1)$ as a local variable (note that the subindex i has been suppressed) and adding a new fifth rule that deletes the previous velocity and stores the new one. Additionally, the position vector only requires a few bits to indicate the presence of a vehicle in a cell. A mark must exist for occupied cells of position vectors, whereas the velocity magnitudes must reside in the velocity vectors. This new representation is depicted in the lower table of Fig. 1.

Going further, an obvious optimization in the classical model is the condensation of the 3 vectors into only two vectors containing current and next velocities, so that non-null cells in current velocity vector are also used as marks to compute d_i. Thus, Fig. 2 represents the same situation as Fig. 1 but using only two

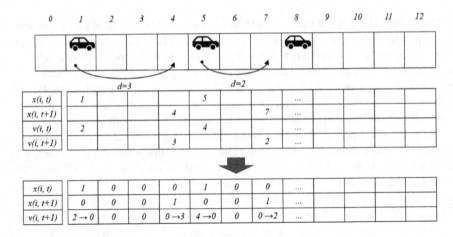

	0	1	2	3	4	5	6		
x(i, t)	1				5			...	
x(i, t+1)				4			7	...	
v(i, t)	2				4			...	
v(i, t+1)				3			2	...	

	0	1	2	3	4	5	6	
x(i, t)	1	0	0	0	1	0	0	...
x(i, t+1)	0	0	0	1	0	0	1	...
v(i, t+1)	2 →0	0	0	0 →3	4 →0	0	0 →2	...

Fig. 1. Example of magnitudes to be computed in the classical Nagel Schreckenberg model for two vehicles.

vectors. Note that the mark in the free cell is now the value -1, because the value 0 must be used for vehicles with null velocity.

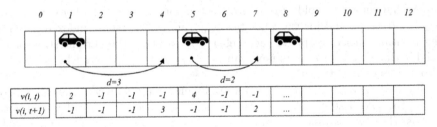

	0	1	2	3	4	5	6	
v(i, t)	2	-1	-1	-1	4	-1	-1	...
v(i, t+1)	-1	-1	-1	3	-1	-1	2	...

Fig. 2. Example of magnitudes to be computed in the optimized Nagel Schreckenberg model for two vehicles.

Another possibility of implementing this model comes from the use of a list that contains (at least) the positions of vehicles. However, the loop that searches for empty cells to compute d_i always implies the necessity of a vector with marks representing the occupied cells, because we cannot guarantee that the vehicle list will be ordered, and the search in a disordered list would be very inefficient.

Obviously, the combination of a list of vehicle coordinates plus a vector of free/occupied cells may be beneficial if the number of vehicles is very small. This is to be analyzed in Sect. 5.

Finally, the re-ordination of two iterations of the rules of the classical model may produce a faster execution (see Sect. 5). Since the most time-consuming part is the search lop that computes d_i, we can reduce the number of iterations of this loop by storing the future velocity of each vehicle. In addition, the future velocity stored in each cell is also the safety distance that must be fulfilled

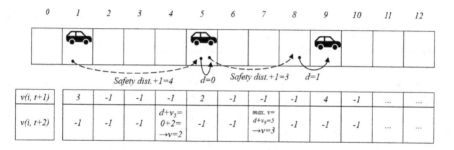

	0	1	2	3	4	5	6	7	8	9		
$v(i, t+1)$	3	-1	-1	-1	2	-1	-1	-1	4	-1	...	...
$v(i, t+2)$	-1	-1	-1	$d+v_s=$ $0+2=$ $\to v=2$	-1	-1	max. $v=$ $d+v_9=5$ $\to v=3$	-1	-1	-1	...	...

Fig. 3. Example of magnitudes to be computed in the novel model for two vehicles.

between vehicles. That is, we must ensure that the stored velocity value implies that the number of cells that are free in front of the vehicle is at least this same value. Thus, the search for the empty cell ahead can begin in the cell situated at the stored velocity plus 1.

Figure 3 represents this case for two vehicles: the first begins its search from cell 5 (because its stored safety distance is 3), where it encounters (in the first iteration) an occupied cell with a (safety distance) velocity of 2. Then its next velocity can be: the amount of cells (d in the figure) where the ahead vehicle was found plus the stored velocity of this ahead vehicle, that is, 0+2 = 2. The second vehicle can begin its search from cell 8 (because its stored safety distance is 2), and it encounters (in the second iteration) an occupied cell with a (safety distance) velocity of 4. Then its next velocity can be: the amount of empty ahead cells ($d=1$) plus the stored velocity of the vehicle ahead, that is, $1 + 4 = 5$. However, the acceleration bound of the model must reduce this new velocity to 3 (one unit more than the previous one).

In summary, the CA dynamic rules for this novel model for a certain vehicle i are as follows:

1. Search (Deceleration) and Bounded Acceleration: $v(t + 2)[i + v(t + 1)[i]] = min(d_i^* + v(t + 1)[i + v(t + 1)[i] + d_i^*], v_{max})$;
2. Randomization: $v(t + 2)[i] = max(v(t + 2)[i] - 1, 0)$ (braking reduces velocity in one unit with probability P_b);

Where d_i^* is the number of empty cells ahead after the safety distance ($v(t + 1)[i]$).

Note that we have used the notation $[i]$ to indicate the element $i - th$ of the velocity vector, while the two (current and next) velocities are expressed with $(t + 1)$ and $(t + 2)$.

4   Efficient Definition of Data Structures

According to the classical Na-Sch model, a complete description of the CA simulation requires up to four vectors with dimensions equal to the number of cells:

$v_i(t+1), v_i(t), x_i(t+1), x_i(t)$. Other quantities do not need to be stored in large data vectors because they are global (v_{max} or can be computed specifically for each cell (d_i, P_b). Besides, when developing a simulation with more complex behavior, e.g. crossroads, different characteristic of vehicles, traffic lights, routing preferences, etc., additional data structures must be inserted.

However, special care must be taken both to maintain the previous fast kernel of simulation and to avoid that complex structures play a significant role in the CA evolution. This is because the memory access locality is usually degraded when using complex structures. In the same way, it is preferable to compact the set of cells into a unique unidimensional vector (which favors memory locality and effective caching if neighboring streets were allocated in adjacent addresses) instead of scattering cells among dynamic lists (which may be allocated in disperse memory addresses). The reason for this decision, as demonstrated in Sect. 5, is that cell vectors would play the most important role in the simulation and probably consume most of the execution time. Thus, we are taking into consideration the lemma "make the common case fast".

Although cell vectors are believed to be a memory waste if the ratio between the number of vehicles and cells is low (around a 10% is generally considered to simulate dense and demanding traffic conditions), note that a complete set of cells simplifies the search for adjacent vehicles. This issue is a crucial, very common, and repetitive task to simulate vehicle movements. In contrast, a search for a smaller but disordered list of cells would be very time-consuming because the search has to be done for the complete disordered list and for each vehicle. Using a cell vector, only the indexes to the new structures (that is, acting like pointers) must be added and updated (as explained below).

In addition to cell vectors, other structures are needed to store the characteristics of vehicles and the shape of the streets that correspond to the city to be simulated. These structures can contain at least the following information to define vehicle and street data. For each vehicle: its routing preferences, its type, the cell where it is at the current step, and other necessary to emulate more complex behaviors, like its length, maximum speed, etc. For each street: the cell indexes where it begins and ends (actually, linear indexes to the cell vector), its maximum allowed speed, a set of indexes to relate this street with its neighboring ones), if it has priority when entering a crossroad, and other necessary to emulate more complex behaviors, like its type, priority changes due to traffic lights, and so on.

In summary, the basic vectors that control the speed of vehicles are two ($v_i(t+1), v_i(t)$) ; the other two ($x_i(t+1), x_i(t)$) are not necessary because the cell index is, in fact, the position $x_i(t)$. Instead of position, a pointer to the vehicle list (namely, $p_{veh_list}(t)$) for each cell must be updated at the end of each simulation step. Note that two vectors for the current (t) and next steps ($t+1$) are not necessary to control vehicle movements. Thus, a minimal set of pointers that relate cell indexes with vehicle and street indexes is also required. Figure 4 represents the minimal set of structures and its relation using indexes among them. Note that Fig. 3 contains the minimal set of structures required for efficient simulation, thus reducing the amount of memory that is frequently accessed.

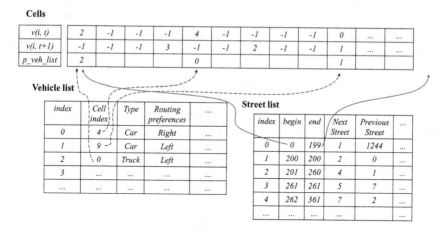

Fig. 4. Minimal set of structures required for an efficient simulation and their main relations.

In the next Section we compare the run-time execution of the different algorithms to get to that with better results. Additionally, we introduce and discuss additional features in the baseline model, to measure the influence of these features on the final execution time.

5   Results and Discussion

The results have been conducted thoroughly to conclude which performance improvement can be reached when changing the CA traffic model. We consider the execution of the classical Na-Sch model as the baseline time, and we proceed to determine the acceleration when parallelizing several cores and when comparing it with different optimizations and additional features.

Before trying to reach extreme performance and making optimizations, a first comparison was made between languages for the classical Na-Sch model. Being Python one of the most common languages nowadays, it is discovered that the algorithm written in this language is around 70× slower than the same algorithm written in C++ for a smaller number of cells (64 Ki cells[2]) when running in only one core. Exactly, a total of $2.89639e + 07$ movements can be run in a second for the C version in contrast to $4.14538e + 05$ reached in Python. The situation is even worse for larger sizes (80× slower for 128 Ki cells). Going further, speedup for the version in C++ is easily achieved using OpenMP, then accelerating a number of times near the number of cores (see next results). This result is even greater than that found as the mean for scientific codes (around 40× slower; see [8]).

---

[2] Ki is the multiplier for 1024×.

Different configurations were also analyzed for the several tests in two stages. In a first stage, we determine the most important parameters and fast models using a simple simulation, mainly consisting of unidimensional vectors. Values for a medium-sized city of a million inhabitants have been used: 5000 streets of around 200 m each, that is, a total of 10^6 m, approx. A common selection for the size of the simulated cell is 4 m, which results in a number of cells of 25×10^4 cells.

In the second stage, we concentrate on the model that yields the best results and compare its performance with that of baseline time for a realistic simulation and for different values of the most important parameters, which were selected in the first stage. These parameters are mainly: a) ratio of the number of vehicles to the number of cells; b) maximum speed.

Throughout the simulations, the different values of the parameters have been chosen to be similar to those in the current literature, except when indicated. An 8% for the ratio of the number of vehicles by the number of cells; for the maximum velocity values, the values are 4, 8 and 12 cells per simulation step. Note that the maximum velocity for cities is around 50 Km/h (15 m/s). If a simulation step counts for a second, this means 4 cells per step. Bigger simulated velocities would mean a finer description of movement, that is, fewer meters per cell. Random braking probability is fixed to 0.10; a common value in most Na-Sch simulations.

We also proceed with two computers (one laptop and a modern desktop PC) to demonstrate whether the machine has an influence on the results. The computers are an Intel Core i7-10750H, 2.60 GHz, 16.0 GB; and a 12th Intel Core i7-12700K, 3.60 GHz, 32.0 GB.

The codes were written in C++ and compiled with Microsoft Visual Studio 2022, allowing all speed optimizations. Each test is repeated ten times, and the minimum times are collected, because the first execution is always slower since the operating system is reallocating the executable (actually the mean times vary less than 5% than the minimum ones).

The main models to be considered are those represented in the three Figures of Sect. 3, that is, the classical Nagel-Schreckenberg, the optimized Nagel-Schreckenberg, and the novel model proposed here.

The main loop that controls the vehicle movement of these models can be two-fold. Obviously, the most basic loop executes one iteration for each cell. However, a second option consists of a loop with one iteration for each vehicle. In this case, we need to go through the vehicle list structure, read the cell index, which points to the corresponding cell where each vehicle is placed, where finally the movement is to be computed.

The main result is obtained by comparing the single-threaded execution with the parallel execution obtained with OpenMP. Speed-up values are very satisfactory even for the laptop, because they are close to the number of physical cores that the machine has. Consequently, and from now on, only results for the parallel OpenMP versions are shown.

Figure 5 shows the number of movements per second for the classical Nagel-Schreckenberg and the novel models when varying the number of cells from 128 Ki to 1024 Ki, and for different maximum velocities (4, 8 and 12 cells per step). Here, the probability of random braking is fixed to 0.1.

It is clear that the number of cells managed for medium cities has very little influence on the sizes that allow the cells to be allocated to the L3 cache. Of course, there is a small performance reduction for much larger sizes. Similar results are encountered for the other models.

Besides, running the same algorithm for different number of steps (bigger than 10) implies little variations in performance. This is evident because each time step is independent from the rest, and once the data vectors have been cached, each execution step does not suffer from important variations.

Therefore, from now on the number of cells to be simulated is that of a medium city (around 256 Ki) and the number of steps is fixed to 160 (a sensible number used, for example, in [12]). Because the achieved speedups are usually near the number of physical cores, OpenMP is active in all the tests.

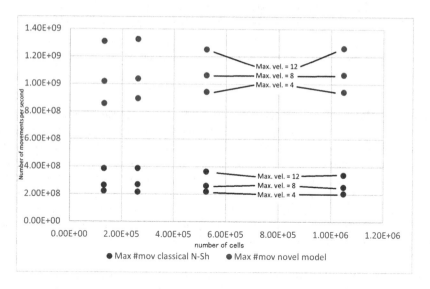

Fig. 5. Number of movements per second for the classical Nagel Schreckenberg and the optimized Nagel Schreckenberg models when varying the number of cells from 128 K to 1024 K. Maximum velocities are 4, 8 and 12 cells per step.

Previous Fig. 5 gives a first idea of the speedup obtained for the models of Sect. 3, which counts for different parameters. The next set of simulations compares the speedup obtained for the models in Sect. 3 for different parameters.

Table 1 shows the number of vehicle movements per second and the speed-up (which is the reference for the classic Na-Sch algorithm) when simulating on the modern PC a total of 160 steps and 256 Ki cells with a ratio of the number of

Table 1. Comparative speed-up using the number of vehicle movements per second for the Classic Na Sch, its optimized version, and the novel model proposed here when varying maximum velocity.

Max. Veloc	Number of vehicle movements per second			Speedup	
	Classic	Optim	Novel	Classic vs Optim	Classic vs Novel
4	2.28177e+08	4.68137e+08	7.09059e+08	2.05	3.11
8	2.17847e+08	4.41291e+08	7.60969e+08	2.03	3.49
12	2.06842e+08	4.06585e+08	8.67613e+08	1.97	4.19

Table 2. Number of vehicle movements per second for different models. r.r. means the reorder ratio of the vehicle list.

Ratio veh/cells	Na-Sch classic	Na-Sch optim	Novel model
5	3.90486e+08	7.58989e+08	1.32079e+09
10	2.73786e+08	5.42995e+08	8.68227e+08
20	1.96049e+08	3.82318e+08	5.9374e+08

Ratio veh/cells	Na-Sch classic using vehicle list (r.r. =0.1)	Na-Sch classic using vehicle list (r.r. =0.2)	Na-Sch classic using vehicle list (r.r. =0.8)
5	5.61475e+08	4.35744e+08	2.83068e+08
10	4.68071e+08	3.60048e+08	2.75381e+08
20	3.84744e+08	2.87258e+08	2.33214e+08

vehicles by the number of cells of 7% and different velocities. Similar speedups are encountered for the laptop. It is clear that the novel model outperforms the rest and that the larger the velocity, the more speedup is reached. This can be understood because the proposed novel algorithm scans for far fewer cells to find each vehicle ahead. In fact, if the vehicles formed a platoon, exactly the next cell (ahead of the stored future velocity) would contain a vehicle, and the scanning would have only one iteration (see Fig. 3). This is clearly more obvious when maximum velocities are greater. On the other hand, classic or optimized Na-Sch models need to scan at least as many cells as the current velocity.

The next interesting effect occurs when simulating different ratios between the number of vehicles and cells: 1 vehicle of 5, 10 and 20 cells is simulated and the results are presented in Table 2. Around a 10% is generally considered to simulate dense and demanding traffic conditions; 1 out of 5 is very dense traffic and 1 out of 20 emulates relaxed traffic conditions.

This table shows the number of movements per second for the following models: the classical Na-Sch, its optimized version, the novel model proposed here, and three tests that implement the classical Na-Sch model with a list of vehicles, so that the main loop is executed (and parallelized) for this list. These three tests vary the reorder ratio (r.r.) of the vehicle list (values r.r. =0.1, 0.2, 0.8), that is, before the simulation, the indexes where the vehicles reside are reordered to emulate the real case: Each entry in the vehicle list may point to disperse positions of the cell vector. The rest of parameters are the same as in the previous table (except the maximum velocity fixed to 4 cell/step).

Several interesting conclusions are drawn from this table, which are enumerated in the next section.

6   Conclusions and Future Work

Experiments carried out for microscopic traffic simulations indicate that compiled languages increase run-time efficiency by more than 70×. In addition, a novel discretized vehicle movement model is proposed that reduces execution time by more than 3× when compared with the classical Nagel-Schreckenberg model. Putting all together, we get to a total run-time for a unidimensional simulation using a 12-core PC that is very close to that reached by supercomputers composed of thousands of cores that use interpreted languages. Other several interesting conclusions that yield from result tables are:

1. If the automata simulates less vehicles, the number of vehicle movements per second is lower for any model that manage cells. This can be understood because the main loop must go through the complete vector cell. If it contained fewer vehicles, there would be an overhead time spent in empty cells. Obviously, this effect is not so significant for the model that includes a vehicle list.
2. Simulations using a vehicle list behave poorer than optimized cases, even for low traffic densities. The effect of sparse accesses to the computer memory hierarchy introduces a very negative effect on lists.
3. As expected, the model using a vehicle list gets much worse when the list is reordered to emulate the above commented real case.
4. The novel model reaches an impressive performance (1.32079e+09 vehicle movements per second) in saturated traffic conditions (due to its reduced scanning task, as explained above). In this sense, we can remark that using only a common PC with 12 cores, we are reaching a performance that is very close to that of [12], which involves a huge amount of 19,200 computing cores. To be exact, in this paper, a total of 160 steps for 11.5M cars were simulated in one second, which means a total of $160 \times 11.5M = 1.84e + 09$ vehicle movements per second, similar to the results of Table 2. Therefore, the waste of energy when using a top HPC system instead of a common PC to get similar performance is enormous. We are aware that some performance degradation is going to occur when introducing more complex situations in the simulations (crossroads, traffic lights, etc.). However, one can estimate that this degradation would not be significant because the ratio between cells and crossing is usually high. For example, in [12] a total of 240K crossroads and 144M cells are simulated, which means $144M/240K = 600$ cells for each crossing.

Future work is twofold. First, making simulations even faster by comprising data cell information into a more reduced number of bits. This can promote efficiency in other platforms like SIMD instructions, GPUs, etc. Second, studying different models of crossroads to make them also time-efficient.

References

1. Brilon, W., Wu, N.: Evaluation of cellular automata for traffic flow simulation on freeway and urban streets. In: Brilon, W., Huber, F., Schreckenberg, M., Wallentowitz, H. (eds.) Traffic and Mobility, pp. 163–180. Springer, Heidelberg (1999). https://doi.org/10.1007/978-3-642-60236-8_11
2. International Energy Agency: Global EV Outlook 2023 (2023). https://www.iea.org/reports/global-ev-outlook-2023
3. Kanezashi, H., Suzumura, T.: Performance optimization for agent-based traffic simulation by dynamic agent assignment. In: 2015 Winter Simulation Conference (WSC), pp. 757–766. IEEE (2015)
4. Klefstad, R., Zhang, Y., Lai, M., Jayakrishnan, R., Lavanya, R.: A distributed, scalable, and synchronized framework for large-scale microscopic traffic simulation. In: Proceedings. 2005 IEEE Intelligent Transportation Systems, 2005, pp. 813–818. IEEE (2005)
5. Nagel, K., Schleicher, A.: Microscopic traffic modeling on parallel high performance computers. Parallel Comput. **20**(1), 125–146 (1994)
6. Nagel, K., Schreckenberg, M.: A cellular automaton model for freeway traffic. J. Phys. I France **2**, 2221–2229 (1992). https://doi.org/10.1051/jp1:1992277
7. O'Cearbhaill, E.A., O'Mahony, M.: Parallel implementation of a transportation network model. J. Parallel Distrib. Comput. **65**(1), 1–14 (2005)
8. Pereira, R., et al.: Ranking programming languages by energy efficiency. Sci. Comput. Program. **205**, 102609 (2021). https://doi.org/10.1016/j.scico.2021.102609. https://www.sciencedirect.com/science/article/pii/S0167642321000022
9. Raney, B., Voellmy, A., Cetin, N., Vrtic, M., Nagel, K.: Towards a microscopic traffic simulation of all of Switzerland. In: Sloot, P.M.A., Hoekstra, A.G., Tan, C.J.K., Dongarra, J.J. (eds.) ICCS 2002. LNCS, vol. 2329, pp. 371–380. Springer, Heidelberg (2002). https://doi.org/10.1007/3-540-46043-8_37
10. Rickert, M., Nagel, K.: Dynamic traffic assignment on parallel computers in transims. Future Gener. Comput. Syst. **17**(5), 637–648 (2001)
11. Strippgen, D., Nagel, K.: Using common graphics hardware for multi-agent traffic simulation with cuda. In: Proceedings of the 2nd International Conference on Simulation Tools and Techniques, pp. 1–8 (2009)
12. Turek, W.: Erlang-based desynchronized urban traffic simulation for high-performance computing systems. Future Gener. Comput. Syst. **79**, 645–652 (2018). https://doi.org/10.1016/j.future.2017.06.003. https://www.sciencedirect.com/science/article/pii/S0167739X17311810

Multi-agent Simulation for Scheduling and Path Planning of Autonomous Intelligent Vehicles

Kader Sanogo[1,2](✉) 📷, M'hammed Sahnoun[3] 📷,
and Abdelkader Mekhalef Benhafssa[1] 📷

[1] CESI LINEACT, EA 7527, Angouleme Campus, 16400 La Couronne, France
ksanogo@cesi.fr
[2] ENSAM, 75013 Paris, France
[3] CESI LINEACT, EA 7527, Rouen Campus, S. E du Rouvray, 76800 Rouen, France
msahnoun@cesi.fr

Abstract. Autonomous and Guided Vehicles (AGVs) have long been employed in material handling but necessitate significant investments, such as designating specific movement areas. As an alternative, Autonomous and Intelligent Vehicles (AIVs) have gained traction due to their adaptability, intelligence, and capability to handle unexpected obstacles. Yet, challenges like optimizing scheduling and path planning, and managing routing conflicts persist. This study introduces a simulator tailored for AIV scheduling and path planning in various production systems. The simulator supports both predictive, where paths are predetermined, and dynamic scheduling, with real-time optimization. Paths are determined using Dijkstra's method, ensuring AIVs use the shortest route. When path-sharing conflicts arise, a multi-criteria priority system comes into play, and its impact on the makespan is assessed. Experimental results highlight the advantage of AIVs over AGVs in most scenarios and the simulator's efficiency in generating effective schedules, incorporating the priority management system.

Keywords: Simulation · AIV · Job-shop scheduling · FMS · Multi-agent System · Industry 5.0

1 Introduction

Research in unmanned ground vehicles has been done for several decades and is continuously creating advancements and capabilities [4]. For more than a decade, AGVs have proven their effectiveness in material handling tasks in manufacturing workshops or logistic warehouses [8]. However, AGV installation is expensive, as it requires modifying the workshop's layout by defining dedicated movement areas [9]. Since AGVs are guided robots, any modification to the workshop's layout requires updating their map and dedicated environment. To alleviate these problems, more intelligent, flexible, and collaborative mobile robots, namely AIVs, are increasingly being used [4].

J.-L. Guisado-Lizar et al. (Eds.): SIMUtools 2023, LNICST 519, pp. 195–205, 2024.
https://doi.org/10.1007/978-3-031-57523-5_15

Unlike AGVs, AIVs do not require dedicated areas in the workshop and can navigate around static and dynamic obstacles, including human operators. Hence, AIVs are relevant in Industry 5.0, which refers to a human-centered industry where humans are working alongside robots and smart machines [5]. They can provide several advantages over traditional transportation methods, such as increased efficiency, flexibility, and safety [4,9]. However, the deployment of AIVs presents some challenges [9], such as the need to efficiently schedule AIVs, plan their paths carefully, and resolve conflicts that may occur in routing.

In this paper, a simulator for scheduling and path planning of AIVs in job-shop production systems is presented. The simulator can be used to simulate both advanced and dynamic scheduling. For predictive scheduling, the AIVs plan their paths based on an optimized schedule that is generated offline. For dynamic scheduling, their paths are planned based on a real-time optimization algorithm that is integrated into the simulator. The simulator uses a path-planning method based on Dijkstra's method for finding the shortest path for AIVs. Routing conflict resolution is based on a multi-criteria system, and the influence of each criterion on the makespan is studied.

Job shop scheduling problems with mobile robots handling materials have been extensively studied by researchers. Indeed, Bilge *et al.* [3] have considered the problem as a simultaneous scheduling of machines and vehicles. They propose four layouts in the literature, each consisting of four machines and one load/unload station, and transportation tasks are carried out by two AGVs. Taking this work as background, Ham [7] proposes a constraint programming approach to solve the Job-Shop Scheduling Problem (JSSP) with AGV-transport. He considers both machines and AGVs as constrained resources. Abderrahim *et al.* [1] tackle the JSSP with automated transportation tasks, treating workstations and vehicles as resources, and employ a Variable Neighborhood Search (VNS) algorithm to optimize makespan by scheduling both manufacturing and transportation tasks.

In recent years, simulation has been used to address various challenges in FMS [2,13]. Simulation is valuable for identifying phenomena that may not have been apparent during theoretical modeling stages [14]. Moreover, some constraints are difficult to model, so simulation is an alternative to overcome this problem. For instance, in [17], the authors used simulation to demonstrate the difference between the simulated and the theoretical schedule in a simple example. Recently, [16] have introduced a simulation approach to solve the Flexible Job-Shop Scheduling Problem (FJSSP) with transportation tasks, a more difficult problem than JSSP with transportation tasks. In [15], the authors developed a multi-agent simulation for the FJSSP, focusing on AGV collision avoidance and testing its influence on AGV fleet and makespan. They then enhanced this approach to simulate predictive and dynamic schedules, incorporating collision avoidance and deadlock resolution algorithms [14]. Current research emphasizes AGV simulation, neglecting the vital role of AIV implementation and management in Industry 5.0

This paper's tackles this problem by proposing the following contributions:

- Address job-shop production systems with transportation tasks carried out by AIVs.

- Proposes a decentralized method for AIV path planning inspired by Dijkstra's method.
- Propose, as well, a decentralized method for managing priorities in AIVs routing conflicts.
- Present an integrated simulation approach for job-shop scheduling optimization with a decentralized AIV's fleet management.

The remainder is organized as follows. Section 2 is dedicated to the problem description, where the job-shop scheduling, path planning, and collision avoidance problems are presented. The study backbone is contained in Sect. 3. Section 4 presents experiments conducted and discusses the results. Finally, a conclusion ends this paper.

2 Problem Description

2.1 JSSP and FJSSP

The JSSP is the problem of sequencing a set of jobs $\mathcal{J} = \{J_1, J_2, ..., J_I\}$ to be processed on a set of machines $\mathcal{M} = \{M_1, M_2, ..., M_M\}$ in a job-shop organization. Each job J_i is composed of a sequence $(O_{i1}, O_{i2}, ..., O_{in})$ of operations to be performed consecutively. The operation O_{ij}, which means operation j of job i, can be performed only on the machine $M_k \in \mathcal{M}$ with the processing time τ_k. Furthermore, a machine can only perform one operation at a time, and preemption of operations is not allowed. However, in FJSSP, an operation O_{ij} is performed by a machine M_k within a subset of eligible machines $\mathcal{M}_{ij} \subset \mathcal{M}$ $(1 \leq card(\mathcal{M}_{ij}) \leq card(\mathcal{M}))$. We have complete flexibility when $card(\mathcal{M}_{ij}) = card(\mathcal{M})$. Otherwise, it is a partial flexibility.

Job transportation between two machines is performed by a single-load AIV. A transportation task is denoted by $T_{i,j}$, which means the transportation of the job J_i to the machine selected to perform the operation $O_{i,j}$. Task preemption is not allowed, i.e., we can not interrupt a task once it starts. Besides, it is assumed that each machine M_k has an input and an output buffer, respectively B_k^I and B_k^O, for storing jobs before processing and after processing. It is also assumed that all the jobs are stored in a load/unload (L/U) station at the beginning/end of the execution.

2.2 Path Planning and Collision Avoidance

Path planning involves finding a suitable path for robots to move between two locations [10]. Several parameters can be taken into account, such as distance, duration [12], risk of collisions and deadlocks [6], and energy consumption [11].

In our case, we have developed a path planning method that searches for either the shortest path or the fastest path. The environment is modeled by an undirected connected graph in which each point of interest (machine, stock, corner, and intersection) is represented by a node, and the edges are the corridors linking them. When a task is assigned to the robot, it plans its path based on this graph.

Collisions are avoided locally by the robots themselves. Indeed, when two robots meet, thanks to our priority management system, one stops and gives way to the other as presented in Fig. 1. Once the path is clear, the robots continue as normal. The difference with our previous work is that no direction of travel is imposed, so AIVs can meet face-to-face. However, the algorithms developed in [14] remain valid and are used to support the priority management system.

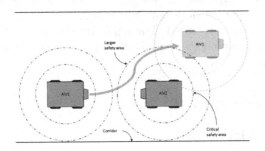

Fig. 1. AIVs collision avoidance mechanism

To ensure safety and prevent collisions between robots, each robot employs two safety radii: a larger radius for obstacle detection and speed reduction, and a smaller radius for immediate stopping. Upon detecting another robot, the priority management system takes over. Within the larger radius, both robots halve their speed. Inside the smaller radius, one robot stops, while the prioritized robot initiates a go-around maneuver, further reducing its speed. Once the path is clear, both robots gradually accelerate back to their cruising speed of 1 m/s.

3   Methods

3.1   Multi-agent System (MAS)

The simulator is based on a MAS involving four (04) main agents: AIVs, machines, stocks, and jobs. The agents are interrelated as follows:

- AIVs pick/deliver jobs from/to stocks.
- Stocks store jobs before/after processing by machines.
- Machines process jobs (Fig. 2).

Table 1 summarize the assumptions made for each agent.

3.2   Framework

The multi-agent system (MAS) and the environment are simulated using Net-Logo 6.2, a programming language and simulator designed for modeling and simulating systems with multiple interacting agents. Each agent is represented

Table 1. Assumptions for each agent's type

AIVs	Machines	Stocks	Jobs
Are independent of each other	Are independent of each other	Machine buffers have an identical limited capacity	Are independent of each other
Can transfer one and only one job at a time	Can perform one and only one operation at a time	L/U station capacity is unlimited	Can be processed on one and only one machine at a time
Job's load/unload time is included in transportation time	Setup times and breakdowns are ignored	Can store products as long as possible	Can be transported by one and only one AIV at a time
Plan path from task scheduling	Process jobs according to the scheduling		Must be processed according to the scheduling
Avoid collisions by their own	Are available at the beginning of the simulation		Preemption of operation is not allowed

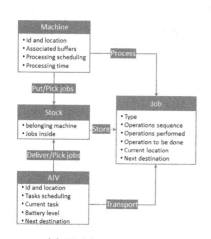

(a) Multi-agent system

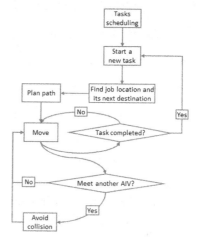

(b) Diagram of AIV performing tasks in the simulator.

Fig. 2. Simulation framework

as a "turtle" belonging to a specific "breed". Global parameters apply to the entire model, while breed-specific parameters are exclusive to that breed. In this simulation, AIVs, machines, jobs, and stocks are considered as four distinct breeds. Simulation time is measured in "ticks", with the assumption that 20 ticks represent one second. AIVs move along the corridors as shown in Fig. 3. The simulator interface is composed by:

- Sliders: for varying the number of jobs or transporters.
- Choosers: for selecting the problem instance, simulation environment, navigation type (shortest or fastest path), and priority type.

- Switches: for activating collision avoidance between robots and for recording simulation results.
- The monitor: for displaying simulation outputs.
- Buttons: The **setup** button initializes (or reinitializes) the simulation, while the **go** button launches it.
- The simulation environment represents the workshop layout. It displays a real-time visualization of the simulation.

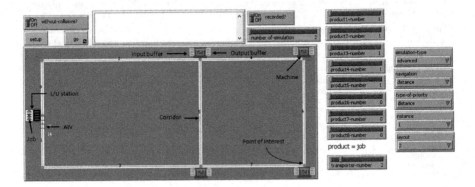

Fig. 3. Simulation interface

3.3   Simulation Model

In our model, the production and transportation tasks are not dependent, which means that AIVs can transfer some jobs while machines are processing others. However, for a job to be processed by a machine, it must first be transported by a robot. Therefore, the problem involves four subtasks:

- Vehicle scheduling: determines which jobs will be transported by a robot and the order in which the jobs will be transported.
- Machine scheduling: determines which jobs will be processed by a machine and the order in which the jobs will be processed.
- Vehicle routing: determines the path a robot will take while carrying out its task.
- Vehicles and machines synchronization: to ensure that precedence constraints and logical sequences are respected.

In the case of predictive scheduling simulation, transportation and production tasks are generated offline after an optimization process. The simulator therefore takes the result of this optimization as input and simulates it. However, in the case of dynamic scheduling simulation, the simulator is embedded with a dynamic scheduling algorithm. As a result, transportation and production tasks are generated dynamically, step by step, throughout the simulation.

3.4   Layout and Instances

Experiments are conducted using the well-known benchmark instances proposed by Bilge and Ulusoy [3]. They proposed four different layouts of the job shop, each consisting of a load/unload (L/U) station and four machines. The L/U station is used as a storage area for all jobs before they are processed (raw materials) and after they have been completed (finished products). Transportation tasks are carried out by two identical uni-charge AGVs. All transportation tasks begin and end at the L/U station. Each layout has a unique travel orientation, travel times, and L/U station and machine locations. For our part, we have replaced AGVs with AIVs. As a result, AIVs don't need to follow a unique travel orientation. They're intelligent enough to plan their own routes. This change has a direct impact on travel times, as shown in Table 2. Note that the values in Table 2b represent the minimum time required to travel between two locations.

Bilge and Ulusoy also proposed 10 different job sets, each of which consists of 5 to 8 jobs. Jobs are made up of several operations that must be performed on specific machines, and each operation has a corresponding processing time. The proposed test instances are denoted as "EX$\alpha\beta$", where α and β represent the job set and the layout, respectively. It is important to note that both travel times and processing times are measured in seconds (Fig. 4).

For this paper, we have limited our experiments to layout 2.

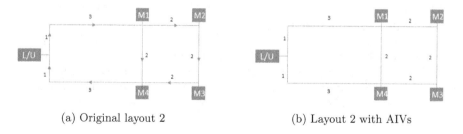

(a) Original layout 2   (b) Layout 2 with AIVs

Fig. 4. Layout 2

Table 2. Travel times

	L/U	M1	M2	M3	M4
L/U	0	4	6	8	6
M1	6	0	2	4	2
M2	8	12	0	2	4
M3	6	10	12	0	2
M4	4	8	10	12	0

(a) Layout 2: original travel times

	L/U	M1	M2	M3	M4
L/U	0	4	6	6	4
M1	4	0	2	4	2
M2	6	2	0	2	4
M3	6	4	2	0	2
M4	4	2	4	2	0

(b) Layout 2: AIVs travel times

3.5   Priority Management System

The priority management system is a rule-based system based on four criteria:

- Distance: The AIV closest to its destination has priority.
- Battery: The AIV with the lowest battery level has priority. In this case, the robots' battery levels gradually decrease as they perform their tasks. It is assumed that the battery level decreases at each simulation time step by 0.0025, 0.00125, and 0.0005 percent of the complete charge, respectively, when the AIVs are at cruising speed, when they reduce speed, and when they are at a complete stop. Nevertheless, robot batteries are initially 100% charged, and have sufficient energy to complete all their tasks.
- Starting time: The AIV that starts its current task earliest has priority.
- Random: AIVs draw a token at random to determine who has priority.

3.6   Experimental Protocol

For our experiments, we used the results obtained with the VNS method by Abderrahim *et al.* [1] presented in [14]. We are only interested in the results obtained considering collision avoidance. We then re-simulated these schedules by replacing AGVs with AIVs, while varying the priority management criterion to study its influence on makespan. We ran each simulation 50 times and recorded the average and the standard deviation. Layout 2 was chosen for the experiments because it presents several interesting challenges for the AIVs, such as deadlocks, intersections, and multiple path alternatives. These challenges provide opportunities to evaluate the performance of different priority strategies. Moreover, We investigated the impact of using shortest or fastest paths for AIV navigation on simulation results. We recorded the average time lost due to collision avoidance maneuvers on each path section (corridors) and used these averages to update the fastest path navigation method.

4   Results and Discussions

The results of the experiments are shown in Table 3. The first column lists the problem instances. The second column refers to the results in [14]. The other columns show the simulation results for the different priority criteria that were adopted. The results presented are the average of the makespan recorded after 50 runs, followed by the standard deviation in brackets.

Overall, AIVs outperform AGVs due to their ability to not follow pre-defined paths, which saves time. However, moving along the shortest path also increases the likelihood of encounters, necessitating collision avoidance maneuvers. Our measurements indicate an average collision avoidance time of 0.8 s for AIVs. Additionally, as noted in [14], lengthy waiting times can disturb other AIVs' activities, particularly evident in EX82, where robots experience significant delays before proceeding with subsequent tasks.

When comparing the different priority criteria, the distance criterion proves most efficient, allowing robots closer to their destinations to complete tasks promptly. This criterion gains further importance when considering deadline constraints for job deliveries. The battery criterion effectively prioritizes the AIV with the lowest battery level, enabling it to complete as many tasks as possible before depleting its energy. The starting time and random criteria, however, yield mixed results. The starting time criterion may prioritize a robot farther from its destination, and the random criterion may not always be relevant.

Furthermore, in general, navigation type has a negligible impact on the makespan. However, it was observed an increase in the number of avoided collisions with fastest path navigation compared to shortest path navigation as presented in Table 4. Similarly, some corridors became more collision-prone with fastest path navigation, because robots always choose the fastest path. In contrast, with shortest path navigation, robots choose a random path if multiple paths have the same length, which can help to distribute traffic more evenly. However, it is important to note that these experiments were conducted with only two AIVs and no external disturbances (moving obstacles or human operators) in order to comply with the benchmark instances [3]. The introduction of external disturbances and/or an increase in the robot fleet could produce different results.

Table 3. Experiment results

Instances	Results from [14]	Priority criteria			
		Distance	Battery	Starting time	Random
EX12	99	81.5 (1.7)	82.0 (1.3)	82.2 (1.6)	80.3 (2.2)
EX22	82.2	83.0 (0.0)	83.0 (0.0)	82.8 (0.0)	83.0 (0.0)
EX32	95	89.3 (0.1)	89.8 (0.3)	89.1 (0.2)	90.0 (0.3)
EX42	109	94.7 (0.8)	95.1 (0.7)	95.1 (1.0)	94.9 (1.7)
EX52	84	70.0 (0.4)	70.0 (0.4)	70.1 (0.4)	70.3 (0.5)
EX62	102.4	102.8 (0.0)	102.8 (0.2)	102.8 (0.1)	102.8 (0.0)
EX72	101	97.2 (0.3)	97.0 (0.3)	97.0 (0.2)	97.1 (0.3)
EX82	155.3	158.3 (1.2)	160.0 (1.0)	159.7 (0.9)	158.0 (0.8)
EX92	106.1	102.6 (1.7)	100.6 (0.7)	101.6 (0.8)	101.2 (1.3)
EX102	145	144.7 (0.1)	144.2 (0.4)	144.5 (0.3)	144.2 (0.4)

Table 4. Navigation type analysis

		Corridors of layout 2							
		0	1	2	3	4	5	6	7
nb. of collisions	Distance	96	404	0	0	159	81	0	873
	Time	105	395	0	0	0	500	0	1000
freq. of collisions	Distance	6%	25%	0%	0%	10%	5%	0%	54%
	Time	5%	20%	0%	0%	0%	25%	0%	50%

5   Conclusion

This paper addresses job-shop scheduling and Autonomous Intelligent Vehicles (AIV) path-planning problems through simulation. The transition from Autonomous and Guided Vehicles (AGVs) to AIVs solves several problems, such as the need for a dedicated environment. AIVs are more intelligent, flexible, and collaborative mobile robots that can navigate in spaces with mobile and/or unexpected obstacles. Therefore, their use is relevant in Industry 5.0, where humans and robots work together. Moreover, the results of the experiments conducted show that, in most of the cases, switching from AGV to AIV improves the makespan (more than 5 s on average).

The simulator presented in this paper is a valuable tool for the study of AIV scheduling and path planning in job-shop production systems. It is able to generate efficient schedules for both predictive and dynamic scheduling, and the priority management algorithm is effective in resolving conflicts between AIVs. This work has a number of implications for the use of AIVs in production systems. First, the simulator can be used to evaluate the performance of different scheduling and path-planning algorithms. Second, AIVs ability to navigate in more complex workshop layouts can be evaluated. Third, it can prepare for the transition to Industry 5.0 by considering the human factor.

Future work will focus on expanding the experiments to other layouts and instances, as well as, improving the performance of the simulator by incorporating more features, such as a battery management system. Humans will be integrated as the fifth agent to study their impact on the scheduling of AIVs.

References

1. Abderrahim, M., et al.: Bi-local search based variable neighborhood search for job-shop scheduling problem with transport constraints. Optim. Lett. **16**, 255–280 (2020)
2. Benhafssa, A.M., et al.: Optimizing energy-conscious dynamic flexible job shop scheduling: Multi-agent simulation approach. In: 2021 1st International Conference on Cyber Management and Engineering (CyMaEn), pp. 1–6 (2021). https://doi.org/10.1109/CyMaEn50288.2021.9497301
3. Bilge, Ü., Ulusoy, G.: A time window approach to simultaneous scheduling of machines and material handling system in an fms. Oper. Res. **43**(6), 1058–1070 (1995)
4. Cronin, C., Conway, A., Walsh, J.: State-of-the-art review of autonomous intelligent vehicles (aiv) technologies for the automotive and manufacturing industry. In: 2019 30th Irish Signals and Systems Conference (ISSC), pp. 1–6 (2019). https://doi.org/10.1109/ISSC.2019.8904920
5. Destouet, C., et al.: Flexible job shop scheduling problem under Industry 5.0: a survey on human reintegration, environmental consideration and resilience improvement. J. Manuf. Syst. **67**, 155–173 (2023). https://doi.org/10.1016/j.jmsy.2023.01.004
6. Drótos, M., et al.: Suboptimal and conflict-free control of a fleet of agvs to serve online requests. Comput. Ind. Eng. **152**, 106999 (2021)

7. Ham, A.: Transfer-robot task scheduling in job shop. Int. J. Prod. Res. **59**(3), 813–823 (2021)
8. Hu, H., et al.: Deep reinforcement learning based agvs real-time scheduling with mixed rule for flexible shop floor in industry 4.0. Comput. Ind. Eng. **149**, 106749 (2020). https://doi.org/10.1016/j.cie.2020.106749
9. Martin, L., et al.: Effect of human-robot interaction on the fleet size of aiv transporters in fms. In: 2021 1st International Conference on Cyber Management and Engineering (CyMaEn), pp. 1–5 (2021). https://doi.org/10.1109/CyMaEn50288.2021.9497273
10. Perez-Grau, F.J., et al.: Introducing autonomous aerial robots in industrial manufacturing. J. Manuf. Syst. **60**, 312–324 (2021)
11. Rapalski, A., Dudzik, S.: Energy consumption analysis of the selected navigation algorithms for wheeled mobile robots. Energies **16**(3), 1532 (2023). https://doi.org/10.3390/en16031532
12. Reith, K.B., Rank, S., Schmidt, T.: Conflict-minimal routing for free-ranging transportation vehicles in in-house logistics based on an a-priori lane design. J. Manuf. Syst. **61**, 97–111 (2021). https://doi.org/10.1016/j.jmsy.2021.07.019
13. Sahnoun, M., et al.: Optimization of transportation collaborative robots fleet size in flexible manufacturing systems. In: 2019 8th International Conference on Modeling Simulation and Applied Optimization (ICMSAO), pp. 1–5. IEEE (2019)
14. Sanogo, K., et al.: A multi-agent system simulation based approach for collision avoidance in integrated job-shop scheduling problem with transportation tasks. J. Manuf. Syst. **68**, 209–226 (2023). https://doi.org/10.1016/j.jmsy.2023.03.011
15. Sanogo, K., et al.: Multi-agent simulation for flexible job-shop scheduling problem with traffic-aware routing. In: Borangiu, T., et al. (eds.) Service Oriented, Holonic and Multi-agent Manufacturing Systems for Industry of the Future, pp. 573–583. Springer, Cham (2022). https://doi.org/10.1007/978-3-030-99108-1_41
16. Xu, Y., et al.: A simulated multi-objective model for flexible job shop transportation scheduling. Ann. Oper. Res. **311**, 899–920 (2020)
17. Zaidi, L., Bettayeb, B., Sahnoun, M.: Optimisation and simulation of transportation tasks in flexible job shop with muti-robot systems. In: 2021 1st International Conference on Cyber Management and Engineering (CyMaEn), pp. 1–6. IEEE (2021)

Medical Sciences

ECG Pre-processing and Feature Extraction Tool for Intelligent Simulation Systems

Manuel Domínguez-Morales[1,2]([✉]) [iD], Adolfo Muñoz-Macho[3] [iD],
and José L. Sevillano[1,2] [iD]

[1] Architecture and Computer Technology Department, E.T.S. Ingeniería Informática,
Universidad de Sevilla, Sevilla, Spain
mjdominguez@us.es
[2] Computer Science Research Institute, Universidad de Sevilla, Sevilla, Spain
[3] Performance and Medical Department at RCD Mallorca SAD, Palma de Mallorca,
Spain

Abstract. Sudden cardiac death events and fatal cardiac problems are
a field of vital importance for physicians working with elite athletes. For
this reason, it is common to periodically perform cardiac monitoring with
professional ECG devices to detect certain risk markers. As these doctors
often work with many athletes (as is the case with professional football
teams), an artificial intelligence-based system would help mass screening
and allow these exams to be carried out more regularly. Because physicians often evaluate the printed reports generated by ECG devices, few
manufacturers provide powerful and configurable software tools. Moreover, for teaching purposes, a simulation tool that would allow working
with previously collected ECG files would be very useful. In this paper,
we present a software tool to be used with General Electric CardioSoft
12SL electrocardiograph. This tool allows importing the XML files generated by this device, perform a manual or automatic signal filtering
process and PQRST peak detection, and finally generate a customisable
report as a CSV file containing the features obtained after signal analysis. This pre-processed information can be used as input of ECG simulators and in artificial intelligence systems to develop diagnostic support
systems.

Keywords: ECG · Signal processing · Feature extraction · Report
generation · Artificial intelligence

1 Introduction

Concerned about cardiac problems in athletes and the sudden deaths caused
by them, international bodies such as the *Fédération Internationale de Football
Association* (FIFA) in the case of football have made an enormous effort to carry

© ICST Institute for Computer Sciences, Social Informatics and Telecommunications Engineering 2024
Published by Springer Nature Switzerland AG 2024. All Rights Reserved
J.-L. Guisado-Lizar et al. (Eds.): SIMUtools 2023, LNICST 519, pp. 209–216, 2024.
https://doi.org/10.1007/978-3-031-57523-5_16

out mass screening of athletes with the use of electrocardiograms (ECG) [11]. According to those tests, sport physicians and cardiologists review ECG Data and determine the players' aptitude [5]. This assessment is performed with professional 12-lead electrocardiographs, which provide the information in printed form (which is the most commonly used), but also in an XML file.

However, due to the high number of professional athletes and the complexity of analysing all the peaks from the 12 leads of an ECG signal, these tests are not carried out many times a year (only one time a year in professional football teams). This fact contrasts with the devastating results of a sudden death, which could require a great precision, and maybe it could be better diagnosed with more frequent screenings.

On the other hand, the use of artificial intelligence (AI) in the field of cardiac disease detection for elite professionals may help to reduce the time needed to detect harmful markers, as has been demonstrated with other physiological signals [7,9]. Therefore, prior to the use of this type of AI systems, the processes of pre-processing and extraction of useful features are essential. Moreover, it is also necessary to provide a simulation tool to teach medical professionals how to detect dangerous markers (in this regard, there are other simulations tools like [6], centred on ECG signals). In addition, such a software tool could help in preprocessing and visualization of ECG signals in a more user-friendly and usable way; or in research, for example, to generate synthetic signals that can be used to enrich databases [8].

For this reason, a new software tool called *ECGVisualizer* is presented. This tool allows loading XML files obtained from General Electric CardioSoft 12SL electrocardiogram, visualising the 12-lead information, filtering the signals, performing PQRST peaks detection, extracting features and generating a summary report. Some manufacturers provide very closed visualization tools without customisation and, in other cases, generic visualization tools are used that do not work properly for all devices.

This tool includes two main features: *1) full customization*, as user can decide what filters to apply, the type of patient for the peaks' detection and what features to be extracted from the signals; and *2) report generation* in a CSV open format, according to the features selected and the baseline information of the patient. This report can eventually be used as input of EGC simulators or in AI-based diagnostic support systems. *ECGVisualizer* can be downloaded from the next URL: https://github.com/mjdominguez/ECGVisualizer.

The objective of this paper is to present the software tool and, using a dataset collected and processed with this tool, to show an example of its use and the results obtained. The effectiveness of this tool has been verified by a cardiac physician.

This paper is organized as follows: firstly, the software tool and the collected dataset are presented; secondly, a use case of this tool is shown with several ECGs obtained from professional soccer players; then, the characteristics of this tool are compared with other similar tools and, finally, the conclusions of this work are shown.

2   Materials

First, the software tool developed (ECGVisualizer) and its functionalities are presented, followed by a summary of the dataset collected for testing with this tool.

2.1   ECGVisualizer Tool

The ECG Visualizer software is a tool that allows to load XML files generated by a professional 12-lead ECG, visualise its content, apply customised filters on the signals and generate a report of the most significative features obtained from the signal. Currently, this tool supports the electrocardiograph CardioSoft 12SL from General Electric, but soon it will support also the Contec 1200G device.

The whole processing chain is fully configurable by the user, allowing to indicate which filters to apply and when, the characteristics of the patient whose ECG we are processing and the characteristics that we want to be included in the final report.

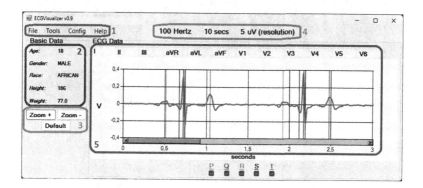

Fig. 1. ECGVisualizer main form.

Software Architecture. This tool has been developed with Visual Studio IDE, using C# language and Windows Forms. In addition to the common operations, all signal filters and peak detection algorithms have been implemented, including some utilities to operate with signals. Finally, regarding the detection of the ECG signal peaks, this task is performed taking into account the maximum and minimum ranges of the usual intervals (QRS, QT and PR) stipulated for the configured patient type. The main form of this tool is presented in Fig. 1. According to it, the tool is divided in:

- Section 1 (red) - Toolbar: options that allow the user loading, filtering, selecting features and configuring the report generated from the ECG file loaded. See the GitHub User Manual[1].
- Section 2 (blue) - Basic patient information: baseline information obtained from the ECG file.
- Section 3 (orange) - Visualization tools: tools that allow to vary zoom.
- Section 4 (green) - Signal information: informative section, where the main characteristics of the loaded ECG signal are shown.
- Section 5 (purple) - ECG signal visualization: the user may select which lead to visualize. The result of the processing is represented here too.

The tool allows an automatic processing (default filter cascade) and manual processing (user can select what filters and when). The usual processing chain is presented in the central part of Fig. 2.

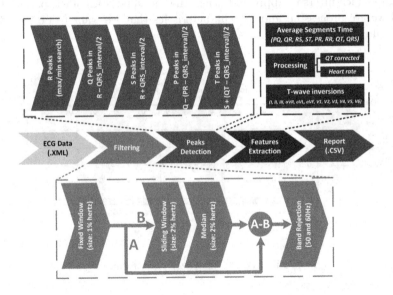

Fig. 2. Summary of the automatic processing chain.

Software Functionalities. The functionalities of this tool are described next:

- Load: XML files from GE CardioSoft 12SL ECG can be loaded. These files include the patient's baseline information and the RAW information of the 12 leads (collected at 500 hz).

---

[1] https://github.com/mjdominguez/ECGVisualizer/tree/main/ECGVisualizer/documentation.

- Visualization: the user can navigate between the 12 leads within the time period. The user can also zoom in and out on those areas he/she wants to enlarge or reduce.
- Filtering: it allows for automatic filtering (Fig. 2-down) and manual filtering. The configurable filters included are:
  - Fixed-window average filter (mean/smoothing filter). It removes the digital noise from the sampling and, as a side effect, reduces the sampling rate.
  - Sliding-window average filter (moving average filter). It removes the high and low-frequency ripples.
  - Sliding-window median filter (moving median filter). It flattens deeply the signal peaks and reduces the noise.
  - Band rejection filter (band-stop filter). It is used to eliminate the persistent noise caused by the electrocardiograph mains connection.
- Peaks detection: it allows selecting the target patient between a common person, an athlete or a custom class [10,11]. The detailed process is described in the upper-left part of Fig. 2.
- Feature extraction & Report Generation: it allows configuring the features included in the report (see Fig. 2 upper-right for the full features list). The result is a CSV file with each feature in a different column.

2.2 Dataset

The dataset collected is named PF12RED[2], including 163 raw ECG data in XML format from 54 football players. It was collected from professional UEFA football players of a team from La Liga EA SPORTS, taken by the co-author *Dr. Adolfo Muñoz-Macho*. It is part of a project focused on using AI in professional football teams for diagnosis aid, inscribed in ClinicalTrials.gov (No. NCT05872945).

3 Results

This section will show a use case of the tool. After that, a comparison with other ECG signal visualization and processing tools is performed.

3.1 Illustrative Example

The tool was configured with the automatic filtering process, patient type "athlete", and with the default features. The result of the peak detection process and the report generated can be seen in Fig. 3.

The tool shows the baseline data on the left and the ECG signals on the right of Fig. 3 top-left, including the peaks detected. The report generated is shown at the bottom of Fig. 3, including a T-wave inversion in *aVL* lead, which can be visually verified by looking closely at *aVL* lead (see Fig. 3 top-right). This process

---

[2] https://github.com/dradolfomunoz/PF12RED.

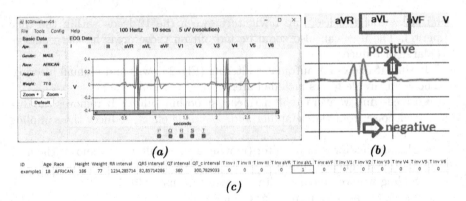

Fig. 3. Visual representation of an ECG processing: (a) peaks detection result, (b) T-wave inversion in aVL, (c) report generated.

was repeated for the whole dataset and verified by *Dr Adolfo Muñoz-Macho*. Results show an accuracy of almost 100% compared with the markers obtained manually: the few discrepancies obtained relies on the confusion between peak T and peak U in some signals (where peak U is an unusual wave, like a T-wave echo).

3.2 Tools Comparison

A search for software tools capable of visualizing ECG information was carried out. A summary of this information can be seen in Table 1.

Table 1. ECG visualization, simulation and processing tools.

Software Tool	Input	Leads	Filtering		Peaks		Features		Free
			Auto	Manual	Auto	Manual	Auto	Manual	
Edelmann et al. (2019) [6]	.mat	1	Yes	No	Yes	No	Yes	No	Yes
Encord ECG (2023) [2]	DICOM	12	No	No	Yes	No	No	No	No
OHIF ECG Viewer (2023) [3]	DICOM	12	No	No	Yes	No	No	No	Yes
Waveform ECG (2008) [4]	.xml	12	No	No	Yes	No	No	No	Yes
ECG-Viewer (2022) [1]	.dat, .txt, .csv	12	Yes	Yes	Yes	No	No	No	Yes
ECGVisualizer (2023) [this work]	.xml	12	Yes	Yes	Yes	Yes	Yes	Yes	Yes

Some of the tools found use DICOM format and, because of this, they cannot perform advanced processing on the information, only visualization and manual labelling. However, it is common that the tools found do not allow filtering and feature extraction: apart from our tool, only two perform some processing:

- Edelmann et al. (2019) [6]: this is the most similar tool compared to ours. However, it has two drawbacks: first, it only allows visualising one lead at a time (and feature extraction is only performed to it); and, second, the input format is specific from MATLAB, requiring the data to be pre-processed with the MATLAB Toolkit before using the software.
- ECG-Viewer (2022) [1]: this is the most widely used, as it allows several open-source input formats and several customisations. However, it has two major drawbacks: first, it does not allow configuration in the peak detection process (not being suitable for athletes); and, second, it does not extract features from the segments and waves (it only includes a general report).

So, our tool has features that are not found in others. Mainly, it is worth highlighting the high degree of customisation of our tool, which allows it to be adapted to the type of user and to select the characteristics that we want to extract from the signals. On the downside, as we use the format of a specific ECG device, we are limited to the information obtained with this type of device.

4   Conclusions

Medical professionals need simulation tools to help them in their learning process. This applies to all areas, including the detection of cardiac problems.

When working with ECG data, it is necessary to pay attention to the PQRST peaks of each of the twelve leads. Moreover, within the sporting environment, the times between peaks and the characteristics to be observed vary in professional athletes.

Therefore, this work presents a free software tool that, thanks to its filtering and peak detection capability, serves as a simulation tool to evaluate the expertise of the future physician.

ECGVisualizer tool includes XMLs loading from a 12-lead ECG, visualization, filtering, feature extraction and fully customized report generation. The two main contributions of this tool are the total customisation of the filtering process and the feature extraction; and, secondly, the possibility of generating a report in a completely open and editable format (being able to join the reports of several patients in a single file).

The results demonstrate the correct feature detection and the future usefulness of this tool.

Declaration of Competing Interest

The authors declare that they have no competing interests that could have appeared to influence this work.

Acknowledgements. This work is part of the project SANEVEC TED2021-130825B-I00, funded by the Ministerio de Ciencia e Innovación (MCIN), Agencia Estatal de Investigación (AEI) of Spain, MCIN/AEI/10.13039/501100011033, and by the European Union NextGenerationEU/PRTR. We also want to thank the professional UEFA football players and the team from La Liga EA SPORTS involved in the collected dataset for allowing us to work with the information from their electrocardiograms.

References

1. ECG-Viewer. https://github.com/CBLRIT/ECG-Viewer. Accessed 29 Sept 2022
2. Encord   ECG.   https://encord.com/try-it-free/?&utm_campaign=cta-blog-medical-light. Accessed 29 Sept 2022
3. OHIF ECG Viewer. https://github.com/RadicalImaging/OHIFExtensionsAndModes/. Accessed 29 Sept 2022
4. Waveform ECG. https://www.cvrgrid.org/tools/waveform-ecg.html. Accessed 29 Sept 2022
5. Drezner, J., et al.: International criteria for electrocardiographic interpretation in athletes: consensus statement. Br. J. Sports Med. **51**(9), 704–731 (2017)
6. Edelmann, J.C., Mair, D., Ziesel, D., Burtscher, M., Ussmueller, T.: An ecg simulator with a novel ecg profile for physiological signals. J. Med. Eng. Technol. **42**(7), 501–509 (2018)
7. Escobar-Linero, E., Domínguez-Morales, M., Sevillano, J.L.: Worker's physical fatigue classification using neural networks. Expert Syst. Appl. **198**, 116784 (2022)
8. Gillette, K., et al.: Medalcare-xl: 16,900 healthy and pathological synthetic 12 lead ecgs from electrophysiological simulations. Sci. Data **10**(1), 531 (2023)
9. Muñoz-Saavedra, L., Luna-Perejón, F., Civit-Masot, J., Miró-Amarante, L., Civit, A., Domínguez-Morales, M.: Affective state assistant for helping users with cognition disabilities using neural networks. Electronics **9**(11), 1843 (2020)
10. School of Health Sciences (The University of Nottingham): A beginners guide to normal heart function, sinus rhythm & common cardiac arrhythmias. https://www.nottingham.ac.uk/nursing/practice/resources/cardiology/function/normal_duration.php. Accessed 1 June 2023
11. Sharma, S., et al.: International recommendations for electrocardiographic interpretation in athletes. Eur. heart J. **39**(16), 1466–1480 (2018)

OTOVIRT: An Image-Guided Workflow for Individualized Surgical Planning and Multiphysics Simulation in Cochlear Implant Patients

Manuel Lazo-Maestre[1]([✉]), Jorge Mansilla-Gil[1], Ma Amparo Callejón-Leblic[1,2],
Cristina Alonso-González[2], Francisco Ropero-Romero[1],
Jesús Ambrosiani-Fernández[3], Javier Reina Tosina[2],
and Serafín Sánchez-Gómez[1]

[1] Servicio de Otorrinolaringología, Hospital Universitario Virgen Macarena, Seville,
Spain
manuel.lazo@faigesco.es, {francisco.ropero.sspa,
serafin.sanchez.sspa}@juntadeandalucia.es
[2] Grupo de Ingeniería Biomédica, Universidad de Sevilla, Sevilla, Spain
cristina.alonso.sspa@juntadeandalucia.es, {mcallejon,jreina}@us.es
[3] Departamento de Anatomía y Embriología Humana, Universidad de Sevilla,
Sevilla, Spain
ambriosiani@us.es

Abstract. In this work, we present a workflow aimed to help ear, nose, and throat (ENT) surgeons in the planning and analysis of inner ear and cochlear implant (CI) surgical interventions. The proposed workflow, OTOVIRT, is based on a multi-modal image registration process with both computer tomography (CT) and magnetic resonance images (MRI) of the patient, followed by the segmentation of anatomical relevant structures. The volumetric images and the 3D anatomic models developed are then used to create virtual surgical simulations of the CI intervention. OTOVIRT modelling workflow proves to be an efficient pipeline to improve surgical outcomes and train surgeons' capabilities. Further advances in OTOVIRT workflow will hopefully allow multimodal data extraction and multiphysics simulation to be systematically conducted in daily clinical practice.

Keywords: 3D models · segmentation · multiphysic simulation

1 Introduction

Last few decades have seen significant improvements in the development of cochlear implants (CI). These devices are capable of converting acoustic stimuli into electrical signals by stimulating auditory nerve fibres through electrodes surgically inserted in the cochlea. CIs allow people with severe hearing loss to develop or regain hearing sensation [1,2].

© ICST Institute for Computer Sciences, Social Informatics and Telecommunications Engineering 2024
Published by Springer Nature Switzerland AG 2024. All Rights Reserved
J.-L. Guisado-Lizar et al. (Eds.): SIMUtools 2023, LNICST 519, pp. 217–226, 2024.
https://doi.org/10.1007/978-3-031-57523-5_17

Regarding CI surgeries, specialists face high inter-subject variability due to the complex anatomical structures embedded within the temporal bone, such as the cochlea, the carotid or the facial nerve [1]. This makes CI surgery a difficult procedure that demands high levels of knowledge and training from ENT specialists [1–3]. The use of modern tools such as virtual reality, haptic feedback, robotics and high-fidelity simulators may prove useful tools to improve surgical performance while preserving patient safety [4–6].

CI virtual surgical simulators have increasingly gained the attention of researchers and ENT surgeons, with different proposals being published in the literature [3,4,7,8]. Most of these simulators are based on the manipulation of expensive synthetic tissues or corpses. Recent proposals also include computer-based solutions relying on virtual reality, haptic feedback, and 3D printing. However, new surgical simulation strategies that can be easily adapted to the clinical practice and systematically used by ENT surgeons are still needed [4].

In this work, a harmonized 3D modeling workflow for realistic virtual simulation of CI surgeries (OTOVIRT) has been designed and implemented. The objective is to provide both novel and specialized surgeons with a modelling and simulation workflow to train and improve surgical capabilities and outcomes while preserving patient safety. We are focused on developing a cost-effective, open and easy-to-use modeling tool to help ENT surgeons in the training and execution of CI surgeries. In this sense, an open-access plugin developed in 3D Slicer will be made available for the community, which can also be used as a part of a more complete multiphysics modeling framework to predict electric field and current distribution in the cochlea and head tissues due to CI stimulation.

The paper is organized as follows: Sect. 2 describes the methods followed for the design and implementation of the OTOVIRT modelling worfklow. Section 3 presents the results obatined for different anatomical models derived from patients medical data using OTOVIRT. Section 4 discusses the results and highlights future improvements of the OTOVIRT pipeline.

2   Material and Methods

Figure 1 shows the OTOVIRT modelling workflow designed. First, a multimodal 3D image registration process is performed based on a CT image of the temporal bone and a full-head MRI. The Landmark Registration module of the open-source 3D-Slicer (https://www.slicer.org/) platform is used to align both images. Subsequently, realistic 3D-anatomical models are obtained using a customized 3D-Slicer module specifically designed for the semi-automatic segmentation of the cochlea and other internal ear structures, including the semicircular canals, carotid artery, sigmoid sinus, internal jugular vein, and facial nerve. Finally, a virtual surgery simulation is carried out in Blender software (https://www.blender.org/) and integrated into the OTOVIRT modelling workflow in order to provide ENT surgeons with more realistic surgical scenarios. In addition, a full-head volume mesh suitable for finite-element-method (FEM), with all internal structures embedded, can be generated for multiphysics simulation.

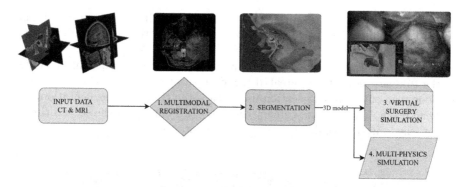

Fig. 1. OTOVIRT modelling workflow. The input data for the OTOVIRT pipeline is an inner-ear CT scan and a full-head MRI. 1) Both CT and MR images are registered and subsequently aligned. 2) A customized 3D-Slicer plugin is used to segment different tissues and create a realistic 3D anatomical model of the inner ear structures. Head tissues are automatically segmented based on SimNIBS software 3) A virtual surgery simulation is conducted in Blender. 4) Finally, a volume mesh suitable for FEM multiphysics analysis can also be obtained from the models.

2.1 Multi-modal Image Registration

Combining structures obtained from different medical images requires a multi-modal registration and co-alignment [9]. In addition, notice that different field of views are supported in our case, with a full-head MRI and a CT scan that only covers the temporal bone. To align both images, the Landmark Registration module of 3D-Slicer is used in the OTOVIRT pipeline. In this module, the user manually places a series of landmarks that are subsequently overlapped using a rigid transformation. The landmarks used in this study were the superior and inferior sections of the cochlea and the semicircular canals, which can be clearly seen in both CT and MR images.

2.2 Segmentation

Semi-automatic Segmentation of the Inner Ear: The segmentation of the inner ear is carried out through a customized plugin coded in 3D Slicer (Fig. 2). It contains a main view with separated sections or tabs to segment each relevant anatomical structure.

The module has been designed to contain the following sections:

– Cochlea segmentation: A simple algorithm is used to segment the cochlea with the use of a bounding box placed by the user in the region of interest (ROI). First, a threshold-based simulation is performed to retain the cochlear bony structures. Second, a morphological opening operation is used to disconnect the cochlea from other spurious elements. Finally, a connectivity-based segmentation is applied to remove these elements.

- Facial nerve segmentation: this tool requires the definition of a series of landmarks, within which a tubular model is interpolated, thus emulating the anatomical profile of the facial nerve.
- Circulatory system segmentation: Similar to the facial nerve simulation tool, the tubular segments are created based on carotid size.
- Bone segmentation: this section uses a two-step threshold segmentation. The first threshold is used to segment the outer contour. With the second threshold, the inner trabeculae is limited to the outer volume.

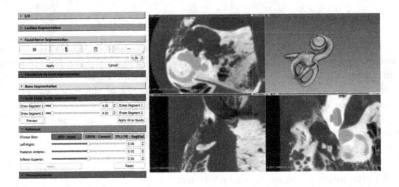

Fig. 2. View of the 3D-Slicer segmentation plugin implemented for the semi-automatic segmentation of inner ear structures.

- Grow from Seeds Segmentation: this is a multi-purpose segmentation tool for complex and irregular anatomical structures, such as the incus, malleus and staples. This section incorporates a set of macros to define inclusion and exclusion criteria of the seeds for a more intuitive and straightforward delimitation of the ROI.
- Reformat: this section includes sliders to rotate the anatomical axes of the volumetric images. This allows the user to observe structures such as the cochlea in real magnitude.
- Measurements: this tool measures relevant data and metrics such as volume segmentation, centroids, roundness, flatness, elongation, principal axes and moments, among others.

Once the segmentation is performed, voxel volume models of the anatomical structures are obtained, which can be later used for the virtual surgical simulation.

Automatic Segmentation of the Full Head: The software selected to segment brain tissues was SimNIBS 3.2.4. From T1 and T2 MRI scans of a patient's head, SimNIBS can automatically generate a range of head structures [10], with greater accuracy in brain tissues [11]. The tissues generated by SimNIBS are: grey matter (GM), white matter (WM), cerebrospinal fluid (CSF), skull (bone), skin, eyes, sinuses, ventricles, and air cavities. SimNIBS uses SPM12 (https://www.fil. ion.ucl.ac.uk//spm/software/spm12/) and CAT12 software (https://neuro-jena. github.io/cat/) for the segmentation [12]. While SPM12 is responsible for modelling tissues based on voxel intensity, CAT12 uses a full segmentation approach to improve surface models such as GM [13].

The main advantange of using SimNIBS as a part of the OTOVIRT modelling workflow is that it provides the user with cleaned and non-intersecting models of head tissues, which are specially useful when creating a non-manifold assembly and a volume mesh suitable for FEM multiphysics simulations.

2.3 Virtual Surgery Simulation

The virtual surgery simulation tool developed in the OTOVIRT pipeline is based on Blender software, which includes: i) a versatile main view that facilitates precise translation and rotation of generated models in space, ii) a data loading tool which automatically assigns a colour and an identifier to each segmented structure, iii) a set of modelling tools to emulate the procedure as closely as possible to the real intervention.

This way, a simulation of a masteidoctomy based on the milling of the temporal bone is performed in Blender. This can be achieved by using a set of tools that mimic a surgical drill. The interaction with the 3D models can be configured in many ways according to size, shape, strength, stroke delay, stroke jitter, among others.

2.4 Multiphysics Simulation

In addition, once the 3D models are obtained, multiphysics simulations can be performed in order to predict the magnitude and distribution of electric fields and currents flowing through a patient's cochlea, as well as extracochlearly through head tissues, depending on different CI stimulation modes. To do that, a non-manifold assembly based on the 3D surface tissue models obtained with OTOVIRT pipeline is created, from which a tetrahedral volume mesh suitable for FEM analyses is subsequently processed. The volume meshes are finally imported into Comsol Multyphyisics software (https://www.comsol.com/ comsol-multiphysics) where the physics of the problem, in this case through Laplace equation, is solved to obtain the voltage distribution across each tissue domain. These models can help us better understand the effect of different stimulation strategies on predicted current distribution, in order to optimize and personalize novel CI stimulation modes.

3 Results

Our results include various 3D anatomical models of the temporal bone and head tissues derived from the OTOVIRT pipeline using patient-specific image data and different CT modalities (see Fig. 3).

Each CT type allows for the visualization of different structures within the cochlea and the temporal bone with varying levels of detail, depending on their spatial resolution. For instance, internal structures of the cochlea such as the *scala timpani* and *scala vestibuli* are only visible in μCT.

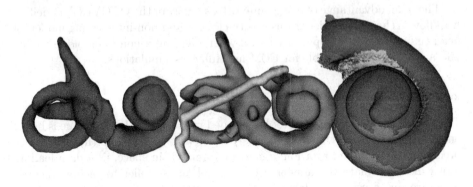

Fig. 3. Comparison of the models obtained from different types of CT scans. Left: cochleovestibular system segmented from a conventional CT scan used in the clinics. Center: CBCT. Right: MicroCT (μCT).

Figure 4 shows an example of a 3D model containing the temporal bone and ear structures. It must be highlighted that this figure emulates a common procedure in CI surgery: a mastoidectomy. It consists in the drilling of the temporal bone in the region beneath the ear pavilion, within the mastoid bone. The surgeon removes irregular bone cells filled with air in order to create the space needed to insert the CI electrode array. Virtual-based simulations were performed in Blender prior to surgery. A virtual mastoidectomy was performed using the sculpting tools in Blender, thus realistically simulating the use of a surgical drill.

To validate the accuracy of the models obtained, various objective volumetric measurements, such as cochlear volume and size, distances A and B, cochlear duct and basal-turn length, were calculated, among others. Table 1 exemplifies a set of relevant morphological data obtained for the pre-operative analysis in a group of patients at different ages, including both adult and children subsets. Through these measures, the required length of the CI electrode array can be estimated based on individual cochlear morphology. This is a relevant clinical parameter which has been reported to be related to clinical post-surgery performance and CI intelligibility measures.

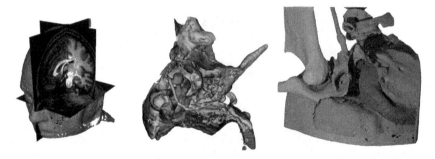

Fig. 4. Left (3DSlicer): 3D model of the head combining a full-head MRI and a CT. Center (3D Slicer) and right (Blender): 3D combined model after a virtual mastoidectomy.

Table 1. A set of features obtained from the 3D models using the Measurements tab of the 3D Slicer plugin developed in this work. A comparison of metrics between young and adult patients is shown. (SD: standard deviation; CDL: cochlear duct length; 2TL: two-turn length; BTL: basal-turn length).

	Adults (> 18 years)		Early Children (< 12 months)	
	mean	SD	mean	SD
Distance A (mm)	9.04	0.37	9.35	0.54
Distance B (mm)	6.70	0.52	7.01	0.43
CDL(lw) (mm)	36.35	1.51	37.59	1.34
2TL(lw) (mm)	33.00	1.38	34.12	1.40
BTL(lw) (mm)	21.97	0.92	22.72	1.07
Cochlear volume (mm^3)	73.57	8.02	69.61	10.45
Temporal volume (mm^3)	45,169.79	1,203.56	10,449.96	456.34

Finally, Fig. 5 shows an example of a multiphyisics simulation in which the 3D models were used to obtain a volume mesh suitable for FEM analysis. Electric field and current spread were computed for two different CI stimulation modes: monopolar and bipolar. This simulation allowed us to predict the different extension of current spread through the complete head for these two stimulation modes. As seen in Fig. 5, while monopolar leads to a higher spread of the current through the scalp and the head, the bipolar mode confines more of the electric current into the region near the cochlea. Therefore, through realistic full head models of the head and inner ear tissues a prediction of both intracochlear and extracochlear voltages and current spread can be obtained in a specific-subject manner, thus paving the way towards the optimization and personalization of CI stimulation strategies and electrode array designs.

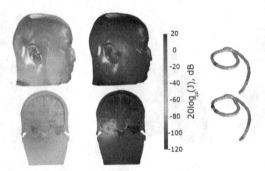

Fig. 5. Current spread through head tissues based on multiphysics simulation for two different CI stimulation modes: monopolar and bipolar.

4   Discussion and Future Work

Conventional CT images of the temporal bone and the proposed OTOVIRT workflow allowed ENT surgeons to easily and intuitively visualize the anatomy of the patient prior to surgery. Virtual modeling surgical tools prove relevant and useful in the training of both novel and specialized surgeons as well as in the planning, optimization, and customization of ENT surgical approaches. The accuracy of the models generated with OTOVIRT was validated subjectively with the help of ENT specialized surgeons and anatomists using a customized questionnaire. The proposed workflow proves to be an useful and intuitive tool to improve the understanding of the anatomy of the patient as well as to optimize surgical planning. The simulation of the intervention showed to be useful for surgeons who improved their knowledge of the subject-specific anatomical region before the procedure. Providing them with the simulated model on a portable device during the actual surgery also proved to be beneficial. However, a more comprehensive and quantitative validation of the accuracy of the OTOVIRT workflow is still needed.

The pipeline was tested in a limited group of seven patients. As future work, we will validate the modelling processes with more patients and surgeon experts in order to systematize and generalize the workflow into the daily clinical practice. This will allow for a systematic preoperative planning that will hopefully improve patient safety and surgical outcomes. More experienced ENT surgeons will be able to process the data faster with the proposed workflow and will have a greater chance to analyze the optimal path for the surgery.

The 3D Slicer plugin developed in this work can also be used to gather individual metrics during preoperative phases and further quantify inter-individual differences in CI patients. Further analysis based on anatomical surgical parameters can be made to predict CI outcomes, e.g., based on characteristics such as electrode depth insertion, type of intervention, etc.

Furthermore, the OTOVIRT pipeline has been shown to be independent of image-type acquisition and has been tested and validated with standard clinical

CT, cone-beam CT, and micro-CT images (Fig. 5). Therefore, its application may provide a multi-purpose tool with high impact in generating large datasets that will help developing automatic methodologies to simplify CI surgeries.

The use of open-source and widely available software and technologies proves possible, efficient in cost and development time. This facilitates the diffusion and provides a solid substrate on which to continue the integration of new tools that complement the workflow in an efficient and targeted manner.

In the future, with the development of artificial intelligence (AI) neural networks and deep learning algorithms, the entire workflow may be a fully automatized process, with validations tools more widely available.

A further step forward will be using the OTOVIRT pipeline to sistematically perform multiphysics simulations, including other modeled tissue data, which will allow us to quantify current spread over the head and optimize CI stimulation strategies in an individual manner.

5 Conclusion

OTOVIRT worflow has been designed and implemented in this work. Its validation with patient-specific image data has proven to be succesful, and provide surgeons with an affordable and easy-to-use pipeline to train surgical capabilities and improve surgical outcomes while preserving patient safety. The proposed OTOVIRT pipeline paves the way for further multimodal analysis and personalized multiphysics simulation to better understand current spread under different cochlear implant stimulation strategies.

Acknowledgements. This work was funded by the OTOVIRT project (PIN-0097-2020): Cirugía Virtual para el entrenamiento por simulación y el ensayo preoperatorio en cirugía otológica y en cirugía endoscópica endonasal by the Andalusian Consejery of Health and Families, co-funded by FEDER Europe.

References

1. Deep, N.L., et al.: Cochlear implantation: an overview. J. Neurol. Surg. B Skull Base **80**(2), 169–177 (2019)
2. Zeng, F.G., et al. Cochlear implants: system design, integration, and evaluation. IEEE Rev. Biomed. Eng. **1**, 115–142 (2008). ISSN 19411189. https://doi.org/10.1109/RBME.2008.2008250
3. Wiet, G.J., Sørensen, M.S., Andersen, S.A.W.: Otologic skills training (2017). ISSN 15578259
4. Alwani, M., et al.: Current state of surgical simulation training in otolaryngology: Systematic review of simulation training models. Arch. Otorhinolaryngol.-Head Neck Surg. **3** (2019). https://doi.org/10.24983/scitemed.aohns.2019.00109
5. Okuda, Y., et al.: The utility of simulation in medical education: what is the evidence? (2009). ISSN 00272507
6. Moglia, A., et al.: A systematic review of virtual reality simulators for robot-assisted surgery (2016). ISSN 18737560

7. Javia, L., Deutsch, E.S.: A systematic review of simulators in otolaryngology (2012). ISSN 01945998
8. Arora, A., et al.: Virtual reality simulation training in Otolaryngology. Int. J. Surg. **12**(2), 87–94 (2014)
9. El-Gamal, F.E.Z.A., Elmogy, M., Atwan, A.: Current trends in medical image registration and fusion (2016). ISSN 11108665
10. Saturnino, G.B., et al.: Simnibs 2.1: a comprehensive pipeline for individualized electric field modelling for transcranial brain stimulation. bioRxiv (2018). https://doi.org/10.1101/500314
11. Thielscher, A., Antunes, A., Saturnino, G.B.: Field modeling for transcranial magnetic stimulation: a useful tool to understand the physiological effects of TMS, pp. 222–225 (2015). https://doi.org/10.1109/EMBC.2015.7318340
12. Farokhian, F., et al.: Comparing cat12 and vbm8 for detecting brain morphological abnormalities in temporal lobe epilepsy. Front. Neurol. **8** (2017). ISSN 16642295. https://doi.org/10.3389/fneur.2017.00428
13. Nielsen, J.D., et al.: Automatic skull segmentation from MR images for realistic volume conductor models of the head: assessment of the state-of-the-art. NeuroImage **174**, 587–598 (2018). ISSN 1053-8119. https://doi.org/10.1016/j.neuroimage.2018.03.001

Network Simulations

Adaptive Sharing of IoT Resources Through SDN-Based Microsegmentation of Services Using Mininet

Angely Martínez[1], José D. Padrón[1(✉)] ⓘ, Jorge Luis Zambrano-Martinez[2] ⓘ, and Carlos T. Calafate[1] ⓘ

[1] Computer Engineering Department (DISCA), Universitat Politècnica de València, Valencia, Spain
anmar74a@inf.upv.es, {jdpadper,calafate}@disca.upv.es
[2] University of Azuay, Cuenca, Ecuador
jorge.zambrano@uazuay.edu.ec

Abstract. As we gradually embrace Smart Cities and the many advantages they can potentially offer, several technical issues arise that should be properly addressed, including security, efficiency, and performance, among others. In this regard, the massive deployment of IoT devices to support the numerous potential applications can consume excessive resources if their use is not optimized; this includes the sharing of some IoT devices whose content has the potential to be shared by many potential applications. One such example are CCTV smart cameras, as their deployment is costly, has a significant impact on urban aesthetics, and also the traffic flow they generate is high. To address such issue, in this paper we propose a novel SDN framework that enables the seamless sharing of streamed CCTV camera contents among multiple users, while adequately accounting for security and privacy restrictions. In particular, we adopt the Zero Trust paradigm to have a fine granularity control of the data-sensitive contents streamed by CCTV cameras. Experiments performed in Mininet using the Ryu controller evidence the potential of our solutions, which is able to achieve the target goals in a resource efficient manner, while introducing a low network updating overhead.

Keywords: Software-Defined Networks · IoT · Microsegmentation · Resource sharing · Zero Trust security

1 Introduction

Smart Cities rely on Information and Communication Technologies (ICT) to create, deploy, and promote sustainable development practices that address the growing urbanization challenges. In this context, Internet of Things (IoT) solutions emerge as key enablers for smart city ecosystems [2,11], as they allow

This work is derived from R&D project PID2021-122580NB-I00, funded by MCIN/AEI/10.13039/501100011033 and "ERDF A way of making Europe".

J.-L. Guisado-Lizar et al. (Eds.): SIMUtools 2023, LNICST 519, pp. 229–242, 2024.
https://doi.org/10.1007/978-3-031-57523-5_18

collecting and analyzing data in real-time, thereby helping municipalities, enterprises, and citizens to make better decisions that improve their overall quality of life.

IoT devices are used in various domains of smart cities, such as infrastructure, mobility, public services, and utilities. For example, connected traffic lights [7] can adjust light cadence and timing to respond to real-time traffic, reducing road congestion. Connected cars can communicate with parking meters and electric vehicle charging docks, and thereby direct drivers to the nearest available spot [9]. Also, smart garbage cans can automatically schedule pick-up as needed, improving upon the existing pre-planned scheduling [23].

While IoT devices offer many benefits for smart cities, they also pose some challenges and limitations that need to be addressed. These challenges include the interoperability of IoT devices from different vendors, platforms, and standards, as well as the security and privacy of IoT devices and the data they generate. Moreover, IoT devices collect large amounts of personal and sensitive data from citizens, which raises concerns about data protection, consent, and ownership. Therefore, IoT devices need to have adequate security mechanisms and follow ethical principles to ensure the trust and safety of smart city stakeholders [1].

One possible solution to overcome some of the challenges of IoT devices in smart cities is to adopt a sharing economy model [17]. A sharing economy is a system where people share access to goods and services rather than owning them individually. Sharing economies can reduce the costs and environmental impacts of owning and maintaining IoT devices by optimizing their utilization and distribution. In the context of Smart Cities, it would be recommendable to share IoT resources that are more expensive to deploy and maintain, that occupy more physical space, or that consume more energy.

Nowadays, Closed-Circuit Television (CCTV) is employed in practically every area of the city, including public spaces, houses, shops, passageways, and even roadways outside the city. Although each of these cameras has a unique role, they are all employed to continuously monitor the area, capturing nearby events for later reference. Also, each of them is usually in a separate network. Currently, there is no collaborative utilization of these devices, which represent a large investment. Yet, in the long run, it appears from a macroeconomic perspective that the existence of parallel networks of CCTVs performing a same task will not be economically beneficial due to the high initial investment and ongoing maintenance expenses [22].

In this work, we focus on CCTV surveillance cameras in the context of IoT, where they are used as yet another IoT resource. In particular, we want to study how such resources can be shared in a controlled and secure manner between multiple users. To this end, we consider that the adoption of Software-Defined Networks (SDN), and specifically the service microsegmentation paradigm, can be helpful to achieve the target goals. Hence, our proposed solution leverages SDN microsegmentation to achieve the desired granular security based on the Zero Trust concept [10], which is applied in the context of IoT resource sharing.

In particular, we develop a full SDN architecture for computing on the edge whereby a web application instructs the Ryu SDN controller on how to enable CCTV camera flows only to authorized clients, being able to create dynamic rules for each CCTV element that benefit from a high-level of management granularity, including the possibility of pinpointing the exact days/times each client is allowed to access the video stream generated by each particular surveillance camera.

The remainder of the paper is organized as follows: in the next section, we provide an overview of some related works. Then, in Sect. 3, we provide an overview of our proposal, including also technical details regarding its implementation. Section 4 details the simulation framework we have set forth in order to undertake the desired study. Experimental results are then presented and discussed in Section 5. Finally, conclusions and future research directions are provided in Sect. 6.

2   Related Work

IoT resources that can be shared with multiple users in a controlled and secure manner are considered one of the main elements of smart city ecosystems. In this regard, several research works address SDN architectures that enable such IoT resource sharing. Li et al. [12] propose an SDN-based IoT architecture to provide data obtained from IoT devices, and their interoperability is supported at different levels, allowing the rapid creation of IoT applications to reuse data and applications. Similarly, Firouzi & Rahmani [6] discuss computational and data sharing among IoT devices, integrating transport network control with distributed cloud and edge resources to provide dynamic and efficient IoT services. On the other hand, Mukherjee et al. [13] propose an SDN-based distributed IoT network with a network functions virtualisation implementation for smart cities; in particular, a residential area uses ICT and IoT networks to improve performance and minimise round trip times through multiple distributed controllers and clusters, thereby improving load balancing, scalability, availability, integrity, and security. Bouloukakis et al. [4] propose a cross-layer middleware system that allows mission-critical data from IoT devices to be shared in a timely and reliable manner with relevant consumers by prioritizing messages.

Osman et al. [14] provide microsegmentation as a means to reduce smart home network attacks with the help of a cloud perimeter by implementing features that create an inventory of all devices and their vulnerabilities, dynamically assigning IoT devices to microsegments to isolate them using security policies at the network level. In [21], the author proposes implementing micro-segmentation to protect smart homes that contain IoT networks from internal attacks that involve lateral movements, thus automatically classifying non-malicious devices based on their functionality to assign them to confined network microsegments.

In the same way, there is a growing number of defenders of the Zero Trust security paradigm linked to micro-segmentation. Syed et al. [18] discuss the conventional micro-segmentation and automation approaches that are available.

In [5], the authors propose a two-layer access control architecture that is compatible with the Zero Trust model to provide automated support for dynamic re-configurations in IoT infrastructures with remote access. Instead, Basta et al. [3] analyze an analytical brand to characterize and quantify the effectiveness of Zero Trust micro-segmentation to improve network security.

In this paper we build upon this Zero Trust micro-segmentation concept to create an IoT-sharing solution whereby the video contents generated by CCTV cameras can be conveyed to multiple receivers (users) depending on their permission levels, which may vary dynamically. In this regard, we develop an application whereby the administrator can have fine grain control over these resources.

3   Proposed Solution

Computer networks are the backbone of our daily activity and of the Internet. The amount of data that circulates through them is uncountable, thus generating the concept and paradigm of "big data". Due to the static nature of the network architecture created by the different network devices (i.e.: routers, switches, firewalls, etc.), a bottleneck is often generated, establishing limitations in terms of scalability and automation. Regarding scalability, traditional networks are limited due to their dependence on the physical hardware of the devices themselves. In terms of automation, they have few capabilities and require a significant amount of manual intervention. Hence, the maintenance of such a large network, especially when it is growing and changing dynamically, is less and less in line with business needs and user demands, while at the same time become very complex to manage.

Regarding the IoT paradigm, it is being included both at a personal level, and in all kinds of industries, from manufacturing to healthcare or transportation; the multitude of Internet-connected devices that this implies contributes to the growth of network traffic, stressing the capacity of cloud data centers. According to Perwej et al. [16], the number of interconnected devices was projected to soar past 34 billion by 2021. Moreover, it is anticipated that these devices will uniquely identify objects, being most connected through an Internet of Things platform. In particular, the dominant areas of data generation are projected to be security systems and video surveillance due to their large file sizes.

This paper attempts to provide a solution based on SDN that allows to flexibly and efficiently manage access to different data sources from different IoT devices, which are to be shared conditionally with different service users. More precisely, we use the micro-segmentation technique, which allows security architects to logically divide the data center into different security segments down to the individual workload level. This allows administrators to program security policies based on where a workload may be used, what type of data it will access, and how important or sensitive the application is, to adequately manage the IoT devices that are part of that network.

Particularly, the network scenario to be implemented consists on: (i) IoT nodes with high data flows (i.e.: video surveillance cameras), and (ii) physically connected nodes (i.e.: servers). The latter will have the role of clients, and will receive the traffic from these cameras according to the agreed service conditions. Thus, the main idea is to allow the operator to add and/or remove nodes dynamically and securely via a web interface, while controlling the flow of the entire network to the different clients.

To understand how our goal is achieved, Fig. 1 shows an example of what would be the communication process in the architecture if the administrator were to perform the operation of adding a client to a camera from the web application. First, the network administrator sends the POST request in a JSON format, to accept the multicast traffic from group 224.0.0.4 to the client. Then, the camera-client relationship table is updated in the database server. Third, the SDN controller processes the request, and sends the rule to the corresponding network devices through the OpenFlow protocol. Finally, when the Access Control List (ACL) table flows are updated, the controller sends an HTTP response with code 200 OK to notify of the success of the request.

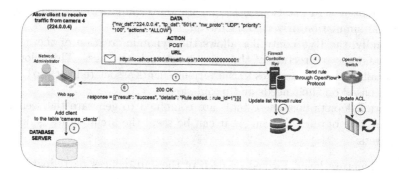

Fig. 1. Example of a triggered update in the context of our solution.

As final remarks regarding this solution, it is worth mentioning two crucial parts of the web app interface. In Fig. 2 we can observe how the allowance period for sending the information of a camera to a specific client is managed. As we can observe, we can set specific rules for a certain time period. Figure 3 presents the main view of the application, where the administrator can see the number of clients and cameras, and also which client(s) is related to the different cameras.

4   Simulation Framework

In this section, we describe the simulation framework used for our study, which involves two different tools:

1. Mininet-WiFi version 2.4.3 [8], in order to emulate the network.
2. Ryu version 4.34 [15], which serves as an external controller to the network.

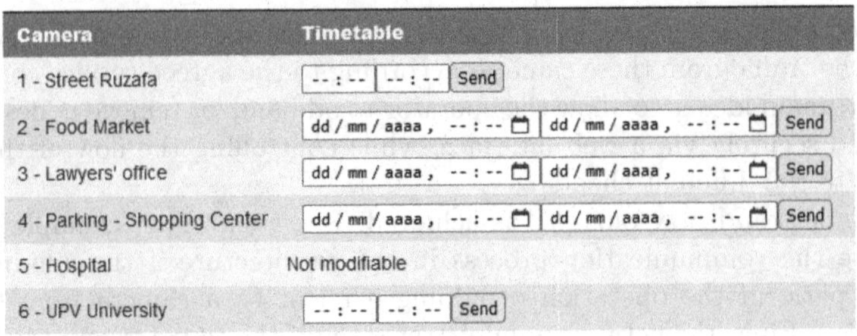

Fig. 2. Interface to detail the allowance period for specific cameras.

Firstly, Mininet-WiFi allows us to design and emulate the proposed network. To this end, we devise a tree topology consisting of 5 switches (Open vSwitch) and 4 Wi-Fi access points. Notice that Mininet-WiFi extends the functionality of Mininet [19] (working with the OpenFlow technology), by adding access points and virtualized Wi-Fi stations based on standard Linux wireless controllers and the 802.11 simulation driver 80211_hwsim.

Secondly, the Ryu controller allows the dynamic creation of the flow table entries, and the redirection of the various network messages. This allows us to dynamically redirect messages to the various clients associated with IoT security cameras based on their needs and permissions.

Figure 4 depicts how these tools are combined to generate the scenario for the evaluation of our solution. As it can be seen, the architecture is divided in three layers:

1. Infrastructure layer: formed by each of the end devices participating in the network. On the left side, 6 video surveillance cameras, connected each one to an AP (Access Point), which then are connected to an Open vSwitch device. Then, on the right side, 5 servers (clients) connected to 4 Open vSwitch devices.
2. Control layer: composed by the Ryu SDN controller.
3. Application layer: web application, which will give the network administrator the flexibility to make changes in the infrastructure. It also allows dynamic addition and deletion of clients, and establishes time-based rules for receiving traffic.

To have a complete view of how our implementation works, Fig. 5 shows the different flow associations and the network topologies involved.

Firstly, Fig. 5a represents the network architecture part related to the IoT Security Cameras, which act as nodes. At the node level, we have that all the cameras are wirelessly connected to their corresponding access point. For the APs, we can see that they are physically connected to a switch which manages the traffic on this network segment based on the flow tables.

Secondly, the client-side network topology is illustrated in Fig. 5b. Here, it becomes evident that the client nodes are not connected to the Access Points

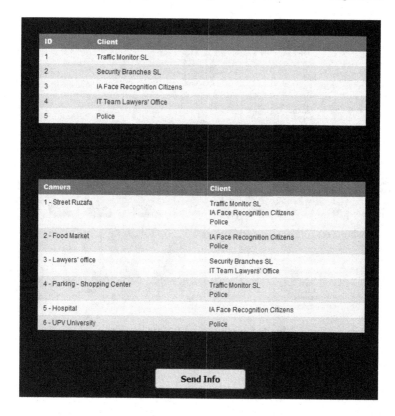

Fig. 3. Global view of the system status.

(APs), but are directly linked to switches. It is crucial to remember that the first level switch is connected to the equivalent first level switch within the camera topology, as we have depicted earlier in Fig. 4. This arrangement guarantees the visibility of both topologies and enables communication, even when the controller is located centrally within the control layer.

Finally, to illustrate our point of view, we present an example showing the data flow transmitted within the network from different cameras to clients 1 and 5, as seen in Fig. 5c. Obviously, this data flow previously traverses the respective network devices. This representation originates from the camera-client relationship that we have established for the initial basic solution. Ultimately, the multicast data stream that is sent follows the camera-client association shown in Table 1.

5   Simulation Results

In this section, we present our simulation results based on the simulation framework described in the previous section. Our goal is to determine the degree of

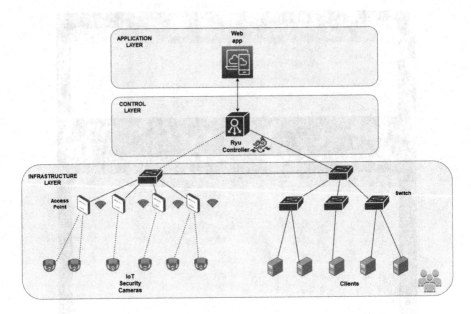

Fig. 4. Scenario used for evaluation.

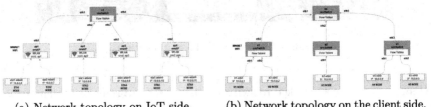

(a) Network topology on IoT side.   (b) Network topology on the client side.

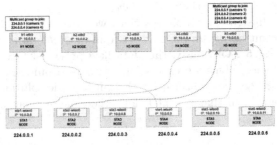

(c) Multicast flow definitions.

Fig. 5. Overview of the different topologies involved, along with the end flow associations.

effectiveness of our SDN-based solution, where the proposed workflow of Fig. 1 is used to share the data flows of the CCTV cameras for the sake of efficiency, while maintaining adequate levels of privacy. To this end, we perform different experiments that measure the network's efficiency. In particular, we assess the performance of UDP multicast connections when a client is receiving data from a camera, along with the efficiency of deploying OpenFlow rules when clients are added or removed. It is important to note that the number of clients and cameras used in this experiment are shown in Table 1.

Regarding resource consumption metrics, we perform a comparative analysis between various packet loads (180, 360, 720, and 1000 pkt/s). The goal of this test is to evaluate whether sending flow rules to network devices substantially raises the CPU load of these devices, and to know their status during traffic redirection. More precisely, our goal is to measure the performance of the primary switch, which is the gateway for all rules and the resulting traffic flow.

Having said this, we start our analysis by examining the performance of the UDP multicast connection when a client receives 1,130 KBytes of data from the camera over a span of 10 s. To facilitate this, we employed the iperf tool [20], which enables the execution of client/server bandwidth tests, and provides various performance parameters of the connection outcome.

Figure 6 displays the results in terms of bandwidth and jitter for the UDP datagram client/server test. More specifically, Fig. 6a represents the bandwidth achieved at each one-second interval. As we can observe, it begins at its peak of 1,000 Kbit/s, then stabilizes at approximately 900 Kbit/s. Subsequently, from the ninth second until the conclusion, it declines by 33%, down to 600 Kbit/s. This primarily occurs because the majority of the file has been transferred, which in turn impacts the bandwidth. So, in general, the bandwidth is maintained consistently stable.

Table 1. Initial client-camera relationship.

Client (IP)	Camera (IP)
1 (10.0.0.1)	1 (224.0.0.1)
	4 (224.0.0.4)
2 (10.0.0.2)	3 (224.0.0.3)
3 (10.0.0.3)	1 (224.0.0.1)
	2 (224.0.0.2)
	5 (224.0.0.5)
4 (10.0.0.4)	3 (224.0.0.3)
5 (10.0.0.5)	1 (224.0.0.1)
	2 (224.0.0.2)
	4 (224.0.0.4)
	6 (224.0.0.6)

Regarding jitter, Fig. 6b shows its performance during the test. As it can be seen, it varies between 6.3 and 12.8 ms. A high jitter has a negative impact on the quality of the video transmission, being more susceptible for applications that process video in real time. When performed on our simulation, we cannot say that the transmission result is poor; however, if implemented on a real environment, it would be convenient to implement measures including network congestion management and adequate allocation of resources, to mitigate jitter as much as possible.

In terms of average results, the test showed an average bandwidth of 854 Kbit/s and a jitter of 10.19 ms, which are acceptable results for this application.

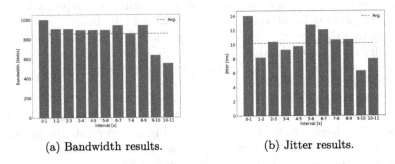

(a) Bandwidth results.   (b) Jitter results.

Fig. 6. UDP client/server traffic test.

In terms of OpenFlow rules performance, Table 2 shows two important parameters to be measured: the time required by the network to fully update when a new rule is added, and the time to delete a client with the use of an OpenFlow rule. In particular, the first time value is the measured time that the client nodes took to receive the traffic from the camera, measured from the time when we send the instructions from the application level. As can be observed, this time is 37.876 ms. This represents the interval required to implement the changes, and ensures that the network reflects the new configurations. It is important to mention that this will vary depending on various factors, such as the size or complexity of the network topology. However, the time obtained for our case shows a high efficiency in terms of updating the network, despite Mininet resource virtualization in the scope of a single standard machine.

Regarding the second time, this measures the time it takes for network devices to update the rules received from the application level, in this case to deny a client from receiving traffic. For this test, client number 5 will be used as the player, since in the initial scenario (see Table 1) it is the one with the most cameras allowed. As shown, the time value achieved is 67.052 ms. This is quite acceptable since the procedure is performed in less than 1 tenth of a second, and was performed on the client that was receiving the most traffic. These results highlight the agility of the SDN architecture in this solution, allowing the overall

Table 2. OpenFlow rules performance.

Time to update network	37.876 ms
Time to delete a client	67.052 ms

system to quickly adapt to the changes and demands of the network environment, while offering efficiency and low latency for this type of requests.

Finally, the question arises as to the solution's ability to manage resource consumption for high network traffic intensities. As depicted in Fig. 7, the results indicate a more than acceptable performance within the tested system. In terms of CPU usage for the main switch, Fig. 7a shows that it remains relatively low, having a peak value of only 16.1% despite an increase in the load, suggesting an efficient utilization of resources. Similarly, the system utilization during the test (load average), as illustrated in Fig. 7b, stays at reasonably low levels, under 0.3, suggesting that the system is not subjected to any excessive load. In particular, this means that the CPU was idle 70% of the time on average for the maximum traffic intensity.

As a sample of the traffic generated from the cameras for the evaluation of the CPU load, Fig. 8 shows the volume of data traversing the network; some traffic flow peaks can be spotted, occurring concurrently with falls, yet maintaining a good stability overall. This is to be expected due to the virtualized nature of all network elements, and performance should be better in actual deployments.

All in all, the results indicate that, as network traffic increases, the parameters assessed tend to increase correspondingly. However, this increase is not very significant. Therefore, we can draw the conclusion that the system demonstrates an acceptable efficiency within the given context, proving that it can manage a higher data flow without a performance drop.

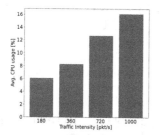 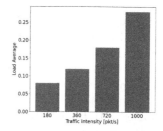

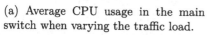

(a) Average CPU usage in the main switch when varying the traffic load.   (b) Load Average comparison.

Fig. 7. Metrics when traffic flows through the network.

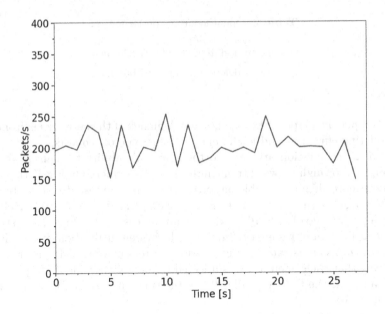

Fig. 8. No. of packets over time for 180 packets/s traffic load.

6   Conclusions and Future Work

As we move towards Smart City scenarios embracing thousands of IoT devices, avoiding further device proliferation is recommendable for the sake of efficiency, energy consumption, economy and aesthetics, among others. Hence, the sharing of data flows generated by IoT devices is recommendable, although it may generate new issues related to security and privacy of such data flows, especially when such devices generate sensitive data like video flows.

In this paper we addressed the aforementioned issue by proposing an SDN framework that allows sharing video flows generated by CCTV cameras. Due to the highly sensitive nature of such data, we devise a solution based on the Zero Trust paradigm that manages such flows with a very high granularity, to have full control on which clients can access the flows of individual cameras, and their allowed time span.

Experimental results using the Mininet platform show that our application, when combined with the Ryu SDN controller, is able to achieve the target goals in a straightforward and yet effective manner. In addition, we find that the time overhead for introducing network updates is maintained rather low: under 40ms for updating the network with new clients, and under 70ms to remove an existing client (receiving multiple flows). In addition, we show that traffic performance is maintained at good levels using our multicast-based solution, to efficiently reach multiple clients simultaneously.

As future work we plan to extend our solution to other types of IoT devices/data flows, and to deploy our solution in a testbed to have more realistic performance data, especially for the wireless part of the network.

References

1. Al-Turjman, F., Zahmatkesh, H., Shahroze, R.: An overview of security and privacy in smart cities' IoT communications. Trans. Emerg. Telecommun. Technol. **33**(3), e3677 (2022). https://doi.org/10.1002/ett.3677
2. Arasteh, H., et al.: IoT-based smart cities: a survey. In: 2016 IEEE 16th International Conference on Environment and Electrical Engineering (EEEIC), pp. 1–6 (2016). https://doi.org/10.1109/EEEIC.2016.7555867
3. Basta, N., Ikram, M., Kaafar, M.A., Walker, A.: Towards a zero-trust microsegmentation network security strategy: an evaluation framework. In: NOMS 2022-2022 IEEE/IFIP Network Operations and Management Symposium, pp. 1–7. IEEE (2022)
4. Bouloukakis, G., et al.: PrioDeX: a data exchange middleware for efficient event prioritization in SDN-based IoT systems. ACM Trans. Internet Things **2**(3), 1–32 (2021)
5. Federici, F., Martintoni, D., Senni, V.: A zero-trust architecture for remote access in industrial IoT infrastructures. Electronics **12**(3), 566 (2023)
6. Firouzi, R., Rahmani, R.: A distributed SDN controller for distributed IoT. IEEE Access **10**, 42873–42882 (2022)
7. Han, J., Shen, D., Karbowski, D., Rousseau, A.: Leveraging multiple connected traffic light signals in an energy-efficient speed planner. IEEE Control Syst. Lett. **5**(6), 2078–2083 (2021). https://doi.org/10.1109/LCSYS.2020.3047605
8. INTRIG: Mininet-WiFi. emulation platform for software-defined wireless networks. (2023). https://mininet-wifi.github.io/. Accessed 29 June 2023
9. KC, Y., Kang, C.S.: A connected car-based parking location service system. In: 2019 IEEE International Conference on Internet of Things and Intelligence System (IoTaIS), pp. 167–171 (2019). https://doi.org/10.1109/IoTaIS47347.2019.8980443
10. Keeriyattil, S.: Microsegmentation and zero trust: introduction. In: Zero Trust Networks with VMware NSX, pp. 17–31. Apress, Berkeley (2019). https://doi.org/10.1007/978-1-4842-5431-8_2
11. Kim, T., Ramos, C., Mohammed, S.: Smart city and IoT. Future Gener. Comput. Syst. **76**, 159–162 (2017). https://doi.org/10.1016/j.future.2017.03.034. https://www.sciencedirect.com/science/article/pii/S0167739X17305253
12. Li, Y., Su, X., Riekki, J., Kanter, T., Rahmani, R.: A SDN-based architecture for horizontal internet of things services. In: 2016 IEEE International Conference on Communications (ICC), pp. 1–7. IEEE (2016)
13. Mukherjee, B.K., Pappu, S.I., Islam, M.J., Acharjee, U.K.: An SDN based distributed IoT network with NFV implementation for smart cities. In: Bhuiyan, T., Rahman, M.M., Ali, M.A. (eds.) ICONCS 2020. LNICST, vol. 325, pp. 539–552. Springer, Cham (2020). https://doi.org/10.1007/978-3-030-52856-0_43
14. Osman, A., Wasicek, A., Köpsell, S., Strufe, T.: Transparent microsegmentation in smart home IoT networks. In: HotEdge (2020)
15. Pemberton, D., Linton, A., Russell, S.: Ryu OpenFlow controller. University of Oregon, Technical report (2014)

16. Perwej, Y., Haq, K., Parwej, F., Mumdouh, M., Hassan, M.: The internet of things (IoT) and its application domains. Int. J. Comput. Appl. **975**(8887), 182 (2019)
17. Rahman, M.A., Rashid, M.M., Hossain, M.S., Hassanain, E., Alhamid, M.F., Guizani, M.: Blockchain and IoT-based cognitive edge framework for sharing economy services in a smart city. IEEE Access **7**, 18611–18621 (2019). https://doi.org/10.1109/ACCESS.2019.2896065
18. Syed, N.F., Shah, S.W., Shaghaghi, A., Anwar, A., Baig, Z., Doss, R.: Zero trust architecture (ZTA): a comprehensive survey. IEEE Access **10**, 57143–57179 (2022)
19. Team, M.: Mininet releases (2021). https://github.com/mininet/mininet/releases. Accessed 10 Sept 2022
20. Tirumala, A.: Iperf: The TCP/UDP bandwidth measurement tool (1999). http://dastnlanr.net/Projects/Iperf/
21. Wasicek, A.: The future of 5G smart home network security is micro-segmentation. Netw. Secur. **2020**(11), 11–13 (2020)
22. Yeganegi, K., Moradi, D., Obaid, A.J.: Create a wealth of security CCTV cameras. J. Phys. Conf. Ser. **1530**(1), 012110 (2020). https://doi.org/10.1088/1742-6596/1530/1/012110
23. Zhou, Z.: IoT-based smart garbage system for efficient food waste management. Sci. World J. (2014). https://doi.org/10.1155/2014/646953

UAV-Assisted Wireless Communications: An Experimental Analysis of A2G and G2A Channels

Kamran Shafafi$^{(\boxtimes)}$ (ID), Eduardo Nuno Almeida (ID), André Coelho (ID), Helder Fontes (ID), Manuel Ricardo (ID), and Rui Campos (ID)

INESC TEC and Faculdade de Engenharia, Universidade do Porto, Porto, Portugal
{kamran.shafafi,eduardo.n.almeida,andre.f.coelho,
helder.m.fontes,manuel.ricardo,rui.l.campos}@inesctec.pt

Abstract. Unmanned Aerial Vehicles (UAVs) offer promising potential as communications node carriers, providing on-demand wireless connectivity to users. While existing literature presents various wireless channel models, it often overlooks the impact of UAV heading. This paper provides an experimental characterization of the Air-to-Ground (A2G) and Ground-to-Air (G2A) wireless channels in an open environment with no obstacles nor interference, considering the distance and the UAV heading. We analyze the received signal strength indicator and the TCP throughput between a ground user and a UAV, covering distances between 50 m and 500 m, and considering different UAV headings. Additionally, we characterize the antenna's radiation pattern based on UAV headings. The paper provides valuable perspectives on the capabilities of UAVs in offering on-demand and dynamic wireless connectivity, as well as highlights the significance of considering UAV heading and antenna configurations in real-world scenarios.

Keywords: Experimental Wireless Channel Characterization · UAV Communications · Air-to-Ground · Ground-to-Air

1 Introduction

Due to the decreasing costs, size, and weight, as well as the increasing endurance, high maneuverability, and ability to hover, Unmanned Aerial Vehicles (UAVs) have emerged as interesting platforms for a wide set of applications, such as surveillance, aerial imagery, operations in unreachable areas, delivery of goods, and search and rescue missions [1]. A key capability envisioned by 5G and beyond cellular networks is quickly deploying and providing on-demand temporary wireless connectivity in emergencies and crowded areas. In this regard, the use of UAVs forming aerial wireless networks has been noted as a cost-effective and flexible solution to carry network hardware and establish a temporary network infrastructure, providing wireless connectivity and enhancing the capacity

© ICST Institute for Computer Sciences, Social Informatics and Telecommunications Engineering 2024
Published by Springer Nature Switzerland AG 2024. All Rights Reserved
J.-L. Guisado-Lizar et al. (Eds.): SIMUtools 2023, LNICST 519, pp. 243–256, 2024.
https://doi.org/10.1007/978-3-031-57523-5_19

of existing networks [2]. Sending non-critical data, such as video transmission, requires the maximization of the throughput between the users on the ground and the UAV while tolerating errors and delays. However, sending critical data such as control signals (e.g., controlling robots for search and rescue missions, UAV controls) requires high Quality of Service (QoS), namely low delay and Packet Loss Ratio (PLR) [3]. In addition to establishing a reliable link, the QoS requirements such as throughput, PLR, and delay should be considered [4]. Still, establishing reliable broadband wireless links faces many challenges. In this regard, wireless channel modeling and characterization are important for designing and optimizing wireless communications systems. Accurate models allow the prediction of the signal quality, the evaluation of the system performance, and the development of new wireless technologies. They enable network designers to identify potential problems and optimize system parameters, making wireless channel modeling a critical area of research in wireless communications.

Comprehensive channel modeling and channel characteristic measurements are essential to ensure a reliable broadband wireless connection. Existing research has primarily focused on Air-to-Ground (A2G) channel modeling, and little attention has been given to critical parameters such as antenna orientation, the Effective Radiation Pattern (ERP) of the antenna system considering the influence of the UAV body, receiver altitude, and UAV heading. These parameters significantly impact wireless channel performance in various environments and altitudes. To address this gap, these parameters should be integrated into channel models and conduct real-world experimental measurements to validate their accuracy. Optimizing antenna orientation, considering receiver altitude, and accounting for UAV heading can improve signal strength and communication performance.

The main contribution of this paper is the experimental characterization of the A2G and Ground-to-Air (G2A) wireless channels in an open environment with no obstacles nor interference. The characterization of the channel is performed at different distances and UAV headings within the context of the H2020 ResponDrone[1] project [5]. We analyze the Received Signal Strength Indicator (RSSI) and the TCP throughput between a user on the ground and a UAV for distances ranging from 50 m to 500 m, and considering different headings of the UAV. Moreover, we provide a more accurate characterization of the channel model, when compared to deterministic models, such as Friis and two-ray. Finally, we characterize the ERP of the antennas based on the headings of the UAV.

The remainder of this paper is organized as follows. The related work is presented in Sect. 2. The system setup is described in Sect. 3. The field trial to model the experimental wireless channels is presented in Sect. 4. The experimental results are analyzed in Sect. 5. Finally, Sect. 6 draws conclusions and points out future work.

---

[1] https://respondroneproject.com/.

2 Related Work

In the context of A2G communications channel characterization for UAVs, different measurement models and approaches are presented in the literature. In the study conducted by [6], the authors performed a comprehensive analysis of A2G, Ground-to-Ground (G2G), and Air-to-Air (A2A) channel measurements and models, specifically focusing on civil aeronautical and UAV communications. Their work primarily delved into the link budget analysis of UAV communications, where they examined and presented design guidelines to effectively manage communication links, taking into account propagation losses and link fading. In [7], the authors presented a model for the characterization of the A2G and G2A channels, while the UAV was hovering at different altitudes including different Line-of-Sight (LoS) distances from the User Equipment (UE). The channel model has been analyzed in terms of path loss and fast-fading components. In [2], A2G channel measurements are presented for small-sized UAVs at different environmental conditions and altitude values between 15 m and 105 m. Path loss, shadow fading, Doppler effect, Power Delay Profile, Root-Mean-Square (RMS) delay spread, RMS Doppler frequency spread, and the Rician K-factor were used to characterize the channel. While their investigation provided valuable insights into the general characteristics of these wireless channels, they did not extensively explore the impact of UAV heading on channel behavior, which is crucial in dynamic UAV scenarios.

In [8], the authors reviewed empirical models for the A2G and A2A propagation channels. Then, they classified the UAV channel modeling approaches as deterministic, stochastic, and geometric-stochastic models. In [9], the authors present experimental results on how the height of the receiver affects Radio Frequency (RF) signal propagation over the sea and the capacity of the radio link. In [10], the authors proposed an architecture of a new model for the A2G channel. The modeling is based on 10 MHz channel-sounding flight measurements. The key advantage of the proposed A2G channel modeling approach is its flexibility to a wide range of potential ground station deployment scenarios. In [11], experimental results in commercial Long-Term Evolution (LTE) deployments were conducted to evaluate the variation of the mean Angle of Arrival (AoA) and Angular Spread (AS) with flying altitude. The authors of [11] used sixteen antennas and LTE cellular signals, to experimentally evaluate the performance of the A2G channel, taking into account the UAV altitude variation. Maximum ratio combining and conventional beamforming techniques have been compared with a single antenna system. In [12], an experimental measurement campaign for the A2G channel at 10 MHz is presented at short (30 m − 330 m) and long (9 km − 11 km) distances between the receiver and the transmitter. In [13], measurements with a helium balloon in stationary positions at altitudes up to 500 m have been considered for the A2G channel model. The Euclidean distance between the base station and the receiver was 1900 m. The experiments have been conducted using passive sounding of Universal Mobile Telecommunications System (UMTS) and Global System for Mobile Communications (GSM) signals in an urban environment at a central carrier frequency of 2120 MHz. Using RSSI values, in [14], the authors calculated the path loss exponent for A2G networks while the UAV was flying over both an open field and a campus area. The authors also measured the UDP throughput of the Air-Ground-Air (AGA) links.

In conclusion, to the best of our knowledge, the existing literature lacks extensive exploration of the influence of UAV heading on wireless channels. To address this limitation, our research aims to provide an experimental characterization of the A2G and G2A wireless channels, considering both distance and UAV heading as critical parameters. By integrating UAV heading as a key parameter in channel characterization, we aim to gain valuable insights into the capabilities of UAVs in offering dynamic wireless connectivity, while also addressing the limitations of previous works in handling UAV heading variations.

3   System Setup

The system setup of this paper consists of one UAV acting as a Flying Access Point (FAP) and one UE on the ground. The ATLAS site, depicted in Fig. 1 served as the location for conducting the experimental measurements. The UAV is an Alpha 800[2] and carries a wireless communications module as payload, based on a PC Engines APU4D4 System Board running OpenWRT 19.07.8, and including a Mikrotik R11E-2HPND Wi-Fi interface capable of Multiple Input Multiple Output (MIMO) 2×2 to provide wireless connectivity to the UE. Two omni-directional 2.4 GHz antennas with a gain of 5 dBi are horizontally mounted directly on the communications payload module, which is fixed in the front of the UAV, depicted in Fig. 2. Both antennas are used for the Wi-Fi link to serve the UE, with one pointing its radiation pattern North/South and the other East/West, considering the "North" as the head of the UAV. The UE is a Xiaomi Mi 9T Android smartphone carried by a person at an altitude of approximately 1.3 m above ground. This UE was selected with single antenna capability as the worst-case scenario. If a smartphone with MIMO (2 antennas or more) was used, better network performance would be expected compared to the baseline assessed in this work. Note that this UE is connected to the UAV only through the Wi-Fi link. The IEEE 802.11n (Wi-Fi 4) standard was used, operating in channel 1 with a bandwidth of 20 MHz. A Tx power of 20 dBm and 30 dBm for the UE and UAV were used, respectively. Finally, Minstrel-HT was used as the Wi-Fi MAC auto-rate adaptation mechanism.

The UAV is connected to the Internet through an LTE link to a local LTE Base Station (BS). This link is supported by two omni-directional triband antennas that are vertically mounted in the rear of the communications payload. The LTE BS is located 120 m away from the hangar as depicted in Fig. 1. This BS provides LTE coverage in Band 3 (1.8 GHz) without carrier aggregation, which leads to theoretical throughput values up to 150 Mbit/s for downlink and 50 Mbit/s for uplink. The real throughput measured in the UAV at a distance of 100 m from the LTE BS averaged 114 Mbit/s for downlink and 55 Mbit/s for uplink.

---

[2] Alpha Unmanned Systems (Spanish company).

Fig. 1. ATLAS site, showing the hangar and runway near which the experimental measurements were performed.

To generate enough traffic to saturate the Wi-Fi link and assess its performance, we used an *iperf3* TCP server installed on the UAV. The traffic flow was generated from the UAV to the UE. To measure the RSSI at each Wi-Fi antenna on the UAV side, we used *tcpdump*. We also used an *iperf3* client application on the UE to monitor the throughput.

Fig. 2. Communications payload installed in the ALPHA 800 UAV.

4   Field Trial

The performance of the wireless channel between the UAV and the UE is characterized in terms of the average throughput of a TCP flow sent from the UAV to the UE. Also, the RSSI (in dBm) of each received packet is measured at each antenna of the UAV, considering different UAV headings and distances. Three experimental scenarios were considered and are detailed in what follows:

Scenario A. In this experiment, the UAV was positioned 200 m away from the UE (horizontal distance), hovering at an altitude of 50 m Above Ground Level (AGL). The Euclidean distance between the UE and UAV was 206 m. The UAV was rotated in incremental steps of 45° up to 360° (a full rotation). At each step, the RSSI was measured at the UAV, and the downlink TCP throughput measured at the UE was recorded. This experiment allowed the evaluation of the antennas' ERP and its impact on the measured throughput, since the UAV's body changes this pattern by obstructing and reflecting the signal, depending on the relative heading between the UAV and the UE.

Scenario B. In this experiment, we moved the UAV away from the UE in steps of 25 m, while maintaining the UAV at 50 m AGL, with a heading of 180° relative to the UE. The UAV then came back towards the UE, repeating the same waypoints as before, but with an opposite heading of 0° (UAV head pointing to the UE). At each step, the RSSI measured at UAV and the downlink TCP throughput measured at UE was evaluated.

Scenario C. In this experiment, the UE was located 1.42 km from the LTE BS, while the UAV was between the UE and the LTE BS (1.2 km away from the LTE BS and 220 m away from the UE). We measured 10 times the Internet throughput achieved when the UE is directly connected to the LTE BS (1.42 km link) compared to when the UE is connected to the LTE BS through the UAV using Wi-Fi (220 m Wi-Fi link + 1.2 km LTE link).

5   Experimental Results

This section shows the results of the three experimental scenarios presented in Section IV. The results are presented in separate plots for each scenario and performance metric. The RSSI measurements along the distance are also compared with theoretical models, such as Friis and two-ray ground-reflection models.

5.1   Scenario A: RSSI and Throughput vs. UAV Heading

Figure 3 presents a radar diagram with the measured RSSI of the packets received at the UAV antennas, depending on the relative heading between the UAV and the UE at an Euclidean distance of 206 m. The 1st Antenna (red color) represents the antenna oriented North/South, and 2nd Antenna (blue color) represents the antenna positioned East/West. A simplified representation of a UAV with a red and a blue antenna, depicted in Fig. 3, was also added to help interpret the radar diagram. The orange line represents the RSSI of the Friis theoretical model, considering an isotropic antenna, and represents the peak RSSI expected for each antenna when aligned with the direction of maximum gain. We can conclude that the radiation pattern is narrow and does not cover the sides of the UAV to provide consistent Wi-Fi coverage to a specific area. Nevertheless, considering

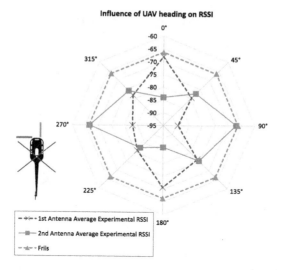

Fig. 3. Scenario A – Measured RSSI of the packets received at both UAV antennas, depending on the relative heading between the UAV and the UE at a Euclidean distance of 206 m, compared to Friis with an isotropic antenna. (Color figure online)

both antennas as a whole, which is possible when considering MIMO, the signal of the same stream being received by multiple antennas can be combined.

Figure 4a shows the effective resulting RSSI for one spatial stream when summing the power (in dB) of the signals received in both antennas. Note that the radar diagrams in Fig. 3 and Fig. 4a can also be interpreted as ERP diagrams if we consider the orange line as the 0 dBm reference. Therefore, since the antennas are dipoles with omni-directional radiation patterns, and considering their mounting orientations, the resulting ERP met our expectations. Furthermore, it was important to see in effect the capability of the MIMO-capable antenna system to be able to transparently combine the signal of both antennas related to a single stream.

In Fig. 4b, the maximum downlink throughput for the same UAV headings is depicted. The values presented depict the best and worst-case scenarios, showing that the throughput can vary from approximately 30 Mbit/s (N, S, E, and W) to approximately 10 Mbit/s (NE, SE, SW, and NW). In general, the relationship between the RSSI and the throughput is complex and depends on various factors such as the Signal-to-Noise Ratio (SNR), Modulation and Coding Scheme (MCS) being used, and other channel conditions such as interference and occupancy. For example, a strong signal may still experience a high level of interference, which can reduce the throughput. However, in this paper, when comparing Fig. 4a and Fig. 4b, we can state that we were achieving the expected values of TCP throughput for the experienced RSSI values due to the low noise floor of −95 dBm and the lack of interference. Additionally, from Fig. 4a we can conclude that at 180°

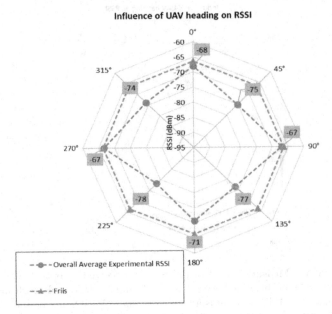

(a) Effective resulting RSSI of the two antennas for one spatial stream when summing the signal received in both of them at a Euclidean distance of 206 m, compared to Friis with an isotropic antenna.

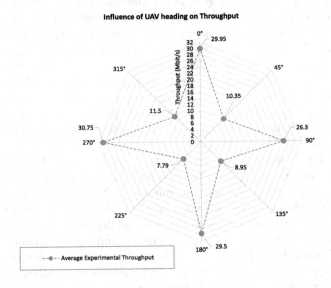

(b) Maximum downlink throughput for the same UAV headings, measured at UE.

Fig. 4. Scenario A – Measured RSSI of the antenna system (sum of both antennas), and downlink TCP throughput at the UE, depending on the relative heading between the UAV and the UE. (Color figure online)

the RSSI is lower than at 0°, which is expected due to the obstruction of the UAV's body.

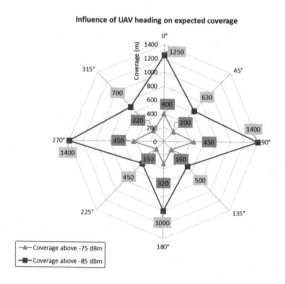

Fig. 5. Scenario A – Resulting expected coverage (in meters) for an RSSI of -85 dBm (link still stable but with low throughput) and -75 dBm (link with still good performance for multiple video streams) cut-offs.

Figure 5 represents the resulting expected coverage for two RSSI cut-offs: i) a -85 dBm link still stable with a SNR of 10 dB, but with low throughput; and ii) a -75 dBm link with 20 dB of SNR, which still provides good performance for multiple video streams. This considers the measurements at the UAV, which is the worst-case scenario due to the link asymmetry of 10 dB.

5.2   Scenario B: RSSI and Throughput vs. Distance

Figure 6a depicts the experimental RSSI results compared to the Friis and two-ray ground reflection propagation loss models, as well as the downlink throughput when the UAV moves away from the UE; Fig. 6b shows these parameters when the UAV comes back toward the UE.

As expected, due to obstruction of the UAV's body, the RSSI was lower when the UAV moved away (180° heading) than when the UAV was coming back to the UE (0° heading). The lower throughput values observed during the UAV's return are attributed to a limitation of the Minstrel-HT auto rate mechanism [15], which is known to delay the increase of the data rate when link conditions improve rapidly. However, upon refueling the UAV at a specific distance and repeating the speed test at the same exact coordinates, the throughput improved significantly as depicted in Fig. 6b at 130 m. In conclusion, it may be necessary

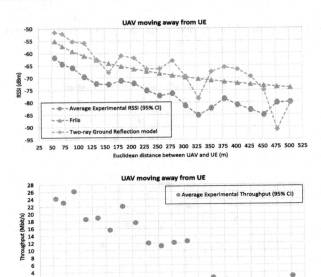

(a) UAV moving away from UE in steps of 25 m, while maintaining a flight at 50 m AGL.

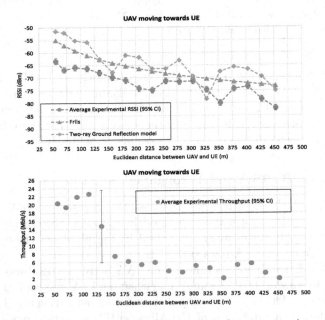

(b) UAV comes back towards the UE, repeating the same waypoints as before.

Fig. 6. Scenario B – Experimental RSSI measured on the UAV compared to the Friis and two-ray ground baselines and the downlink throughput measurements on the UE when the UAV is moving away from the UE and vice-versa.

to restart the Wi-Fi card to clear the Minstrel-HT history and expedite the process of finding an optimal rate. Furthermore, when the UAV moves away from the UE, a steep decline in throughput occurs, as shown in Fig. 6a between the distances of 300 m and 325 m. This decline is primarily due to the asymmetry of the link, with a 10 dB advantage in favor of the downlink resulting from the differences in Tx power. Specifically, the MAC acknowledgments (ACKs) are sent at 24 Mbit/s whenever data packets are received at 24 Mbit/s or higher using the fast ACK mechanism. Although there is a favorable SNR for higher MCSs in the A2G direction, eventually the G2A SNR becomes too low to support successful acknowledgments at 24 Mbit/s. Consequently, the data packets are "forced" to be sent at lower MCSs to ensure that the ACKs are generated below 24 Mbit/s.

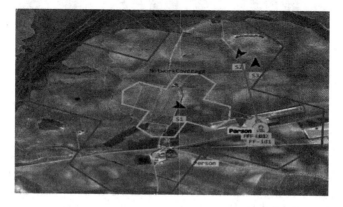

Fig. 7. Overlay polygon used in the H2020 ResponDrone project Command Center interface. The blue and green colors represent the same −85 dBm and −75 dBm cut-offs, respectively. (Color figure online)

Figure 7 represents an overlay polygon of the experimental effective Wi-Fi network coverage provided by a UAV (as depicted in Fig. 5) for a UE with a single antenna, considering its position and heading. The blue and green lines represent, respectively, the same −85 dBm and −75 dBm cut-offs discussed above. For the green area, the throughput was expected to be between 10 Mbit/s and 30 Mbit/s, and the coverage for the N, S, E, and W directions had a range of up to 400 m. Coverage in the NE, SE, SW, and NW directions had a range of up to 200 m. For the blue area, the coverage for the N, S, E, and W directions had a range of up to 1100 m. Coverage in the NE, SE, SW, and NW directions had a range of up to 550 m. For UEs with two antennas, the coverage range is expected to be higher, since we have successfully tested a coverage range of 1500 m, with an RSSI at the UAV side averaging −90 dBm while being able to successfully browse web pages.

5.3   Scenario C: Internet Throughput Vs LoS

As depicted in Fig. 8, when the UE was connected directly to the LTE BS, it achieved an average of 13 Mbit/s. However, when the UE was connected to UAV by Wi-Fi, which was relaying traffic to the LTE BS, it reached an average of 21 Mbit/s at the same location, representing a gain of 1.6×. The terrain topography and existing trees blocked the radio LoS between the UE and the LTE BS. However, by going through the UAV, those obstacles were circumvented and radio LoS was ensured.

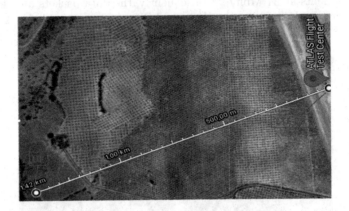

Fig. 8. Scenario C – Distance of the UE to the LTE BS at the hangar. The UE was connected to the Internet either directly via LTE or via Wi-Fi through the UAV, which is then connected to the LTE BS.

6   Conclusions

This work provided an accurate experimental model that describes the A2G and G2A channels. Our experiments revealed that real-world antenna radiation patterns can be heterogeneous, and the impact of the UAV's body and heading on RSSI should be considered when designing airborne communications systems. As an example, in this specific setup used in the ResponDrone project, the RSSI is generally lower when the UAV is oriented away from the UE compared to when it is pointing towards the UE. We found that UEs with different antenna configurations can affect the connectivity range of the UAV, emphasizing the importance of optimizing antenna design for UAV communications systems. Our findings also showed that Minstrel-HT was able to quickly reduce the MCS being used when the SNR was getting lower (i.e. when the UAV was moving away from the UE), but the opposite was not true since it remained using sub-optimal MCSs in higher SNR link conditions. Clearing the Minstrel-HT link statistics helped it converge faster to an optimal MCS for the observed link SNR. Furthermore, we also concluded that the Fast-ACK mechanism of Wi-Fi was actually degrading the link throughput due to the observed link asymmetry.

In conclusion, this study offers valuable insights into the potential of UAVs for providing on-demand and dynamic wireless connectivity and the importance of considering UAV heading and antenna configurations in real-world scenarios. Our findings are valuable for future research and development of UAV communication systems and contribute to the optimization of wireless connectivity in various applications.

Future works include optimizing antenna designs for UAV communications systems and different UE antenna configurations. Additionally, to enhance rate adaptation mechanisms such as Minstrel-HT to better handle rapidly changing link conditions and address the degradation caused by the Fast-ACK mechanism in asymmetric links.

Acknowledgments. This work is financed by National Funds through the Portuguese funding agency, FCT - Fundação para a Ciência e a Tecnologia, within project LA/P/0063/2020.

References

1. Shafafi, K., Coelho, A., Campos, R., Ricardo, M.: Joint traffic and obstacle-aware UAV positioning algorithm for aerial networks. arXiv preprint arXiv:2307.16490 (2023)
2. Rodríguez-Piñeiro, J., Domínguez-Bolaño, T., Cai, X., Huang, Z., Yin, X.: Air-to-ground channel characterization for low-height UAVs in realistic network deployments. IEEE Trans. Antennas Propag. **69**(2), 992–1006 (2021). https://doi.org/10.1109/TAP.2020.3016164
3. Huda, S.A., Moh, S.: Survey on computation offloading in UAV-enabled mobile edge computing. J. Netw. Comput. Appl. **201**, 103341 (2022). https://doi.org/10.1016/j.jnca.2022.103341. https://www.sciencedirect.com/science/article/pii/S1084804522000108
4. Pundir, M., Sandhu, J.K.: A systematic review of quality of service in wireless sensor networks using machine learning: recent trend and future vision. J. Netw. Comput. Appl. **188**, 103084 (2021). https://doi.org/10.1016/j.jnca.2021.103084. https://www.sciencedirect.com/science/article/pii/S1084804521001065
5. Friedrich, M., Lieb, T.J., Temme, A., Almeida, E.N., Coelho, A., Fontes, H.: Respondrone-a situation awareness platform for first responders. In: 2022 IEEE/AIAA 41st Digital Avionics Systems Conference (DASC), pp. 1–7. IEEE (2022). https://doi.org/10.1109/DASC55683.2022.9925792
6. Yan, C., Fu, L., Zhang, J., Wang, J.: A comprehensive survey on UAV communication channel modeling. IEEE Access **7**, 107769–107792 (2019). https://doi.org/10.1109/ACCESS.2019.2933173
7. Almeida, E.N., Coelho, A., Ruela, J., Campos, R., Ricardo, M.: Joint traffic-aware UAV placement and predictive routing for aerial networks. Ad Hoc Netw. **118**, 102525 (2021). https://doi.org/10.1016/j.adhoc.2021.102525
8. Khuwaja, A.A., Chen, Y., Zhao, N., Alouini, M.S., Dobbins, P.: A survey of channel modeling for UAV communications. IEEE Commun. Surv. Tutorials **20**(4), 2804–2821 (2018). https://doi.org/10.1109/COMST.2018.2856587

9. Teixeira, F.B., Campos, R., Ricardo, M.: Height optimization in aerial networks for enhanced broadband communications at sea. IEEE Access **8**, 28311–28323 (2020). https://doi.org/10.1109/ACCESS.2020.2971487

10. Schneckenburger, N., et al.: Modeling the air-ground multipath channel. In: 2017 11th European Conference on Antennas and Propagation (EUCAP), pp. 1434–1438 (2017). https://doi.org/10.23919/EuCAP.2017.7928222

11. Izydorczyk, T., Tavares, F.M., Berardinelli, G., Bucur, M., Mogensen, P.: Angular distribution of cellular signals for UAVs in urban and rural scenarios. In: 2019 13th European Conference on Antennas and Propagation (EuCAP), pp. 1–5. IEEE (2019)

12. Schneckenburger, N., et al.: From l-band measurements to a preliminary channel model for APNT. In: Proceedings of the 27th International Technical Meeting of the Satellite Division of The Institute of Navigation (ION GNSS+ 2014), pp. 3009–3015 (2014)

13. Goddemeier, N., Daniel, K., Wietfeld, C.: Role-based connectivity management with realistic air-to-ground channels for cooperative UAVs. IEEE J. Sel. Areas Commun. **30**(5), 951–963 (2012). https://doi.org/10.1109/JSAC.2012.120610

14. Yanmaz, E., Kuschnig, R., Bettstetter, C.: Channel measurements over 802.11 a-based UAV-to-ground links. In: 2011 IEEE GLOBECOM Workshops (GC Wkshps), pp. 1280–1284. IEEE (2011). https://doi.org/10.1109/GLOCOMW.2011.6162389

15. Xia, D., Hart, J., Fu, Q.: On the performance of rate control algorithm minstrel. In: 2012 IEEE 23rd International Symposium on Personal, Indoor and Mobile Radio Communications - (PIMRC), pp. 406–412 (2012). https://doi.org/10.1109/PIMRC.2012.6362819

Trajectory-Aware Rate Adaptation
for Flying Networks

Ruben Queiros[1,2]($\boxtimes$) (iD), Jose Ruela[2], Helder Fontes[2](iD), and Rui Campos[1,2](iD)

[1] Faculdade de Engenharia da Universidade do Porto, Porto, Portugal
[2] INESC TEC, Porto, Portugal
{ruben.m.queiros,jose.ruela,helder.m.fontes,
rui.l.campos}@inesctec.pt

Abstract. Despite the trend towards ubiquitous wireless connectivity, there are scenarios where the communications infrastructure is damaged and wireless coverage is insufficient or does not exist, such as in natural disasters and temporary crowded events. Flying networks, composed of Unmanned Aerial Vehicles (UAV), have emerged as a flexible and cost-effective solution to provide on-demand wireless connectivity in these scenarios. UAVs have the capability to operate virtually everywhere, and the growing payload capacity makes them suitable platforms to carry wireless communications hardware. The state of the art in the field of flying networks is mainly focused on the optimal positioning of the flying nodes, while the wireless link parameters are configured with default values. On the other hand, current link adaptation algorithms are mainly targeting fixed or low mobility scenarios.

We propose a novel rate adaptation approach for flying networks, named Trajectory Aware Rate Adaptation (TARA), which leverages the knowledge of flying nodes' movement to predict future channel conditions and perform rate adaptation accordingly. Simulation results of 100 different trajectories show that our solution increases throughput by up to 53% and achieves an average improvement of 14%, when compared with conventional rate adaptation algorithms such as Minstrel-HT.

Keywords: Flying Networks · UAV · Wireless Communications · Rate Adaptation · Simulation

1 Introduction

Even though the concept of ubiquitous wireless connectivity is becoming a reality, there are scenarios where wireless communications coverage is insufficient or does not exist. In natural and man-made disaster scenarios, communications infrastructures may be damaged and become unavailable. In temporary crowded events, the existing infrastructure may not have been designed to cope with the additional traffic demand, resulting in overload. In maritime scenarios, environmental monitoring activities using autonomous vehicles will take place in offshore zones, typically not in range of existing onshore communications infrastructures.

© ICST Institute for Computer Sciences, Social Informatics and Telecommunications Engineering 2024
Published by Springer Nature Switzerland AG 2024. All Rights Reserved
J.-L. Guisado-Lizar et al. (Eds.): SIMUtools 2023, LNICST 519, pp. 257–271, 2024.
https://doi.org/10.1007/978-3-031-57523-5_20

Flying networks, composed of Unmanned Aerial Vehicles (UAV), are emerging as a flexible and cost-effective solution to provide on-demand wireless connectivity in such scenarios. UAVs have the possibility to operate virtually everywhere, and the growing payload capacity makes them suitable platforms to carry wireless communications hardware, playing the role of mobile base stations, access points or relay nodes. A flying network may typically be composed of a fleet of UAVs, organized in a multi-tier topology with so-called Flying Edge Nodes (FENs) and Flying Gateways (FGWs) [4]. Figure 1 shows a flying network example where FENs can play the role of Flying Access Points that provide the access network to the users on the ground, or the role of Flying Sensor Nodes that can perform video surveillance missions, for example. The FENs forward the traffic to the FGWs, that act as relay nodes and are responsible for forwarding the traffic to/from the backhaul (BKH) network and ultimately to/from the Internet.

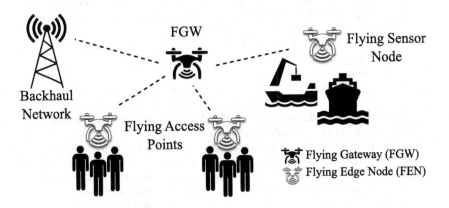

Fig. 1. Flying Network multi-tier topology example.

Most of the state of the art works propose rate adaptation solutions that do not consider the specific characteristics of flying and vehicular networks [18]. In flying networks, the nodes need to be properly positioned and their wireless link configuration dynamically adjusted in order to ensure the Quality of Service (QoS) expected by the end users. In addition, these scenarios are typically highly unpredictable due to the varying locations as well as the concentration/dispersion of end-users served by the Flying Access Points and their movements regarding direction and velocity – e.g., vehicles or pedestrians. Therefore, a static wireless link configuration and UAV positioning are not adequate.

The ResponDrone project [6] defined different flying network use cases (e.g., Follow-me missions) where the future trajectory of flying nodes is known, as requested by the mission commander. However, the usage of this information to predict future wireless channel conditions has been overlooked. State of the art work has been mainly focused on the optimal positioning of the flying nodes, having most of the wireless link parameters statically configured with default values. The Rate Adaptation challenge is well-known in fixed or low mobility IEEE 802.11 networks, and Minstrel High Throughput (HT) [5] is the default Wi-Fi rate adaptation algorithm used in the Linux kernel since the IEEE 802.11n version. Yet, it performs inefficient random sampling of the environment and reacts with significant delays in situations where the link quality improves [8]. The authors in [7,17] consider information of UAV sensors to estimate wireless channel conditions for unknown environments and perform rate adaptation, but they do not use the information about the UAV trajectories as input. To the best of our knowledge, a solution that uses the node trajectory information to predict the wireless channel conditions and perform rate adaptation is yet to be developed.

The main contribution of this paper is the Trajectory-Aware Rate Adaptation (TARA) approach. TARA takes advantage of knowing the trajectory of all nodes in the flying network to estimate future changes in the wireless link quality and perform rate adaptation accordingly. The network performance improvement achieved with TARA was evaluated using ns-3 [14]. The simulation results show significant throughput gains when compared with conventional rate adaptation algorithms.

The rest of the paper is organized as follows. Section 2 explains the TARA approach and its implementation. Section 3 evaluates TARA by means of simulation. Finally, Sect. 4 provides some concluding remarks and points out the future work.

2 Related Work

With the increasingly popular usage of UAVs as relay nodes in wireless networks, several relevant problems have been addressed recently. Typically, rotor-wing UAVs are used in flying networks due to their capability of hovering a given area. The position and trajectories of UAVs have a strong impact on the QoS experienced by the end users, thus playing an important role when investigating solutions aimed at optimizing the network performance under the restrictions imposed by the movement of the flying nodes.

In [2], the authors had the objective of establishing a communication link between a control station and a UAV not directly connected by using a UAV acting as a communication relay in maritime environment. However, only the UAV positioning was considered. In [1,3] the authors jointly optimize the UAV placement with the routing protocols and backhaul network design, but network snapshots are assumed and static default values for MAC and PHY parameters are used.

In [7,10] the authors use online learning methods to adjust the training algorithm to cope with unforeseen wireless channel changes in vehicular scenarios and adapt accordingly. Yet, it is not clear whether the solutions would work in real hardware, where the computational requirements necessary to train deep learning algorithms online are typically not met.

In [15] the authors used ns-3 to evaluate several state of the art rate adaptation algorithms, in terms of mobility and interference. However, most proposed rate adaptation algorithms are typically proprietary, non-compliant with the IEEE 802.11 standard, or lack technical information to be replicated. Minstrel HT [5] is the default Wi-Fi Rate Adaptation algorithm used in the Linux kernel since IEEE 802.11n. Yet, it performs inefficient random sampling of the environment and reacts with significant delays in situations where the link quality improves [8], such as when a moving wireless device gets closer to an Access Point or Base Station, or when a FEN is moving towards the FGW. Both problems lead to slower responses in dynamic and fast changing channel conditions, as it may happen in flying networks.

Existing research has mostly focused on UAV positioning and has overlooked the use of trajectory information for predicting wireless channel conditions. Additionally, many proposed rate adaptation algorithms lack technical information to be reproduced and are not standard compliant.

3   Trajectory-Aware Rate Adaptation Approach

TARA is a standard-compliant solution that builds on top of Minstrel-HT and aims at overcoming the Minstrel-HT limitations by taking advantage of the knowledge about the future movement of the flying nodes. It predicts the future Modulation and Coding Scheme (MCS) index to use (MCS_{TARA}) and changes the Minstrel-HT retry chain table to consider the predicted MCS_{TARA}.

The problem involves the dynamic data rate optimization to maximize the throughput of a flying network composed of FENs, one or more FGWs and the respective BKH link(s). The movement of a particular FEN is determined by its mission, which can be either predefined or adjusted based on specific objectives during the mission. In order to react to the movements of FENs, the FGWs must move to new positions that are calculated based on one or more criteria so that the network performance is optimized.

The TARA approach is depicted in Fig. 2. Table 1 defines the notation used hereafter. TARA has an instance associated to each wireless link and uses the trajectory information of every node in the flying network as input for the $SNR(t)$ estimation function. This function is then used to predict the $MCS(t)$ value that is applied in an improved version of the Minstrel-HT algorithm. TARA is a standard-compliant solution, because it only changes the existing rate adaptation mechanism running locally in each communicating node, without requiring the exchange of any additional information between them. Despite its design being based on IEEE 802.11 and related rate adaptation algorithms, with the proper adjustments, TARA can also be applied to other wireless communications technologies.

In what follows, the movement of a flying node is modeled and an estimation method of wireless link quality is proposed, based on trajectory information. Next, the prediction of MCS_{TARA} is explained; it determines the PHY rate for the next frame transmission(s) in the respective link. Finally, the improvement of the Minstrel-HT rate adaptation algorithm is detailed.

Table 1. Defined notations

Notation	Description
T_n	nth node trajectory
pos_n	nth node current position: $(x, y, z)m$
v_n	nth node velocity: $(v_x, v_y, v_z)m/s$
f_n	nth node flight duration in seconds
SNR_k	kth link Signal to Noise Ratio
$SNR_{threshold}$	Min. SNR value for target (BER, MCS)
MCS_{TARA}	TARA MCS prediction for time interval t
MCS_{MaxTP}	Minstrel-HT best throughput MCS
MCS_{MaxTP2}	Minstrel-HT 2nd best throughput MCS
$MCS_{MaxProb}$	Minstrel-HT best probability MCS
TX_{MCS}	Minstrel-HT current transmission MCS

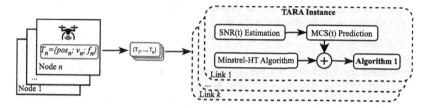

Fig. 2. Illustration of the TARA approach.

3.1 SNR Estimation Based on Node Trajectories

The trajectory of a node n is defined as the data tuple $T_n = \{pos_n; v_n; f_n\}$, as shown in Fig. 2, where pos_n is the current position of the node, v_n is the node velocity and f_n is the node flying time. With the trajectory information we can calculate the position function for any node in the network as $pos_n + v_n t$ as long as $t \leq f_n$. This is because, by then, the node has stopped flying and its position does not change.

The communication channel between two flying nodes, characterized by a strong line of sight component, is modeled using the Friis path loss model [9]. Considering a link k, which connects nodes a and b, $SNR_k(t)$ in dB is given by:

$$SNR_k(t) = P_t^{dB} + G_t^{dBi} + G_r^{dBi} - P_n^{dB} - FSPL^{dB}(t) \qquad (1)$$

$$FSPL^{dB}(t) = 20 \log_{10} \left(\frac{4\pi}{\lambda} d(pos_a(t), pos_b(t)) \right) \qquad (2)$$

where P_t^{dB} is the transmission power, G_t^{dBi} and G_r^{dBi} are respectively the transmitter and receiver antenna gains, P_n^{dB} is the noise power and $d(pos_a(t), pos_b(t))$ is the Euclidean distance between nodes a and b. Note that the computed SNR_k

values assume a discretized t that is synchronized with the update frequency of the rate adaptation algorithm; this is detailed in the following sections.

3.2 Calculation of MCS Predicted Value

The optimal MCS to use in a wireless communications link is often a complex task due to unpredictable factors – other than SNR – that impact the channel conditions, such as interference, shadowing and multipath fading, to name a few. In [11], emulation trials in a physical-layer testbed showed significant differences from ns-3 simulation results. Motivated by this, in [12] the *NistErrorRateModel* is proposed to model orthogonal frequency division multiplexing transmissions with generally $\pm 1 \, dB$ margin when compared with emulation data, in interference-free scenarios.

To calculate the optimal MCS of each communications link, we use the *NistErrorRateModel*, to define a target Bit Error Ratio (BER), ρ_{BER}. Then, a look-up table that maps $(MCS_i, \rho_{BER}) \mapsto SNR_{threshold}$ is built. $SNR_{threshold}$ is the minimum SNR value that is required to achieve the required BER for the specified MCS, and i is the MCS index.

The output of Eq. 1, SNR_k, is used to choose the best achievable MCS_i for each communications link, given the previously calculated $SNR_{threshold}$, as long as the condition $SNR_k \geq SNR_{threshold}$ is verified. Herein, we refer to the best achievable MCS_i as MCS_{TARA}, which uses the SNR estimation based on the flying nodes' movement defined in Sect. 3.1. MCS_{TARA} is used to modify the original Minstrel-HT algorithm, as shown in Fig. 2.

3.3 Minstrel-HT Algorithm Improvement

Minstrel-HT is the evolution of the Minstrel algorithm [16,19], which incorporates new IEEE 802.11n features such as the configuration options of Number of Spatial Streams (NSS), Guard Interval (GI) and Channel Bandwidth (CB). In [8,16] the authors observe that both Minstrel and Minstrel-HT underperform in scenarios with dynamic channel conditions.

To overcome the problem, we propose a novel version of Minstrel-HT to improve its overall performance in dynamic scenarios such as Flying Networks, without adding significant complexity to the original algorithm. Algorithm 1 highlights the main modifications that were implemented so that the original Minstrel-HT algorithm uses the MCS_{TARA}, without compromising its original operation, in situations where the MCS_{TARA} calculation is inaccurate and the retry chain table is necessary. This inaccuracy, expressed by the need of frame retransmissions, is due to the selection of an optimistic MCS value. The existing functions that were modified are detailed in the following.

UpdateStats. It is called every τ milliseconds to update the link-specific statistics. These include the number of successes and attempts for each MCS in each

Algorithm 1. Improvement of Minstrel-HT with trajectory-aware MCS prediction, MCS_{TARA}.

1: **procedure** UPDATESTATS(*link*)   ▷ from Minstrel-HT
2:     ...   ▷ current algorithm
3:     **if** $MCS_{TARA} > MCS_{MaxTP}$ **then**
4:         $MCS_{MaxTP2} \leftarrow MCS_{MaxTP}$
5:         $MCS_{MaxTP} \leftarrow MCS_{TARA}$
6:     **end if**
7: **end procedure**
8: **procedure** UPDATERATE(*link*)   ▷ from Minstrel-HT
9:     **if** $retries < 2$ **then**
10:         $TX_{MCS} \leftarrow MCS_{TARA}$
11:     **else if** $retries < RetryCount_{MaxTP}$ **then**
12:         $TX_{MCS} \leftarrow MCS_{MaxTP}$
13:     **else if** $retries < RetryCount_{MaxTP2}$ **then**
14:         $TX_{MCS} \leftarrow MCS_{MaxTP2}$
15:     **else if** $retries < RetryCount_{MaxProb}$ **then**
16:         $TX_{MCS} \leftarrow MCS_{MaxProb}$
17:     **end if**
18: **end procedure**

(NSS, GI, CB) group, which impact both the expected throughput and exponentially weighted moving average probability of success of each MCS. Finally, the decision of Minstrel-HT's MCS $(MCS_{MaxTP}, MCS_{MaxTP2}, MCS_{MaxProb})$ is updated, for the following τ period.

MCS_{TARA} is compared with MCS_{MaxTP}. If MCS_{TARA} is higher than the current best throughput MCS, the Minstrel-HT's MCS is updated to $(MCS_{TARA}, MCS_{MaxTP}, MCS_{MaxProb})$, in that specific order. Otherwise, the TARA suggestion is used to modify the original retry chain table; this is explained next.

UpdateRate. It implements the retry chain table. Considering that a transmitted frame is lost for any reason, Minstrel-HT will attempt to retransmit that lost frame, with the previously used MCS, or any other in the retry chain table, until the maximum number of *retries* is reached. Minstrel-HT calculates the amount of retries ($RetryCount$) for each of its MCS values. For MCS_{TARA}, a fixed amount of 2 retries is defined, before resuming the original Minstrel-HT retry chain table. In this way, we impose the trajectory-aware MCS without disrupting the original operation of the algorithm, since after 2 retries – 3 frame transmissions attempts – the algorithm falls back to its original behavior.

4 Performance Evaluation

The flying network performance achieved with TARA is presented in this section, including the simulation scenario, the simulation setup and the analysis of results.

4.1   Simulation Scenario

Herein, we aim to evaluate the performance of the new proposed Rate Adaptation algorithm; for this purpose, a simple simulation scenario with a single FEN and FGW is sufficient. This choice allows for a preliminary evaluation of the TARA feasibility and provides valuable insights for future work involving more complex scenarios with multiple FENs.

In this scenario, the BKH and the access links must carry the same amount of traffic, except for possible losses that should be kept as low as possible. For that reason, the position of the FGW was assumed to remain in the midpoint between the BKH and the FEN. In this way, it equalizes the SNR value on both links, which is only affected by the distance, and thus the same MCS index. However, such an assumption is not generalizable to scenarios with multiple FENs with heterogeneous traffic demand.

Extending the problem to scenarios with multiple FENs will be part of future work, which will include the development of a novel positioning algorithm for the FGWs, aimed at optimizing the system performance, while relying on the TARA approach.

4.2   Simulation Setup

In order to evaluate the flying network performance achieved with TARA, ns-3 (version ns-3.38) was used. A summary of the most relevant configuration parameters is presented in Table 2. Different Wireless Local Area Network (WLAN) channels were used for each link, to ensure that there are no frame losses due to interference. Traffic was generated using User Datagram Protocol (UDP), with a constant packet size of 1400 bytes and a data rate above link capacity, to saturate the communication link. The TARA performance was compared with the original Minstrel-HT and Ideal [14], considering its use in both wireless links (FEN-FGW and FGW-BKH).

The Ideal algorithm implementation maintains for every link the SNR value of every packet received and sends back this SNR value to the sender by means of an out-of-band mechanism. Each sender keeps track of the last SNR value sent back by a receiver and uses it to pick a transmission mode based on a set of SNR thresholds derived from a target BER, and transmission mode-specific SNR/BER curves, as it was explained in Sect. 3.2. In the following simulations, we defined the same target BER for both Ideal and TARA algorithms.

The dynamic network topology is represented in Fig. 3; uplink traffic generation by the FEN is relayed by the FGW, with BKH as destination. Random FEN movements were defined for each simulation run using different seeds, which provide a broad and rich sequence of independent events [20] that put stress on the Rate Adaptation algorithm, in order to evaluate its performance. A complete trajectory (for the duration of a simulation run) is a sequence of elementary movements along a linear path. Every simulation run starts with a new random position of the FEN and its trajectory is randomly updated every Δ seconds. Each movement starts at the final position of the previous one, and a new path is randomly generated (direction and length). When moving, the FEN velocity

Table 2. ns-3 Simulation Parameters

Configuration Parameter	Value
Wi-Fi Standard	IEEE 802.11n
Propagation Delay Model	Constant Speed
Propagation Loss Model	Friis
Error Rate Model	NistErrorRateModel
Channel Bandwidth	20 MHz
Transmission Power	20 dBm
RX/TX antenna gains	0 dBi
Wi-Fi MAC	Ad-hoc
ρ_{BER}	1e-6
τ	50 milliseconds
Δ	30 s

remains constant at 8 m/s. The duration of each movement is $t_m \leq \Delta$. For the FGW a different approach was used. As said, the final position of each FGW movement (along a linear path, as well) must be at the midpoint of the straight line between the BKH and the final position of the corresponding FEN movement. Moreover, the FGW moves with a constant velocity, such that both the FEN and the FGW arrive at the same time to their final positions. By imposing these conditions, all the intermediate FGWs positions have the same property. The BKH node is fixed at the edge of the scenario, which is a square with 1000 by 1000 m.

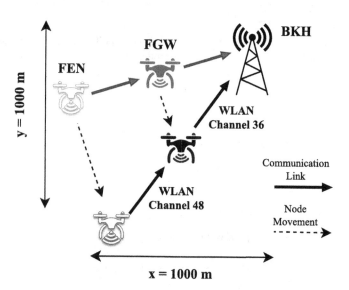

Fig. 3. Network topology. The communication links are represented by full lines, with two non-interfering WLAN channels.

We defined simulation runs with a duration of 300 s, which were evaluated using 100 different random seeds. These random seeds impact the initial position of the FEN, the sequence of random elementary movements (paths) as well as the average values of throughput. The results are expressed using mean values of the throughput measured at the MAC layer every simulation second, and their relative percentage gains. The measured throughput is link-specific. We present results for both the relay link (between the FGW and BKH node) and the access link (between the FEN and the FGW). However, the end-to-end network performance is best characterized by the relay link since the effective throughput of the system is determined by the packets delivered to the BKH after being forwarded by the FGW.

4.3   Simulation Results

Simulation results are presented in this section, first those referring to a particular random scenario (seed) and then results of the extensive simulations. Finally, a discussion of the results is provided.

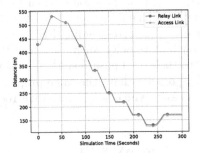
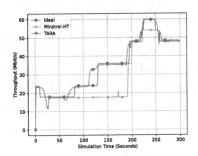

(a) Distance between nodes throughout the simulation period.

(b) Relay link Throughput, throughout the simulation period.

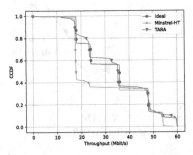

(c) Relay link Throughput CCDF.

Fig. 4. Selected Seed Results.

Example Scenario. A random seed was selected, which generated a simulation scenario covering a wide range of distances, as shown in Fig. 4a. The throughput achieved in the relay link measured throughout the simulation period is shown in Fig. 4b. As expected, the throughput increases as the distance between nodes in each link decreases, since the SNR value is higher, which makes the use of higher MCS indexes possible. We can also observe that TARA, despite being based on Minstrel-HT, changes MCS indexes with a faster reaction time, which can be directly compared with the reaction time of the Ideal algorithm. In Fig. 4c we represent the Complementary Cumulative Distribution Function (CCDF) of the throughput for the same seed. The CCDF $F(x)$ represents the percentage of time for which the mean throughput was higher than x. From the results we observe the significant throughput gains of TARA.

The reason for slight improvement of TARA over the "not so" Ideal algorithm, is because the Ideal algorithm is optimized towards minimizing the BER, while the results are comparing the solutions in terms of throughput. With these results we can observe that TARA's slight gains are due to few decision instants, where specific conditions are met. These conditions are observed when the decision of adapting MCS could result in a higher BER probability, but the throughput would still be better.

The corresponding results for the access link are not presented since they were similar due to the fact that both links have the same distance, which optimizes performance. However, these results are heavily biased by the initial position of the nodes and their trajectory. To address the impact of different random trajectories, we present in the following section the results for 100 different random seeds.

Extensive Simulations. Figure 5 represents the distribution of distances that were observed during the extensive simulations that were carried out. The higher frequency of distances between 300 and 500 m can help justify the distribution of the observed distribution of throughput values as well.

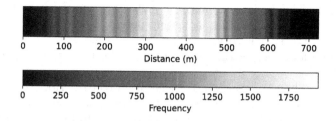

Fig. 5. Link distance distribution, with $3 * 10^4$ total samples.

Figure 6a represents the CCDF of the throughput for the relay link. In this analysis three different percentiles, 70th, 50th and 30th are considered. For the 30th percentile, there is a throughput improvement of 31.5% when compared to

Minstrel-HT and a throughput deterioration of 2.7% when compared to Ideal. If we consider the 50th percentile (median), the throughput results are all within 2% difference of each other. However, for the 70th percentile, there is a through-put improvement of 48.4% when compared with Minstrel-HT and a throughput deterioration of 2.1% when compared with Ideal.

Figure 6b represents the 99% confidence interval of the mean throughput for both links. Regarding the relay link, the mean throughput increases by 13.9% and by 3.2% when compared with Minstrel-HT and Ideal respectively. Regarding the access link, the performance is similar to the relay link.

Figure 6c represents the CCDF of the percentage gains of TARA throughput when compared with Minstrel-HT and Ideal. The gains were calculated consider-ing the mean throughput of each random seed. The CCDFs are similar for each link, thus its analysis will be made considering solely the relay link results, since it better represents the end-to-end network performance. Positive throughput gains of TARA relatively to Minstrel-HT and Ideal occurred in 92% and 86% of the seeds, respectively. The highest throughput gain of TARA, on a partic-ular seed, was 52.8% and 13.2%, when comparing with Minstrel-HT and Ideal, respectively.

4.4   Discussion

In this section we address the observations regarding the average throughput values in the access link and relay link, the comparison between TARA and Ideal throughput, and the significance of the 14% average throughput gain over Minstrel-HT algorithm:

- The average throughput in the access link was slightly higher than in the relay link. This is an expected result since frame loss can occur in both access and relay link.
- When comparing TARA and Ideal throughput, it might be surprising that the average throughput of TARA is 3.2% higher than that of Ideal. However, upon analyzing the CCDF curves, the TARA curve either coincides or lies above the Ideal curve. This finding explains the higher average throughput of TARA. Despite the lower percentiles indicating potential discrepancies, the overall behavior of the CCDF curves suggests that TARA achieves comparable or superior performance to the Ideal algorithm, leading to the higher average throughput.
- Note that a 14% gain over Minstrel may seem modest. However, it is impor-tant to consider the stability of TARA's performance and the potential for greater gains when the algorithm needs to adapt to frequent improvements in the connection quality. The selected seed represents a case where succes-sive increases in the modulation and coding scheme (MCS) were necessary, resulting in a throughput percentage gain of 21.2% when compared with Minstrel-HT. These findings suggest that TARA's stability and adaptability provide benefits beyond a simple percentage gain, and the actual gains can be more significant in scenarios with frequent improvements in the link quality.

In summary, the results demonstrate that TARA matches the performance of the Ideal algorithm. This is relevant because the Ideal algorithm can be considered as a benchmark algorithm; it is not implementable since it assumes the knowledge of the SNR at the receiver before deciding which MCS to use for the transmission. Despite the 14% gain over Minstrel-HT, the stability and adaptability of TARA make it a promising algorithm, particularly in situations where frequent enhancements to link quality occur. Further investigation into the extreme case with successive MCS increases or different target BER could provide additional insights into TARA's performance.

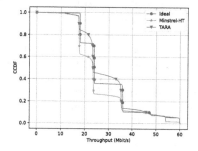
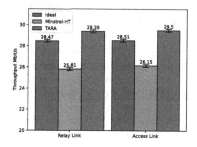

(a) Throughput CCDF for the Relay Link, between the BKH and the FGW.   (b) Mean Throughput with 99% confidence interval.

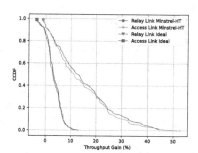

(c) Throughput CCDF Gains for both links, comparing TARA with Minstrel-HT and Ideal rate adaptation algorithms.

Fig. 6. Extensive simulation results.

5   Conclusions and Future Work

This paper proposes TARA, a trajectory-aware rate adaptation approach for flying networks. TARA takes advantage of the knowledge of future movements of UAVs to predict how the quality of wireless links will change, and perform rate adaptation accordingly. The proposed solution was evaluated using ns-3 simulations. Simulation results showed consistent gains when compared with state of the art algorithms, such as Minstrel-HT, with a throughput increase of up to 53% for the simulated scenarios. The results for each seed and the TARA source code[1] are publicly available [13].

As future work, we plan to evaluate TARA experimentally and address the complexity of scenarios with multiple FENs and more than one FGW. These challenges include achieving an equal throughput on both sides of the FGW, considering the trade-off between distance and throughput in multi-link scenarios, handling cases where optimal positioning cannot guarantee target throughput on all links, and accounting for variable and time-dependent traffic characteristics. Finally, we aim at improving TARA to take into consideration stochastic path loss models, scenarios with communication interference, and drone movements that consider the inertia that exists in real world systems.

Acknowledgements. This work is co-financed by Component 5 - Capitalization and Business Innovation, integrated in the Resilience Dimension of the Recovery and Resilience Plan within the scope of the Recovery and Resilience Mechanism (MRR) of the European Union (EU), framed in the Next Generation EU, for the period 2021 - 2026, within project Produtech_R3, with reference 60. The second author thanks the funding from FCT, Portugal under the PhD grant 2022.10093.BD.

References

1. Almeida, E.N., Coelho, A., Ruela, J., Campos, R., Ricardo, M.: Joint traffic-aware UAV placement and predictive routing for aerial networks. Ad Hoc Netw. **118**, 102525 (2021)
2. Braga, J., Braga, J., Alessandretti, A., Aguiar, A.P., de Sousa, J.B.: A feedback motion strategy applied to a UAV to work as an autonomous relay node for maritime operations. In: 2017 International Conference on Unmanned Aircraft Systems (ICUAS) (2017). https://doi.org/10.1109/icuas.2017.7991434
3. Coelho, A., Fontes, H., Campos, R., Ricardo, M.: Traffic-aware gateway placement for high-capacity flying networks. In: 2021 IEEE 93rd Vehicular Technology Conference (VTC2021-Spring), pp. 1–6. IEEE (2021)
4. Coelho, A., Campos, R., Ricardo, M.: Traffic-aware gateway placement and queue management in flying networks. Ad Hoc Netw. **138**, 103000 (2023). https://doi.org/10.1016/j.adhoc.2022.103000, https://www.sciencedirect.com/science/article/pii/S157087052200172X
5. FietKau, F.: Minstrel_HT: new rate control module for 802.11n [LWN.net], March 2010. https://lwn.net/Articles/376765. Accessed 30 May 2023
6. Friedrich, M., Lieb, T.J., Temme, A., Almeida, E.N., Coelho, A., Fontes, H.: Respondrone - a situation awareness platform for first responders. In: 2022 IEEE/AIAA 41st Digital Avionics Systems Conference (DASC), pp. 1–7 (2022). https://doi.org/10.1109/DASC55683.2022.9925792
7. He, S., Wang, W., Yang, H., Cao, Y., Jiang, T., Zhang, Q.: State-aware rate adaptation for UAVs by incorporating on-board sensors. arXiv: Networking and Internet Architecture (2019). https://doi.org/10.1109/tvt.2019.2950285

---

[1] https://gitlab.inesctec.pt/pub/ctm-win/tara.

8. Karmakar, R., Chattopadhyay, S., Chakraborty, S.: SmartLA: reinforcement learning-based link adaptation for high throughput wireless access networks. Comput. Commun. **110**, 1–25 (2017)

9. Khuwaja, A.A., Chen, Y., Zhao, N., Alouini, M.S., Dobbins, P.: A survey of channel modeling for UAV communications. IEEE Commun. Surv. Tutor. **20**(4), 2804–2821 (2018). https://doi.org/10.1109/COMST.2018.2856587

10. Liu, H., He, J., Gupta, S., Rajan, D., Camp, J.: FIT: on-the-fly, in-situ training for snr-based rate selection. IEEE Trans. Veh. Technol. (2020). https://doi.org/10.1109/tvt.2020.3009198

11. Papanastasiou, S., Mittag, J., Ström, E.G., Hartenstein, H.: Bridging the gap between physical layer emulation and network simulation. In: 2010 IEEE Wireless Communication and Networking Conference, pp. 1–6 (2010). https://doi.org/10.1109/WCNC.2010.5506341

12. Pei, G., Henderson, T.R.: Validation of OFDM model in ns-3 (2011). https://www.nsnam.org/~pei/80211ofdm.pdf. Accessed 10 June 2023

13. Queiros, R., Ruela, J., Fontes, H., Campos, R.: Trajectory-Aware Rate Adaptation for Aerial Networks Simulation Results, June 2023. https://doi.org/10.5281/zenodo.8099173

14. Riley, G.F., Henderson, T.R.: The ns-3 Network Simulator. In: Wehrle, K., Gunes, M., Gross, J. (eds.) Modeling and Tools for Network Simulation, pp. 15–34. Springer, Berlin, Heidelberg (2010). https://doi.org/10.1007/978-3-642-12331-3_2

15. Sammour, I., Chalhoub, G.: Evaluation of rate adaptation algorithms in IEEE 802.11 networks. Electronics (2020). https://doi.org/10.3390/electronics9091436

16. Xia, D., Hart, J., Fu, Q.: Evaluation of the minstrel rate adaptation algorithm in IEEE 802.11G WLANs. In: 2013 IEEE International Conference on Communications (ICC), pp. 2223–2228 (2013). https://doi.org/10.1109/ICC.2013.6654858

17. Xiao, X., Wang, W., Jiang, T.: Sensor-assisted rate adaptation for UAV MU-MIMO networks. IEEE ACM Trans. Netw. (2021). https://doi.org/10.1109/tnet.2021.3136911

18. Yin, W., Hu, P., Indulska, J., Portmann, M., Mao, Y.: Mac-layer rate control for 802.11 networks: a survey. Wirel. Netw. (2020). https://doi.org/10.1007/s11276-020-02295-2

19. Yin, W., Hu, P., Indulska, J., Portmann, M., Mao, Y.: Mac-layer rate control for 802.11 networks: a survey. Wirel. Netw. **26**, 3793–3830 (2020)

20. Yuan, X., et al.: Capacity analysis of UAV communications: cases of random trajectories. IEEE Trans. Veh. Technol. **67**(8), 7564–7576 (2018). https://doi.org/10.1109/TVT.2018.2829726

Rate Adaptation Aware Positioning for Flying Gateways Using Reinforcement Learning

Gabriella Pantaleão[✉] , Rúben Queirós , Hélder Fontes ,
and Rui Campos

INESC TEC and Faculdade de Engenharia, Universidade do Porto, Porto, Portugal
{gabriella.pantaleao,ruben.m.queiros,helder.m.fontes,
rui.l.campos}@inesctec.pt

Abstract. With the growing connectivity demands, Unmanned Aerial
Vehicles (UAVs) have emerged as a prominent component in the deployment of Next Generation On-demand Wireless Networks. However, current UAV positioning solutions typically neglect the impact of Rate
Adaptation (RA) algorithms or simplify its effect by considering ideal
and non-implementable RA algorithms. This work proposes the Rate
Adaptation aware RL-based Flying Gateway Positioning (RARL) algorithm, a positioning method for Flying Gateways that applies Deep Q-
Learning, accounting for the dynamic data rate imposed by the underlying RA algorithm. The RARL algorithm aims to maximize the throughput of the flying wireless links serving one or more Flying Access Points,
which in turn serve ground terminals. The performance evaluation of the
RARL algorithm demonstrates that it is capable of taking into account
the effect of the underlying RA algorithm and achieve the maximum
throughput in all analysed static and mobile scenarios.

Keywords: Aerial networks · Rate Adaptation · UAV positioning ·
Deep Reinforcement Learning

1 Introduction

Unmanned Aerial Vehicles (UAVs), commonly known as drones, have emerged
as a promising technology for ensuring cost-effective on-demand wireless connectivity [6,18]. The ability of UAVs to fly and navigate autonomously allow them
to provide access to communications services where no infrastructure coverage
exists, which can be particularly useful in remote or difficult-to-reach areas.
UAVs are especially relevant in the context of sudden fluctuations in traffic
demands that impair the effective allocation of radio resources, a scenario frequently seen in crowded events, for instance. Thus, UAVs are suitable platforms
for delivering and enhancing connectivity in heterogeneous scenarios, carrying
communications hardware to deploy Wi-Fi or cellular coverage. UAVs are highly

© ICST Institute for Computer Sciences, Social Informatics and Telecommunications Engineering 2024
Published by Springer Nature Switzerland AG 2024. All Rights Reserved
J.-L. Guisado-Lizar et al. (Eds.): SIMUtools 2023, LNICST 519, pp. 272–286, 2024.
https://doi.org/10.1007/978-3-031-57523-5_21

adaptable and can be quickly deployed and optimally positioned, in contrast to conventional ground-based solutions [8].

In flying networks, relays are often employed to improve network coverage and capacity, as represented in Fig. 1. The distance between UAVs directly influences the communications range between the flying nodes, as well as the Quality of Service (QoS) associated to the inter-UAV wireless links. Therefore, the use of intermediate UAVs, herein named Flying Gateways (FGWs), enables the extension of the communication range between the Backhaul network and the Flying Access Points (FAPs), while preserving the quality of the established connection [7]. By optimizing the positioning of the FGWs, there is an effective balance of the load in the network while improving coverage, resulting in a more efficient and reliable flying network. Nevertheless, the optimization of the positions of UAVs in flying networks according to specific link metrics is still a challenge, considering their dynamic nature.

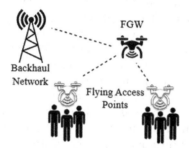

Fig. 1. Relay network topology example, adapted from [12].

Machine Learning approaches can be employed to enhance various aspects of the performance and operation of flying networks, including delay, throughput, transmission power, and cache resource utilization [1,3,5,11,15]. Reinforcement Learning (RL) techniques are particularly useful, as they are intrinsically related to control theory, given its feedback-driven optimization process. RL represents a relevant approach to handle the continuous changing environment of flying networks, taking into account long-term, sequential and cumulative rewards, as it maps states into the effectiveness of the actions [10]. With RL, decisions are based on the current states of the environment, meaning that the agent can be trained using real-time network measurements instead of relying on approximations [1]. This allows the agent to have a more accurate response to the current environment conditions.

The main contribution of this paper is the Rate Adaptation aware RL-based Flying Gateway Positioning (RARL) algorithm, which addresses the problem of finding the position for the FGW that maximizes the throughput obtained in the FAPs, considering the influence of the underlying RA algorithm. The selected RA algorithm was the Minstrel-High Throughput (HT), designed as the evolution of the Minstrel algorithm for the IEEE 802.11n standard [13,16,17].

The effectiveness of the RL approach was validated through simulations using Network Simulator 3 (ns-3), which served as the platform for training, validating and testing the model.

The rest of the paper is organized as follows. Section 2 presents the related work on UAV positioning in flying networks. The design of the RARL algorithm is detailed in Sect. 3. Section 4 introduces the ns-3 simulation setup, as well as the simulation results on the performance of the RARL algorithm. Finally, Sect. 5 presents the conclusions and points out the future work.

2   Related Work

With the advancements made in the context of flying networks, many studies have been conducted to improve the positioning of the flying nodes. The work reported in [7] includes the implementation of centralized on-demand Gateway UAV positioning algorithm, relying on the awareness of the incoming traffic behaviour. Based on a mathematical approach, the goal is to minimize the capacity of the bidirectional wireless link between the FGW and the FAPs, while ensuring the bitrates required by each FAP. The results indicate that the position of the FGW is an essential aspect of the Backhaul network configuration, since constant FGW position updates can improve network performance. However, the authors consider an ideal underlying RA algorithm.

In [5], a solution for flying Base Stations, serving a region with numerous users, was proposed. This deployment relies on RL techniques for the UAV to be able to learn how to optimize its trajectory, contouring obstacles and reaching the intended service area. In this study, the UAV is assumed to return to its landing location when reaching the limit period of the flight. With a Q-Learning approach, the system was implemented based on making direct movement decisions, allowing the optimization of the sum rate of the transmission over the duration of the flight. With this solution, the algorithm needs no prior knowledge of the environment and has the ability to learn the structure of the network, resulting in improved performance. However, a limiting factor of this study is that it considers a static environment, with no changes in the course of the flight.

Overall, the main UAV positioning approaches include brute-force searching, mathematical optimizations [2,7,19], heuristics [9], and Machine Learning algorithms [1,3,5,11,15]. Despite their importance, optimizing UAV positions in a network to maximize one or more link metrics remains a challenging task, given the multiple factors to consider. From the literature review, Deep Reinforcement Learning (DRL) emerges as a promising approach for UAV positioning, supporting the choice of the Q-Learning approach in the implementation of the RARL algorithm.

It is worth noting that few solutions have considered the impact of the Backhaul network on the QoS experienced by ground terminals [7]. In addition, they are focussed on static and invariant scenarios, assuming mostly symmetric links. Moreover, none of the studies analysed included a realistic RA algorithm, which limits the applicability of these methods. Our work aims to address the aforementioned shortfalls, by considering a continuous analysis of the network state and accounting for the implementation of realistic and dynamic adjustments of the data rate in the network.

3   RARL Algorithm Design

The RARL algorithm relies on the implementation of Deep Q-Learning, a Deep RL method that has been proven to be highly applicable in continuous control tasks, making it well-suited for addressing the positioning of UAVs within flying networks. Three different scenarios were defined to test the RARL algorithm, as presented below:

1. **Asymmetric links scenario:** with three static nodes corresponding to the Backhaul, the FGW and the FAP, considering that the link between the FGW and the Backhaul node and the link between the FAP and the FGW are asymmetric, meaning that they have different values for the transmission power. This scenario is illustrated in Fig. 2a.
2. **Moving FAP scenario:** with the same network topology as the **asymmetric links** scenario, where the link between the FAP and the FGW and the link between the FGW and the Backhaul node are symmetric, but the FAP moves, as presented in Fig. 2b.
3. **Two FAPs scenario:** with four static nodes, corresponding to the Backhaul, the FGW and two FAPs, where the link between the FGW and the Backhaul node handles the traffic of the two symmetric links between the FGW and the FAPs, as shown in Fig. 2c.

Without loss of generality, in the two last scenarios we have considered symmetric wireless links in order to isolate the problems. The learning process was adapted for each of the three scenarios. For all the cases, the agent was instantiated in the FGW node, which is responsible for performing the different actions selected. Nevertheless, the algorithm modelling was tailored for each scenario. The action space, the observation space and the reward functions defined for each scenario are described below.

3.1   Action Space

The actions of the FGW are based on discrete sequential movements, based on incrementing the position in the 2D venue in the selected direction by 25 m, a distance defined as a compromise between the training time and the impact of the FGW's movement on the link metrics, selected every 1 s, defined as the decision interval. Thus, the action space comprises five movement options, including the possibility of remaining in the same position: *Left, Right, Up, Down,* and *Same*.

3.2   Observation Space

The observations must characterize the system so that the agent can recognize the best positions for maximizing and balancing the throughput values in the FGW and FAP nodes. For the **asymmetric links** and **moving FAP** scenarios, the observations are defined as:

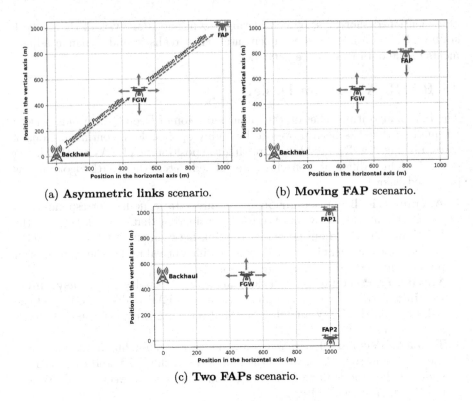

(a) **Asymmetric links** scenario.

(b) **Moving FAP** scenario.

(c) **Two FAPs** scenario.

Fig. 2. Three scenarios analysed.

- the coordinates of the FGW;
- the distances between the FGW and the Backhaul node and between the FGW and the FAP;
- the throughput values measured in each link, calculated as the number of bytes received throughout the course of a decision interval, i.e. every second.

For the **two FAPs** scenario, the approach to sense the environment is different, given the existence of more than one FAP. In this case, the observations do not include the throughput values.

3.3 Reward Function

The underlying Minstrel-HT RA algorithm has a significant impact on the obtained throughput values, heavily influenced by the distances travelled by the FGW. This means that even if it travels to the same final position, the initial conditions imposed by the link metrics in the starting point impact the final throughput value obtained at the destination point. This means that the closer the UAV originally is to the final position, the fewer fluctuations are seen in the observed throughput. This is due to the fact that, when using Minstrel-HT, the throughput variation has a slow response in cases where the link quality improves, as shown in [4,13,14,16]. Hence, modelling the system becomes challenging due to the need to identify positions that optimize and balance the throughput values, which in turn requires addressing the peaks and variations introduced by the Minstrel-HT algorithm.

To better understand the variation of the network metrics under the effect of Minstrel-HT in the ns-3 simulations for the reward function design, a preliminary study was carried out to understand the Signal-to-Noise Ratio (SNR) and the throughput. For this purpose, the Backhaul node was positioned in (0, 0) and the FAP in (1000, 1000), with the configuration showed in Fig. 2a. The FGW was set to move from the coordinates (25, 25) to (975, 975). The position of the FGW was increased incrementally, both horizontally and vertically, by 25 m every 1 s. This approach was employed to precisely examine the impact of distance on link metrics.

For the **asymmetric links** and **moving FAP** scenarios, since the SNR, shown in Fig. 3b, has greater sensitivity to changes in position when compared to the throughput, presented in Fig. 3a, the SNR was considered as a more suitable measure of the environment's state. This means that, the objective can be modelled according to the SNR, with the reward functions translating into maximizing the SNR values and minimizing the difference between the SNR obtained in both the link connecting the Backhaul node and the FGW and in the link between the FGW and the FAP.

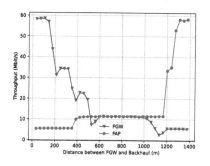

(a) Throughput variation in nodes FAP and FGW.

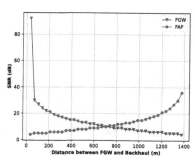

(b) SNR variation in nodes FAP and FGW.

Fig. 3. Link metrics comparison for the **asymmetric links** and **moving FAP** scenarios.

The goal is to maximize the throughput values and to minimize possible throughput imbalances between the two nodes acting as receivers in each wireless link. For this purpose, the objective is then to maximize the SNR value in the FGW, SNR_{FGW}, and the SNR value in FAP, SNR_{FAP}, and penalize the difference between them, by multiplying it by a weight of 2. This constant was chosen empirically, as it allows the penalty to be sufficient to impact the reward value when the links are imbalanced, without impacting negatively the learning process. The reward function is defined in Eq. 1:

$$Reward = SNR_{FGW} + SNR_{FAP} - 2|SNR_{FGW} - SNR_{FAP}| \qquad (1)$$

In the case of the **two FAPs** scenario, the objective remains the same: to maximize the throughput values while minimizing throughput imbalances between the two nodes. However, in this scenario, variations in throughput and SNR values differ due to differences in the network topology and to the need to route traffic through the FGW node. As the distance between the FGW and the Backhaul node increases, there is an increase in the Packet Loss Ratio, which implies a reduction of the link capacity. This is demonstrated by the results obtained from the same preliminary study conducted for this scenario, where the Backhaul node was positioned in (0, 500), the FAP1 in (1000, 1000) and the FAP2 in (1000, 0), as represented in Fig. 2c. The results of the throughput variation in Fig. 4a and the SNR variation in Fig. 4b show that the throughput and SNR are not proportional, due to the interdependency of the links. For instance, if we move the FGW closer to the Backhaul node, the links between the FGW and the FAPs get stretched, thus leading to a reduction in the throughput obtained in the link between the FGW and the Backhaul node.

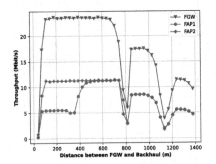

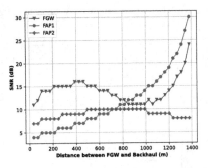

(a) Throughput variation in FAPs and FGW.

(b) SNR variation in FAPs and FGW.

Fig. 4. Link metrics comparison for the **two FAPs** scenario.

Hence, in this scenario, the reward was designed to rely directly on the throughput values obtained in the FAPs. As in the first reward function, the reward was designed to penalize the possible throughput imbalances obtained in the FAPs and favour higher throughput values. Similarly, a factor of 2 was considered. The reward function for the **two FAPs** scenario is defined in Eq. 2, where T refers to the throughput.

$$Reward = T_{FAP_1} + T_{FAP_2} - 2|T_{FAP_1} - T_{FAP_2}| \qquad (2)$$

4   Simulation Configuration and Results

The simulations performed to validate the proposed RARL algorithm were carried out using ns-3. This section presents the configuration of the simulation environment and the simulation results obtained for each scenario.

4.1   Simulation Configuration

The ns-3 simulator played a crucial role in simulating real-world behaviour in various scenarios. It served as the foundation for the DRL agent to gather relevant information from the environment, specifically the link metrics of interest. It is worth noting that the different connections were designed as independent links, and downlink traffic was considered. Table 1 summarizes the most relevant parameters applied in the simulation.

In this study, the simulations utilized the IEEE 802.11n Wi-Fi standard, commonly referred to as Wi-Fi 4. Moreover, the antenna gain was defined to have 0 dBi, meaning that for simplicity the antenna is considered to be isotropic. When it comes to the propagation loss model, the Friis Free Space Propagation Model was applied as it offers an approximation of the line-of-sight path loss that occurs in free space environments. Finally, to avoid the overhead associated with the robustness of Transmission Control Protocol, the traffic protocol chosen was the User Datagram Protocol (UDP), with a fix packet size of 1400 bytes. Moreover, in all the defined scenarios, the UDP data rate was set to be 70 Mbit/s to ensure that there was always traffic being generated, meaning that the links were saturated, maintaining a consistent load.

Table 1. Simulation parameters considered for the three scenarios.

ns-3.37 Simulator Parameters	
Wi-Fi Standard	IEEE 802.11n
Channel Bandwidth	20 MHz
Antenna Gain	0 dBi
Propagation Loss Model	Friis
Rate Adaptation Algorithm	Minstrel-HT
Application Traffic	UDP
UDP Data Rate	70 Mbit/s
Packet Size	1400 bytes

4.2   Simulation Results

The initial positions of the FGW were defined as extreme locations, tailored to each specific scenario. The results are presented below according to the scenario.

Asymmetric Links Scenario. Regarding the **asymmetric links** scenario, the aim was to assess the impact of the asymmetric links in the optimal positioning of the FGW. Thus, the Backhaul and the FAP nodes were stationary, located at the coordinates $(0, 0)$ and $(1000, 1000)$, respectively. Furthermore, the initial position for the FGW was at the coordinates $(500, 500)$, to show that the model was able to recognize the asymmetry between the links and find the optimal position in the new scenario, following the trajectory shown in Fig. 5a, as depicted below:

- Initial position of the FGW: $(500, 500)$;
- Final position of the FGW: $(175, 525)$;
- Final distance between FGW and FAP: 950 m;
- Final distance between FGW and Backhaul: 550 m.

Regarding the **asymmetric links** scenario, it is possible to see that the FGW recognizes the asymmetry of the links, as the final position is significantly closer to the Backhaul node, given that its transmission power was lower than the transmission power of the FGW. After a few iterations, the throughput in the FAP and in the FGW reached the value of around 17 Mbit/s, as seen in Fig. 5b. Nevertheless, the instabilities with the Minstrel-HT RA algorithm were evident, with fluctuations occurring during the Modulation and Coding Scheme data rate changes.

Figure 5a also presents the baseline solution, with the optimal trajectory to the optimal final position, determined as the point that ensures the SNR values in both links are the same, following Eq. 3, where P refers to the transmission power, G to the antenna gain, D to the distance between nodes and f to the frequency of operation. The throughput variation for the baseline solution, shown in Fig. 5c, follows a pattern similar to the one achieved with the RARL algorithm. Still, RARL converges faster (cf. Fig. 5b), validating the RA aware implementation of the RARL algorithm, as it was able to quickly meet the objective of throughput convergence and maximization in the different links.

$$P_{Rx} = P_{Tx} + G_{Tx} + G_{Rx} + 20 \log \left(\frac{c}{4\pi D f} \right) \tag{3}$$

Moving FAP Scenario. The FAP movement in the **moving FAP** scenario relied on the use of the Waypoint Mobility Model available in ns-3. For the evaluation presented herein, the movement was defined to evidence the behaviour regarding the FGW positioning when the FAP moves closer and further away. The following movement was defined:

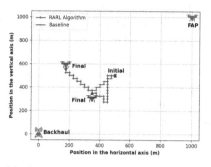

(a) Trajectory of the FGW to final position.

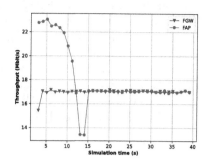

(b) Throughput values evolution for the RARL algorithm.

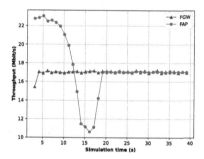

(c) Throughput values evolution for the baseline model.

Fig. 5. Analysis of the RARL algorithm performance for the **asymmetric links** scenario.

1. The FAP is stationary during the first Waypoint, at (600, 600), for the initial 20 s, as observed in Fig. 6a. The final results are:
   - Initial position of the FGW: (400, 400);
   - Final position of the FGW: oscillation between the coordinates (250, 450) and (275, 450);
   - Final distance between FGW and FAP: 380 m;
   - Final distance between FGW and Backhaul node: 500 m.
2. When it comes to the second Waypoint, represented in Fig. 6b, the movement of the FAP from (600, 600) to (1000, 1000). The FGW behaviour is described below:
   - Initial position of the FGW: (275, 450);
   - Final position of the FGW: the FGW adapts progressively to the FAPs position, finally oscillating between (550, 450) and (575, 450). The final position of this trajectory validates the RARL algorithm, given the proximity to the geometric centre between the FAP and the Backhaul node;
   - Final distance between FGW and FAP: 700 m;

– Final distance between FGW and Backhaul node: 730 m.
3. Finally, in the third part of the movement, displayed in Fig. 6c, the FAP moves to the coordinates (700, 300). The FGW behaviour is described below:
    – Initial position of the FGW: (575, 450);
    – Final position of the FGW: the final position of the FGW resulted in the oscillation between the coordinates (300, 450) and (325, 450).
    – Final distance between FGW and FAP: 400 m;
    – Final distance between FGW and Backhaul node: 550 m.

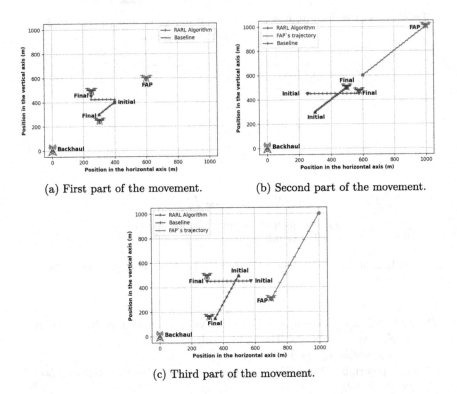

(a) First part of the movement.   (b) Second part of the movement.

(c) Third part of the movement.

Fig. 6. Trajectory of the FGW to final position for the **moving FAP** scenario.

When it comes to the evolution of the throughput values throughout the simulation in the **moving FAP** scenario, it is possible to observe in Fig. 7a that the throughput in the FGW node remained overall constant, having a uniform behaviour. On the other hand, the throughput measured in the FAP suffered multiple variations. Given that the FAP movement begins at 20 s, the fluctuations occurred just in the initial moments. As soon as the FGW is able to adjust the position to the movement, the throughputs converge, reaching around 17 Mbit/s. Due to the convergence occurring during the movement of the FAP, it can be concluded that the FGW was able to successfully follow the trajectory of the FAP.

A baseline model was also tested to evaluate the RARL algorithm performance. In the baseline model, the FGW defines a trajectory that follows the movement of the FAP node, maintaining the same distance between the FAP and the Backhaul node. The throughputs in the receiving nodes are presented in Fig. 7b and lead to the conclusion that the RARL was able to learn how to converge and maximize the throughput values even when the environment is constantly changing. As an RA aware algorithm, the RARL algorithm was able to detect the throughput imbalances and ensure the convergence of the throughputs throughout the FAP, outperform the baseline solution.

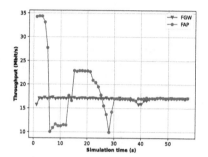 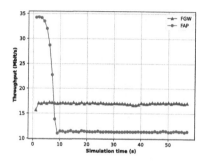

(a) Throughput values evolution for the RARL algorithm.

(b) Throughput values evolution for the baseline model.

Fig. 7. Throughput values evolution for the **moving FAP** scenario.

Two FAPs Scenario. When it comes to the **two FAPs** scenario, given the presence of an additional FAP node, the distribution of the nodes through the venue included the Backhaul node at (0, 500), FAP1 at (1000, 1000) and FAP2 at (1000, 0). The analysis of the implementation with the Minstrel-HT, shown in Fig. 8a, was based on placing the FGW at a considerable distance to all the nodes in this configuration, having the following results:

- Initial position of the FGW: (25, 25);
- Final position of the FGW: (325, 375);
- Final distance between FGW and FAP1: 920 m;
- Final distance between FGW and FAP2: 770 m;
- Final distance between FGW and Backhaul: 350 m.

Overall, in the **two FAPs** scenario, the first link between the Backhaul node and the FGW can act as a bottleneck, limiting the maximum throughput achievable in the FAPs. The throughput variation in the different nodes is shown in Fig. 8b, showcasing the effect of the applied underlying RA algorithm with the instabilities associated with data rate transitions. It is possible to observe that the throughput in the FGW is constantly higher, showing values around 23 Mbit/s. However, around the moment when there is a transition to a higher data rate in FAP1, there is a significant fluctuation in all the values. Finally, the throughput values in the FAPs converge to approximately 11 Mbit/s, accomplishing the objective of reaching higher values.

A baseline optimal trajectory leading to the geometric centre of the three nodes is presented in Fig. 8a. This implementation was able to converge the throughput values throughout most of the simulation time. Nevertheless, the FGW eventually gets to a position where its throughput decreases, consequently decreasing the throughputs achieved at the FAPs. This evidences that the final position was not optimal, showcasing that the RARL algorithm indeed maximized the throughput values in the nodes, while minimizing imbalances.

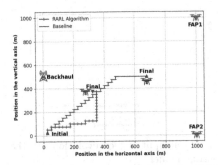

(a) Trajectory of the FGW to the final position.

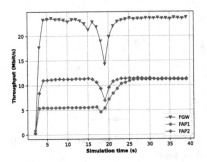

(b) Throughput values evolution for the RARL algorithm.

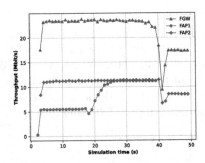

(c) Throughput values evolution for the baseline model.

Fig. 8. Analysis of the RARL algorithm performance for the **two FAPs** scenario.

5   Conclusions

Given the great impact on the network performance, the optimal positioning of the FGW is a critical element in the flying network design. This paper proposes the RARL algorithm, a DRL-based FGW positioning approach that considers the effect of two aspects that have been overlooked in the state of the art: the influence of underlying RA algorithms and the impact of the Backhaul network configuration.

The evaluation of the performance of the RARL algorithm was carried out in ns-3. It was possible to observe that the fluctuations and instabilities, associated with the influence of Minstrel-HT in the link metrics, were overcome. This is supported by the trajectory of the FGW leading to a maximization of the defined reward functions, despite potential interference caused by the underlying RA algorithm in the throughput measured throughout the displacement of the FGW.

The comparisons of the RARL algorithm with the baseline models demonstrate its capability of converging and maximizing the throughput values in the nodes in all the three scenarios studied, meaning that this work endorses the possibility of implementing an RA aware positioning algorithm for real-world deployments. As future work, we intend to enhance the trajectory performed by the FGW, as it was overall not fully optimized, in order to reduce resource consumption and the time to converge to the optimal position. Moreover, given that this work is an initial evaluation of the position optimization of UAVs considering the influence of RA algorithms, after performing the necessary steps into scaling the complexity of the network configuration and topology, a real-world implementation should be carried out. For this, after the model being trained in the simulation environment, it will be implemented in the FGW through transfer learning.

Acknowledgements. This work is co-financed by Component 5 - Capitalization and Business Innovation, integrated in the Resilience Dimension of the Recovery and Resilience Plan within the scope of the Recovery and Resilience Mechanism (MRR) of the European Union (EU), framed in the Next Generation EU, for the period 2021 - 2026, within project Produtech_R3, with reference 60. The second author thanks the funding from FCT, Portugal under the PhD grant 2022.10093.BD.

References

1. Almeida, E.N., Campos, R., Ricardo, M.: Traffic-aware UAV placement using a generalizable deep reinforcement learning methodology. In: 2022 IEEE Symposium on Computers and Communications (ISCC), pp. 1–6 (2022). https://doi.org/10.1109/ISCC55528.2022.9912770

2. Alzenad, M., El-Keyi, A., Yanikomeroglu, H.: 3-D placement of an unmanned aerial vehicle base station for maximum coverage of users with different QoS requirements. IEEE Wirel. Commun. Lett. **7**(1), 38–41 (2018). https://doi.org/10.1109/LWC.2017.2752161

3. Anokye, S., Ayepah-Mensah, D., Seid, A.M., Boateng, G.O., Sun, G.: Deep reinforcement learning-based mobility-aware UAV content caching and placement in

mobile edge networks. IEEE Syst. J. **16**(1), 275–286 (2022). https://doi.org/10.1109/JSYST.2021.3082837

4. Arif, T.Y., Munadi, R., et al.: Evaluation of the minstrel-HT rate adaptation algorithm in IEEE 802.11 n WLANs. Int. J. Simul. Syst. Sci. Technol. **18**(1) (2017)

5. Bayerlein, H., De Kerret, P., Gesbert, D.: Trajectory optimization for autonomous flying base station via reinforcement learning. In: 2018 IEEE 19th International Workshop on Signal Processing Advances in Wireless Communications (SPAWC), pp. 1–5 (2018). https://doi.org/10.1109/SPAWC.2018.8445768

6. Cicek, C.T., Gultekin, H., Tavli, B., Yanikomeroglu, H.: UAV base station location optimization for next generation wireless networks: overview and future research directions. In: 2019 1st International Conference on Unmanned Vehicle Systems-Oman (UVS), pp. 1–6 (2019). https://doi.org/10.1109/UVS.2019.8658363

7. Coelho, A., Fontes, H., Campos, R., Ricardo, M.: Traffic-aware gateway placement for high-capacity flying networks. In: 2021 IEEE 93rd Vehicular Technology Conference (VTC2021-Spring), pp. 1–6 (2021). https://doi.org/10.1109/VTC2021-Spring51267.2021.9448966

8. Fotouhi, A., et al.: Survey on UAV cellular communications: practical aspects, standardization advancements, regulation, and security challenges. IEEE Commun. Surv. Tutor. **21**(4), 3417–3442 (2019). https://doi.org/10.1109/COMST.2019.2906228

9. Lagum, F., Bor-Yaliniz, I., Yanikomeroglu, H.: Strategic densification with UAV-BSs in cellular networks. IEEE Wirel. Commun. Lett. **7**(3), 384–387 (2018). https://doi.org/10.1109/LWC.2017.2779483

10. Li, Y.: Deep reinforcement learning: an overview. arXiv preprint arXiv:1701.07274 (2017)

11. Liu, X., Liu, Y., Chen, Y.: Reinforcement learning in multiple-UAV networks: deployment and movement design. IEEE Trans. Veh. Technol. **68**(8), 8036–8049 (2019). https://doi.org/10.1109/TVT.2019.2922849

12. Queiros, R., Ruela, J., Fontes, H., Campos, R.: Trajectory-aware rate adaptation for flying networks. arXiv preprint arXiv:2307.06905 (2023)

13. Queirós, R., Almeida, E.N., Fontes, H., Ruela, J., Campos, R.: Wi-Fi rate adaptation using a simple deep reinforcement learning approach. In: 2022 IEEE Symposium on Computers and Communications (ISCC), pp. 1–3 (2022). https://doi.org/10.1109/ISCC55528.2022.9912784

14. Sammour, I., Chalhoub, G.: Evaluation of rate adaptation algorithms in IEEE 802.11 networks. Electronics **9**(9), 1436 (2020)

15. Saxena, V., Jaldén, J., Klessig, H.: Optimal UAV base station trajectories using flow-level models for reinforcement learning. IEEE Trans. Cogn. Commun. Netw. **5**(4), 1101–1112 (2019). https://doi.org/10.1109/TCCN.2019.2948324

16. Xia, D., Hart, J., Fu, Q.: Evaluation of the minstrel rate adaptation algorithm in IEEE 802.11g WLANs. In: 2013 IEEE International Conference on Communications (ICC), pp. 2223–2228 (2013). https://doi.org/10.1109/ICC.2013.6654858

17. Yin, W., Hu, P., Indulska, J., Portmann, M., Mao, Y.: Mac-layer rate control for 802.11 networks: a survey. Wirel. Netw. **26**, 3793–3830 (2020)

18. Zeng, Y., Zhang, R., Lim, T.J.: Wireless communications with unmanned aerial vehicles: opportunities and challenges. IEEE Commun. Mag. **54**(5), 36–42 (2016). https://doi.org/10.1109/MCOM.2016.7470933

19. Zhang, S., Zhang, H., He, Q., Bian, K., Song, L.: Joint trajectory and power optimization for UAV relay networks. IEEE Commun. Lett. **22**(1), 161–164 (2018). https://doi.org/10.1109/LCOMM.2017.2763135

RateRL: A Framework for Developing RL-Based Rate Adaptation Algorithms in ns-3

Ruben Queiros[1,2]($\boxtimes$) , Luís Ferreira[1,2] , Helder Fontes[2] ,
and Rui Campos[1,2]

[1] Faculdade de Engenharia da Universidade do Porto, Porto, Portugal
[2] INESC TEC, Porto, Portugal
{ruben.m.queiros,luis.m.martins,helder.m.fontes,rui.l.campos}@inesctec.pt

Abstract. The increasing complexity of recent Wi-Fi amendments is making the use of traditional algorithms and heuristics unfeasible to address the Rate Adaptation (RA) problem. This is due to the large combination of configuration parameters along with the high variability of the wireless channel. Recently, several works have proposed the usage of Reinforcement Learning (RL) techniques to address the problem. However, the proposed solutions lack sufficient technical explanation. Also, the lack of standard frameworks enabling the reproducibility of results and the limited availability of source code, makes the fair comparison with state of the art approaches a challenge. This paper proposes a framework, named RateRL, that integrates state of the art libraries with the well-known Network Simulator 3 (ns-3) to enable the implementation and evaluation of RL-based RA algorithms. To the best of our knowledge, RateRL is the first tool available to assist researchers during the implementation, validation and evaluation phases of RL-based RA algorithms and enable the fair comparison between competing algorithms.

Keywords: Wireless Networks · ns-3 · Deep Reinforcement Learning · Machine Learning Tool

1 Introduction

The new configuration parameters available in the most recent Wi-Fi amendments allied to the high variability and asymmetry of the radio channel, make Rate Adaptation (RA) and the optimal configuration of these parameters challenging. Recent RA algorithms in Wi-Fi are often developed considering simplified simulations that are not always well described. This poses a challenge for the implementation and comparison of different RA algorithms. For example, the Network Simulator 3 (ns-3) implements a significant amount of existing state-of-the-art RA algorithms. However, only a few of these algorithms can be used for recent Wi-Fi versions subsequent to IEEE 802.11n. Additionally, many

J.-L. Guisado-Lizar et al. (Eds.): SIMUtools 2023, LNICST 519, pp. 287–298, 2024.
https://doi.org/10.1007/978-3-031-57523-5_22

recent RA algorithms are based on Machine Learning (ML), which can make them difficult to implement and understand. In some cases, the authors of these algorithms do not even provide the source code or the training dataset, which poses an obstacle to accurately reproduce the obtained results. When developing novel ML-based solutions the authors should consider the following practices: 1) clearly describe the problem that the proposal is trying to solve and justify any underlying assumptions; 2) systematically devise procedures that ensure the reproducibility of results; 3) clearly state and justify the metrics used for the evaluation; 4) expose the dataset used in the training process of the algorithm; and 5) have one or more baseline models to compare with.

The use of Reinforcement Learning (RL) and other ML techniques within the wireless networks research area has emerged as a way to further improve the network Quality of Service (QoS). Leveraging these techniques, the research community has been optimising the network performance, reducing latency, and ensuring efficient resource allocation [11,17]. A high percentage of the current telecommunications infrastructures have begun to invest and test ML algorithms for supporting the network operation and business decisions [12]. However, the techniques employed are not standardized, resulting in a lack of foundational principles that would enable the transfer of knowledge from previous initiatives to more recent ones. When compared with other fields that pioneered the use of ML, such as computer vision or natural language processing, wireless networks research started using ML at a later stage. Thus, it is common within the existing literature to identify ML-based solutions that lack the use of good practices stated above. A predominant challenge relates to the scarcity of technical details provided in published works, which hampers the reproducibility of results. Furthermore, the limited availability to the source code and the dataset used, precludes the validation and extension of prior findings. These issues collectively emphasize the need for a more cohesive and systematic approach to integrate RL into wireless networks.

The main contribution of this paper is RateRL, a framework to support the development of RL-based RA algorithms. We illustrate the use of RateRL through a practical use case, employing the Data Driven Algorithm for Rate Adaptation (DARA) proposed in [15]. Our framework integrates well-known RL libraries, such as TensorFlow Agents and OpenAI Gym [3] with ns-3 [16], using ns3-gym [8] to interface all the components. RateRL enables the task automation to identify the hyperparameter configuration that maximizes the expected cumulative reward of the RL algorithm, while offering real-time feedback of the training process. The code and ns-3 scripts are publicly available, facilitating the efforts of future research works to build upon RateRL.

The rest of the paper is organised as follows. Section 2 presents the background. Section 3 addresses the related work. Section 4 explains the RateRL framework. Section 5 illustrates the use of RateRL considering DARA as the use case. Finally, Sect. 5 provides some concluding remarks and points out the future work.

2   Background

This section refers to some background concepts that are necessary to understand RateRL. It starts with an overview of RL, namely the Q-learning algorithm and existing frameworks to implement these techniques. Then, a brief description of the network simulator ns-3 is provided.

2.1   Reinforcement Learning

The Fig. 1 illustrates the RL model, which consists of the environment and agent elements. These elements communicate based on action, state and reward signals. Based on the observations (states) retrieved from the environment, the agent learns to make decisions (actions) and it evaluates these decisions by considering a reward. Learning the policy that maps an action for an environment state that maximises the total cumulative reward for each (action, state) combination, is the objective of RL. The literature has a variety of learning algorithms available. The recent works that address the RA problem [5,6,14,15] use the classic Q-learning algorithm and show better results when compared to traditional algorithms such as Minstrel-HT [7], the default RA algorithm for Linux systems.

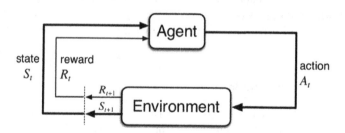

Fig. 1. Reinforcement Learning loop diagram.

As a model-free algorithm, Q-learning [18] learns by making mistakes and does not rely on any past environment information. It is only in a discrete action space that Q-learning works. Finding the best policy that maximises the expected cumulative reward is the objective of Q-learning. The Q-function values are updated using Eq. 1, through trial and error. The expected cumulative reward when the agent selects action a in state s is represented using $Q(a, s)$, considering that following actions are chosen according to the policy that was learnt. The reward for taking action a in state s is represented by $r(a, s)$, and $\max_{a \in A} Q(a, s_{new}), \forall a \in A$ is the maximum possible reward of the new state s_{new}, which is the result of the current action; s_{new} is the new state and a_{all} represents every $a \in A$. The learning rate α determines the rate at which new values update the total Q-value. Finally, the discount factor $\gamma \in [0, 1]$ determines the importance of future rewards in the calculation of the expected cumulative reward.

$$Q(a,s) \leftarrow (1-\alpha)Q(a,s) + \alpha[r(a,s) + \gamma \max_{\forall a \in A} Q(a, s_{new})] \tag{1}$$

2.2 Reinforcement Learning Frameworks

There are multiple and extensively validated frameworks available to implement Q-learning or other RL-based learning algorithm. TensorFlow [1] and PyTorch [13] are two prominent deep learning frameworks widely adopted for building and training ML models, including RL agents. TensorFlow, developed by Google, offers a comprehensive ecosystem of tools and libraries that facilitate the creation of neural networks and the optimisation of their parameters. TensorFlow Agents (TF-Agents) is an extension of TensorFlow specifically designed to enable the construction of RL agents. TF-Agents [9] provides reusable components for defining agent behaviour, defining the environment interaction loop, and implementing various state-of-the-art RL algorithms. Similarly, PyTorch, developed by Facebook's AI Research lab, provides a dynamic computational graph that simplifies model development and experimentation. Gym is an open-source toolkit developed by OpenAI, designed to facilitate the development and testing of RL algorithms. It provides a collection of environments (simulated scenarios) that allow researchers and developers to experiment with and benchmark various RL techniques as well as to develop their own custom environment making it a valuable resource that can interface with the popular network simulator ns-3.

2.3 The Network Simulator 3

ns-3 [16] is a well-known open-source network simulation tool and one of the most used wireless network simulators. ns-3 was driven by a desire to model networks in a way that best suits network research and learning. It aims to provide highly accurate and scalable network simulation capabilities for studying various aspects of networking protocols, communications methods, and network behaviour. Hence, it was not developed with ML or artificial intelligence in mind. There is currently no official framework for integrating with prevalent ML tools. Initial community efforts [8,19] were made to bridge the gap between the network simulator and popular ML frameworks such as TensorFlow, PyTorch and Gym. The resulting tools, named ns3-ai and ns3-gym, are detailed in Sect. 3.

3 Related Work

The related work is presented in this section. First, we overview existing reinforcement learning frameworks for networking and then we review the state of the art in RL-based solutions for the RA problem.

3.1 Reinforcement Learning Frameworks for Networking

To the best of our knowledge, few frameworks that integrate Reinforcement Learning frameworks with network simulators have been proposed in the state of the art. In [8] the authors develop a sockets-based interface between ns-3 and OpenAI Gym to encourage the usage of RL in networking research. To overcome the lack of flexibility imposed by ns3-gym, the authors in [19] proposed ns3-ai, a Python module that allows the interconnection between any artificial intelligence framework with ns-3, using a higher efficiency mechanism based on shared-memory. However, since this is a high flexibility and efficiency data interaction framework researchers using ns3-ai have to adapt to implement their own development environment to address their specific problem, resulting in slower algorithm development or simplistic simulation environments, which reduces the solution realism. On the other hand, the authors in [2] developed the PRISMA framework, which is tailored to the distributed packet routing problem, on top of ns3-gym, extending the problem to a Multi-Agent Deep Reinforcement Learning approach. Therefore, researchers would need to modify PRISMA's design if the objective was to address the RA problem.

3.2 Reinforcement Learning for Rate Adaptation

The RA problem has been addressed using several different solutions, in particular for Wi-Fi networks. Some use classical heuristic approaches [4, 7] while recent works have been using RL-based techniques [5, 6, 10, 14, 15]. In [5], the authors developed a Q-learning based link adaptation solution that addresses RA together with other configuration parameters such as the channel bandwidth and number of spatial streams, outperforming state of the art solutions in terms of throughput. Despite implementing it in a network interface card and evaluating their solution in an experimental setting, the authors do not mention any standard framework that was used to implement their solution. Also, the source code is not publicly available. In [6, 14] the authors use ns-3 to implement their RL-based RA solutions with the help of ns3-gym and ns3-ai frameworks. However, both works do not provide any information with regards to the training process or hyperparameter configuration. Moreover, despite simplistic simulation scenarios for evaluation, they are not sufficiently well described, posing an obstacle to accurately reproduce the obtained results.

3.3 Summary

Despite the good results of recent works that boost the overall network performance, the difficulty to replicate the results of the proposed solutions is common among existing works. Typically, they lack implementation details – i.e. the code is not open source – and training process description. Moreover, within the identified works, the results of the proposed solutions are not compared with other RL-based RA algorithms.

4   RateRL Framework

In this section, we present the RateRL framework, including its architecture and components.

The RateRL framework was designed considering design principles similar to the PRISMA framework [2], such as the achievement of realistic wireless networks simulation environments due to the usage of ns-3 and the development with a modular approach, which makes fast prototyping of RL-based RA algorithms possible.

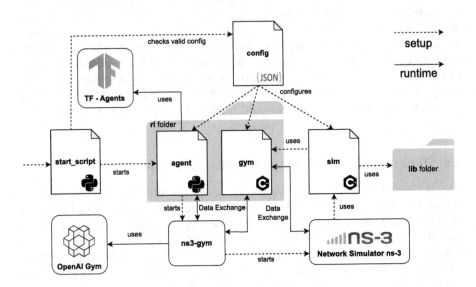

Fig. 2. RateRL architecture diagram.

In Fig. 2 we present the RateRL architecture and how its components interact with each other. The programming languages used to code RateRL were Python and C++. The Python files hold every essential setup procedures and parsing mechanisms required for the proper execution of the system, the core ML components and most of the data collection processes. The files written in C++, are mainly related to the configuration and utilisation of the ns-3 simulator together with some files that interact with the ns3-gym interface.

We now detail the RateRL components and instruct the reader on how to use RateRL. The starting point of the RateRL framework is the start_script file. A detailed description of the role of each component is presented below:

– start_script checks if the configuration file is valid. It also sets up the results folder where the logs of the simulation or training are stored. Finally, it starts the agent component.
– config is a JSON file that holds the configuration parameters relevant for each of the other files within the framework, such as the agent, gym and sim.

- **agent** interacts with the TF-Agents framework using the environment data that is retrieved from the ns-3 simulation. It starts the ns-3 environment using the ns3-gym interface.
- **sim** defines the ns-3 simulation script. It uses the lib folder, where multiple utility functions are defined to ease aspects such as the simulation configuration and data collection.
- **gym** configures the ns-3 environment defining the observation and action data shapes. It executes the action that comes from the **agent**, and establishes the data collection methods that are used to collect the observation from the ns-3 simulation as well as the metrics to calculate the reward.

The installation process is documented in the public repository, inside the install folder, and it assumes the user does not have any of the required dependencies installed. The user can run the agent in two different modes:

- **Training Mode** begins by addind the trajectories gathered from the simulation to the replay buffer. A trajectory comprises three components: 1) a time step which represents the first observation of the environment; 2) the action step which represents the chosen action after taking into account the previous time step; and 3) the subsequent time step, which represents the new observation and the reward consequent from the previous action step). Until the end of the episode, which in this case also signifies the conclusion of the simulation, this replay buffer is filled while the simulation is running. During this procedure, the agent is trained by randomly selecting a set number of trajectories defined by the hyperparamenter *batch size* from the replay buffer, updating the weights accordingly and raising the train step counter. Next, the user can modify how frequently training occurs, how many episodes the simulation runs, and how epsilon greedy adapts during training. It is feasible to save the progress using a checkpoint so that the policy's present state can be received at a later time, should the user choose to pause the training or finish it earlier.
- **Evaluation Mode** assumes a fixed epsilon greedy factor of 0 to avoid exploratory attempts, and loads the previously trained policy. However, this mode is not prepared for simulation scenarios that dynamically change requiring an online learning approach. This will be the subject of future work.

Regardless of the mode used, RateRL saves simulation logs with the throughput of every existing communication link as well as the nodes positions, with a configurable periodicity.

5   Using the RateRL Framework

In this section we use the implementation, training and evaluation of the DARA algorithm [15] as a use case to illustrate the utilisation of the RateRL framework.

5.1 DARA Overview

DARA [15] is a RL-based RA algorithm developed for the IEEE 802.11n amendment. It considers scenarios with Single Input Single Output and fixed channel bandwidth of 20 MHz, using long Guard Interval. The valid actions are the first 8 Modulation and Coding Schemes (MCS). The state is the average SNR value considering the Acknowledgement frames that originate from the receiver node. Finally, the reward is a function of the Frame Success Ratio (FSR) and the chosen MCS, to value the highest possible MCS without compromising the FSR.

5.2 Simulation Settings

We configured the preliminary validation scenario defined in [15]. In this scenario, we have a stationary node and a moving node. In the beginning of the simulation, the nodes start close to each other, and their distance increases throughout the simulation period. In this way we stimulate the algorithm with a wide range of SNR values. The algorithm is then compared in terms of throughput with other RA algorithms implemented in ns-3 such as Minstrel-HT (MIN) and the Ideal (ID) algorithm. All the other main simulation configuration parameters are presented in Table 1.

Table 1. Simulation Configuration Parameters.

Configuration Parameter	Value
Wi-Fi Standard	IEEE 802.11n
Propagation Delay Model	Constant Speed
Propagation Loss Model	Friis
Frequency	5180 MHz
Channel Bandwidth	20 MHz
Transmission Power	20 dBm
Wi-Fi MAC	Ad-hoc
Traffic	UDP, generated above link capacity
Packet Size	1400 Bytes of UDP Payload

5.3 Training and Hyperparameter Tuning

DARA was trained and evaluated on a ASUS ROG G14 Laptop with a Ryzen 9 5900HS (8 cores up to 4.6 GHz), 32 GB RAM and a NVIDIA RTX 3060 GPU. In this illustrative example the hyperparameter configuration chosen is defined in Table 2. The simulations were 60 s long, for a total of 15 episodes.

The hyperparameter tuning is an essential part of any machine learning model training. To this end, we assess how different values could benefit the

Table 2. DQN Learning Algorithm main Parameters.

Parameter	Value
Observation Space	One-dimensional scaled float (0.0–1.0)
Action Space	One-dimensional integer (0–7)
Optimiser	Adam
Loss Function	Mean Square Error
Epsilon Greedy	Fixed at 0.1
Discount Factor	Fixed at 0.5
Replay buffer	size of 10^6
Batch Size	64

final DARA performance. In this work, comparisons between different values of learning rate and the hidden layer architecture of the neural network were carried out.

These comparisons were not extensive, thus the performance of DARA could be further improved with a more in depth tuning, despite the simple scenario, which shows that good results are achievable with few training episodes. However, the objective of this work is to show that RateRL can be used to compare different hyperparamenter configurations and assess their impact in the performance of the algorithm.

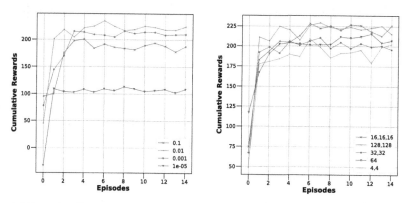

(a) Learning Rate comparison training. (b) Hidden Layer architecture training.

Fig. 3. Hyperparameter tuning trainings.

Figure 3a shows the cumulative reward over 15 training episodes with 4 different learning rate configurations, using two hidden layers with 32 units each. The results show that a learning rate of 0.01 is consistently better than the other options. After defining the used learning rate value, additional trainings were performed to fine tune the hidden layer architecture.

Figure 3b shows the results of this training, with 5 different options being evaluated. Despite the similarities in performance it was decided to choose as the final configuration the one which finished with highest cumulative reward by the end of the 15 episodes training. Therefore, a learning rate of 0.01 and a neural network with 3 hidden layers of 16 units each was defined.

5.4   Simulation Results

Using the resulting policy from the training that was detailed in the previous sections, we used RateRL to evaluate how the performance of DARA is compared to other popular RA algorithms such as Minstrel and Ideal. Fig. 4a shows the throughput throughout the simulation period and Fig. 4b its complementary cumulative distribution function.

The results show that RateRL can be used to evaluate the performance and comparison of RL-based RA algorithms with other state of the art RA solutions. The average throughput of Ideal was of 13.45 Mbit/s and Minstrel was of 13.07 Mbit/s. DARA achieved an average throughput of 13.52 Mbit/s, an increase of 3.4% over Minstrel and similar throughput when compared with Ideal. To conclude, we managed to successfully implement train and evaluate DARA using RateRL.

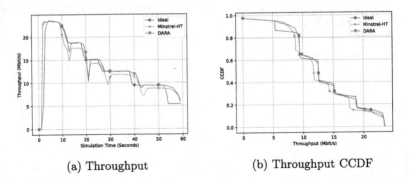

(a) Throughput   (b) Throughput CCDF

Fig. 4. Simulation Results using the resulting hyperparamenter configuration.

6   Conclusion

This paper presented RateRL, the first framework designed for assisting the development, validation and evaluation of RL-based RA algorithms. We demonstrated the use of RateRL in the whole development cycle of an RL-based RA algorithm, using the state of the art DARA algorithm as a use case. Our objective with RateRL is to provide a framework for developing future RL-based RA solutions and enable their direct comparison with state of the art or related solutions. The RateRL framework is open source and it is publicly available on Gitlab[1].

As future work, we plan to migrate to ns3-ai to support other popular ML frameworks. Also, we aim to extend RateRL to use other popular RL algorithms such as Deep Deterministic Policy Gradient and Proximal Policy optimisation.

Acknowledgements. This work is financed by National Funds through the Portuguese funding agency, FCT - Fundação para a Ciência e a Tecnologia, within project LA/P/0063/2020. The first author thanks the funding from FCT, Portugal under the PhD grant 2022.10093.BD.

References

1. Abadi, M., et al.: {TensorFlow}: a system for {Large-Scale} machine learning. In: 12th USENIX Symposium on Operating Systems Design and Implementation (OSDI 16), pp. 265–283 (2016)
2. Alliche, R.A., Barros, T.D.S., Aparicio-Pardo, R., Sassatelli, L.: PRISMA: a packet routing simulator for multi-agent reinforcement learning. In: 2022 IFIP Networking Conference (IFIP Networking), pp. 1–6. IEEE (2022)
3. Brockman, G., et al.: OpenAI gym (2016)
4. Byeon, S., Yoon, K., Yang, C., Choi, S.: STRALE: Mobility-aware PHY rate and frame aggregation length adaptation in WLANs. In: IEEE INFOCOM 2017 - IEEE Conference on Computer Communications, pp. 1–9 (2017). https://doi.org/10.1109/INFOCOM.2017.8056965
5. Chen, S.C., Li, C.Y., Chiu, C.H.: An experience driven design for IEEE 802.11ac rate adaptation based on reinforcement learning. In: IEEE INFOCOM 2021 - IEEE Conference on Computer Communications, pp. 1–10 (2021). https://doi.org/10.1109/INFOCOM42981.2021.9488876
6. Cho, S.: Reinforcement learning for rate adaptation in CSMA/CA wireless networks. In: Park, J.J., Fong, S.J., Pan, Y., Sung, Y. (eds.) Advances in Computer Science and Ubiquitous Computing. Lecture Notes in Electrical Engineering, vol. 715, pp. 175–181. Springer, Singapore (2021). https://doi.org/10.1007/978-981-15-9343-7_24
7. FietKau, F.: Minstrel_HT: new rate control module for 802.11n [LWN.net] (2010). https://lwn.net/Articles/376765. Accessed 20 May 2022
8. Gawłowicz, P., Zubow, A.: ns-3 meets OpenAI gym: the playground for machine learning in networking research. In: Proceedings of the 22nd International ACM Conference on Modeling, Analysis and Simulation of Wireless and Mobile Systems, pp. 113–120 (2019)
9. Guadarrama, S., et al.: TF-Agents: A library for reinforcement learning in TensorFlow. https://github.com/tensorflow/agents (2018), https://github.com/tensorflow/agents. Accessed 25 June 2019
10. Karmakar, R., Chattopadhyay, S., Chakraborty, S.: SmartLA: reinforcement learning-based link adaptation for high throughput wireless access networks. Comput. Commun. **110**, 1–25 (2017)
11. Kulin, M., Kazaz, T., De Poorter, E., Moerman, I.: A survey on machine learning-based performance improvement of wireless networks: PHY, MAC and network layer. Electronics **10**(3), 318 (2021)

---

[1] https://gitlab.inesctec.pt/pub/ctm-win/raterl.

12. Mahmoud, H.H.H., Ismail, T.: A review of machine learning use-cases in telecommunication industry in the 5G era. In: 2020 16th International Computer Engineering Conference (ICENCO), pp. 159–163 (2020). https://doi.org/10.1109/ICENCO49778.2020.9357376

13. Paszke, A., et al.: PyTorch: an imperative style, high-performance deep learning library. In: Advances in Neural Information Processing Systems, vol. 32 (2019)

14. Pratama, M.H.B., Nakashima, T., Nagao, Y., Kurosaki, M., Ochi, H.: Experimental evaluation of rate adaptation using deep-Q-network in IEEE 802.11 WLAN. In: 2023 IEEE 20th Consumer Communications & Networking Conference (CCNC), pp. 668–669. IEEE (2023)

15. Queirós, R., Almeida, E.N., Fontes, H., Ruela, J., Campos, R.: Wi-fi rate adaptation using a simple deep reinforcement learning approach. In: 2022 IEEE Symposium on Computers and Communications (ISCC), pp. 1–3 (2022). https://doi.org/10.1109/ISCC55528.2022.9912784

16. Riley, G.F., Henderson, T.R.: The ns-3 network simulator. In: Wehrle, K., Gunes, M., Gross, J. (eds.) Modeling and Tools for Network Simulation, pp. 15–34. Springer, Berlin (2010). https://doi.org/10.1007/978-3-642-12331-3_2

17. Szott, S., et al.: Wi-Fi meets ML: a survey on improving IEEE 802.11 performance with machine learning. IEEE Commun. Surv. Tutorials **24**(3), 1843–1893 (2022)

18. Watkins, C.J., Dayan, P.: Q-learning. Mach. Learn. **8**, 279–292 (1992)

19. Yin, H., et al.: ns3-AI: fostering artificial intelligence algorithms for networking research. In: Proceedings of the 2020 Workshop on ns-3, WNS3 2020, pp. 57-64. Association for Computing Machinery, New York (2020). https://doi.org/10.1145/3389400.3389404

On the Analysis of Computational Delays in Reinforcement Learning-Based Rate Adaptation Algorithms

Ricardo Trancoso$^{(\boxtimes)}$ ⓘ, João Pinto, Ruben Queiros ⓘ, Helder Fontes ⓘ, and Rui Campos ⓘ

INESC TEC and Faculdade de Engenharia, Universidade do Porto, Porto, Portugal
{ricardo.j.espirito,ruben.m.queiros,helder.m.fontes,
rui.l.campos}@inesctec.pt

Abstract. Several research works have applied Reinforcement Learning (RL) algorithms to solve the Rate Adaptation (RA) problem in Wi-Fi networks. The dynamic nature of the radio link requires the algorithms to be responsive to changes in link quality. Delays in the execution of the algorithm due to implementional details may be detrimental to its performance, which in turn may decrease network performance. These delays can be avoided to a certain extent. However, this aspect has been overlooked in the state of the art when using simulated environments, since the computational delays are not considered. In this paper, we present an analysis of computational delays and their impact on the performance of RL-based RA algorithms, and propose a methodology to incorporate the experimental computational delays of the algorithms from running in a specific target hardware, in a simulation environment. Our simulation results considering the real computational delays showed that these delays do, in fact, degrade the algorithm's execution and training capabilities which, in the end, has a negative impact on network performance.

Keywords: Reinforcement Learning · Rate Adaptation · Computational Delay

1 Introduction

The IEEE 802.11 standard, commonly known as Wi-Fi, enables the establishment of Wireless Local Area Networks. The standard has had many amendments to keep it up-to-date with the growing requirements of the vast application scenarios. For example, new configuration parameters, such as more spatial streams and larger channel bandwidth, were introduced in the recent standard amendments [1]. When configured correctly for a given link quality, these parameters may increase the efficiency of Wi-Fi networks. One of the parameters that can be changed is the Modulation and Coding Scheme (MCS). Since the link conditions are not static, the MCS has to be changed dynamically. To address this

© ICST Institute for Computer Sciences, Social Informatics and Telecommunications Engineering 2024
Published by Springer Nature Switzerland AG 2024. All Rights Reserved
J.-L. Guisado-Lizar et al. (Eds.): SIMUtools 2023, LNICST 519, pp. 299–310, 2024.
https://doi.org/10.1007/978-3-031-57523-5_23

challenge, multiple Rate Adaptation (RA) algorithms are proposed in the state of the art.

There are multiple heuristic-based RA algorithms. The most commonly used in practice are Minstrel [2] and Iwlwifi [3]. However, these algorithms have shortcomings [4], which limit their ability to select the optimal MCS rate. Algorithms that employ Reinforcement Learning (RL) techniques have emerged as an alternative [4–10]. RL techniques collect observations from the environment. With these observations, the algorithm makes a decision on the best action. Finally, the algorithm calculates a numerical reward, which indicates how suitable the action was. The algorithm learns to repeat actions that yielded a high reward and to avoid actions which led to the opposite. Through this process, the algorithm can eventually find solutions to a problem autonomously and even adapt to unforeseen circumstances. In the context of RA, the environment is the radio link, and the algorithm learns how to configure the Wi-Fi parameters to increase efficiency in dynamic link conditions. Since link conditions are constantly changing, an RL algorithm requires up-to-date observations and actions. Therefore, delays during the execution of an RL-based RA algorithm may be detrimental to its performance.

In the state of the art, computational delays of RL-based RA algorithms have been overlooked. Usually, only the conceptual stages of the algorithms are described, such as the RL model used and the information collected for the observations and the reward; other implementational details are typically not referred. In [4], the authors mention the use of an asynchronous framework to prevent halting of the algorithm while waiting for a process to finish, but do not provide more details. In [5–10], computational delays are not even mentioned. Characterizing the computational delays, which are not modeled in simulation, is relevant since they may impact the algorithm's real-world performance.

The main contributions of this paper are three-fold. First, we bring up awareness to the execution time problem and the importance of considering computational delays when it comes to RL-based RA algorithms; this has been overlooked in the state of the art and may reveal that several existing algorithms can experience degraded performance, when considering the real computational delays. Second, we describe the methods we use to reduce the computational delays of DARA [10], an RL-based RA algorithm, without deviating from its original conceptual design. This can guide implementation alternatives that may be used to reduce the execution time and improve the realistic achievable performance of other RL-based RA algorithms. Finally, we measured the delays of the DARA algorithm in a real scenario and created a framework to simulate these delays. We use this augmented simulation to evaluate and compare the effect these computational delays have on the algorithm's performance in terms of network throughput and other metrics.

The paper is structured as follows. Section 2 characterizes the problem. Section 3 discusses the methods used to reduce the delays of an RL-based RA algorithm, as well as proposes a methodology for comparing the impact of these delays. Section 4 presents the results of the previous comparison. Finally, in Sect. 5, we draw the conclusions.

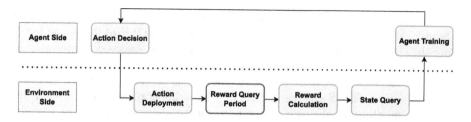

Fig. 1. Overview of the DARA algorithm with its main operations highlighted, and split between agent and environment side.

2   Problem Characterization

In this section, we characterize the problem, using the Data-driven Algorithm for Rate Adaptation (DARA) [10] as a representative state of the art RL-based RA algorithm for Wi-Fi networks. As previously stated, RL relies on observations from the environment, so in a dynamic environment such as the radio link, delays in those observations affect the performance of the algorithm. However, the processes of an RL agent are not instant and have computational delays associated. These delays may not be present in simulation, with the processes instead being functionally instant, as the simulation pauses for the agent to calculate its action, before resuming as normal. This may lead to a significant difference in performance between a simulated and a real environment.

After performing a solution-agnostic analysis of different RL-based RA algorithms, we have identified that they share five key operations: 1) **action decision**, using the agent to choose the optimal expected action; 2) **agent training**, using the reward so that the agent may learn from its previous actions; 3) **action deployment**, applying the chosen action; 4) **reward calculation**, gathering information and calculating the numerical value of the reward; and 5) **state query**, gathering data on the current state of the environment.

In Fig. 1, we can see an overview of the DARA operations, based on the well known RL loop, with the aforementioned five operations highlighted in orange. DARA uses a Deep Q-Network (DQN) [11] algorithm that decides an action out of the eight possible MCS rates defined in IEEE 802.11n, considering a static configuration with Single Input Single Output, 20 MHz channel bandwidth and 800 ns guard interval. DARA decides an action every 100 ms. In [10] DARA was implemented in simulation without taking any computational delays into account. Given that it shares the five key operations with other state of the art algorithms, hereafter we consider it as an application example of this work.

First, DARA was implemented in a real environment to measure experimentally how long was each of its execution steps. This was done on the w-iLab.2 testbed [12] provided by the Fed4FIRE+ project. Our network topology consisted of two nodes: a ZOTAC node as the access point, and a DSS node as the client. The DARA algorithm was deployed on the client node. The client node was equipped with an Intel Core i5 2.6 GHz 4-core CPU, a 60 GB SSD hard drive, and a 4 GB DDR2 800 MHz PC2-6400 CL6 RAM. The devices ran a Ubuntu 14.04 Linux distribution, on kernel version 3.13.0. Note that the hardware the algorithm is executed on is strongly tied to the observed computational delays. To be able to run DARA in an experimental setting, it required some modifications to collect data regarding the status of the real Wi-Fi link and apply its actions (MCS changes). This first experimental version of DARA did not focus on the optimization of computational delays, as they were thought to be potentially negligible, and would be an object of study. Further details about this implementation will be provided in Sect. 3. This version of DARA will be addressed in this paper as "base DARA", as it serves as an example of an algorithm that overlooks the effect of computational delays on its performance. We performed a preliminary measurement of ten thousand execution steps, and found that the average execution step time of one RL loop was 528.8 ms. This is substantially above the intended 100 ms interval of action which is also used by Minstrel and is related to the coherence time of the Wi-Fi channel. Therefore, this motivated us to study computational delays, possible ways to reduce them, and what their impact in network performance is. For this reason, in this paper we highlight factors that can reduce computational delays and gather information on how much these computational delays impact the performance of RL-based RA algorithms, since the resulting network performance is highly dependent on their responsiveness.

3   Methodology and Alternative Implementations

In this section, the process to reduce these computational delays is described, which can be applicable to a wide range of other RL-based RA algorithms. Afterwards, the methodology to evaluate the impact of computational delays is explained.

3.1   Delay Reduction

DARA's average execution time of 528.8 ms was significantly above the 100 ms step time goal. Our goal was to minimize these delays without changing the algorithm's conceptual design, and without changing the hardware that was used. In what follows, we describe some of the techniques that were applied to reduce delays. We will discuss three different implementation alternatives for data collection, three alternatives for data parsing, a kernel module modification and a configuration parameter through which the more significant delay decreases were achieved. These techniques are focused on the environment side of the DARA algorithm, as shown in Fig. 1. This is because we wanted to preserve DARA's original design, and changes to the agent side imply changes to this design, such as using different agents or neural network model sizes. Because the DARA algorithm is implemented in Python, we could measure the time the program spends inside its functions using the *timeit* module [13]. For the techniques with multiple implementation alternatives, we measured the time their respective functions took to execute, and performed a preliminary analysis to pick the fastest option.

In the course of the reward and state query, the DARA algorithm needs to gather information. This information comes from files in the device that are dynamically updated and need to be read and processed. The files often contain information beyond what is needed, or they are read based on a non-ideal data type (e.g., as a string rather than as an integer). For this reason, in addition to reading the files, it is also important to parse them in order to extract the required data. Because this is a crucial step in the algorithm's functioning, it is worthwhile to explore efficient ways for both collecting the information and parsing it.

We considered three alternative implementations to collect the information:

- **Subprocess** – A Python module to spawn and interact with Linux shells, which enables the use of bash commands. This option was used in the base DARA implementation.
- **Pure Python** – A pure Python approach that uses the built-in *read* function in order to access the files. This method may avoid the overheads of the previous option.
- **Rust extension** – A Rust-based approach. Rust is a compiled language and thus may be faster than Python. This option attempts to leverage the potential benefits of using a compiled language to extend Python, since replacing it would require rewriting the algorithm entirely.

As for parsing the information, we evaluated three alternative implementations:

- **Subprocess** – It enables the use of bash commands and it can pipe the output through multiple filtering commands. This option was used in the base DARA implementation to serve as a baseline for comparison.
- **Pure Python** – We considered the use of Python built-in string functions on the output to filter it.
- **Regex** – We considered the use of Regex search patterns to find and extract the information required from the output.

These alternatives are not an exhaustive list of possible implementations. Also note that both the reward and the state information need to be parsed, and the way their data is obtained is different. Therefore, we evaluated the information parsing alternatives in these two scenarios: parsing the reward, and parsing the state information. Our goal is to demonstrate how implementation differences affect computational delays, and compare the alternatives. The results of our preliminary analysis are shown in Fig. 2.

The file read by the algorithm for the state query is present on a Linux Ubuntu 14.04 distribution. However, the file containing statistics for the calculation of the reward is not. The base DARA implementation obtained this information through Minstrel, a heuristic RA algorithm implemented in Linux. Minstrel is implemented using the *mac80211* Linux kernel module. This module is used for managing wireless devices, thus having access to low-level information on wireless connections. Nevertheless, this low-level information is usually locked

304 R. Trancoso et al.

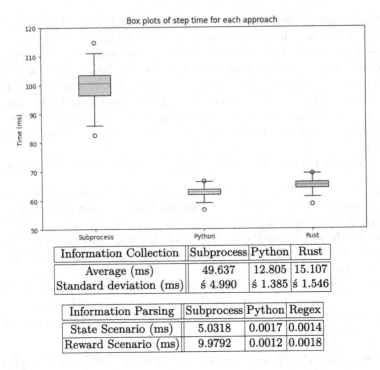

Information Collection	Subprocess	Python	Rust
Average (ms)	49.637	12.805	15.107
Standard deviation (ms)	ś 4.990	ś 1.385	ś 1.546

Information Parsing	Subprocess	Python	Regex
State Scenario (ms)	5.0318	0.0017	0.0014
Reward Scenario (ms)	9.9792	0.0012	0.0018

Fig. 2. Statistics on information collection and parsing alternatives.

to the kernel, and cannot be readily accessed. The base DARA implementation read a table that is computed every 100 ms, even if Minstrel is disabled. This table, unlike the data in the kernel module, is accessible in user-space, although the data is not as up-to-date due to the 100 ms period. This step alone forces the base implementation to take at least 100 ms on each action decision.

For these reasons, our enhanced implementation of DARA modifies the mac80211 module to create a virtual empty file that when read from user space, runs a kernel space function that exposes the values stored in the variables related to frame transmission successes and attempts directly from the kernel. We obtain accurate and current information for the calculation of the reward without being limited by the 100 ms waiting period associated with the table update. For the sake of testing other approaches, we used a preliminary time period of 50 ms instead. However, in practice, this query can be done during the "sleep" time of the algorithm between execution steps, i.e., after the algorithm finishes applying its chosen MCS, but before the next execution step starts. Therefore, this delay can be reduced to functionally zero, which is only possible because the algorithm no longer has to wait for the table update as a result from this kernel module modification.

In Fig. 2, we have a box plot for each approach (Subprocess, Python and Rust) that represents the time of a full execution step. The approaches are represented on the x-axis, while the y-axis represents the time in milliseconds that each approach takes for each algorithm execution step. Do note that the box plot accounts for the total execution step, which includes the 50 ms mentioned previously. This is why the y-axis starts at 50 ms. The lower and upper boundaries of the boxes represent the first and third quartiles, respectively. The lower and upper whiskers represent the minimum and maximum recorded value within 1.5 times the interquartile range below or above the first and third quartiles, respectively. The dots represent the minimum and maximum recorded values. We also have two tables with the time each approach takes for information collection, and parsing. The tables only aggregate the time spent specifically for the collection or parsing instead of the total time. Given the results in Fig. 2, our final implementation used Python to read the files and parse the reward statistics file, and Regex to parse the state query file. Additionally, it made use of the changes to the mac80211 module, which removed the previous limitation of taking 100 ms minimum.

In the end, while the base version of DARA that did not factor computational delays had a response time of 528.8 ms, after changes to the implementational details, we managed to achieve an average response time of 34.8 ms in the same hardware, while maintaining the algorithm's conceptual design. This new version of DARA with reduced delays was called Enhanced DARA or E-DARA.

3.2   Simulation of Delays

After successfully reducing the delays by an order of magnitude, we had two versions of DARA ready that we could compare in addition the original simulation version without delays, those being the base DARA version and E-DARA. The execution time of ten thousand steps of each version were collected experimentally on real devices. To evaluate the impact of computational delays in network performance, we also measured the throughput of each version of DARA. To ensure the reproducibility of wireless channel conditions, we developed a simulation scenario in ns-3. However, this time, the delays will also be simulated, based on the data received from the experimental implementation. This was done by creating a normal distribution of the delays based on the collected average and variance of the measured delays. In this new simulation, after the agent receives the observation, a random delay based from its normal distribution is introduced before the action is applied. Therefore, the resulting effect is as if the simulation no longer stopped for the agent to function, similar to a real environment.

We collected the data on 100 simulations with different seeds and thus, random delays. The simulated scenario has two nodes, one static where the agent is deployed, and another one moving away at a constant velocity, up to a distance of 1100 m, and the throughput between the two nodes is measured. This results in a smooth decrease of SNR throughout the simulation which ensures that the node will cover the whole spectrum of MCS usage, starting with a high MCS at short distances, and ending on a low MCS at longer distances. The nodes communicate using the IEEE 802.11n standard, with a 20 MHz channel bandwidth at a frequency of 5180 MHz. The Friis propagation model and a constant propagation delay are considered.

We then compared the network throughput and frame loss statistics achieved by multiple versions of the DARA algorithm. Those DARA versions are: 1) Simulation DARA with no delays during training and exploitation; 2) DARA with its base 528.8 ms delays during training and exploitation; 3) E-DARA with its reduced 34.8 ms delays during training and exploitation; and 4) E-DARA with no delays during training but 34.8 ms delays during exploitation. This last version of DARA was included to provide a preliminary perspective on training an algorithm in ideal simulated conditions, but then applied to a real scenario. If this training process without delays is more effective, it could be a helpful resource to keep in mind since as long as the simulation is accurate enough, it may be worthwhile to train an agent in simulation before deploying it to a real environment. For further comparison, we also include the simulated network performance from using the ns-3 Ideal RA algorithm, and the ns-3 implementation of Minstrel-HT, as those were the points of reference in the original DARA paper [10].

4   Results

In Fig. 3 we have a complementary cumulative density function of the throughput of each version of the DARA algorithm, as well as a table displaying the average throughput and the average frames lost, which refers to the average number of frames that are lost in total for each simulation. The Minstrel-HT and Ideal RA algorithms are shown just as a reference, and do not consider any computational delays. In Fig. 4, we have the throughput over time of an example of one of the hundred simulations that were performed. Note that due to a warm-up time in the simulation, the plot starts at 4 s. DARA with no delays and with enhanced delays are very similar, both performing consistently better in throughput than Minstrel-HT. They are even better than ns-3 's Ideal algorithm in a few cases. This is because Ideal's goal is not to maximize throughput, but to maintain the Frame Error Ratio below a given threshold. However, DARA with base delays falls drastically behind all the other algorithms, being 49.54% worse than DARA with enhanced delays. The original implementation in a simulation that did not take the delays into account failed to portray this poor performance.

These results indicate that considering and reducing computational delays is important due to their impact on the performance of the algorithm. Completely overlooking the delays may result in simulations that cannot identify the inadequacy of an algorithm for real scenarios, such as was the case for DARA with base delays. Although delays can be reduced and result in a negligible difference in throughput, the version of DARA with enhanced delays still had 5.36% higher frame losses than the version without any delays. It is important to note that these results come from a well-behaved scenario where one device slowly moves away from another, in ideal propagation conditions. In the real world, a more dynamic environment may prove that the network performance is even more sensitive to delays.

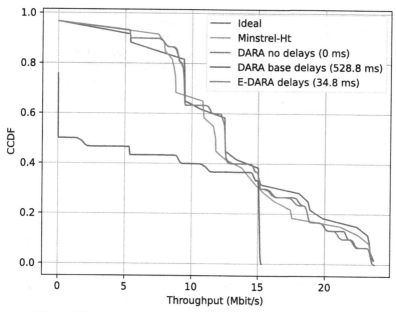

Algorithm	Average throughput (Mbit/s)	Average frames lost
Ideal step average	13.27	
Minstrel-HT	12.74	
DARA no delays	13.04	1128.5
DARA base delays	6.44	4661.8
DARA enhanced delays	13.00	1189.0

Fig. 3. Comparison of network performance of Ideal, Minstrel-HT, DARA with no delays, DARA with base delays and DARA with reduced delays.

In Fig. 5 we show a comparison between E-DARA versions, in which one was trained with no delays, and the other was trained with 34.8 ms delays. During exploitation, however, both versions had similar delays. Despite this, we can see that the version that was trained with no delays performs slightly better. One interesting implication of this result is that if the simulation environment is accurate enough, it is possible to train the algorithm with no delays to achieve a higher performance when it is deployed to a real environment afterwards.

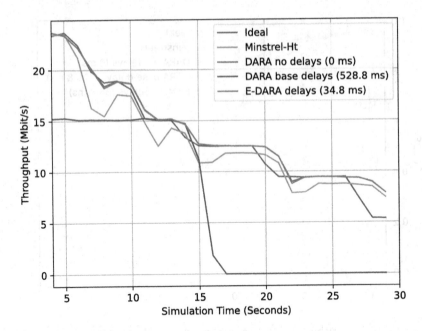

Fig. 4. Example of the throughput of Ideal, Minstrel-HT, DARA with no delays, DARA with base delays and DARA with reduced delays in one simulation.

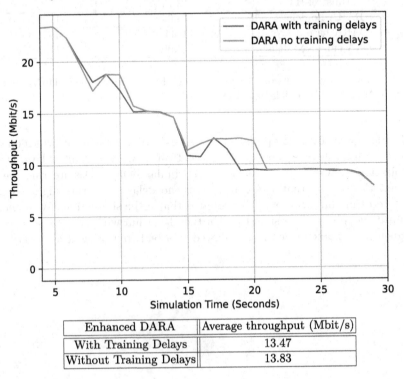

Enhanced DARA	Average throughput (Mbit/s)
With Training Delays	13.47
Without Training Delays	13.83

Fig. 5. Comparison of throughput between DARA trained with and without delays.

5   Conclusions

Computational delays on RL-based RA algorithms are often overlooked in the state of the art. Information about their impact on the performance of these algorithms is hard to find, and this work intends to fill this void and encourage further work on the topic. We measured experimentally the computational delays of DARA, an example of an RL-based RA algorithm. Afterwards, we managed to reduce the execution time by one order of magnitude, without changing the hardware or the algorithm's core functionality.

The data on the delays allowed us to replicate them and their effect in simulation, bridging the gap between results obtained experimentally and those obtained in simulated scenarios. The importance of these delays was evidenced by comparing different versions of the DARA algorithm, which showed there is a difference in algorithm performance that may not be immediately apparent, between when computational delays are considered, and when they are not. It may be possible to reduce the delays to the point where their effect is close to negligible in terms of throughput and frames lost. However, they may impact separate metrics differently. This emphasizes that more attention on computational delays when discussing RL algorithms may be warranted. Furthermore, the lack of analysis of an algorithm's delays may result in its unsuitability for experimental scenarios to go unnoticed.

Acknowledgments. This work is financed by National Funds through the Portuguese funding agency, FCT - Fundação para a Ciência e a Tecnologia, within project LA/P/0063/2020. The third author thanks the funding from FCT, Portugal under the PhD grant 2022.10093.BD

References

1. IEEE standard for information technology–telecommunications and information exchange between systems local and metropolitan area networks–specific requirements part 11: Wireless LAN medium access control (MAC) and physical layer (PHY) specifications amendment 1: Enhancements for high-efficiency WLAN. IEEE Std. 802.11ax-2021 (Amendment to IEEE Std. 802.11-2020), pp. 1–767 (2021). https://doi.org/10.1109/IEEESTD.2021.9442429
2. The minstrel rate control algorithm for mac80211. https://wireless.wiki.kernel.org/en/developers/documentation/mac80211/ratecontrol/minstrel. Accessed 1 Feb 2022
3. Grünblatt, R., Guérin-Lassous, I., Simonin, O.: Simulation and performance evaluation of the Intel rate adaptation algorithm. MSWiM (2019). https://doi.org/10.1145/3345768.3355921
4. Chen, S.C., Li, C.Y., Chiu, C.H.: An experience driven design for IEEE 802.11ac rate adaptation based on reinforcement learning. In: IEEE INFOCOM 2021 (2021). https://doi.org/10.1109/infocom42981.2021.9488876
5. Karmakar, R., Chattopadhyay, S., Chakraborty, S.: SmartLA: reinforcement learning-based link adaptation for high throughput wireless access networks. Comput. Commun. (2017). https://doi.org/10.1016/j.comcom.2017.05.017

6. Karmakar, R., Chattopadhyay, S., Chakraborty, S.: IEEE 802.11ac Link adaptation under mobility. In: 2017 IEEE 42nd Conference on LCN (2017). https://doi.org/10.1109/lcn.2017.90
7. Karmakar, R., Chattopadhyay, S., Chakraborty, S.: An online learning approach for auto link-configuration in IEEE 802.11ac wireless networks. Comput. Netw. (2020). https://doi.org/10.1016/j.comnet.2020.107426
8. Peserico, G., Fedullo, T., Morato, A., Vitturi, S., Tramarin, F.: Rate adaptation by reinforcement learning for Wi-Fi industrial networks. In: 2020 25th IEEE International Conference on ETFA (2020). https://doi.org/10.1109/etfa46521.2020.9212060
9. Karmakar, R., Chattopadhyay, S., Chakraborty, S.: Dynamic link adaptation in IEEE 802.11ac: a distributed learning based approach. In: 2016 IEEE 41st Conference on LCN (2016). https://doi.org/10.1109/LCN.2016.20
10. Queiros, R., Almeida, E., Fontes, H., Ruela, J., Campos, R.: Wi-Fi rate adaptation using a simple deep reinforcement learning approach. In: 2022 IEEE ISCC (2022). https://doi.org/10.1109/iscc55528.2022.9912784
11. Mnih, V., et al.: Playing Atari with deep reinforcement learning. arXiv preprint arXiv:1312.5602 (2013)
12. w-iLab.2 hardware and inventory. https://doc.ilabt.imec.be/ilabt/wilab/hardware.html. Accessed 26 Jan 2022
13. Timeit module documentation. https://docs.python.org/3/library/timeit.html. Accessed 21 Dec 2022

Author Index

J.-L. Guisado-Lizar et al. (Eds.): SIMUtools 2023, LNICST 519, pp. 311–312, 2024.
https://doi.org/10.1007/978-3-031-57523-5

Printed in the United States
by Baker & Taylor Publisher Services